Maker Mark

on

British Silver Plated Wares

ARS-Verlag - Munich

© Copyright 2012

ARS Verlag
C. M. Baur, Munich

ISBN 978-3-9814009-4-6

Cover design:
ARS Verlag, Munich
Photo: Stellan Gottschalk, Munich

Contents:

Brief historical introduction

Documentation shows that the first form of silver plating used for commercial purposes can be traced back to the 15th century. This earliest form of plating was highly illegal and was used by unscrupulous artisans to pass off hammered silver covered tin as Sterling silver. A practice that eventually led to the hallmarking system, that is still in use today.

Old Sheffield Plate or fused plate

This is the technique of rolling a heated sheet of Sterling silver onto a heated sheet of copper. This process was interestingly found quite by accident in c1743 by Thomas Boulsover. A craftsman, undertaking an everyday repair to a damaged knife handle. He used a copper coin to support his work and in doing so found that the two metals fused together and so an industry was born that lasted almost 100 years.
This new process allowed for articles formally crafted from Sterling silver to be produced in a less expensive manner, with no loss of the desired silver effect. Such items initially consisted of buttons, belt and shoe buckles. Over a relatively short period of time this small industry grew and produced a fused plated version of just about everything that was made in Sterling silver. The introduction of electroplating in 1843, allowed for mass-production at a substantially lower cost, finally killing off the already dying trade in c1860.

French Plating

A long forgotten process that was invented during the early fused plating period. Rather like the art of French polishing in the cabinet-making business, it was used to make good areas of fused plate that had not properly adhered during the rolling process. Once the offending "bubble" had been removed from the finished sheet of fused plate, small patches of thin silver sheets were made to fit into the void. Using a hot iron these small sheets were worked and layered on top of each other until level with the original finished work, rendering the repair near invisible.

Electroplating or galvanic plating

This technique first appeared commercially in Birmingham c1843 although trials (both good and bad) had been going on behind the scenes since 1834.
George Richard Elkington (1801 – 1865) and his cousin Henry Elkington (1810 – 1852) were the English pioneers of this new method. It was however, an Italian, Luigi Brugnatelli who in 1805 brought his findings to the French academy of scientists who swiftly dismissed the idea. Ironically, it was a French company who purchased the first International license from Elkington! Back in England, this new form of plating could be used for both gold and silver. This was an important breakthrough that was to save countless lives which would have otherwise been cut short because of the process used. Heated mercury (and the deadly toxins involved in its use) was previously used in the gilding of articles. Electroplating brought an end to this slow, labour intensive and life threatening method. At the same time allowing for the massive increases in the production and therefore reduction in production costs needed to supply the rapidly rising worldwide demand for luxury goods.

Close Plating

This method was basically to iron a sheet of silver to a sheet of steel with a layer of tin used as a flux in between. During the heating process the tin would run away leaving the silver and steel co-joined. Pieces are marked CP (close plated) or PS (plated steel) to show that steel is the base metal.

Base metal

This is the term used to describe the underlying metal on plated items, be they covered by gold or silver. Concentrating on silver plating, there are four main base metals used in the manufacture of English silver plated wares. Shown here in a loose chronological order. It should be noted at this point that all of them co-existed, and while slightly modified, fall into the following cathegories.

Steel

This metal is considered to be the first base metal and was used in the close plating industry during the period 1750 – 1910 for items requiring an extra element of strength. Such items produced were for example cutlery, spurs, buckles and buttons.

Copper

Probably the easiest base metal to work with again used from the mid 18th century. However as supplies of the raw material became more expensive to mine, it was less frequently used. Copper was easily formed and worked and so allowed artisans to produce the most wonderful pieces both in fused plate and electroplate. Pieces marked for example EPC (Electroplated copper) or more recently EPCA (Electroplated copper alloy) and EP on C (Electroplated on copper).

Britannia Metal or White Metal

First produced c1770 by James Vickers in Sheffield, this is one of the more frequently found base metals consisting of 93% tin, 5% antimony and 2% copper. In these early days, articles were produced wholly in Britannia Metal without plating. Along with Vickers, James Dixon made great use of it and many pieces can be found with their names appearing on the bases. In its new and highly polished state, this alloy resembled silver. Much softer and more plyable than other base metals, artisans found that intricate and highly decorative items were far better suited to this metal. After c1847 pieces started to appear with an electroplated silver covering, these articles were marked Britannia Metal electroplated. Then like other base metals the full name was abbreviated, this one being EPBM. Some makers produced their own variant of this alloy and marks like: "Brittanoid" and "Martinoid" can be found. The use of this alloy eventually declined around the start of WWII, with only a couple of better known makers producing articles so based after that period. Interestingly it is still in use today for the Acadamy Award better known as the "Oscar".

German Silver, Nickel Silver or British Plate

This base metal, quite confusingly, bears no silver content. In use from c1840 it rapidly became the most prominent base metal in electroplating production. First mined in Saxony it could also be used without an electroplated silver covering. On the Continent and also in South America this metal is better known as ALPACA, a trademark belonging to Arthur Krupp of Berndorf, Austria. Marks to be found are for example NS (Nickel silver), EPGS (Electroplated German silver) and the famous EPNS (Electroplated Nickel silver).

Diamond Registration Marks

A little understood marking system, that was first introduced by the British Patent Office in September 1842. Importantly the diamond registration mark was used to protect the design of a product. In addition these marks showed the material, maker and exact date the design was first registered by using a set series of letters and numbers. There are two cycles to this form of marking, although similar in appearance but there are distinct differences between the marks, detailed below.

Pieces of silver plate bearing either of these marks are highly desirable for collectors, by whom, they are considered to be the forerunners to the later registered makers' mark. Sometimes it is found that pieces will bear both a makers' mark and a diamond registration mark. Generally this occurs on the second (later) cycle, rather than the earlier first one.

First Cycle (1842 – 1867)

Starting from the top, read in a clockwise direction:

I – Material used in construction, in this case metal.
(II = Wood, III = Glass, IV = Ceramic, V = Wallpaper, VI=Carpets & VII – XIII = Fabrics)
D   - Year of registration.
11   - Day of registration.
3   - Number of registered pieces (In this case a set of three).
H   - Month of registration.

Letter coding for month of registration:

A	December (except 1860)
B	October
C	January
D	September
E	May
G	February
H	April
I	July
K	November/December 1860
M	June
R	August untill 19th September
W	March

Letter coding for year of registration:

A	1845	J	1854	S	1849
B	1858	K	1857	T	1867
C	1844	L	1856	U	1848
D	1852	M	1859	V	1850
E	1855	N	1864	W	1865
F	1847	O	1862	X	1842
G	1863	P	1851	Y	1853
H	1843	Q	1866	Z	1860
I	1846	R	1861		

Second Cycle (1868 – 1883)

Starting from the top, read in a clockwise direction:

I – Material used in construction, in this case metal.
(II = Wood, III = Glass, IV = Ceramic, V = Wallpaper, VI=Carpets & VII – XIII = Fabrics).
11   - Day of registration.
D   - Year of registration.
H   - Month of registration.
3   - Number of registered pieces (In this case a set of three).

Letter coding for month of registration:

A	December
B	October
C	January
D	September
E	May
G	February
H	April
I	July
K	November
M	June
R	August
W	March

Letter coding for year of registration:

A	1871	F	1873	K	1883
C	1870	H	1869	L	1882
D	1878	I	1872	P	1877
E	1881	J	1880	S	1875
U	1874	V	1876	X	1868
Y	1879				

Registration numbers (1884 – 1964)

The diamond registration mark was discontinued in 1884 being replaced by a series of numbers, starting from the number 1. These followed a continuing rising numerical sequence through the dates shown annually below.

For the purposes of this publication these stop at 1964, but the sequence continues to this day.

Example shown can be dated to the year 1911

Year	Numbers	Year	Numbers	Year	Numbers
1884	1 - 19755	1911	574817 - 594194	1938	825231 - 832609
1885	19756 - 40479	1912	594195 - 612430	1939	832610 - 837519
1886	40480 - 64519	1913	612431 - 630189	1940	837520 - 838589
1887	64520 - 90482	1914	630190 - 644934	1941	838590 - 839229
1888	90483 - 116647	1915	644935 - 653520	1942	839230 - 839979
1889	116648 - 141272	1916	653521 - 658987	1943	839980 - 841039
		1917	658988 - 662871	1944	841040 - 842669
1890	141273 - 163766	1918	662872 - 666127	1945	842670 - 845549
1891	163767 - 185712	1919	666128 - 673749	1946	845550 - 849729
1892	185713 - 205239			1947	849730 - 853259
1893	205240 - 224719	1920	673750 - 680146	1948	853260 - 856998
1894	224720 - 246974	1921	680147 - 687143	1949	856999 - 860853
1895	246975 - 268392	1922	687144 - 694998		
1896	268392 - 291240	1923	694999 - 702670	1950	860854 - 863969
1897	291241 - 311657	1924	702671 - 710164	1951	863970 - 866279
1898	311658 - 331706	1925	710165 - 718056	1952	866280 - 869299
1899	331707 - 351201	1926	718057 - 726329	1953	869300 - 872530
		1927	726330 - 734369	1954	872531 - 876066
1900	351202 - 368153	1928	734370 - 742724	1955	876067 - 879281
1901	368154 - 385179	1929	742725 - 751159	1956	879282 - 882948
1902	385180 - 403199			1957	882949 - 887078
1903	403200 - 424399	1930	751160 - 760582	1958	887079 - 891664
1904	424400 - 447799	1931	760583 - 769669	1959	891665 - 894999
1905	447800 - 471859	1932	769670 - 779291		
1906	471860 - 493899	1933	779292 - 789018	1960	895000 - 899913
1907	493900 - 518639	1934	789019 - 799096	1961	899914 - 904637
1908	518640 - 535169	1935	799097 - 808793	1962	904638 - 909363
1909	535170 - 551999	1936	808794 - 817292	1963	909364 - 914535
1910	552000 - 574816	1937	817293 - 825230	1964	914536 - 919606

Trademarks

The Trademark Registation Act of 1875 enabled silversmiths to register their own design of trademark.
Beware, there may be marks on pieces made before this time. These are markers' marks and not trademarks.

(Makers' mark belonging to Matthew Boulton, Birmingham)

Looking at the given image I will explain its construction.

THE "HYGENIA"
PATENT № 257541
E.P. ⚜ N.S
UNITY
QUALIT. PLATE
3 9 0 5 0

The name THE "HYGENIA" is a patented name given to a specific piece with the associated patent number shown below.
E.P.N.S shows the base metal used and that it has a silver covering. The clover leaf containing three stars is a registered trademark belonging to Barker Brothers, Birmingham.
UNITY QUALITY PLATE is also a registered trade name of this company and in this case shows that this piece was made at their Unity Works in Paradise St, Birmingham.

Finally, there is a series of numbers. This is the Makers´ internal catalogue or serial number.
NB: This should not be used as a dating tool.

Among some of the makers of Great Britain they wanted to introduce a standardised level of quality.

A1 = Superior Quality = 1.028 ozt per 12 pieces of cutlery
A = Standard Quality = 0.771 ozt per 12 pieces of cutlery
B = Third Quality = 0.541 ozt per 12 pieces of cutlery
C = Fourth Quality = 0.385 ozt per 12 pieces of cutlery
D = Fifth Quality = 0.192 ozt per 12 pieces of cutlery
(Source: Catalogue Barker Brothers, Birmingham)

Specialisations of makers:

(EP) Electro Plater
(OSP) Old Sheffield Plater
(CU) Cutler
(CP) Close Plater

(FP) French Plater
(T) Retailer
(BM) Britannia Metal
(WG) Water Guilder

References:
(See also page 450)

J·Q&Cº	*(See also)* J. **Quixall & Co.**	**(OSP)** (WTD) (HTD)
J.R & S	*(See also)* John **Round &Son** (**Tudor Works & Arundel Works**)	**(EP)** (PDB) (WAB) (CD) (DOB) (WDOB)
J. R. McC.	*(See also)* James Robert **McClelland**	**(EP)** (CD) (DOB) (WDOB)
JR & Co S / J.R & Cº	*(See also)* Joseph **Ridge & Co.** (**Ridge, Allcard & Co**) (**Lion Works**)	**(EP)** (HTD) (WDB) (PDB)
JR	*(See also)* John **Roberts**	**(OSP)** (WTD)
JR JR	*(See also)* Joseph **Rodgers & Sons** (George)	**(EP)** (PDB) (WAB) (CD) (DOB) (WDOB)
J R J G R	*(See also)* John **Rogers & Sons** (George)	**(CP/CU)** (CD) (DOB) (WDOB)
J R E R	*(See also)* John **Round & Son** (**Truro Works/Arundel Works**)	**(EP)** (DOB) (WDOB)
JR & S S / JR & S W / J R & S	*(See also)* John **Round &Son** (**Tudor Works & Arundel Works**)	**(EP)** (WTD) (HTD) (WDB) (PDB) (WAB) (CD) (DOB) (WDOB)
J R W L	*(See also)* James Rankine **Laing &** William **Laing**	**(EP)** (WTD)
J.S.&S.	*(See also)* John **Shaw & Sons Ltd.**	**(EP/CU)** (WTD) (DOB) (WDOB)
J.S.S	Not assigned!	**(EP)** (DOB) (WDOB)
J.SHARPE SHEFFIELD	*(See also)* John **Askham**	**(CU/EP)** (WAB) (CD) (DOB) (WDOB)
J.S J.S	*(See also)* John **Smallwood**	**(CP)** (WTD)

J

Prologue

For ease of research each section letter is, if required, separated by either an ampersand (&), full stop (.) decimal point (·) or a sign/symbol (∗).

eg is for section A:

A & B
A · B
A ∗ B
A
AA
AA & Co S

Those makers listed without an accompanied trademark or other markings will follow on from the preceding trademark as if they have one, using their trading name.
ie: ADAMANTINE would be followed by Adams which would be followed by Adams Brothers (see page 16/17).

In some cases only pictures will be used within a mark, searching towards to the back of this book, within the pictorial mark section (PM), can help to identify these.

Additionally some pieces may bear more than one mark or other name, often in full and containing an address. A prime example of this occurrence is the Atkin Brothers Plume-in-Hand trademark in combination with a retailer. This appears along with many different names, either above or below the trademark. These are mostly retailers' stamps and not necessarily the maker. eg:

Other instances of double marks have also been found. One such case was a teapot bearing both Mappin & Webb's and Walker & Hall's trademarks!
It is assumed that one or the other had been commissioned to refurbish the piece and replating had been undertaken. In these rare cases, the mark with the serial (catalogue) number beneath should be considered as the original maker.

Where *(See also)* is shown the references will be at the name/trademark to which you are directed.

A&Cº	*(See also)* **Asprey & Co. Ltd.**	(EP)
A & D S H **A&D S**	*(See also)* Charles James **Allen &** Sidney **Darwin**	(EP)
A. & F. Pears	*(See also)* A. & F. **Pears**	(EP)
A & L M	*(See also)* **Arnold & Lewis**	(EP)
A & N CS L **A & N C S L** **A&N.C.S.L**	*(See also)* **Army & Navy Cooperative Society**	(EP)
A&O	*(See also)* **Atkin & Oxley**	(OSP)
A & S	*(See also)* **Armstrong & Scott**	(EP)
A&S **A & S**	*(See also)* T. **Aston & Son**	(EP)
A.&J.Z	*(See also)* Arthur & John **Zimmerman**	(EP)
A·A EP	*(See also)* Andrew **Allison**	(CP)
A.B	*(See also)* Albert J. **Beardshaw**	(EP)
A·B	*(See also)* A. **Brailsforth & Co.**	(OSP)
A.BRIGHT & Co.	*(See also)* **Atkinson Brothers** **(Milton Works)**	(EP)
A·B·S	*(See also)* **Atkinson Brothers** **(Milton Works)**	(EP)
A·C	*(See also)* A. **Crawshaw**	(OSP)

A

Mark	Description	Category
A·C A.C A1	*(See also)* Alexander **Clark Manufacturing Co.**	(EP)
A·C &Cº	*(See also)* J. **Ashforth**, J. **Cutts** & T. **Anderton**	(OSP/CU)
A.E.POSTON&CºLTD LONDON Lonsdale Plate	*(See also)* A.E. **Poston & Co. Ltd.**	(EP)
A·G&Cº	*(See also)* Alex. **Goodman**, Rob. **Gainsford & Co.**	(OSP)
A·G&Cº	*(See also)* Alexander **Goodman & Co.**	(OSP)
A·GOODMAN&Cº	*(See also)* Alexander **Goodman**, Robert **Gainsford** & George **Fairbairn**	(OSP)
A·H	*(See also)* Aaron **Hatfield**	(OSP)
A·H	*(See also)* Aaron **Hatfield & Sons**	(OSP)
A·H	*(See also)* A. **Hunt**	(OSP)
A·H	*(See also)* **Ashforth & Harthorn**	(OSP)
A·H	*(See also)* **Martin Brothers & Co.**	(OSP)
A. MANDARIN A.	*(See also)* Adolphe **Arbenz**	(CU)
A. ROSLING	*(See also)* Albert J. **Beardshaw**	(CU/EP)
A·S	*(See also)* R. **Sutcliffe** & A. **Sporle**	(OSP)
A·S	**Not assigned!** Sheffield 1818 ...	(OSP) (B)
A.S ✠ G.R Ⓢ EP A.S & G.R	*(See also)* Alexander **Scott** & George **Randle**	(EP) (E)(S)

14

n;w]9]9:9<::::>:?>?>?>?>?>?>?>?>?>

A.S.J.&Cᵒ	Not assigned!	(EP) ⁽ᴱ⁾

A

A.S.P.Cᴼ	*(See also)* Angora Silverplate Co.	(EP)
A·W	Not assigned!	(EP) ⁽ᴱ⁾
A	*(See also)* George **Barnsley & Sons**	(CP)
A	*(See als)* Jonathan **Crookes & Son**	(CU)
A	*(See also)* Frederick **Ward & Co.**	(CU)
AB&Cᵒ / A B & Co S / A B & Cᵒ	*(See also)* Albert J. **Beardshaw & Co.**	(EP)
AB.	*(See also)* Albert J. **Beardshaw & Co.**	(EP)
A B ❋ S	*(See also)* **Atkin Brothers** **(Truro Works)** (Only on Britannia Metal)	(BM/EP)
AB	*(See also)* Albert J. **Beardshaw & Co.**	(EP)
A B ⬚ ⬚ ◀	*(See also)* Alfred **Browett**	(BM/EP)
A B ♡ ❀ ◀	*(See also)* **Browett, Ashberry & Co.**	(EP)
✠ ABBA	*(See also)* Jacob & Samuel **Roberts**	(CU)
ABBEY	*(See also)* **Osborne & Co.**	(EP)
AB FB	*(See also)* **Briddon Brothers** (Alfred & Frederick) **(Victoria Plate Works)**	(EP)

15

ABOYEUR	*(See also)* **Henley Silver Rolling & Wire Mills Ltd.**	**(EP)**	
	Barnett Henry **Abrahams** London (Houndsditch) 1885 - 1928 1928 - 1974 (**Ltd.**) *(See also figures: BHA, B.H.A)*	**(EP)**	(S) (M)
🅰 🅱 🅢 🅴🅿 DEFIANCE	*(See also)* Abram **Brooksbank & Co.** (**Malinda Works**)	**(EP)**	
🅰 🅒 &🅒⁰	Not assigned!	**(CU/EP)**	(E)
ACLEA ✕	*(See also)* A.C. **Lea**	**(OSP)**	
AC MC⁰	*(See also)* Alexander **Clark Manufacturing Co.**	**(EP)**	
A C M E .	*(See also)* Henry **Williamson**	**(EP)**	
A C M E	*(See also)* John **Bedford & Son**	**(CU)**	
AD	*(See also)* A. **Dyson**	**(OSP)**	
ⵏ	*(See also)* **Austin & Dodson Ltd.**	**(CP/CU)**	
ADAMANTINE	*(See also)* John Patterson **Smith**	**(EP)**	
	Benjamin **Adams** Birmingham (Ludgate Hill/2, Cannon St) - 1829 - 1833 ...	**(CU)**	(WAB) (HTD) (DOB)
	Edward James **Adams** Birmingham (81a, Bull St/76, Spencer St) - 1878 - 1884 ...	**(EP)**	(K78) (K80) (K84)
	John **Adams** Birmingham (72, Newhall St) - 1833 ...	**(CP)**	(DOB)

Thomas **Adams**　　　　**(CP/EP)** ^{(WAB) (HTD)} ^(K78)
Birmingham (Lionel St/13, Upper Hockley St)
- 1829 - 1878 ...

Adams Brothers　　　　**(EP)** ^(K80)
Sheffield (13, Norfolk Ln)
- 1880 ...

William **Adams Inc.**　　　　**(EP)**
Birmingham/New York (USA)
1865 - 1966 *(See also figure: W A)*
(Then: Henry Jenkins & Sons Ltd. USA)

Henry **Adamson**　　　　**(EP)** ^{(K82) (K84)}
Birmingham (38, Spencer St)
- 1882 - 1884 ...

AD **&** **CO** **LTD**　　**Not assigned!**　　**(EP)** ^(E)

G. **Addy & Son**　　　　**(OSP)** ^(B) SAOR)
Sheffield (Pea Croft)
1825 ... *(See also figure: G · A)*

ADELANTE　*(See also)*　　**(EP)**
Gunston Sons & Co.

" Eagle "　*(See also)*　　**(EP)**
ADELANTE　H. **Schü(ue)rhoff & Co.**

ADELPHI PLATE　*(See also)*　　**(EP)**
James **Hardy & Co.**

Charles J. **Adie**　　　　**(CU/EP)**
(Lion Works)
London (57 - 60, Holborn Viaduct)
Birmingham (156, Warstone Ln)
1890 - 1918 *(See also figure: C J A)*
- 1896 - 1936 ... **(& Nephew)** ^{(PC) (K36)}
(See also figure: CJA & N)

Adie Brothers Ltd.　　**(EP)** ^(K36)
(Atlas Works)
Birmingham (Soho Hill)
London
1906 - 1936 ...
(See also figure: BROS A Ltd)

Henry **Adkins & Sons** Birmingham (12, Weaman Rw/75, Bath Rw) - 1862 - 1896 ...	**(EP)**	(BDB) (GS) (MDG) (POB) (K72) (K78) (K80) (K82) (K84) (K88) (K92) (PC)

ADMIRAL

(See also)   **(EP)**
 Larder & Burgess

𝓐 Ɛ 𝓒°   *(See also)*   **(CU/OSP)**
 Ashforth, Ellis & Co.

Ⓐ Ⓔ Ⓕ Ⓐ Ⓢ   *(See also)*   **(EP)**
 Arthur E. **Furniss & Sons**

🅐 🅒 🅕 ⬬ 🅢   *(See also)*   **(BM/EP)**
 Arthur Edward **Furniss**

ÆNEAS

(See also)   **(EP)**
 John **Round & Son Ltd.**

AEROPLANE

(See also)   **(CU)**
 William **Jessop & Sons Ltd.**

AEWH **GH** **IH** **EE**   **Not assigned!**   **(OSP)** (B)
 1790 - 1800

AFRICAN SILVER

(See also)   **(EP)**
 Spittle & Heape
 and
 Hills, Menke & Co.   **(EP)**

AGUILA   *(See also)*   **(CU/EP)**
 Frederick **Barnes & Co.**

A H.T (heart device)   *(See also)*   **(EP)**
 Albert Henry **Thompson**

Ⓐ Ⓗ ✠ Ⓙ Ⓗ   *(See also)*   **(CP/OSP)**
 Aaron **Hatfield & Sons**

(cup device A H)   *(See also)*   **(CU)**
 Moss & Gamble Brothers

AIGO.

(See also)   **(EP)**
 Joseph **Peace & Co.**

William **Ainsworth** Birmingham (Ford St) - 1872 ...	**(EP)**	(K72)

	Ainsworth, Taylor & Co. Birmingham (78, Ford St/Park Rd/ 40 & 42, Spencer St) - 1878 - 1903 ... *(See figure: A T & Co)*	**(EP)**	(K78) (K80) (K82) (K84) (K88) (K92) (PC) (K03)
	William **Aitken** Birmingham (15a, Pitsford St) - 1892 ...	**(EP)**	(K92)
A·J·B	Andrew John **Bailey** **(Everest Works)**	**(EP)**	
AJAX	*(See also)* Benjamin **Huntsmann**	**(CP)**	
	(See also) Abraham **Kemp**	**(EP)**	
AKROS	*(See also)* John James **Saville & Co.**	**(CU)**	
	Not assigned! - 1897 (Possibly: Alfred Lindley, period and styling would match)	**(EP)**	(E)
ALBANY PLATE	**Not assigned!** ~ 1920 ...	**(EP)**	(E)
ALBION SILVER	*(See also)* Thomas **Tillotson**	**(CU)**	
ALBION SILVER	*(See also)* George Shadford **Lee &** Henry **Wigfull Ltd.** **(John Street Works)**	**(BM/EP)**	
	Richard **Albrighton** Birmingham (Pritchett St) - 1815 ...	**(CU/CP)**	(WTDB)
A L D	*(See also)* A. L. **Davenport Ltd.**	**(EP)**	
	Thomas **Aldridge** London (57, Brompton Rd) 1865 ... *(See also figure: Thomas ALD-RIGE)*	**(EP)**	(M)

19

William **Alexander & Sons**   **(EP)**
Glasgow
~ *(See also figure: WA & S G)*

James **Alexanders**   **(CP/EP)**   (HGDB) (HDG)
Birmingham (12, Gt. Charles St/160, New   (K82) (K84)
Hall St)
- 1849 - 1884

ALEXANDER SCOTT
   (See also)   **(EP)**
   Alexander **Scott**

ALEXᴿ CLARK Cᴼ.Lᴰ
   (See also)   **(EP)**
   Alexander **Clark Manufacturing Co.**
   (Welbeck Works)

ALFRED GREEN
   (See also)   **(CP/CU)**
   George **Barnsley & Sons**

ALFRED LINDLEY
SHEFFIELD
   (See also)   **(BM/EP)**
   Alfred **Lindley**
   (Richmond Works)

ALLADIN
   (See also)   **(EP)**
   John **Round & Son Ltd.**

Frederick **Allan**   **(BM/EP)**
Birmingham (2, Ellis St/Freeth St/85, Icknield Sq)   (MDG) (K80)
- 1866 - 1880 ...   (K82) (K84)
- 1882 - 1884 ... **(& Son)**

James **Allan**   **(CU/BM/EP)**
Sheffield (Johnson Ln/Andrew St)
- 1854 ...
(See also figure: James Allan)   (POS) (K54)
1855 - 1872 **(& Co.)**   (M)
(See also figure: James Allan &Co)

W. **Allanson & Co.**   **(OSP)**   (B) (SAOR)
Sheffield (Norfolk St)
1832 ... *(See also figure: W.A & Co)*

Allanson & Machon   **(CP)**   (GDS)
Sheffield (19, Norfolk St)
- 1833 ...

A

(See also) **(CU)**
Richard **Thomas & Co. Ltd.**

Allcard & Co. **(CU/EP)** (K93) (WDS01)
(Formerly: Arthur Culf & Co)
Sheffield (34 & 36, Charlotte St/161-167,
Howard St)
- 1893 - 1901 ...

Alldays & Onions Pneumatic (EP)
Engineering
Sheffield
~ 1878 ...
(See also figure: S. LINLEY)

Edgar **Allen & Co.** **(CU)**
(Well Meadow Steel Works)
(Imperial Steel Works)
Sheffield (Tinsley)
London (9, Ducksfoot Ln) (K72) (WDS79)
- 1872 - 1888 ... (K88AD) (K93)
- 1893 - 1901 ... **(Ltd.)** (SBW)
(See also figures: LSD, IMPERI- (WDS01)
AL, K9, HOOLE)

Charles James **Allen &** Sidney **Darwin (EP)** (SOAR) (K93)
(Portland Works) (WDS01) (WDSR)
Sheffield (55, Arundel St) (Rd 143384) (M)
- 1887 - 1928 *(See also figures: A &*
D, symbol "hour glas")
(Then: Charles James Allen)

Allen & Daws **(EP)** (K80)
Norwich (45, London St)
- 1880 ...

Allen & Martin **(EP)** (B) (M)
Sheffield
~ 1888 ... *(See also figure: MARTIN)*

Allen & Smith Ltd. **(EP)** (K36)
Birmingham (33, Hall St)
- 1936 ...

John **Allen & Son** **(CU)** (K03)
Birmingham (7, Vyse St)
- 1903 ...

Charles James **Allen** **(EP)**
(Formerly: Allen & Darwin)
Sheffield
1928 ... *(See also figure: CJA S)*

Edwin Alfred **Allen** **(EP)**
Birmingham (67 & 68, Mott St)
- 1888 ...
- 1892 - 1903 ... **(& Co.)** (K88)
(See also figure: CARPATHIAN (K92) (PC) (K03)
SILVER)

George **Allen** **(EP)**
Birmingham (39, Harford St/15 & 39, (K72) (K03)
Victoria St) (K78) (K80) (K82)
- 1872 - 1903 ... (K84) (K88) (PC)
- 1878 - 1896 ...

Henry **Allen** **(EP)** (K82)(K88) (K92)
Birmingham (147, Park Ln/59, Icknield St/ (K03) (K36)
169a, Hockley Hill/ 234, Brearley St/
63, Caroline St)
- 1882 - 1903 ...

J. **Allen** **(EP)** (MDG)
Birmingham (Park Rd)
- 1866 ...

James **Allen** **(BM/EP)** (GDBS) (WDOS)
Sheffield (11, Wicker/Andrew St) (K93)
- 1849 - 1893 ...

Joseph **Allen** jun. **(CU)** (K80)
Birmingham (Branston St)
- 1880 ...

T. **Allen** **(OSP)** (B)
Sheffield (Bailey St)
1777 ... *(See also figure: TA)*

William **Allen** **(WG/CP)** (WTDB)
Birmingham (Loveday St)
- 1815 ...

William Henry **Allen** **(EP)** (K03)
Birmingham (Warstone Ln)
- 1903 ...

ALL GOOD	John **Allgood** Birmingham (Essex St/Coleshill St/Vauxhall Ln) 1812 - 1830 ...	**(CP)**	(B) (CD) (WTD) (WDB) (WAB) (HTD) (SBW) (M)
	Andrew **Allison** Glasgow 1852 - 1862 *(See also figure: A · A)*	**(CP)**	(S)
	J. **Allison** London (Castle St/Holborn) - 1808 ...	**(T)**	(POAD)
*** allport*** **R** ***allport***	Edward **Allport** Birmingham (Cannon St/Gt. Charles St/ 9, Bartholomew St) 1812 - 1830 ...	**(Coach/CP)**	(B) (WTDB) (WTD) (PDB) (WAB) (HTD) (SBW) (M)
	James **Allport** Birmingham (12, Weaman Rw) - 1835 - 1850 ...	**(CP/EP)**	(WWDB) (WDOB) (HGDB) (HDG)
	Francis **Allum** London (99, Strand) - 1808 ...	**(OSP)**	(POAD)
ALMADA SILVER	*(See also)* Joseph **Gilbert** **(Sun Works)**	**(CP/EP)**	
ALO ✱	*(See also)* Robert **Youle**	**(CU)**	
ALPHA	*(See also)* **Harrison Brothers & Howson**	**(CU/EP)**	
ALPHROID **E.P. B.M. A**1	**Not assigned!** - 1920 ...	**(EP)**	(E)
ALPIN	*(See also)* **Pinder Brothers**	**(EP/CU)**	
ALUMINIUM SILVER	*(See also)* Thomas H. **Daniel &** Thomas R. **Arter** **(Globe Nevada Silver Works)**	**(EP)**	
ALVA	*(See also)* Richard **Loy**	**(OSP/CU)**	

A M & C° (symbol)	**Not assigned!** Manchester ~	(EP)
A M (symbol)	*(See also)* Arthur **Marsh**	(CU)
	Amatt & Son Portsea (15, Union St) - 1880 ...	(EP) (K80)
(AMAZON symbol)	*(See also)* **Rosing Brothers & Co.**	(EP)
" Ambassador "	*(See also)* **Gladwin Ltd.** **(Embassy Works/Montgomery Works)**	(EP)
AMERICAN SILVER ALLOY	*(See also)* **Perry & Co. Ltd.**	(EP)
AMINTO	*(See also)* John **Round & Son Ltd.**	(EP)
A M S (symbols)	*(See also)* **Silver & Fleming Ltd.**	(EP)
	Charles **Anderton** Sheffield (Union Ln/43 - 47, Cooper St) - 1863 - 1880 ...	(EP) (GS) (WDS79) (K80)
	Willi Athol **Anderton** Sheffield (173, Eyre St) - 1901 ...	(EP) (WDS01)
	John Henry **Andrew & Co.** **(Toledo Steel Works)** Sheffield (Neepsend Ln) ~ 1860 - 1893 ... - 1901 ... **(Ltd.)** *(See also figure: TOLEDO)*	**(CU/CP)** (W) (K93) (WDS01)
	Francis Sidney **Andrews** Birmingham (16, Branston St) - 1903 ...	(EP) (K03)
ANGLE △ PLATE	*(See also)* William **Hutton & Sons**	(EP)

ANGORA ◄ **EPNS**	**Angora Silverplate Co.** Sheffield Birmingham (Regent St) 1928 - 1936 ... 1937 - 1941 (**Ltd.**) *(See also figure: A.S.P. & Co)*	**(EP)**	(K36) (S) (W)
	William **Angus** Liverpool (17, Lord St) - 1880 ...	**(EP)**	(K80)
	George B. **Anscombe** Birmingham (53a, Northwood St) - 1936 ...	**(EP)**	(K36)
	Anstey & Wilson Ltd. **(Standard Plate Works)** Birmingham (18, Kenyon St) London (93 & 94, Hatton Garden) - 1936 ...	**(EP)**	(K36)
	Samuel **Anstey** Birmingham (Gt. Charles St) - 1815 ...	**(CU/CP)**	(WTDB)
	Antrobus & Co. Birmingham (27, Victoria St) - 1903 ...	**(EP)**	(K03)
A O T	*(See also)* Albert **Oates**	**(CU)**	
APEX	*(See also)* John **Biggin & Co. Ltd.**	**(CU)**	
AQUA	*(See also)* **Kayser, Ellison & Co.** **(Carlisle Works)**	**(CU)**	
ARARA	*(See also)* John Henry **Potter** **(Rockingham Works)**	**(CU)**	
ARATOR	*(See also)* John **Round & Son Ltd.** **(Tudor Works & Arundel Works)**	**(EP)**	

Adolphe **Arbenz** **(EP)** ^(W)
Birmingham
~ 1892...
(See also figure: A. MANDARIN. A)

Archer & Co. **(EP)** ^(SOAR)
(Formerly: Archer, Marchin & Marsh)
Sheffield (Fargate)
1855 ...

James **Archer** **(CU)** ^(WWDB)
Birmingham (14, Gt. Hampton St)
- 1835 ...

Archer, Machin & Marsh **(EP)** ^{(B) (SBW) (M)}
Sheffield (Fargate)
1854 - 1855 *(See also figure: HA)*
(Then: Archer & Co.)

Alfred **Arculus** **(EP)** ^{(GS) (MDG) (POB)}
Birmingham (42 - 45, Broad St)   ^(K72)
- 1863 - 1872 ...

S. **Ardron & Son** **(BM)** ^{(GDBS) (WDOS)}
Sheffield (12, Holly St)
- 1849 - 1852 ...

ARENAM	*(See also)* John **Round & Son Ltd.** **(Tudor Works/Arundel Works)**	**(EP)**
ARGENLINE	*(See also)* Thomas H. **Daniel &** Thomas R. **Arter** **(Globe Nevada Silver Works)**	**(EP)**
ARGENT LAW L&Co	*(See also)* Thomas **Law & Co.**	**(CU)**
ARGENTINA SILVER	*(See also)* Joseph **Gilbert** **(Sun Works)**	**(CP/EP)**
ARGENTINE PLATE	*(See also)* William **Hutton & Son**	**(CP/EP)**
ARGOSY SILVER	*(See also)* Solomon Lewis **Gorer** and **Gilding & Silvering Co.**	**(EP)** **(EP)**

ARGUS	*(See also)* **Crookes, Roberts & Co.**	**(CU)**	**A**

ARGYLE PLATE	*(See also)* John **Sanderson**	**(EP)**	

ARISTOCRAT MADE IN ENGLAND	**Not assigned!** Birmingham ~ 1960 ...	**(EP)**	(E)

ARIZONA SILVER	*(See also)* W. S. **Savage & Co.** (W. **Savage, Smith & Co)**	**(EP)**	

W. H. **Armitage & Co.** **(Vesuvius Works)** Sheffield - 1878 ... *(See also figures: CAPS ANY, VE* *SEVIUS,* WILLIAM SYKES & Co.*)*	**(EP)**	(W) (K88)

Thomas W. **Armitage** Sheffield (51, Rockingham St) - 1893 ...	**(GS)**	(K93)

Armitages & Standish Sheffield (Eyre Ln) - 1829 ...	**(CU)**	(PD)

Armstrong & Scott Birmingham ~ 1895 ... *(See also figure: A & S)*	**(EP)**	(B) (M)

Armstrong, Stevens & Son Birmingham ~	**(EP)**	(SBW)

Army & Navy Cooperative Society (EP) London (Westminster/Victoria St) 1871 - 1930 *(See also figures: A & N, symbol* *"flag")*		(SBW) (M)

ARNOLD&LEWIS **MANCHESTER**	**Arnold & Lewis** Manchester (7, St. Ann's Sq) 1875 - 1897 *(See also figure: A&L)* 1898 - 1905	**(EP)**	(M)

John **Arnot** **(GS)** ^(DSRR)

Sheffield (Ct. 9, Carver St)
- 1841 ...

Walter Jason **Arnott** **(EP)** ^(K03)

Birmingham (78 & 79, Unett St)
- 1903 ...

ART

(See also) **(EP)**
George **Butler & Co. Ltd.**
(Trinity Works)

Arundel & Mappin **(CU)** ^(PD)

Sheffield (Eyre Ln)
- 1829 ...

ARUNDEL PLATE   *(See also)* **(EP)**
Charles William **Fletcher & Sons Ltd.**

ASAY   *(See also)* **(CU)**
John **Hallam**

ASCEND   *(See also)* **(CU)**
William Thomas **Staniforth**
(Eldon Works & Ascend Works)

J. **Ash & Co.** **(EP)** ^(K96)

Birmingham
- 1896 ...

Joseph **Ash & Son** **(CU/EP)** ^{(W) (WDS01)}

Sheffield (57, Trafalgar St)
~ 1850 - 1901 ... *(See also figure: TB2)*

Philip **Ashberry** **(CU/BM/EP)** ^(B)

Sheffield (15, Copper St/19 & 21, Bowling
Green St)
- 1833 - 1852 ...
- 1863 - 1893 ... **(& Sons)**
- 1901 - 1911 ... **(& Sons Ltd.)**
(See also figures: BRITANNIA,
PA&S, symbol "Britannia", NA-
CZI, symbol "gaunlet and flag")

^{(GDS) (GDBS)}
^(WDOS)
^{(GS) (SOAR)}
^{(WDS79) (K80)}
^{(K93) (SBW) (M)}
^{(WDS01) (WDSR)}
^(WDS11)

ASH BER RY

EP ASHBERRY

Henry William **Ashford** **(EP)** ^(GS)

Birmingham (27 & 28, Snape St)
- 1861 ...

G. **Ashforth & Co.** **(OSP)** (B) (M) SAOR)

Sheffield (Holy St)
1773 ... *(See also figure: GA&Co)*
1784 ...

Ashforth & Harthorn **(OSP)** (B) (SAOR) (PD)

Sheffield (16, Silver St)
1826 -1829 ... *(See also figure: A.H)*

G. & R. **Ashforth** **(BM)** (WAB)

Birmingham (Moland St)
- 1829 ...

J. **Ashforth** **(BM)** (DOB)

Birmingham (Ct 13, Moland St)
- 1833 ...

James & William **Ashforth** **(BM)** (WAB)

Birmingham (Ct 14, Moland St)
- 1829 ...

John **Ashforth** **(OSP)**

Sheffield
1787 ... *(See also figure: Z WA)* (B)
1825 ... **(& Co.)** (SAOR)

Robert **Ashforth** **(BM/EP)** (HDG) (CDB) (GS)

Birmingham (13, Edgbaston St/2, Jamaica Rw)
- 1850 - 1863 ...

Samuel **Ashforth** **(OSP)** (B)

Sheffield
1787 - 1797 ...
(See also figures: + + IE, X IE SA)

Ashforth, Creswick & Hartshorn (OSP) (SAOR) (SDG)
(PG)
Sheffield (16, Silver St)
- 1828 - 1829 ...

J.**Ashforth**, J.**Cutts** & T.**Anderton** (B) (NGDS) (PD)

Sheffield (16, Silver St) **(CU/OSP)**
- 1825 - 1829 ...
(See also figure: AC & Co)

Ashforth, Ellis & Co. **(CU/OSP)** (B) (M)

Sheffield (Holy Croft)
1770 - 1774 ...
(See also figures: AE&Co, L' ES-PAGNE)

29

Ashforth, Ellis, Wilson & Hawksley (GM) (UBD)
Sheffield (Angel St) **(OSP)**
- 1787 - 1791 ...

Ashley **(CP)** (B) (M)
Birmingham
1816 ...

Charles **Ashley** **(EP)** (K80)
Birmingham (24, Hockley Hill)
- 1880 ...

Frederick **Ashmore** **(GS)** (WDS11)
Sheffield (230, Edmond Rd)
- 1911 ...

Richard **Ashton** **(OSP)** (DSRR)
Sheffield (12, Rock St)
- 1841 ...

Thomas **Ashton** **(CU/EP)**
Birmingham
1841 ... (SAOR)
1858 ... *(& Son)* (B) (SBW) (M)
(See also figure: A & S) (SAOR)

Joseph **Ashworth** **(EP)**
Sheffield
~ 1892 *(See also figure: J A S)*

ASKEW **Askew** **(OSP)** (B) (M)
MAKER Nottingham
NOTTINGHAM 1828 ...

John **Askham** **(CU/EP)**
Sheffield (57, Bailey St)
~ 1864 ... (W)
- 1901 ... (WDS01)
*(See also figures: JOHN ASK-
HAM, J.SHARPE)*

Frederick Charles **Asman** **(EP)**
Sheffield (20, Cambridge St/34, Eyre St/
299, Western Bank/6, Lawson Rd)
~ 1876 - 1905 (WDS01) (WDSR)
1906 - 1936 ... **(& Co.)** (WDS01) (WDS11)
(See also figures: FA&Co, symbol (K36) (W)
"bird cage")

	Asprey & Co.	**(EP)**	(S)
	London		
	1900 - 1909		
	(See also figure: A & Co.)		
	1909 - heute (**Ltd.**)		
ASPREY	William **Asprey**	**(CU)**	
	Mitcham, Surrey		
	1781 - 1840		
	(Then: Kennedy & Asprey)		
	Charles **Asprey**	**(EP)**	
	London		
	1843 - 1872		
	1872 - 1888 (**& Sons**)		
	C.& G. E. **Asprey**	**(EP)**	
	London		
	1888 - 1900		
	Henry H. **Aston**	**(CU/CP)**	(GS)
	Birmingham (12, Regent Pl)		
	- 1863 ...		
	Joseph **Aston**	**(CP/CU)**	(WTDB) (CD) (WTD) (WDB) (PDB) (WAB) (HTD)
	Birmingham (16, Coleshill St)		
	- 1815 - 1830 ...		
	(See also) **Ainsworth, Taylor & Co.**	**(EP)**	
	(See also) A. T. **Cannon Ltd.**	**(EP)**	
ATHENA	*(See also)* Walter A. **Lyndon**	**(CU)**	
	Atkin & Oxley	**(OSP)**	(B) (SAOR)
	Sheffield (Eyre St)		
	1829 ... *(See also figure: A & O)*		
	Atkin & Oxley & Co.	**(CU)**	(GDS) (WD37)
	Sheffield (43, Howard St)		
	- 1833 - 1837 ...		

Charles Herbert **Atkins &** Ernest **Wigley (EP)** [E]
Birmingham (171, Hockley Hill)
~ 1920 ...

Charles **Atkin** **(OSP)** (WDOS)
Sheffield (East View)
- 1852 ...
(Junior partner of Broadhead & Atkin)

Henry **Atkin** **(CU/OSP/BM/EP)**
Sheffield (32, Howard St/19, Eyre St)
1841 - 1846 ... *(See also figure: H.A)* (B) (SBW) (SAOR)
1833 - 1853 ... **(&Co.)** (SD)
*(See also figure: HA*S)* (B) (M) (WDOS)

Atkin Brothers **(BM/EP)**
(Truro Works) (Harry, Edward, Frank)
Sheffield (169, Matilda St)
London (11, Charterhouse St)
Glasgow (75, Buchanan St)
1853 - 1925 (SAOR) (B) (GS)
1925 - 1936 ... **(Ltd.)** (K80) (K93)
*(See also figures: A B * S, HA EA* (WDSR) (SBW)
FA, TRUROX, symbol "feather
hand") (K36)

ATKIN BROS   NS
ATKIN BROTHERS.
SHEFFIELD

Thomas **Atkins** **(CP)** (WAB) (HTD)
Birmingham (Moor St)
- 1829 - 1830 ..

Walter **Atkins** **(EP)** (K88)
Birmingham (84, Gt. Hampton St)
- 1888 ...

Atkinson Brothers **(CU/EP)**
(Milton Works)
Sheffield (Nowbray St/80 - 92, Milton St/ (WDS79) (K80)
1, Sarah St/19, Creswick Walk) (K93) (E) (SBW)
- 1879 - 1905 .... (W) (WDSR) (M)
- 1901 ... **(Ltd.)** (WDS01)
(See also figures: A.BRIGHT &
Co, A.B.S, BRILLO, IN MIND,
symbol "bear", IN MIND)

ATKINSON BROS.

ATLAS *(See also)* **(EP)**
John **Brown**

ATTRACT	*(See also)* **Bromley & Fisher**	**(CU)**
	Henry **Attrill** Birmingham (260, Icknield St) - 1903 ... - 1936 ... (**Ltd.**)	**(EP)** (K03) (K36)
	Charles **Attwood** Durham ~ 1892 ... *(See also figure: C . ATTWOOD)*	**(CU/EP)** (M)
AURICHALCUM	*(See also)* **Morewood & Co. Ltd.**	**(CU)**
AURORA	*(See also)* John **Shaw & Sons Ltd.**	**(EP/CU)**
	Henry W. **Auster** Birmingham (59, Skinner Ln) - 1872 - 1880 ...	**(EP)** (K72) (K80)
	Austin & Dodson Ltd. (Cambia Works) Sheffield (191, Arundel St) - 1879 - 1893 ... *(See also figures: AD, DA)*	**(CP/CU)** (W) (WDS79) (K93)
AUSTRALIAN SILVER	*(See also)* William **Naylor & Co. (Caledonian Works)**	**(BM/CP/GS/EP)**
AUTO	*(See also)* James **Deakin (Sidney Works)**	**(BM/EP)**
AVENA	*(See also)* **John Round & Son Ltd. (Tudor Works & Arundel Works)**	**(EP)**
	Thomas **Avern** Birmingham (Paradise St) - 1815 - 1818 ...	**(CP)** (WTDB) (WTD)
AW&JH S EP A	**Not assigned!** Sheffield ~ 1920 ...	**(EP)** (E)

A W	*(See also)* Arthur **Willis**	(EP)
A**X**1	*(See also)* Sharman Dermott **Neill** and Ellis **Newton**	(EP) (EP)
AZTEC	*(See also)* **James Deakin** **(Sidney Works)**	(BM/EP)

(B&AS)	*(See also)* **(BM/OSP)** Roger **Broadhead &** Henry **Atkin**
B & B S	*(See also)* **(EP)** **Bradley &** T H. **Blake**
B & C B & C	*(See also)* **(EP)** **Biddle & Collingwood** or **Brookes & Crookes** **(CU/EP)** **(Atlantic Works)**
B&C	*(See also)* **(EP)** **Brown & Clark**
B & Co.	*(See also)* **(EP)** **Bewlay & Co. Ltd.**
B & C	*(See also)* **(EP)** Edwin James **Buxton & Co.**
B & C L	*(See also)* **(EP)** **Benetfink & Co.**
B &/S Co	*(See also)* **(EP)** **Bramwell & Co.** **(Bramwell Brownhil & Co. Ltd.)**
B&F	*(See also)* **(OSP)** Matthew **Boulton & Fothergill**
B&G GS **B** **E** **B&G/S** **P** **M**	*(See also)* **(EP)** Charles **Boardman, Glossop & Co.** **(Clarence Work)**
B & K	*(See also)* **(EP)** C. F. **Barnes &** A.D. **Kirkby**
B&O'N	*(See also)* **(EP)** Henry **Bourne &** Daniel J. **O'Neil**
B&P	*(See also)* **(CU/OSP)** **Blackwell & Parkin**
B & S	*(See also)* **(EP)** **Bracher & Sydenham**

Mark	(See also)	Type
B&W EPNS S / **B&W**	*(See also)* **Burton & Waters**	(EP)
B.B	*(See also)* **Briddon Brothers**	(EP)
B·B	*(See also)* B. **Brockslesby**	(EP)
B·B	*(See also)* B. **Brodderick**	(OSP)
B.BROS / **B BROS** STRIPES	*(See also)* **Burgess Brothers**	(EP)
B.GRAYSON & SON SHEFFIELD	*(See also)* Benjamin **Grayson & Son**	(EP)
B.G.L™	*(See also)* **Birmingham Guild of Handicrafts Ltd.**	(EP)
B.HUNTSMAN	*(See also)* Benjamin **Huntsmann**	(CP)
B.J.R&S	*(See also)* Benjamin J. **Round & Son**	(EP)
B·M	*(See also)* B. **Martin**	(OSP)
BON · ACCORD	*(See also)* **Slack & Grinold (Bath Works)**	(CU/EP)
B·R	*(See also)* Benjamin **Rooke & Sons**	(OSP)
B.R	*(See also)* B. **Rowlings**	(OSP)
B·S	*(See also)* Benjamin **Smith**	(OSP)
B·W	*(See also)* B. **Withers**	(OSP)
B.W & Co	*(See also)* **Bingley, Bower & Co.**	(EP)

(See also) William **Batt & Sons**	**(EP)**	
(See also) **Bravingtons Ltd.**	**(EP)**	
(See also) Thomas H. **Daniel &** Thomas R. **Arter** **(Globe Nevada Silver Works)**	**(EP)**	
(See also) Frederick **Ward & Co.**	**(CU)**	
Thomas **Bacon & Son** Sheffield (45, Hollis Croft) - 1825 ...	**(CU)**	(NGDS)
Thomas **Badger & Co.** **(Badger, Worrall & Armitage)** Sheffield (Shales Moor) 1844 ... *(See also figures: TB&Co, BW&A)*	**(OSP)**	(B) (SAOR) (SBW) (M)
Badger & Worrall Sheffield (253, Moorfields) - 1846 ...	**(OSP)**	(SD46)
Thomas **Badger** Sheffield 1847 ...	**(OSP)**	(SAOR)
John **Bagley & Co.** **(Bagley & Hipwood)** Birmingham (6, Regent Pd) - 1872 - 1884	**(EP)**	(K72) (K78) (K80) (K82) (K84)
William **Bagley** Birmingham (66, Lw. Loveday St/ 7, Caroline St) - 1861 - 1866 ... **(& Co.)** - 1867 - 1872 ...	**(EP)**	(CDB) (BDB) (MDG) (POB) (K72)
Alfred **Bagnall** Birmingham (60, Northampton St) - 1892 - 1903 ...	**(EP)**	(K92) (PC) (K03)

B

w. **Bagshaw** Sheffield (Spring St) 1820 ... *(See also figure: WB)*	**(OSP)**	(B) (SAOR)	
William **Bagshaw** Leeds (8, Lambert's Yard) - 1893 ...	**(EP)**	(K93)	
Bagshaw Brothers Sheffield (48, Button Ln) - 1936 ...	**(EP)**	(K36)	
William **Baily & Sons** London (Gracechurch St) ~ 1860 ... *(See also figure: W.BAILY)*	**(T/EP)**		
Andrew John **Bailey** **(Everest Works)** Birmingham (3, Pope St/53, Tenby St) - 1882 - 1903 ... *(See also figure: A.J.B)*	**(EP)**	(K82) (K84) (K88) (K92) (PC) (K03)	
Henry **Bailey** Birmingham (234, Colmore St) - 1880 - 1884 ...	**(EP)**	(K80) (K82) (K84)	
George **Bailey** Birmingham (35, Northampton St) - 1888 ...	**(EP)**	(K88)	
John **Bailey** Birmingham (72, Lionel St/Frederick St) - 1882 - 1892 ...	**(BM)**	(K82) (K84) (K88) (K92)	
Joseph **Bailey** Sheffield (West Bar) 1786 ... *(See also figure: IB)*	**(OSP)**	(B) (SAOR)	
Bailey Brothers Birmingham (34, Frederick St/21, Newhall Hill) - 1896 - 1903 ...	**(EP)**	(PC) (K03)	
John **Bain** Edinburgh (11, Elder St) - 1880 ...	**(EP)**	(K80)	
BAINCO	**Not assigned!** ~ 1900	**(EP)**	(E)

John **Baines** **(OSP)** (GDS)
Sheffield (Fitzwilliam St)
- 1833 ...

Thomas **Bains** **(OSP)** (DSRR)
Sheffield (Broomhall Field St)
- 1841 ...

Baker & Co. **(EP)** (K78)
Birmingham (15, George St)
- 1878 ...

John **Baker & Sons** **(EP)** (WDS79) (K93 AD)
(Monmouth Works)
Sheffield (Harmer Ln)
1837 - 1937 ...
(See also figure: J.B&S)

Baker & Staniforth **(EP)** (K93) (WDS01)
Sheffield (22, George St)
- 1893 - 1901 ...

I. **Baker** **(OSP/CU)** (HGDB) (HDG)
Birmingham (110, Gt. Hampton St)
- 1849 - 1850...

John **Baker** **(EP)** (K80)
Birmingham (13 & 35, Mott St)
- 1880 ...

John **Baker** **(EP)** (CDB) (BDB) (GS) (MDG) (POB) (K72) (K80)
Birmingham (Summer Hill/33, Powell St)
- 1861 - 1880 ...

John **Baker** **(CP/CU)** (WDOB) (HGDB) (HGD)
Birmingham (Hall St/57, Graham St)
- 1839 - 1850 ...

John **Baker** **(GS/OSP)** (GDBS) (WDOS)
Sheffield (40/42, Carver St)
- 1849 - 1852 ...
(See also figure: John Baker)

John **Baker** **(CU/BM/EP)**
(Wheeldon Works)
Sheffield (Wheeldon St/38, Arundel St)
- 1872- 1911 ... (K72) AD
- 1893 ... (**& Co.**) (WDS11)
(See also figure: MERIT) (K93) (SBW) (M)

	Samuel **Baker**	**(EP)**	(K80)
	Birmingham (77, Carver St)		
	- 1880 ...		
	Thomas **Baker**	**(EP)**	(K80)
	Birmingham (13, Gt. Hampton St)		
	- 1880 ...		
	William **Barker**	**(EP)**	(K82) (K84) (K88)
	Birmingham (10, Smith St/Gt. Hampton Rw)		(K92)
	- 1882 - 1892...		
	William Edwin **Baker**	**(EP)**	(K03)
	Birmingham (35, Mott St)		
	- 1903 ...		
	William T. **Baker**	**(CU/EP)**	(HGDB) (HGD)
	Birmingham (42 & 43, Paradise St)		(GS)
	- 1849 - 1863		
	Baker Brothers	**(EP)**	(K03)
	Birmingham (12, 14 & 16, Constitution Hill)		
	- 1903 ...		
BALAZO	*(See also)*	**(EP)**	
	John **Round & Son Ltd.**		
	(Tudor Works/Arundel Works)		
BALFOUR " Phoenix "	Arthur **Balfour & Co.**	**(EP)**	(SBW)
	Sheffield		
	~ 1865 *(See also figure: GRIFFIN)*		
	James **Ballantyne & Son**	**(T)**	(S)
	Glasgow (Virginia St)		
	- 1897 - 1910		
	(See also figure: JB & S EP)		
BALL BROS	**Ball Brothers**	**(EP)**	(K82) (K84) (K88)
	Birmingham (14, Regent Pd)		(K92) (K93) (PC)
	- 1882 - 1896 ...		
	John **Balleny**	**(EP)**	(GS) (SAOR)
	Birmingham (43 & 44, St. Paul's Sq)		
	- 1844 - 1861 ...		
	Balt, Addis & Co.	**(EP)**	(PC) (K03)
	(Bolt, Addis & Co)		
	Birmingham (Price St)		
	- 1896 - 1903 ...		

BANDOLA	*(See also)* **(EP)** John **Round & Son Ltd.** **(Tudor Works/Arundel Works)**	
	Banister & Griffiths **(CU/EP)** Birmingham (Quest St/Hockley Hill) - 1863 ...	(GS)
	William **Banister** **(CP)** Birmingham (17, Lench St/116, Lancaster St) 1788 - 1839 ...	(B) (AB) (WTDB) (CD) (WTD) (PDB) (DOB) (WWDB) (WDOB) (M)
	Charles **Bannister** **(CU)** Birmingham (16, Moland St) - 1835 ...	(WWDB)
	Arthur **Banks & Co.** **(EP)** Birmingham (14, Buckingham St) - 1888 ...	(K88)
	Henry **Barber** **(CP)** Birmingham (190, Bradford St) - 1833 ...	(DOB)
	I. & James **Barber** **(EP)** Sheffield ~ 1890 *(See also figure: James Barber)*	
	John **Barber** **(OSP)** Birmingham 1816 ...	(SAOR)
	Thomas **Barber** **(CP)** Birmingham (Cock St) - 1815 ...	(WTDB)
	Edward **Bardell** **(CP)** Birmingham (Prospect Rock) - 1815 ...	(WTDB)
	Barker & Allen **(GS)** Sheffield (77, Surrey St) Birmingham (16, Oozells St North) - 1884 - 1892 ...	(K84) (K88) (K92) (K93)

Barker & Creed (CU) ^{(WAB) (HTD)} ^{(DOB) (WWDB)}

Birmingham (87, Caroline St/Carver St)
- 1829 - 1835 ...

BARKER
DAVY

Barker & Davy (CU/OSP) (B)
Sheffield
~ 1787

Barker
Ellis

Barker & Ellis Silver Co. Ltd. (EP)
Sheffield
- 1906 - 1960 ...
(See also figures: symbol " pineap-
ple", "gate", "shell", "candelab-
ra", "MS")

Barker & England (CU/EP) (W)
Sheffield
~ 1874 .. *(See also figure: B M E)*

Mary **Barker** (CP) (WAB)
Birmingham (Lionel St)
- 1829 ...
(Then: William Barker)

William **Barker** (EP) (CDB) (BDB) (MDG)
Birmingham (42 & 43, Paradise St)
- 1861 - 1866 ...
(Then: Barker Brothers)

Barker Brothers (BM/EP)
(Unity Works) (Herbert Edward & Matthias)
(Formerly: William Barker)
Birmingham (42 & 43, Paradise St/Constitu-
tion Hill)
London (45-50, Holborn Viaduct)
- 1867 - 1903 ...
1907 - 1960 (**Silversmiths Ltd.**)
(See also figures: BB, BB S Ld.,
GRIEL, BRITANNOID, Unity
*Quality Plate, EP *** NS, EP*NS)*
(Then: Barker Ellis Silver Co.Ltd.)

(B) (POB) (K72)
(K78) (K80) (K82)
(K84) (K88) (K92)
(PC) (K03) (M)

(K36) (M)

Benjamin **Barlow & Son** (CP) (WTDB) (CD)
(WTD) (WDB)
Birmingham (14, Cannon St)
- 1815 - 1825 ... (PDB) –

42

	John **Barlow** **(CP/CU)** (WWDB) (WDOB) Birmingham (27, Little Hampton St) 1819 - 1839 ... (SAOR)
BARNARD	Edward **Barnard & Sons Ltd.** **(CU/EP)** London 1829 - heute
	R. **Barnard &** W. **Hadfield** **(OSP)** (B) (SAOR) Sheffield (Grindlegate) 1792 ... *(See also figure: R·B)*
	Edward & John **Barnard** **(EP)** London 1851 - 1868 *(See also figure: EB JB)*
	Edward, Ed. jun. John & William **Barnard (EP)** London 1846 - 1868 *(See also figure: EE B W)*
	Robert **Barnard** **(OSP)** (B) (SAOR) Sheffield (Furnace Hill) 1788 ... *(See also figure: RB)*
	Daniel **Barnard** J. **Settle & Co.(OSP)** (B) (SAOR) (Daniel **Barnard & Co.)** Sheffield (Scotland St) 1799 ... *(See also figure: DB&Co)*
	Henry **Barnascone** **(EP/CU)** Sheffield ~ 1868 - 1883 (W) (M) - 1901 - 1934 (**& Sons**) (WDS01) *(See also figures: .BARNASCONE,* *EMPIRE, HB & S, HENRY* *BARNASCONE)*
	Lewis **Barnascone** **(CU)** (WDS01) Sheffield (13, Tudor St) - 1901 ... *(See also figure: MULBER-* *RY CUTLERY & Co.)*
	Barnby & Rust **(EP)** (K80) Hull (15, Market Pl) - 1880 ...

**BARNES & Cº.
SHEFFIELD**

Frederick **Barnes & Co.**   **(CU/EP)**
Birmingham
Sheffield   (SBW) (M)
London
~ 1890 ...
*(See also figures: AGUILA, DURA-
TION, RECTO, SENRAB)*

C.F. **Barnes &** A.D. **Kirkby**   **(EP)**
Sheffield
- 1897 *(See also figure: B & K)*

Thomas **Barnes & Sons**   **(CU)** (W)
Smithfield
1787 - 1797 *(See also figure: LOVE
NER)*

George **Barnes** jun.   **(FP)** (WTD)
Birmingham (Fox St/Bartholomew St)
- 1818 ...

Isaac **Barnes**   **(EP)** (W)
Sheffield
~ 1890 ... *(See also figure: U * S)*

Joseph **Barnes**   **(OSP)**
Sheffield
~ 1787 ... *(See also figure: IB)*

BARNETT

A. **Barnett & Son**   **(EP)** (GS)
Birmingham (30, Newhall St)
- 1863 ...

George **Barnett**   **(OSP)** (SAOR)
Birmingham
1815 ...

John **Barnett**   **(EP)** (CDB) (GS)
Birmingham (Kenion St/Upper Hockley St)
- 1861 - 1863 ...
*(See also figure: JOHN BAR-
NETT)*

W. **Barnett**   **(EP/CU)** (HGDB) (HGD)
Birmingham (Smallbrook St/14, Inge St)   (BDB)
- 1849 - 1862 ...

George **Barnsley & Sons**   **(CU/CP)**   (K93)
Sheffield (Cornish St)
- 1860 - 1893 ...
(See also figures: A symbol "shoe",
ALFRED GREEN, H.HARROP,
STOIC)

Joseph **Barraclough &** J. **Rowbotham**   (B) (SAOR)
(Joseph **Barraclough & Co.)**   **(OSP)**
Sheffield (Scotland St)
1787 ... *(See also figure: I·B)*

Z. **Barraclough & Sons**   **(EP)**
Leeds
1888 ...   (SAOR)
1914 ... **(Ltd.**)
(See also figure: Z. Barraclough &
Sons)

Barrett & Mackenzie   **(EP)**   (POB)
Birmingham (23, Lower Loveday St)
- 1867 ...

George **Barrett**   **(EP)**   (BDB) (MDG)
Birmingham (42, Warstone Ln/101, Buckingham St)
- 1862 - 1866 ...

W. **Barretta**   **(EP)**   (K36)
Sheffield (32, Mappin St)
- 1936 ...

Thomas **Bartleet**   **(OSP)**   (SAOR)
Birmingham
1816 ...

John **Bartleman**   **(CU)**   (HTD)
Birmingham (Exeter Rw)
- 1830 ...

John **Bartleman**   **(EP)**   (K80)
Edinburgh (30, Hanover St)
- 1880 ...

John **Bartlett**   **(EP)**   (K36)
Birmingham (27, Mary St)
- 1936 ...

B

Thomas **Bartlett** (OSP) ^(SAOR)
Birmingham
1812 ...

George **Barton** (EP) ^{(K84) (K82)}
Birmingham (10, Frederick St)
- 1882 - 1884 ...

John **Barton** (CP) ^(WAB)
Birmingham (Exeter Rw/Frederick St)
- 1829 ...

John **Barton** (EP) ^(K80)
Edinburgh (80, Hanover St)
- 1880 ...

Samuel **Barton** (CU/EP) ^(W)
Sheffield
~ 1892 ... *(See also figure: BUSY B)*

Albert Edward **Bate** (EP) ^(K03)
Birmingham (50, Caroline St)
- 1903 ...

George **Bate** (CP) ^{(DOB) (WDOB)}
Birmingham (23, Navigation St /Suffolk St)
- 1833 - 1839 ...

Ralph **Bateman** (CU)
Sheffield
- 1787 ...

Robert **Bateman** (CU/CP) ^{(K72) AD}
(Don Works)
Sheffield (Penistone Rd)
- 1872 ... *(See also figures: T, ROD)*

George **Bates** (CP/CU) ^(WWDB)
Birmingham (Navigation St)
- 1835 ...

Albert **Batt** (EP) ^(WDS01)
Sheffield (77, Watkin St)
- 1901 ...

46

John **Batt**   **(CU/BM/EP)**
Sheffield (20, Cambridge St/33, Broad St/
14, Sycamore St/463, Selbourne Rd)   (WDS79) (SAOR)
- 1879 - 1901 ...   (K80) (K93)
1896 - 1938 **(& Co. Ltd.)**   (WDS01)
(See also figures: JB&Co. Ltd.,   (WDSR)
JOHN BATT)

Thomas **Batt**   **(EP)**   (WDS01)
Sheffield (4, Elmore Rd)
- 1901 ...

William **Batt**   **(EP)**
Sheffield (69, Broom Spring Ln/17, Sycamore St.)   (GS) (SAOR)
- 1863 - 1881   (SAOR) (K80)
1881 - 1901 ... **(& Sons)**   (K93) (WDS01)
(See also figures: WB & S, W. Batt
& Sons)

G. **Battie & Brothers**   **(OSP)**   (B) (SAOR)
Sheffield (Furnace Hill)
1801 ... *(See also figure: G·B&B^{rs})*

Battie, Howard & Hawksworth (OSP)   (B) (SAOR) (CD)
Sheffield (Charles St)
1815 - 1818 ...
(See also figures: B H & H, HB&H)

Maurice **Baum**   **(BM/CU/EP)**
(Albert Works)
Sheffield (189 - 191, Norfolk St)   (SAOR) (W)
1884 - 1897   (SBW) (K93)
1897 - 1904 *(See also figures: B M*   (WDS01)
Rd. S, Maurice Baum, MB*S, SIL-
VERINE)

Baum Brothers   **(EP/CU)**   (WDS01)
Sheffield (101, Eyre St)
- 1901 ... *(See also figure: STRIPES)*

E. **Bawen**   **(EP)**   (MDG)
Birmingham (34, Ludgate Hill)
- 1866 ...

Alfred **Baxter & Co.**   **(EP)**   (K82) (K84) (K88)
Birmingham (21, Broad St)
- 1882 - 1888 ...

Robert **Baxter & Co.** (CU/OSP) (E)
Sheffield
~ 1850 ... *(See also figure: ROB^T BAXTER)*
(Then: Lockwood Brothers Ltd.)

Baxter & Co. (EP) (K92)
Birmingham (78 & 80, Pershore St)
- 1892 ...

William J. **Bayley** (EP) (GS) (MDG) (K80)
Blackpool (7, Caroline St/Abingdon St)
- 1863 - 1880 ...

Coulthard **Bayliss & Co.** (EP) (K36)
Birmingham (60, Branston St)
- 1936 ...

Ernst Hubert **Bayliss** (EP) (K03)
(Norfolk Works)
Birmingham (46, Buckingham St)
- 1903 ...

Thomas **Bayliss** (CP) (WAB) (HTD)
Birmingham (45, Summer Ln)
- 1829 - 1830 ...

(See also (BM/EP)
Barker Brothers
(Unity Works)

(See also) (EP)
Briddon Brothers

(See also) (EP)
Henry Arthur **Goodall**

(See also) (OSP)
B. **Blonk**

(See also) (EP)
Briddon Brothers

(See also (BM/EP)
Barker Brothers
(Unity Works)

BB S.LD	*(See also)* **Barker Brothers (Unity Works)**	**(BM/EP)**

BEACH & MINTE

Beach & Minte (Beach & Co) **(EP)** (K78) (W) (SBW) (M)
Birmingham (8, Caroline St)
- 1878 ...

BEACON PLATE

Not assigned! **(EP)** (E)
~ 1900

Joseph **Beal & Sons** **(EP)**
Sheffield
~ 1876 ...
(See also figure: JOSH BEAL)

J. & J. **Beal** **(EP)** (M)
(Redhill Works)
Sheffield
~ 1876 *(See also figures: ENDURE, symbol "boar head")*

Michael **Beal** **(EP)** (B) (SAOR) (SBW) (M)
Sheffield (Market Pl)
1867 ... *(See also figure: MB)*

T. **Beardman** **(EP)** (PC)
Birmingham (14, Vyse St)
- 1896 ...

T. **Beardmore** **(EP)**
Birmingham
~ 1895 ... *(See also figure: T.B)*

BEARDSHAW, SHEFFIELD

Albert J. **Beardshaw** **(CU/EP)**
(Baltic Steel Works)
Sheffield (12, Mulberry St/32 - 35, Victoria St/ Effingham Rd)
- 1871 - 1880 ... *(See also figure: A.B)*
1864 - 1901 ... **(& Co./& Son)**
- 1901 ... **(Ltd.)**
(See also figures: A B & Co, A.ROSLING, CONQUERER, CHARLES CALOW, STEVENS)

(WDS71) (K80)
(M) (SBW)
(B) (SAOR) (K80)
(K93) (WDS01)
(SBW) (M)

(WDS01)

John **Beattie** **(OSP)** ^(DSRR)
Sheffield (62, Edward St)
- 1841 ...

William Henry **Beaumont & Co. (BM/EP)** ^{(GS) (K80)}
(Beaumont & Joiner)
Sheffield (1a, Wicker)
- 1861 - 1880 ...
(See also figure: WHB)

Charles Henry **Beaumont** **(EP)** ^(WDS01)
Sheffield (39, Infirmary Rd)
- 1901 ...

Henry **Beaumont** **(EP)** ^(K36)
Sheffield (Joiner Ln, Wicker)
- 1936 ...

Joseph **Beaumont** **(EP)** ^(WDS01)
Sheffield (273, Shoreham St)
- 1901 ...

Beaumont Brothers **(EP)** ^{(WDS79) (K93)}
Sheffield (Joiner Ln/108, Rockingham St/ ^{(WDS01) (WDSR)}
106, Sackville Rd) ^(WDS11)
- 1879 - 1911 ...

BEBARA

(See also) **(EP)**
John **Round & Son Ltd.**
(Tudor Works/Arundel Works)

William **Beckett & Co.** **(CU/EP)**
Sheffield
~ 1860 ...
(See also figures: William Beckett
& Co, W.J.BELCHER)

Alfred **Beckett & Sons** **(EP/CU)** ^(W)
Sheffield
~ 1900 ...
(See also figures: M.B MOULSON,
R. VERNON & SONS, T. JOWITT)

John **Bedford & Sons (Lion Works)** (CU)
Sheffield (Mowbray St)
1865 - 1893 ...
- 1901 ... (**Ltd.**)
(See also figures: ACME, INDUS-TRIA ACME, symbol "lion")

(W) (WDS79)
(K93)
(WDS01)

John **Bednall & Co.** (CU/EP) (W)
Sheffield
~ 1860 ... *(See also figures: CHRIS, JB & Co)*

John **Bee** (OSP) (CD) (WTD)
Birmingham (Mount St)
- 1818 ...

R. **Beech** (CP) (WDOB)
Birmingham (Cecil St)
- 1839 ...

Thomas **Beely** (CU)
Sheffield
1787 ... *(See also figure: MARS)*

W. **Beeston** (EP) (GS)
Sheffield (West St)
- 1863 ...

Edward **Beet** (OSP) (B)
Sheffield
1787 -

Widow **Beet & Sons** (CP/CU) (B)
Sheffield
1787 ...

John **Beet** (CU/OSP) (W)
Sheffield
1787 ... *(See also figure: CIR CLE)*

BELANZA

(See also) (EP)
John **Round & Son Ltd.**
(Tudor Works/Arundel Works)

G. **Beldon** (OSP) (B) (W) (M)
Sheffield
1809 ...

Beldon, Hoyland & Co. **(OSP)** (B) (GM) (M) (W)
Sheffield (Burgess St)
1785 - 1787 ... *(See also figure: PLU-TUS)*

Robert **Belfitt** **(EP)**
Sheffield
~ 1892
(See also figure: THE CAVEN-DISH)

Walter **Belk & Son** **(EP)**
(Kingsley Works)
Sheffield (Young St)
1915 - 1923
1923 - 1931 (**Ltd.**) *(See also figures: W.BELK, KINGSLEY PLATE)*

Charles **Belk** **(EP)** (WDS79) (M)
(Samuel **Roberts &** Charles **Belk**)
(Formerly: Roberts & Briggs)
Sheffield (Kenwood Rd)
1863 - 1900
ab 1901 ... (**Ltd.**) *(See also figure: C B E P)*

John **Bell** **(CU/EP)** (B) (SAOR)
(WDOS) (SBW)
Sheffield (Stoker Cottage) (M)
- 1852 - 1854 ... *(See also figure: IB)*

John & Jonathan **Bell** **(OSP)** (B) (SAOR) (SBW)
(M)
Sheffield (South St, Moor)
1843 ... *(See also figure: J&JB)*

Jonathan **Bell** **(EP)** (B) (SAOR)
(SBW)
Sheffield (South St, Moor)
1854 ... *(See also figure: JB)*
1897 ... (**& Sons**) *(See also figure: JB&S)*

Richard **Bell** **(CU/EP)** (WDOB) (HGDB)
Birmingham (Gt. Charles St/13, Gt. Hampton Rw)
- 1839 - 1849 ...

Samuel **Bell** **(EP)** (K80)
Birmingham (11, Mary St/Caroline St)
- 1880 ...

	W. **Bell** (EP) (MDG) Birmingham (87, Lower Tower St) - 1866 ...
	Bellamy & George **Gordon** (EP) Sheffield ~ 1894 - 1896
	Ben & Jones (EP) London ~ 1845 - 1851 *(Then: Benefink & Co)*
BENAROID	*(See also)* (EP) John **Round & Son Ltd.** **(Tudor Works/Arundel Works)**
	James **Bendall** (CU/CP) (WDB) (PDB) Birmingham (20, Steelhouse Ln) - 1823 - 1825 ...
BENETFINK&Co **CHEAPSIDE**	**Benetfink & Co.** (EP) (M) (B) London (83, Cheapside) 1852 - 1861 ... 1891 - 1915 ... *(See also figure: B & Co)* *(Then: Benetfink & Fox)*
	Benetfink & Fox (EP) London (83, Cheapside) 1861 - 1890 *(Then: Benetfink & Co.)*
BENGALL	*(See also)* (EP) (W) Thomas Radley **Cadman & Sons**
BENGAL SILVER	*(See also)* (EP) Thomas H. **Daniel &** Thomas R. **Arter** **(Globe Nevada Silver Works)**
	Samuel **Bennett &** Peter **Spurr** (OSP) (B) (SAOR) Sheffield (Arundel St) 1801 ... *(See also figure: S·B)*
	Edward **Bennett** (OSP) (CD) Sheffield (Rockingham St) - 1818 ...

Edwin T. **Bennett** **(EP)** (K80)
Barton/Bristol (131, Ducie Rd)
- 1880 ...

John **Bennett** **(EP)** (K78)
Birmingham (15, Summer Ln)
- 1878 ...

Bennett Brothers **(EP)** (K80)
Liverpool
- 1880 ...

H. J. A. **Bensley** **(EP)** (K36)
London (57a, Holborn Viaduct)
- 1936 ...

Benson & Ryland **(EP)** (BDB)
Birmingham
- 1861
(Then: Benson Brothers)

John Daniels **Benson** **(EP)** (K80) (K82) (K84)
Birmingham (64, Vyse St/6, Hylton St)   (K88) (K92) (K03)
- 1880 - 1903 ...

J. W. **Benson** **(EP)**
London
1884 ...   (SAOR)
London (62 & 64, Ludgate Hill)
- 1936 ...**(Ltd.)** *(See also figure: J.W.*   (K36) (SBW)
Benson)

William H. **Benson** **(EP)** (POB) (MDG)
Birmingham (13, Weaman St)   (K72) (K78) (K80)
- 1867 - 1888 ...   (K82) (K84) (K88)

Benson Brothers **(EP)** (CDB) (BDB) (GS)
(Formerly: Benson & Ryland)   (MDG)
Birmingham (13, Weaman St)
- 1861 - 1866 ...

Bent & Tagg **(CP)** (SAOR) (DOB)
Birmingham (42, Lionel St/Newhall St)   (WDOB)
1832 - 1839 ...

Joseph **Bent** **(GS/BM)** (SAOR) (HGD)
Birmingham (59, Newhall St)
1842 - 1850 ...

Thomas **Bentley & Co.** **(EP)** ^(K80)
Margate (31, High St/New St)
- 1880 ...

BEN TON

George & Frederick **Benton** **(EP)** ^(K93)
Sheffield (13, Norfolk Ln)
- 1893 ...

J. H. **Benton & Co.** **(EP)** ^(PC)
Birmingham (40, Augusta St)
- 1896 ...

Benton & Okey **(EP)** ^(K03)
Birmingham (61, Kenyon St)
- 1903 ...

Henry **Benton & Son** **(EP)** ^(K92)
Birmingham (53, Gt. Hampton Rw)
- 1892 ...

G. **Benton** **(EP/CP)** ^(PC)
Birmingham (53, Gt. Hampton Rw)
- 1896 ...

Harriet **Benton** **(EP)** ^{(K80) (K82) (K84)}
Birmingham (54, Barr St)
- 1880 - 1884 ...

Henry William **Benton** **(EP)** ^{(K88) (K92)}
Birmingham (128, Well St)
- 1888 - 1892 ...

John **Benton** **(OSP/CU)** ^{(WTDB) (WTD) (WDB)}
Birmingham (James St/Livery St)
- 1815 - 1823 ...

John **Benton** **(EP)** ^{(K88) (K92)}
Birmingham (118, Barr St)
- 1888 - 1892 ...

Thomas **Benton** **(EP)** ^{(CDB) (POB) (K72) (K78)}
Birmingham (54, Barr St)
- 1861 - 1878 ...

Benton Brothers **(GS)**
Sheffield (Rodley Ln)
- 1893 ...

James **Beresford & Co.** **(BM/EP)** (BDB) (GS)
(Eagle Works) (MDG) (POB)
Birmingham (42, Summer Rw/31, Charlotte (K72) (K78) (K80)
St/36, Ludgate Hill) (K82) (K84) (K88)
- 1861 - 1896 ... (K92) (PC)

Berkeley & Co. **(EP)** (PC)
Birmingham (Henry St)
- 1896 ...

Berlyn & Wicker **(EP)** (K03)
Birmingham (49, Branston St)
- 1903 ...

Berndorf **(GS/EP)** (K82) (K84)
(Nickel & German Silver Works)
Birmingham (53, St. Paul's Sq)
- 1882 - 1884 ...

Berndoy Metal Works **(GS)** (K93)
Sheffield (9, Eyre St)
- 1893 ...

Charles **Besancon** **(EP)** (K72)
Birmingham (2, Hockley Hill)
- 1872 ...

Bessant & Holloway **(EP)** (K78)
Birmingham (75, Caroline St)
- 1878 ...

Thomas **Bessant** **(EP)** (K80)
Birmingham (75, Caroline St)
- 1880 ...

BESSEMER Henry **Bessemer Co. Ltd.** **(CU/EP)** (WDS79) (WDS01)
(Bessemer Steel Works)
Sheffield (Carlisle St East)
- 1879 - 1901 ...

BEST **Best & Wastidge** **(CU)** (B) (M)
Sheffield
1816 ...

B E S T H. **Best** **(CU/OSP)** (B) (M) (W)
Birmingham (Gt. Charles St)
1814 ...

	George **Best** Birmingham (31a, St. George's Pl) - 1888 - 1892 ...	**(EP)**	(K88) (K92)
	Thomas **Best** Sheffield (45, Howard St) 1819 - 1825 ... *(See also figure: T·BEST)*	**(CU/OSP)**	(B) (SAOR) (HDG) (NGDS)
BEST ELECTRO PLATE	*(See also)* John **Morton & Co.**	**(EP)**	
" BEST PLATE "	**Not assigned!** ~ 1770 - 1790	**(OSP)**	(B) (SBW)
	John **Bettridge** Coventry 1817 ...	**(OSP/CU)**	(SAOR)
	Betts & Sons Birmingham (James St/Charlotte St) - 1815 - 1818 ...	**(CP)**	(WTDB) (WTD)
	James R. **Betts** Sheffield (39, Eyre St) - 1936 ...	**(EP)**	(K36)
	Beverley Hall Ltd. Birmingham (16, Regent Pd) - 1936 ...	**(EP)**	(K36)
	Bewlay & Co. Ltd. London 1903 - 1910 *(See also figure: B&Co)*	**(EP)**	(S)
BEXRA	*(See also)* John **Round & Son Ltd.** **(Tudor Works/Arundel Works)**	**(EP)**	
	(See also) **Birmingham Guild of Handicrafts Ltd.**	**(EP)**	
B. H. A	*(See also)* Barnett Henry **Abrahams**	**(EP)**	
	(See also) **Battie, Howard & Hawksworth**	**(OSP)**	

B

BH	*(See also)* J. **Brammer** & S. **Horrabin**	(OSP)	
B H	*(See also)* B. **Hounsfield**	(OSP)	
BHA Ⓑ Ⓗ Ⓐ	*(See also)* Barnett Henry **Abrahams**	(EP)	
B H L⁽ᵀᴰ⁾ EP NS	**Not assigned!** ~ 1920	(EP)	
	Bickley & Pickett London (12, President St) - 1936 ...	(EP)	(K36)
	Biddle & Collingwood Birmingham - 1875 - 1897 *(See also figure: B & C)*	(EP)	(M) (SBW)
	William Adolphus **Biddle** Birmingham (70 & 138, Cheapside) - 1884 - 1892 ... - 1872 ... **(& Co.)**	(GS/EP)	(K84) (K88) (K92) (K72)
	Frank **Biddle** Birmingham (26, Constitution Hill) - 1878 ...	(EP)	(K78)
BIGGIN	John **Biggin & Co. Ltd.** Sheffield (10, Milk St) 1825 - 1893 ... *(See also figure: APEX)*	(CU)	(B) (GS) (K93) (SBW)
	Henry **Biggin & Co.** **(Matilda Works)** Sheffield (45, Matilda St) - 1880 - 1884 ... *(See also figure: HENRY BIGGIN & Co)*	(BM/EP)	(M) (K80)
	John **Biggin** Sheffield (Mulberry St/23, Sycamore St/ 10, Milk St) 1855 - 1905 ... *(See also figure: JB)*	(GS/EP)	(B) (K84) (K93) (WDSR) (SBW) (M)

Samuel **Biggin** **(EP)**
(Matilda Works)
Sheffield (117, Matilda St)
~ 1892 - 1905 ...
1888 ... **(& Son)**
(See also figure: G.TURNER)

(W) (WDSR)
(SAOR)

John Walter **Biggins** **(EP)**
Sheffield (70, Ashland Rd/34, Arundel St)
- 1879 - 1901 ...

(WDS79) (K93)
(WDS01)

Frank **Bill** **(EP)**
Birmingham (53, Branston St)
- 1882 - 1884 ...

(K82) (K84)

Bingham & Ogden **(CU)**
Sheffield (188, Rockingham St)
- 1879 ... *(See also figure: SELECT)*

(WDS79)

John Edward **Bingham** **(EP)**
Sheffield (Ranmoor Park Rd)
- 1879 - 1901 ...

(WDS79) (WDS01)

William. J. **Bingham** **(CU)**
(Clough Works)
Sheffield
- 1887 *(See also figure: OLD O)*

(K88AD)

John **Bingley** **(CU/OSP)**
Birmingham (Newhall St)
- 1818 ...

(WTD)

William **Bingley** **(CU/OSP)**
William **Bingley & Son**
Birmingham (Bishopsgate St/Newhall St)
1787 - 1818 ...
(See also figure: W.BINGLEY)

(B) (CD) (W)
(WTD) (WTDB)
(M)

Bingley, George **Bower & Co.** **(EP)**
Sheffield
~ *(See also figure: B.W & Co)*

(SBW) (M)

R. **Binnall & Co.** **(EP)**
Shrewsbury
~

(SBW) (M)

John **Binney** **(OSP)**
Sheffield (Woodhead Rd)
- 1871 ...

(WDS71)

Birch & Mason	**(EP)** [BDB]

Birmingham (13, Coleshill St)
- 1862 ...

Walter **Birch** (CU/EP) [W]
Sheffield
~ 1875 *(See also figure: PRACTICAL)*

BIRD

Bird & Co. (EP) [W]
Sheffield
~ 1900

Bird & Blake (CU/EP) [W]
Sheffield
~ 1892 ...
(See also figure: DUCHESS)

Bird & Feran (EP) [K03]
Birmingham (55, Frederick St)
- 1903 ...

Frank **Birkett & Co.** (EP) [K82] [K84] [K88] [K92] [K03]
Birmingham (2, Whittall St)
- 1882 - 1903 ...

W. **Birks & Co.** (CU/OSP) [B] [SAOR]
Sheffield (Pincin Ln/Norfolk St)
1773 ... *(See also figure: W.B & Co)*
1781 ... (**& Son**)
(See also figure: WB & S)

William & John **Birks** (CU/OSP) [B]
Sheffield (Norfolk St)
1787 ... *(See also figure: FABRE)*

Birks, Withers & Sykes (CU) [B]
Sheffield (Pinston Croft Ln)
1774 ...
1787 ...
*(See also figures: SK & Co,
SYKES)*

Birmingham Electro Plating Co. (EP) [K80] [K03]
Birmingham (40, St. Paul's Sq/160, Angelina St)
- 1880 - 1903 ...

Birmingham Excelsior Plating Co. (EP) [K03]
Birmingham (54, Staniforth St)
- 1903 ...

Birmingham Guild of Handicrafts Ltd. (M) (S)
(EP)
Birmingham
1895 - 1910
(See also figures: BGLtd., BGH Ld.)
(Then: E. & R. Gittings)

Birmingham Silver Plate Ltd. (EP) (S)
(Mappin & Webb, Walker & Hall, Elkington)
Birmingham
1964 ... *(See also figure: B S L)*

BIRTS&SONS

Birts & Sons **(EP)** (W) (SBW) (M)
Woolwich
~ 1878 ...

Thomas **Bishop** **(CP/OSP)** (CD) (PDB) (M)
(B)
Birmingham (Rockingham St/Furnival St/
24, St. Paul's Sq)
- 1818 - 1830 ...

George **Bishop & Sons** **(EP)** (WDSR) (SBW)
Sheffield (216, Rockingham St)
1894 - 1940
(See also figures: GB & S, G.B & S)

W. **Bishop & Sons** **(EP)** (WDS01)
Sheffield (Joiner Ln)
- 1901 ...

Herbert **Bishop** **(EP)** (WDS01)
Sheffield (117, Alderson Rd)
- 1901 ...

William Arthur **Bishop** **(EP)** (WDS01)
Sheffield (9, Eyre Ln/47, Bramall Ln)
- 1901 ...

Thomas **Bishton** **(EP)** (K36)
Birmingham (87, Victoria St)
- 1936 ...

John **Biven** **(EP)** (K82) (K84)
Birmingham (34, Theodore St)
- 1882 - 1884 ...

Blackford & Lawson **(CU/CP)** (DOB) (WWDB)
(WDOB)
Birmingham (2, Bread St/Gt. Charles St)
- 1833 - 1839 ...

Blackham & Matthews   **(EP)**   (K03)
Birmingham (27, Northampton St)
- 1903 ...

John **Blackham**   **(CP)**   (DOB) (WDOB)
Birmingham (33, Church St/Hanley St)
- 1833 - 1839 ...

William Henry **Blackstaff**   **(EP)**   (K80)
Birmingham (Warstone Ln)
- 1880 ...

Blackwell & Parkin   **(CU/OSP)**   (B) (SAOR) (CD)
Sheffield (Hicks Ln, Westbar)
1816 - 1818 ... *(See also figure: B & P)*

Joseph **Blackwell**   **(OSP)**   (GDS) (WDS37)
Sheffield (25, Arundel St/Pye Bank)
- 1833 - 1837 ...

William **Blackwell**   **(OSP)**   (B) (SAOR) (CD)
Sheffield (Tower Hill/Bridge Houses)   (HDG) (PDY)
1816 - 1825 ... **(& Co.**)   (PDB)
(See also figure: WB & Co)   (NGDS) (SDG)
- 1825 - 1829 ... **(& Son**)   (PD) (GDS)
- 1833 - 1837 ...   (HGDY) (WDS37)

William **Bladder**   **(EP/CU)**   (HGDB) (HGD)
Birmingham (21, Mary Ann St/Peel St/   (CDB) (K72)
Winson Green/Ct. 3, Mount St)
- 1849 - 1872 ...

J. **Bladon**   **(EP)**   (MDG)
Birmingham (122, Lodge Rd)
- 1866 ...

Thomas **Blagden**   **(OSP)**
Sheffield (Nursery Walk/White Rails)
1798 ... *(See also figure: T·B)*   (B) (SAOR)
1808 - 1830 ... **(&Co.**)   (B) (SAOR)
(See also figure: T·B&Co)

Blagden, Hodgson & Co.   **(OSP)**   (HDG) (PDY)
Sheffield (White Rails/ 20 & 3, Nursery St)   (NGDS) (SDG)
- 1822 - 1833 ...   (PD) (GDS)
(See also figure: symbol "globe")
(Then: Hawksworth, Eyre & Co)

Blagden, Hodgson, Kirby & Co. (OSP) ^(CD)
Sheffield (Nursery St)
- 1818 ...

Hammond **Blake**   **(OSP)**   (SAOR) (M)
Sheffield (Queen St)
1798 ... *(See also figure: H.B)*

John **Blake**   **(CU)**   (POAD)
London (16, Long Acre)
- 1808 ...

Thomas Henry **Blake**   **(EP/CU)**   (WDS01) (W)
Sheffield (Holly St/19, Carver Ln)
1887 - 1911
(See also figures: THBS, BROOM)
(Then: Castle & Turton)

Thomas **Blakemore**   **(OSP)**   (CD)
Sheffield (Gt. Charles St)
- 1818 ...

William **Blakeway & Son**   **(OSP/CU)**   (WTD)
Birmingham
- 1818 ...

Solomon **Blanckensee & Sons Ltd. (EP)**
(Acquisition of Nathan & Hayes)
Birmingham (Gt. Charles St)
- 1863 ... *(See also figure: S.B & S L^D)*

Lionel **Blanckensee**   **(BM/EP)**   (K92) (PC) (K03)
Birmingham (55, Buckingham St/18, 19, 35, Northwood St)
- 1892 - 1903 ...

E. **Blaydes & Co.**   **(CU)**   (WDS79)
Sheffield
- 1879 ... *(See also figure: symbol "bat")*

William **Blews & Sons**   **(BM/GS)**   (HGD)
Birmingham (9, Bartholomew St)
- 1850 ...

Jesse **Blocksidge**   **(OSP)**   (CD) (WTD)
(WDB) (PDB)
Birmingham (Northwood St/36, Branston St)
- 1818 - 1825 ...

Benjamin **Blonk** **(OSP)** (B) (SAOR)
Sheffield (Change Alley)
1779 ... *(See also figure: BB)*

Benjamin **Bloomer** **(CP)** (WAB) (HTD) (DOB)
Birmingham (6, Little Charles St)
- 1829 - 1833 ...

George Henry **Bloomer** **(EP)** (WDS01)
Sheffield (Ct. 2 & 4, Furnival St)
- 1901 ...

Henry George **Bloor** **(EP)** (WDS79) (K80)
(Orchard Works)
Sheffield (7, Orchard Ln)
- 1879 - 1880 ...

W. **Blows & Sons** **(BM)** (HGD)
Birmingham (Bartholomew St)
~ 1850 ...

Edwin **Blyde & Co.** **(EP)** (WDS01) (Rd)
Sheffield (32, Lambert St)
1872 - 1910 *(See also figures: E.B & Co., Faugh-A-Ballagh, Volunteer, Edwin Blyde)*
1910 - 1940 (**Ltd.**)
(See also figure: E.Blyde & Co Ltd.)

John **Blyde** **(EP)** (SBW) (M)
(Clintock Works)
Sheffield
~ 1873 ...
(See also figures: GENIUS, J.B)

John **Blyth** **(CP)** (DOB) (WDOB)
Birmingham (Woodcock St)
- 1833 - 1839 ...

ⒷⓂⒺ *(See also)* **(CU/EP)**
Barker & England

BMMTS **Britannia Metal Mounts** **(BM)**

B

(circles: M, Rᵈ, S, B, crown symbol)

(See also) **(EP)**
Maurice **Baum**
(Albert Works)

Charles **Boardman &** A. O. **Glossop**
(Clarence Work)   (BM/EP/CU)
Sheffield (54 and then 169 & 171, Pond St)   (B) (SAOR)
London (16, Ely Pl, Holborn)
1861 - 1871 ...
1887 - 1895 (**& Co.**)   (K80) (K93)
1895 - 1924 (**& Co. Ltd.**)   (WDS01) (WDSR)
(See also figures: B&G, B&G S)   (SBW) (M)

Charles **Boardman**   **(GS/EP/BM)**   (WDS37) (B)
Sheffield (Norfolk Ln/128, Allan St/54,   (SAOR) (DSRR)
Pond St)   (GDBS) (WDOS)
- 1837 - 1852 ... *(See also figure: C B)*   (M)

Bocock & Wilkinson   **(EP)**   (K92) (PC)
Birmingham (123, Gt. Hampton St)
- 1892 - 1896 ...

William **Bocking**   **(EP)**   (W)
Sheffield
~ 1900 *(See also figure: TRUE)*

Joseph **Boler**   **(EP)**   (K36)
Sheffield (8, Brown Ln)
- 1936 ...

BOLIVIAN SILVER   *(See also)*   **(EP)**
William **Page & Co.**

Bolt, Addis & Co.   **(EP)**   (K82) (K88) (K92)
Birmingham (3, St. Mary's Rw/Price St)
- 1882 - 1892 ...

Herbert Henry **Bolton & Co.**   **(EP)**   (K92) (PC)
Birmingham (Caroline St./24, Mary St./
24, Augusta St)
- 1892 - 1896 ...

James **Bolton**   **(EP)**
(Parade Works)   (CDB) (POB)
Birmingham (20, Barr St/Villa St/64, George St)   (K72) (K78)
- 1861 - 1878 ...   (GS) (K80) (K82)
- 1863 - 1884 ... (**& Co./& Son**)   (K84)

William **Bolton** (CP) ^(DOB)
Birmingham (Ct. 23, Lionel St)
- 1833 ...

BONA-FIDE *(See also)* (CU)
John **Wigfall & Co.**

Bonser & Son (EP) ^(SBW)
London
~

Thomas **Booker** (BM/GS) ^(HGD)
Birmingham (160, Gt. Hampton Rw)
- 1850 ...

Henry C. **Booth & Co.** (CU) ^{(K72) AD}
(Norfolk Works)
Sheffield (Norfolk Ln)
- 1872 ...

Booth & Deakin (CU/OSP) ^(PD)
Sheffield (Holly St)
- 1829 ...

William Bruce **Booth** (EP) ^(K80)
Bolton/Lanes (89, Derby St)
- 1880 ...

Borries & Co. (EP) ^{(PC) (K03)}
Birmingham (10, Augusta St)
- 1896 - 1903 ...

J. **Borwick** (OSP) ^(B)
Sheffield (Lambert Croft)
1788 ... *(See also Meister: I·B)*

Boswell, Hatfield & Co. (EP) ^(SBW)
(Hope Works)
Sheffield
~ 1900 ... *(See also figures: OPOBA, XY)*

Botteley & Lilly (CP) ^(WTDB)
Birmingham (St. Paul's Sq)
- 1815 ...

Botteley & Richards (CP) ^{(WTD) (WDB)}
Birmingham (2, James St) ^(PDB)
- 1818 - 1825 ...

Thomas **Botterley**   **(CP)**   (WAB) (HTD)
Birmingham (43, Water St)   (DOB)
- 1829 - 1833 ...

Boucher Brothers   **(EP)**   (WDS79)
Sheffield (1, Cadman Ln)
- 1879 ...

Matthew **Boulton & Fothergill (OSP)**
Birmingham (Soho Hill)
1764 - 1773 ... *(See also figure: B&F)*

BOULTON

✹   ✹

Matthew **Boulton & Plate Co.** **(OSP)**   (B) (SAOR) (CD)
Birmingham (Soho Manufactory)   (MB) (WTDB)
1784 - 1851   (WTD) (WDB)
    (PDB) (M)

Bourne & Chambers   **(OSP/CU)**   (WTD)
Birmingham (Broad St)
- 1818 ...

Henry **Bourne &** Daniel J. **O'Neil** **(EP)**   (K80) (M)
Birmingham (18 & 19, Ludgate Hill)
- 1880 - 1886 ... *(See also figure: B & O'N)*

Arthur James **Bourne**   **(EP)**   (WDS01)
Sheffield (165, Abbeydale Rd)
- 1901 ...

Herny H. **Bourne**   **(EP)**   (K72) (K78) (K80)
Birmingham (18 & 19, Ludgate Hill)   (K92) (K93) (PC)
- 1872 - 1903 ... *(See also figure: H.B)*   (K03) (M)

James **Bourne**   **(OSP)**
Coventry
1813 ...   (SAOR)
Birmingham
1819 ...   (SAOR)

James Huggart **Bourne**   **(EP)**
Sheffield (8, Sycamore St)
- 1880 ...   (K80)
- 1893 .. **(& Son)**   (K93)

William Henry **Bourne**   **(EP)**   (WDS01)
Sheffield (8, Sycamore St)
- 1901 ...

John **Bourne** **(EP)** (MDG) (K72)
(K78) (K80) (K82)
Birmingham (72, Spencer St/48, Newhall (K84) (K88) (K92)
Hill)
- 1866 - 1892 ...

R. **Bourne** **(EP)** (MDG)
Birmingham (Federick St)
- 1866 ...

BOVAL James **Woolley, Sons & Co.** **(EP)** (SBW) (M)
Manchester
~ 1900 ...

George **Bowen** **(EP)**
(Victoria Works)
Birmingham (15, Victoria St)
- 1862 ... (BDB)
Birmingham (33, Lw. Loveday St/46, Au- (K78) (K80) (K82)
gusta St) (K84) (K88) (K92)
- 1878 - 1896 (**& Son**) (M)
(See also figures: GB&S, symbol (PC) (K03) (K36)
"bow")
1896 - 1936 ... (**& Sons**)

J. **Bowen** **(EP)** (HGDB) (HGD)
Birmingham (127, Hospital St)
- 1849 - 1850 ...

Jonas **Bowen** **(EP)**
Birmingham (38, Ludgate Hill/15, Victoria
St) (GS) (K80)
- 1861 - 1880 ...
Birmingham (28 & 29, Summer Rw/Fleet St) (K80)(K92) (K03)
- 1880 - 1903 ... (**& Son(s)**)
(See also figure: JB&S)

Jonas & George **Bowen** **(EP)** (CDB) (MDG)
(POB) (K72) (M)
Birmingham (15, Victoria St/29 and then 23,
Summer Rw)
-1861 - 1872 ...
(See also figures: J.B G.B, J&GB)

Miss Emma **Bowen** **(EP)** (POB)
Birmingham (34, Ludgate Hill)
- 1867 ...

Joseph **Bower** **(CP)** (SAOR) (CD) (WTD) (WDB) (PDB) (WAB) (HTD) (DOB) (WWDB) (WDOB)
Birmingham (Gt. Charles St/141, Snow Hill)
- 1818 - 1839 ...

Thomas **Bowers** **(EP)** (K80)
Oldham (3, Horsedge)
- 1880 ...

Bowes & Mincher **(EP)** (K78)
Birmingham (82, Lichfield St)
- 1878 ...

Richard Taylor **Bowes** **(EP)** (K80) (K82) (K84)
Birmingham (14, Mary's Rw/14, Franchise St)
Walsall (18, Lower Rushall St)
- 1880 - 1884 ...

William **Bowker & Son (Orchard Works)** **(EP)** (K93) (WDS01)
Sheffield (Orchard Ln/68 & 70, Division St)
- 1893 - 1901 ...

Arthur **Bowker** **(EP)** (WDS01)
Sheffield (294, Northumberland Rd)
- 1901 ...

Thomas **Bowker** **(EP)** (WDS01)
Sheffield (292, Northumberland Rd)
- 1901 ...

W. R. **Box & Co.** **(EP)** (M)
Dublin
~ *(See also figure: SILVERSTEIN)*

Charles **Boyton & Son Ltd.** **(EP)**
Birmingham
1907 ...
(See also figures: CB&S, CB&S Ltd.)

BP B. **Polack** **(OSP)** (B)
Sheffield (High St)
1807 ...

Bracher & Sydenham **(EP)** (SAOR)
Reading (Queen Victoria St)
1888 ...
(See also figures: B&S, ROYAL COUNTY PLATE)

Thomas **Bradbury & Co. (CU/OSP/EP)** (HDG)
Sheffield (Surry St/22 & 24, Arundel St) (SAOR)(GDS)
- 1822 ... (HGDY) (SD46)
1832 - 1858 *(& Son)* (WDS37) (SAOR)
(See also figure: TB&S) (GDBS) (WDOS)
1863 - 1905 *(& Sons*) (K54) (POS)
(See also figures: JBTB, TB JH, (B) (GS) (K80)
TB&SS, Thos Bradbury) (K93) (M)
1905 - 1943 *(& Sons Ltd.*) (K36)
(Then: Atkin Brothers)

James **Bradbury** **(CU)** (B)
Sheffield (57, Eyre St)
1833 ...
*(See also figure: G*R BRADBURY)*

Joseph **Bradbury** **(EP)** (M)
Sheffield
~ 1889 - 1892 *(See also figure: J.B.)*

Thomas **Bradbury** jun. **(CU/OSP)** (GDS) (DSRR)
Sheffield (Nether Heeley/Arundel St)
London (30, Bouverie St)
- 1833 - 1841 ...

Bradley & T. H. **Blake** **(EP)** (SAOR)
Sheffield
1883 - 1886 *(See also figure: B&B)*
(Then: Thomas Henry Blake)

Edward **Bradley & Co.** **(CU)** (B) (SAOR)
Sheffield (77, Arundel St) (DSRR) (SBW)
1841 ... *(See also figure: EB)* (M)

Albert Samuel **Bradley** **(CU)** (SBW)
Sheffield
~ *(See also figure: TOPAZ)*

Thomas **Bradley** **(CU/OSP)** (PD) (HDG)
Sheffield (39, New Field/39/79, Osborne St) (WDS37) (DSRR)
- 1822 - 1846 ... (SD46)

BRADSHAW

William **Bradshaw & Son**   **(CU/EP)**
Sheffield
1849 - 1864

Joseph **Bradshaw**   **(CU)**   (B) (M)
Birmingham (3, Goff St)
1822 ...

Bragg & Baldwin   **(CU/OSP)**   (SAOR)
Birmingham
1817 ...

Bragg & Co.   **(EP)**   (K72)
Birmingham (9, Ellis St)
- 1872 ...

William Eaton **Bragg**   **(EP)**   (MDG) (K78)
Birmingham (55, St. Paul's Sq/13, Suffolk   (K80) (K82) (K84)
St/49, Ellis St/Caroline St)   (K88) (K92) (K03)
- 1866 - 1903 ...

Alexander **Brailsforth & Co.**   **(OSP)**   (B) (SAOR)
Sheffield
1800 ... *(See also figure: A.B)*

John **Bramich**   **(OSP)**   (WTD)
Birmingham (Bath Rw)
- 1818 ...

J. **Brammer &** S. **Horrabin**   **(OSP)**   (B) (SAOR)
Sheffield (Holy Croft)
1810 ... *(See also figure: BH)*

Bramwell & Co.   **(BM/EP)**   (WDS01) (WDSR)
(Bramwell, Brownhil & Co. Ltd.)   (SBW) (M)
Sheffield (15, Henry St)
- 1901 - 1926 *(See also figures:*
B&Co., RELIABLE, THE MAS-
HER)

Edwin Stovin **Bramwell**   **(EP)**   (WDS01)
Sheffield (19, Eastgrove Rd)
- 1901 ...

John H. **Branson**   **(EP)**   (GS)
Sheffield (Sycamore St)
- 1863 ...

Bravingtons Ltd. (EP) (S)
Sheffield/London
1926 - 1946 *(See also figure: B's)*

J. **Brazier** (EP) (MDG)
Birmingham (343, Icknield Port Rd)
- 1866 ...

BRAZILIAN SILVER

(See also) (EP)
Thomas H. **Daniel &** Thomas R. **Arter**
(Globe Nevada Silver Works)

William **Brearley** (EP) (B) (SAOR) (SBW)
Sheffield (Carver St)
1868 ... *(See also figure: W.B)*

BRENADA SILVER

(See also) (EP)
James Robert **McClelland**

George **Briddock & Co.** (OSP) (B) (SAOR)
Sheffield (Lambert Croft)
1781 ... *(See also figure: GB&Co)*

Briddon Brothers (Alfred & Frederick)
(Victoria Plate Works) **(EP/CU)**
Sheffield (7, Eyre Ln/77, Arundel St)
1863 - 1901 ...   (B) (SAOR)
1904 - 1910 ... **(Co. Ltd.)**   (WDS79) (K80)
(See also figures: B.B, AB FB,   (K93) (WDS01)
B.Bros.)   (SBW) (M)

Charles **Bridgens** (GS) (K93)
Sheffield (112, Arundel St)
- 1893 ...

Alfred **Bridger** (EP) (K88) (K92) (K03)
Birmingham (7, Regent Pd)
- 1888 - 1903 ...

John Charles **Bridger** (EP) (K78) (K80) (K82)
Birmingham (7, Regent Pd)   (K84)
- 1878 - 1884 ...

Jonathan **Briggs & Co.** (OSP) (B) (SAOR)
Sheffield (Button Ln)
1821 ... *(See also figure: IB&Co)*

William **Briggs & Co.**   **(BM/EP)**
Sheffield (35, 50 & 52, St. Andrew St)
1873 - 1893 ...
- 1901 - 1922 (**Ltd.**)
(See also figures: WB&Co, W^M
BRIGGS &Co)
(Then: James Allen)

(SAOR) (WDS79)
(K80) (K93)

(WDS01)

Briggs & Smith   **(CU/OSP)**
Sheffield (Carver St)
- 1822 ...

(HDG) (PDY)

Lewis **Briggs**   **(EP)**
Leeds (116, Woodhouse Ln/147, Marsh Ln)
- 1880 ...

(K80)

William **Briggs**   **(CU/OSP/EP)**
(Formerly: Furniss, Poles & Turner)
Sheffield (Button Ln/21, Carver St/13, Carver
Ln/38, Furnival St)
1823 - 1858 ... *(See also figures: W.B,*
W B)
(Then: S.Roberts & W.Briggs)

(B) (SAOR)
(NGDS) (PDB)
(SDG) (PD) (GDS)
(HGDY)(DSRR)
(E)

S. **Bright & Co.**   **(EP)**
Sheffield (St. James St)
- 1863 ... *(See also figures: SB&Co,*
Brillo)

(B) (SAOR) (GS
AD) (SBW) (M)

J. **Bright & Sons**   **(OSP)**
Sheffield (Market Pl)
- 1822 - 1829 ...

(HDG) (PD)
(NGDS)

John **Bright**   **(T)**
London (37, Bruton St)
- 1808 ...

(POAD)

Brightside Plating Co.   **(EP)**
Birmingham (23, Gt. Hampton Rw)
- 1903 ...

(K03)

(See also)   **(EP)**
S. **Bright & Co.**

(See also)   **(EP)**
Atkinson Brothers
(Milton Works)

J. W. **Bristol & Co.**   **(BM)** (K92)

Birmingham (Back of William Edward St)
- 1892 ...

BRITANNIA

(See also)   **(BM/EP)**
Philip **Ashberry & Sons**

(See also)   **(BM/EP)**
Barker Brothers
(Unity Works)

British Oneida Community Ltd. (K36)
(Community Plate)   **(EP)**
London (264, Regent St)
- 1936 ...

British Xilonite Co. Ltd.   **(EP)** (W)

Middlesex
~ 1890 .... *(See also figure: FIBRO-*
LOID)

George **Brittain & Co.**   **(OSP)** (B) (SAOR)

Sheffield (Arundel St)
1784 ... *(See also figure: G · B)*

S. S. **Brittain & Co.**   **(CU)** (WDS79) (WDS01)
(St. George's Work) (M)

Sheffield (Shoreham St)
- 1879 - 1901 ...
(See also figure: Symbol "swan")

W. H. **Brittain &** William **Hall & Co.** **(EP)** (W)

Sheffield
~ 1900 ...
(See also figures: Broadhead, Hall
& Co)

Richard **Brittain**   **(OSP)** (SAOR)

Birmingham
1812 ...

BRITTAIN WILKIN SON & BROWNILL	**Brittain, Wilkinson & Brownill (OSP)** Sheffield 1785 - 1797 *(See also figures: EXCELLENT, G * B)*	(B) (M) (SBW)
	Frederick **Britton** (EP) Birmingham (100, Vyse St) - 1888 - 1903 ...	(K88) (K92) (K03)
	Britzius & Goldstrass (EP) Sheffield ~ 1870 ... *(See also figure: CINDE-RELLA)*	(W)
BROADHEAD &ATKIN **BROADHEAD & ATKIN SHEFFIELD**	Roger **Broadhead &** Henry **Atkin (EP/BM)** Sheffield (1, Love St) - 1849 - 1852 ... *(See also figure:B&AS)*	(GDBS) (GE) (WDOS) (M)
BROADHEAD & Co SHEFFIELD	Roger **Broadhead & Co.** (BM/EP) **(Britannia Works)** Sheffield (Love St/Pond St) - 1863 - 1893 ... *(See also figure: R.BROADHEAD)*	(GS) (K80) (K93) (M)
	Broadhead & Rodgers (BM) Sheffield (16, Queen St) - 1833 ...	(GDS)
	Samuel **Broadhead** (BM) Sheffield (15, Queen St) - 1825 - 1829	(PDB) (SDG) (PG)
BROADHEAD HALL & Co	*(See also)* (EP) W. H. **Brittain &** William **Hall & Co**	
	William **Broadhurst & Son** (CU) Sheffield (Westfield Terrace) - 1841 ...	(SD46)
	Thomas **Broadhurst** (EP) Walsall (25, Birmingham St) - 1880 ...	(K80)
	Charles **Broadman** (EP) Sheffield (54, Pond St) - 1854 ...	(POS)

Brockington Brothers   **(EP)**   (K80) (K82) (K84)
Birmingham (250, New John St/44, Hylton St)
- 1880 - 1884 ...

Benjamin **Brockslesby**   **(OSP)**   (B) (SAOR)
Sheffield (Castle St)
1792 ...

Benjamin **Brodderick**   **(OSP)**   (B) (SAOR)
Sheffield (Fargate)
1782 ... *(See also figure: B.B)*

H. **Brodie**   **(T)**   (POAD)
London (30, Aldersgate St)
- 1808 ...

Bromley & Fisher   **(CU)**   (K93) (W)
Sheffield (Shoreham St)
~ 1870 - 1893 ...
(See also figure: ATTRACT)

Brook Brothers   **(EP)**
(Albert Works/Cambridge Works)
Sheffield (28, Cambridge St)
- 1893 - 1905 ...   (K93)(WDSR)
- 1901 ... **(Ltd.)**   (WDS01)

Benjamin **Brooke & Son**   **(OSP)**   (HDG)
Sheffield (Sycamore St)
- 1822 ...

Brookes & Crookes   **(CU)**   (B) (MHM)
(Atlantic Works)   (SBW) (M)
Sheffield (St. Philip's Rd)   (SAOR) (WDS79)
1862 - 1901... *(See also figures: B & C,*   (WDS01)
symbol "bell")

William **Brookes & Son**   **(CU)**   (SD46)
Sheffield (29, Rockingham St)
- 1846 ...

F. J. **Brookes**   **(EP)**   (PC)
Birmingham (20, Caroline St)
- 1896 ...

Richard **Brookes**   **(OSP)**   (POAD)
London (10, Salisbury St)
- 1808 ...

Abram **Brooksbank & Co.** **(EP/CU)** (K93) (WDS01)
(Malinda Works)
Sheffield (Malinda St)
- 1893 - 1901 ... *(See also figures: AB*
S EP, DEFIANCE, symbol "can-
non")

B R O O M
DAVID MILLER & SON
SHEFFIELD

(See also) **(CU/EP)** (W)
Thomas Henry **Blake**

Thomas **Broomhead** **(CU/OSP)** (HDG)
Sheffield (55, Nursery St)
- 1822 ...

(See also) **(EP)**
Adie Brothers Ltd.
(Atlas Works)

Thomas **Brough** **(EP)** (HGDB) (HGD)
Birmingham (32, Sun St/3, Howard St) (BDB)
- 1849 - 1862 ...

Thomas & George **Brough** **(EP)** (CDB) (GS)
Birmingham (195, Warstone Ln/Howard St) (MDG)
- 1861 - 1866 ...

Alfred **Browett** **(CP/GS/BM/EP)**
Birmingham (14, Dean St) (K72) (K78) (K80)
London (46, Little Britain) (K82) (K84) (PC)
- 1872 - 1903 ... (K03) (SBW) (M)
~ 1926 - 1936 ... **(Ltd.)**
(See also figure: AB***) (K36)

Browett, Ashberry & Co. **(EP)** (K80) (K84) (K88)
Birmingham (14, Dean St) (K92) (SBW) (M)
- 1880 - 1892 ...
(See also figure: A.B.***)

Brown & Clark **(EP)** (B) (SAOR) (SBM)
Birmingham (Richard St) (M)
1859 ... *(See also figure: B & C)*

William **Brown &** John **Hands** **(OSP)** (SAOR)
Coventry
1819 ...

Brown & Hardman   **(BM/CP/CU)**   ^{(CD) (WTD)} ^(HGD)
Birmingham (Paradise St)
- 1818 - 1850 ...

Brown & Tyler   **(BM)**   (GDS)
Sheffield (Andrew St)
- 1833 ...

J. & F. **Brown**   **(EP)**   (K80)
Liverpool (5, Mount Pleasant)
- 1880 ...

James **Brown**   **(BM)**   (WDB) (WDB)
Birmingham (10, Paradise St)   (WAB) (PDB)
- 1823 - 1839 ...   (DOB) (WDOB)

James **Brown**   **(EP)**   (HGD)
Birmingham (Easy Rw)
~ 1850 ...

John **Brown**   **(EP)**   (K80)
Stonehouse/Plymouth (120, Union St)
- 1880 ...

John **Brown**   **(CU)**
Sheffield (Baker's Hill/Savile St/141, Penistone Rd)   (GS) (WDS79)
- 1863 - 1905 ...   (WDS01) (WDSR)
- 1901 ... **(& Co. Ltd.)**   (WDS01)
(See also figure: ATLAS)
(Then: Parker & Brown)

Joseph **Brown**   **(EP)**   (GDBS) (WDOS)
Sheffield (229, Rockingham St)   (GS) (M)
- 1849 - 1863 ...
(See also figure: J.BROWN)

William **Brown**   **(BM)**   (SAOR) (PDB)
Coventry/Sheffield (Bailey St)
1817 - 1825 ...

Luke **Brownell**   **(OSP)**   (B) (SAOR)
Sheffield (Howard St)
1790 ... *(See also figure: LB)*

George **Brownhill**   **(CP/EP)**   (MDG) (K72)
Birmingham (Ct. 3, 50, Gt. Charles St)   (K78) (K80) (K84)
- 1866 - 1888 ...   (K88)

BRUMBY + MIDDLETON SHEFFIELD

Brumby & Middleton (Charleston Works) **(EP)**
Sheffield (Orange St)
~ 1889 - 1905 ...
(WDSR) (M)

George **Bryan & Co.** **(EP)**
Birmingham (Gt. Hampton St)
~ 1900

Thomas **Bryan** **(EP)** (MDG) (POB)
Birmingham (13, Gough St) (K72)
- 1866 - 1872 ...

BSL
Silver Plate
ENGLAND

(See also) **(EP)**
Birmingham Silver Plate Ltd.

George **Buckley & Co. Ltd.** **(EP)**
Birmingham (7, Caroline St/10, Newhall St/
130, Barr St)
- 1882 ... (K82) (K84)
- 1896 ... **(& Co.)** (PC)

Buckley & Hope **(EP)** (HGDB) (HGD)
Birmingham (33, Hockley Hill)
- 1849 - 1850 ...

John **Buckley** **(EP)** (HGD) (GS)
Birmingham (32 & 35, Hockley Hill) (MDG) (K80)
- 1850 - 1880 ...

P. H. **Budgen** **(EP)** (K03)
Birmingham (52, Frederick St)
- 1903 ...

Reubin William **Buggins** **(OSP/CU)** (SAOR)
Birmingham
1814 ...

Thomas **Bullock** **(OSP)** (WDB) (PDB)
Birmingham (5, Briddle St)
- 1823 - 1825 ...

H. **Bunn & Son** **(EP)** (K36)
Birmingham (62, Hockley St)
- 1936 ...

Bunney & Wright **(EP)** [BDB]
Birmingham (Floodgate St)
- 1862 ...

J. **Burburry** **(OSP)** [B] [SAOR]
Sheffield (Union Ln)
1830 ... *(See also figure: J.B)*

John **Burdekin** **(OSP)** [B]
(Workman at Walker, Knowles & Co)
Sheffield
~ 1845 ... *(See also figure: I·B)*

A. **Burgess & Co.** **(EP)** [K36]
Birmingham (38, Frederick St)
- 1936 ...

Charles **Burgess** **(CU)** [MDG] [POB]
Birmingham (Bucknal/82, Spencer St)
- 1866 - 1867 ...

Henry **Burgess** **(EP)** [K80]
Leeds (New Briggate)
- 1880 ...

Thomas **Burgess** **(OSP)** [CD] [WTD]
Birmingham (Dale's End & Gt. Brook St)
- 1818 ...

William **Burgess** **(CP)** [WDB] [WAB] [HTD]
Birmingham (Dale's End)
- 1823 - 1830 ...

Burgess Brothers **(EP)** [Rd 133518] [SBW]
Birmingham (43, Northampton St)
- 1888 ... *(See also figure: B.Bros.)*

William **Burgin** **(EP)** [WDS01]
Sheffield (34, Elmore Rd)
- 1901 ...

William **Burkinshaw & Son** **(EP)** [WDS79]
Sheffield (66, Eyre St)
- 1879 ...

Burley & Glover **(EP)** [MDG] [POB]
Birmingham (44, Warstone Ln)
- 1866 - 1867 ...

	John **Burley** Birmingham (44, Warstone Ln) - 1861 - 1888 ...	(EP)	(CDB) (BDB) (GS) (MDG) (K72) (K78) (K80) (K82) (K84) (K88)
BURMAROID	*(See also)* Thomas H. **Daniel &** Thomas R. **Arter** **(Globe Nevada Silver Works)**	(EP)	
	Charles **Burn** Birmingham (38, Hill St) - 1815 - 1818 ...	(CP)	(WTDB) (CD) (WTD)
	James **Burnand & Co.** **(Leicester Works)** Sheffield (Leicester St) - 1880 ...	(EP)	(K80)
	Burnand, Booth & Co. Ltd. Sheffield (27, Carver Ln) - 1901 ...	(EP)	(WDS01)
BURNL'S **REVUE**	*((See also)* William **Burnell** Sheffield - 1881 ...	(CU)	(W) (No K80)
	Burrell, Holland & Co. **(Eclipse Oak Works)** Sheffield (80, Arundel Ln) - 1901 - 1905 ...	(EP)	(WDS01) (WDSR)
	Charles Truman **Burrows & Sons** Birmingham (59, Branston St) - 1903 - 1936 ... *(See also figure: CT B)*	(EP)	(K03) (K36)
	Burton & Co. Birmingham (34, Spencer St) - 1903 ...	(EP)	(K03)
	Burton & Waters Birmingham 1921 - 1939 *(See also figure: B & W)*	(EP)	(S)
	Anthony **Burton** Sheffield (23, Furnival St/124, Broomhall St) - 1901 ...	(EP)	(WDS01)

George **Burton** **(EP)** (K80) (K82) (K84)
(Vales Mill) (K88) (K92) (K03)
Birmingham (Warstone Ln/Scotland St/
64, Edward St)
- 1880 - 1903 ...

William S. **Burton** **(OSP/EP)** (GE)
London (Oxford St)
1820 - 1851 ...
(See also figure: William S. Burton)

BURVIS

(See also) **(EP)**
John **Round & Son Ltd.**
(Tudor Works/Arundel Works)

BURYS & C⁰
SHEFFIELD

Burys & Co. **(CU)** (W)
Sheffield
~ 1850 - 1919

Harold **Bushell & Co. Ltd.** **(EP)** (K36)
Birmingham (28, Tenby St North)
1925 - 1936 ...

George **Bushell** **(EP)** (POB)
Birmingham (66, Spencer St)
- 1867 ...

G. & J. **Bushell** **(EP)** (K80)(K88) (K92)
Birmingham (Regent Pd/53, Frederick St) (PC) (K03)
- 1880 - 1903 ... *(See also figure: G &*
J B)

J. **Bushell** **(GS/BM)** (HGDB) (HGD)
Birmingham (Morley's Buildings)
- 1849 - 1850 ...

John **Bushell** **(EP)**
Birmingham (39 & 40, Tenby St)
- 1892 ... (K82) (K84) (K88)
- 1896 - 1903 ...(**& Co.**) (K92)
(PC) (K03)

Joseph Edward **Bushell** **(EP)** (K92) (PC) (K03)
Birmingham (66, Branston St./12, Caroline St/ (K36) (M)
76, Tower St)
- 1892 - 1936 ... *(See also figure: J.E.B)*

BUSY
B

(See also) **(CU/EP)**
Samuel **Barton**

B

Thomas **Butcher**   **(OSP)**   (WDB) (PDB)
Birmingham (Pritchett St)
- 1823 - 1825 ...

Thomas **Butcher**   **(EP)**   (WDS01)
Sheffield (15, Red Hill)
- 1901 ...

William & Samuel **Butcher**   **(CP/CU)**   (WDS79) (WDS01)
Sheffield (41, Eyre Ln/13, Furnival St/
72, Arundel St)
- 1879 - 1901 ... *(See also figures:*
WADE & BUTCHER, .BUTCHER,
W. & S. BUTCHER)

BUTLER
SHEFFIELD

George **Butler & Co.**   **(CU/EP)**   (W)
(Trinity Works)
Sheffield (105, Eyre St)
Glasgow (184, Buchanan St)
- 1852 - 1880 ...   (WDOS AD)
1880 - 1922 **(Ltd.)**   (SAOR) (WDS79)
(See also figures: GB&Co., ART,   (K80) (K93)
THE CAVENDISH)   (K80)
(Then: Arthur Price & Co)

T. A. **Butler & Co. Ltd.**   **(EP)**   (K36)
Birmingham (48 & 50, Victoria St)
1927 - 1936 ...

Charles **Butler**   **(EP)**   (K80)
Sheffield (7, Mulberry St)
- 1880 ...

Butler Brothers   **(BM/CU)**   (WTD) (WDB)
Birmingham (19, Lionel St)   (PDB)
- 1818 - 1825 ...

BUTTS

Thomas **Butts**   **(CU)**   (CD) (B) (WTD)
Birmingham (Hill St/24, Coleshill St)   (WDB) (PDB)
1807 - 1830... *(See also figure: TB*S)*   (WAB) (HTD) (M)

Edwin James **Buxton & Co.**   **(EP)**   (GS)
Sheffield (5, Duke St/Matilda St)
~ 1859 - 1863 ... *(See also figures:*
B&Co, E.J.BUXTON)

83

BUXTON & RUSSELL	Edwin James **Buxton &** Samuel **Russel** Sheffield (5, Duke St/Matilda St) **(BM/EP)** - 1852 - 1863 ...	(WDOS) (POS) (K54)(GS) (M)
	Benjamin **Buxton** **(EP)** **(Moor Plate Works)** Sheffield (1, Alexandra Rd/149a, South St) - 1879 - 1880 ...	(WDS79) (K80)
BW&A	*(See also)* **(EP)** **Badger, Worrall & Armitage**	
𝔅 𝔚 & 𝔖	*See also)* **(EP)** B. **Worth & Sons**	

C & C **GO AHEAD.**	*(See also)* **Colquhoun & Cadman** **Arundel & Co**	**(EP)**
C & Co	*(See also)* E. J. **Carnelly & Co.**	**(EP)**
C&Co C P N S	*(See also)* John Bodman **Carrington**	**(EP)**
C & C° **C&Co**	*(See also)* **Creswick & Co.**	**(EP)**
C&Co C P G S	*(See also)* George Richmond **Collis & Co**	**(OSP/EP)**
C & K ♛ ❧ **C&K S**	*(See also)* **Culf & Kay**	**(EP)**
C. ATTWOOD'S **PATENT STEEL**	*(See also)* Charles **Attwood**	**(CU/EP)**
C.B & S L ᴸᴰ	*(See also)* **Cooper Brothers & Sons Ltd.**	**(EP)**
C.BROS **L**	*(See also)* **Cooper Brothers & Sons Ltd.**	**(EP)**
C·E **N**	*(See also)* Charles Edward **Nixon** **(Street Wolfram's Works)**	**(EP)**
C.F.Y	*(See also)* C. F. **Younge**	**(CU)**
C.H.C	*(See also)* Charles Howard **Collins**	**(EP)**
C.J.A & N	*(See also)* Charles J. **Adie & Nephew**	**(EP)**
C.JOHNSON & Co. **S H E F F I E L D**	*(See also)* Christopher **Johnson & Co.**	**(EP)**
C·L **P**	*(See also)* C. & L. **Proctor**	**(OSP)**
C.M&P	*(See also)* **Castleton, Parkin & Milner** **(Castleton, Milner & Co.)**	**(OSP)**

C·N
C.NEEDHAM
MAKER
SHEFFIELD

(See also)
Charles **Needham**

(CP)

C ✠ C

(See also)
Joseph **Elliot & Sons**

(CU/EP)

C $\overset{+}{\underset{+}{X}}$

(See also)
Lockwood Brothers

(CU/EP)

James **Cadby**
Birmingham (3, James St)
- 1829 - 1830 ...

(CP) ^{(WAB) (HTD)}

George **Cadman & Co.**
Sheffield
1786 ...

(OSP) ^(SAOR)

Thomas Radley **Cadman & Sons**
Sheffield (211, St. Mary's Rd)
- 1901 ... *(See also figure: BEN-GALL)*

(EP) ^{(WDS01) (W)}

David **Cadman**
Sheffield (Coalpit Ln)
1780 ... *(See also figure: D · C)*

(OSP) ^{(B) (SAOR)}

John **Cadman**
Sheffield (Trafalgar St)
1833 ...

(CU) ^(GDS)

Henry **Caldicutt**
Birmingham (Lench St)
- 1839 ...

(CP) ^(WDOB)

Frederick **Calow**
Sheffield (Rockingham Ln)
- 1893 ...

(EP) ^(K93)

(See also)
E. H. **Parkin & Co.**
(Cornwall Works)

(EP)

Charles **Cammell & Co. Ltd.** **(CU)** (WDS79) (K93) AD) (WDS01)
(Cyclops Steel & Iron Works)
Sheffield (Savile St)
- 1879 - 1901 ... *(See also figures:*
CYPLOPS, symbol "camel", sym-
bol "three crowns")

Charles **Campbell** **(EP)** (K80)
Glasgow (37, Nelson St)
- 1880 ...

William **Camsell** **(GS)** (WDSR)
Sheffield
1905 ...

A. T. **Cannon Ltd.** **(EP)** (S)
Birmingham
1965 - 1986 *(See also figure: A T C)*

D. **Capell** **(EP)** (MDG)
Birmingham (46, Pershore St)
- 1866 ...

" CAPITAL " *(See also)* **(EP)**
Hawksworth, **Eyre & Co. Ltd.**

"CAPS ANY" *(See also)* **(EP)**
W. H. **Armitage & Co.**
(Vesuvius Works)

𝖢𝖺𝗋𝖽𝗂𝗇𝖺𝗅 𝖯𝗅𝖺𝗍𝖾 *(See also)* **(EP)**
Elkington & Co. Ltd.
(See also Elkington's History)

CARDINAL PLATE *(See also)* **(EP)**
Northern Goldsmiths Company

Joseph **Carnall** **(CP)** (SAOR) (WAB) (HTD) (DOB)
Birmingham (25, Rea St)
1828 - 1833 ...

E. J. **Carnelly & Co.** **(EP)** (MDG) (K78) (K80) (K82) (K84) (K88) (K92) (PC)
Birmingham (2, Caroline St/20 & 22, Hylton St)
- 1866 - 1896 ... *(See also figure: C & Co)*

Carnelly & Lamb **(EP)** (CDB) (BDB) (GS)
Birmingham (2, Caroline St)
- 1861 - 1863 ...

Ellen **Carnelly** (EP) (K03)
Birmingham (116, Heaton St)
- 1903 ...

Jarvis **Carnelly** (EP) (POB) (K72)
Birmingham (2, Caroline St)
- 1867 - 1872 ...

E. **Carnley** (EP) (K88) (K92)
Birmingham (81, Ford St)
- 1888 - 1892 ...

CARPATHIAN SILVER

(See also) (EP)
E. A. **Allen & Co.**
and (K36)
(See also) (EP)
Frank **Hawker Co. Ltd.**

John **Carpendale** (EP) (GS)
Sheffield (Scotland St)
- 1863 ...

Harry **Carr** (EP) (WDS01)
Sheffield (390, Ecclesall Rd)
- 1901 ...

John **Carr** (OSP/CP) (SAOR) (HDG) (GDS)
Sheffield (64 and then 50, Scotland St)
1816 - 1833 ...

John Bodman **Carrington** (EP)
Sheffield ()
London (130, Regent St)
1882 ... *(See also figure: J.B.C)* (SAOR)
1888 ... **(& Co.)** (SAOR)
(See also figure: C&Co)
- 1922 ...**(Ltd.)**
(Then: Collingwood Group Ltd.)

W. **Carter** (OSP) (B) (SAOR)
Sheffield (New Church St)
1839 ... *(See also figure: WC)*

George **Cartwright &** Joseph **Hirons**
Birmingham (CU/EP)
- 1853
(Then: Cartwright, Hirons & Woodward)

Charles **Cartwright & Sons** **(BM/EP)** ^{(MDG) (K80)}
Birmingham (22 & 13, Edgbaston St)
- 1866 - 1880 ...

Cartwright & Woodward **(EP)** ^{(CDB) (BDB) (GS)}
(Atlas Works) ^{(MDG) (K72)}
(Formerly: Cartwright, Hirons & Woodward)
Birmingham (138 & 139, Gt. Charles St)
- 1861 - 1872 ...
(Then: Horance Woodward & Co.)

Cartwright, Hirons & Woodward (EP) ^{(B) (M)}
(Formerly: Cartwright & Hirons)
Birmingham (Gt. Charles St)
1853 - 1859 *(See also figure: C H & W)*
(Then: Cartwright & Woodward)

W. F. **Casewell** **(EP)** ^(M)
Birmingham
~ 1890 ... *(See also figure: W.F.C)*

Castle & Turton **(CU)** ^(W)
(Premier Works)
(Formerly: Thomas Henry Blake)
Sheffield (Wentworth St)
- 1900
(Then: Thomas Staniforth & Co.)

Castleton, Parkin & Milner (OSP) ^{(B) (SAOR) (HDG)}
(Castleton, Milner & Co.)
Sheffield (Carver Ln)
1821 - 1822 ... *(See also figure: C·M&P)*

J. F. **Causer** **(CU/OSP)** ^{(B) (M)}
Birmingham (4, Nicholson St)
1824 ...

CAUSER

Cavendish Plate

(See also) **(CU/EP)**
George **Butler & Co.**
(Trinity Works)

Josiah **Cawton** **(OSP)** ^{(B) (SAOR)}
Sheffield (Snow Hill)
1782 ... *(See also figure: I.C)*

CB

(See also) **(OSP)**
Charles **Boardman**

C₈B S **A I E P** C.B & S Lᵀᴰ	*(See also)* Charles **Boyton & Son Ltd.**	**(BM/EP)**
C B **E P**	*(See also)* Charles **Belk**	**(EP)**
C Bros S EPNS	*(See also)* **Cooper Brothers & Sons Ltd. (EP)**	
CBRS	*(See also)* **Clifford Brothers**	**(EP)**
C B S	*(See also)* **Cooper Brothers**	**(EP)**
C C Cᴰ S	*(See also)* George **Hawksley & Co.**	**(EP)**
C C S LTD	**Not assigned!**	**(EP)** ⁽ᴱ⁾
CDW G S C P	**Not assigned!**	**(EP)** ⁽ᴱ⁾
C E & Co BP C E & Cᵒ	*(See also)* Charles **Ellis & Co.**	**(EP)**
CENTURYPLATE	*(See also)* James **Walker**	**(EP)**
C F & Cᵒ	*(See also)* Charles **Favell & Co.**	**(EP)**
C G & Cᵒ	*(See also)* Charles S. **Green & Co. Ltd.**	**(EP)**
CG W " animal "	**Not assigned!**	**(EP)**
CH&C	*(See also)* M. **Clark,** J. **Hall &** C. **Clark**	**(CU/CP)**
	John **Challener** Birmingham (Hampton St/8, Snowhill) - 1835 - 1850 ...	**(OSP/EP)** ⁽ᵂᵂᴰᴮ⁾ ⁽ᴴᴳᴰ⁾

Charles **Chamberlain**   (CP)   (WAB) (HTD)
Birmingham (Camden St)
- 1829 - 1830 ...

John **Chamberlain**   (OSP)   (WWDB)
Birmingham (Gt. Hampton St)
- 1835 ...

Thomas **Chamberlain**   (CP)   (DOB)
Birmingham (12, Little Hampton St)
- 1833 ...

T. **Chambers & Co.**   (EP)   (K88) (K92)
Birmingham (15, St. Paul's Sq/1, Graham St.)
- 1888 - 1892 ...

Wm. **Chambers &** Wm. **Cottrell (CP)**   (SAOR) (WAB)
Birmingham (44, Newhall St)   (HTD)
1829 - 1830 ...

Thomas **Champion & Son**   (OSP)   (B) (SAOR)
Sheffield (High St)
1826 ... *(See also figure: T.C&S)*

CHAMPION   *(See also)*   (EP)
Thomas Spendelow **Richards & Co.**

David **Chapman**   (EP)   (K36)
Birmingham (56, Albion St)
- 1936 ...

Charles & Warner   (EP)   (K36)
Sheffield (122, Scotland St)
- 1936 ...

Andrew **Charles**   (EP)   (SBW) (M)
Birmingham
~ 1895 ... *(See also figure: Hessin)*

CHARLES CALOW.   *(See also)*   (CU/EP)
Albert J. **Beardshaw**

Y. **Charlewood**   (CU)   (POAD)
London (Ct 17, Russel St)
- 1808 ...

John **Charlton**   (OSP)   (GDS) (DSRR)
Sheffield (26, Charles St)
1833 - 1841 ...

Charlton Brothers   **(EP)**   (SBW)

Birmingham

~

CHAR^S OWEN & Co

(See also)   **(EP)**
Charles **Owen & Co.**
(Wellington Works)

CHAR^S OWEN

(See also)   **(EP)**
Charles **Owen**
(Wellington Works)

John Bishop **Chatterley**   **(EP)**
(Albert Works)
Birmingham (57 & 58/119, New Town Rw/
11 & 13, Pitsford St)
London (87, Hatton Garden)   (K80) (K84) (K88)
- 1880 - 1892 ...   (K92)
(See also figure: J.B.C&S)   (K82) (PC) (K03)
- 1882 - 1936 ... **(& Sons Ltd.)**   (K36) (M)
(See also figure: JBC&S Ld)

Ebenezer **Cheatle**   **(EP)**   (K72) (K78)
Birmingham (28, Summer Rw/46, Buckingham St.)
- 1872 - 1878 ...

John **Cheetham**   **(BM/GS)**   (HGD)
Birmingham (22, New St)
- 1850 ...

E. **Cheetham Ltd.**   **(EP)**   (K36)
Sheffield (24, Mary St)
- 1936 ...

CHELTENHAM
AND COMPANY LTD

Cheltenham & Co. Ltd.   **(EP)**   (E)
Sheffield
~ 1910

Colen H. **Cheshire**   **(EP)**   (K72) (K78) (K80)
Birmingham (3, Northampton St)   (PC)
- 1872 - 1896 ...

Chester Electro Plating Co.   **(EP)**   (K36)
Chester (City Rd)
- 1936 ...

	James **Chesterman & Co. (Bow Works)** (CU) Sheffield (Nursery St/Pomona St) 1862 ... - 1901 ...*(See also figure: JC&Co)*	(B) (SAOR) (SBW) (M) (WDS01)
Ches-ton	Thomas **Cheston** (OSP) Birmingham (13, Jamaica Rw) ~ 1800 - 1825 ...	(B) (SAOR) (CD) (WTD) (WDB) (PDB) (M)
E P CHH S N S	*(See also)* (EP) Charles Henry **Hattersley (Snider Works)**	
	Child & Cooper (EP) Birmingham (10, Northampton St) - 1867 - 1872 ...	(POB) (K72)
CHILD	Thomas **Child** (CP) Birmingham (37, Coleshill St) 1821 - 1833 ...	(B) (WAB) (HTD) (M)
	R. **Chippendall** (OSP) London (1, Salisbury St/Bell's Building) - 1808 ...	(POAD)
C H & J E	*(See also)* (EP) **Hawksworth, Eyre & Co.**	
C H & W	*(See also)* (EP) **Cartwright, Hirons & Woodward**	
CHS	*(See also)* (OSP) C. **Hammond**	
CINDERELLA	*(See also)* (EP) **Britzius & Goldstrass**	
CIR CLE	*(See also)* (CU/OSP) John **Beet**	
	City Replating Co. (EP) Birmingham (13, Summer Rw) - 1903 ...	(K03)
CIVIC	*(See also)* (EP) Thomas **Land & Sons (Colonial Works)**	

C

CJ & Co S ET / **CJ & Co**	*(See also)* Christopher **Johnson & Co.**	**(EP)**
C. J. A	Charles J. **Adie** **(Lion Works)**	**(CU/EP)**
🐘 C J A	**Not assigned!** ~ after 1920 (Possibly successor of Th. Hands & Sons because of using their Trademark)	**(EP)**
CJA ⊛ ⌛	*(See also)* Charles James **Allen**	**(EP)**
& Co LTD	*(See also)* J. **Collyer & Co. Ltd.**	**(EP)**
CLARBOUR	*(See also)* **Hoyland, Clarbour & Barnard**	**(CU)**
	William **Clare** Birmingham (Dale's End) 1818 ...	**(CU)** [WTD]
	Clark & Richardson Birmingham (14, Vittoria St) - 1878 ...	**(EP)** [K78]
	Clift Alexander M. **Clark** London (138, Frenchurch St) - 1891 ... *(Then: A. Clark Manufacturing Co)*	**(EP)**
	E. & J. **Clark** London (Fleet St) - 1808 ...	**(CU)** [POAD]
	W. **Clark** Birmingham (Victoria St) - 1866 ...	**(EP)** [MDG]
	M. **Clark,** J. **Hall &** C. **Clark (CP/CU)** Sheffield (South St) 1808 ... *(See also figure: CH&C)*	[B] [SAOR]

Alexander **Clark Manufacturing Co. (EP)** (K36)
(Welbeck Works)
(Formerly: Clift Alexander M. Clark)
Sheffield (Randall St./Hill St./Sycamore St.)
Birmingham (Hylton St)
London (125 & 126, Frenchurch St)
1891 - 1911
1912 - 1936 ... **(Ltd.)**
(See also figures: A .C, AC MC⁰,
ALEX CLARK, Welbeck Plate)

Shirley **Clarke & Co.**   **(CU)** (WDS01)
(Boston Works)
Sheffield (Eyre Ln)
- 1901 ... *(See also figure: OIO)*

Charles **Clarke**   **(EP)**
Birmingham (7 & 8, Washington St/
59a/ 42, Northampton Rd)
- 1878 - 1892 ...   (K78) (K80) (K88)
- 1903 ... **(& Son)**   (K92) (K03)

James **Clarke**   **(OSP)** (CD)
Birmingham (4, Temple St)
- 1818 ...

J. H. & R.C. **Clarke**   **(CU/OSP)** (WDB) (PDB)
Birmingham (128, Moor St)
- 1823 - 1825 ...

William **Clarke**   **(EP)** (M)
London
~ 1885 ... *(See also figure: WC**)*

John **Clarke & Sons**   **(CU/EP)** (B) (WDS01) (M)
Sheffield (Mowbray St)
~ 1894 - 1905

CLARKE'S PATENT

(See also figures: JC&S, NEVA,
EXPRESS)
1905 - 1923 **(Ltd.)**
(See also figures: JC&Sons, NEVA,
EXPRESS)

CLARK'S JUBILEE GOLD

John **Clark**   **(EP)** (SBW) (M)
Birmingham
~ 1892

William **Clarkson** (CP) ^(WTDB)
Birmingham (St. Martin's Pl)
- 1815 ...

George **Clayton & Co.** (CU) ^{(K72) AD}
Sheffield (7, Workhouse Ln)
- 1851 - 1872 ...

Thomas **Clayton** (OSP) ^{(B) (SAOR) (HDG)} ^{(PDY) (PDB)}
Sheffield (15, Solly St)
1820 - 1825 ... *(See also figure: T·C)*

John **Clemmens** (EP) ^{(K72) (K78) (K80)} ^{(K82) (K84) (K88)} ^{(K92) (K03)}
Birmingham (45, Hampton St)
- 1872 - 1903 ...

W. & E. **Clewe** (EP) ^(K03)
Birmingham (56, Gt. Hampton St)
- 1903 ...

Mrs. Caroline **Clewer** (EP) ^(POB)
Birmingham (40, Caroline St)
- 1867 ...

Clifford Brothers (EP)
Birmingham
1911 ... *(See also figure: CBRS)*

Levesley Brothers (EP) ^{(B) (K80) (K36)} ^(SBW)
Sheffield (West St./Mary St./203, Arundel St.)
1868 - 1936 ...

Henry **Clulee** (EP) ^(GS)
Birmingham (88, Cheapside)
- 1863 ...

Henry **Coar** (OSP) ^{(B) (SAOR)}
Sheffield (Carver Ln)
1803 ... *(See also figure: HC)*

Frank **Cobb & Co.** (EP) ^(M)
Sheffield (35 - 37, Howard St)
1905 - 1911 ...
(See also figure: F.C&Co)

Cocks & Bettridge (CU/OSP) ^(SAOR)
Birmingham
~ 1800 - 1813 ...

William **Coghill**   **(EP)**   ^(K80)
Glasgow (38, Queen St)
- 1880 ...

G. **Coldwell**   **(GS)**   ^(MDG)
Birmingham (65, Legge St)
- 1866 ...

William **Coldwell**   **(OSP)**   ^{(B) (SAOR)}
Sheffield (Howard St)
1806 ..
(See also figures: W·C, W.COLDWELL)

Richard **Cole**   **(OSP)**   ^(WWDB)
Birmingham (New Summer St)
- 1835 ...

Coles & Fryer Ltd.   **(EP)**   ^(K03)
Birmingham (12, St. Paul's Sq)
- 1903 ...

Thomas **Colley**   **(OSP)**   ^{(B) (SAOR)}
Sheffield (Burgess St)
1783 ... *(See also figure: T.C)*

P. **Collignon**   **(EP)**   ^(MDG)
Birmingham (18, Fleet St)
- 1866 ...

Henry **Collingwood**   **(EP)**   ^{(K82) (K84) (K88) (K92)}
Birmingham (115, King Edward Rd)
- 1882 - 1892 ...

B. H. **Collins & Co.**   **(EP)**   ^(K36)
Birmingham (38, Frederick St)
- 1936 ...

James **Collins & Son**   **(EP)**   ^(GS)
Birmingham (57, Frederick St/Newhall St)
- 1861 ...

Collins & Wallis   **(EP)**   ^(SBW)
Birmingham
~ 1900 ...
(See also figure: MONTANA SILVER)

Charles Howard **Collins** **(EP)** (SBW) (M)
Birmingham
1889 ... *(See also figure: C.H.C)*

Daniel George **Collins** **(EP)**
London (95 - 97/118, Newgate St)
1896 - 1904
1904 - 1936 ... (**Co. Ltd.**)
(See also figure: DGC) (K36)

George **Collins** **(EP)** (K72)
Birmingham (25, Branston St)
- 1872 ...

James **Collins** **(OSP)** (SAOR) (CD)
Birmingham (4, Cock St)
1816 - 1839 ...

John **Collins** **(EP)** (K82) (K84) (K88)
Birmingham (42, Augusta St)
- 1882 - 1888 ...

George Richmond **Collis** **(CU/MP/EP)** (WDOB) (HGDB)
Birmingham (28, Church St/57, Cambridge (HGD) (GE) (GS)
St) (K72)
London (130, Regent St)
- 1839 - 1872 ... (SAOR) (CDB)
1837 - 1896 ... (**& Co.**) (MDG) (POB)
(See also figures: C&Co., (K78) (K80) (K82)
G.R.Collis & Co., G.R.C) (K84) (K88) (K92)
(Then S. W. Smith & Co) (PC) (M)

John **Collyer & Co.** **(EP)** (K36)
Birmingham (133, Hockley Hill)
~ 1920 ...
- 1936 ... (**Ltd**.)
(See also figure: C.J.&Co Ltd)

S. **Colmore** **(CU)** (B)
Birmingham
1790 ... *(See also figure: SC)*

Colquhoun & Cadman **(CU/EP)** (WDS01)
(Douglas Works)
Sheffield (Arundel St)
1878 - 1901 ...
(See also figures: C&C, GO
AHEAD)

C O M A	*(See also)* A.T. H. **Coward**	**(EP)**
𝕮𝖔𝖒𝖒𝖔𝖓 𝖘𝖊𝖓𝖘𝖊	*(See also)* John **Shaw & Sons Ltd.**	**(EP/CU)**

C

Zadock **Congreaves**
(E. Congrave)
Birmingham (245, Icknield St)
- 1880 -1896 ...　**(EP)** (K80) (PC)

Connought	*(See also)* Thomas H. **Daniel &** Thomas R. **Arter** **(Globe Nevada Silver Works)**	**(EP)**
CONQUEROR	*(See also)* Albert J. **Beardshaw & Co.**	**(EP)**

Richard **Constantine**　**(BM)** (PDB) (SDG) (PD)
Sheffield (16, Scotland St)
- 1825 - 1829 ...

A. E. **Cook & Co.**　**(EP)** (K82) (K84) (K88)
(Lionel Street Plating Works) (K92) (K03)
Birmingham (2, Lionel St)
- 1882 - 1903 ...

I. & B. **Cook**　**(CU)** (SAOR)
Birmingham
1814 ...

John **Cook**　**(CU/OSP)** (SAOR)
Birmingham
1819 ...

Benjamin **Cooke**　**(OSP)** (WDB) (PDB)
Birmingham (20, Summer St)
- 1823 - 1825 ...

Charles **Cooke**　**(EP)** (K72) (K78)
Birmingham (113, Warstone Ln)
- 1872 - 1878 ...

Henry Mark **Cooke**　**(EP)** (K80) (K82) (K84)
Birmingham (46 & 48, Albert Rd) (K88) (K92) (PC)
- 1880 - 1903 ... (K03)

John **Cooke**　**(CP)** (WAB) (HTD)
Birmingham (Fleet St)
- 1829 - 1833 ...

Frank **Cookes** **(EP)** (K03)
Birmingham (116, Hockley St)
- 1903 ...

Cooper & Son **(CP)** (DOB)
Birmingham (22, Moland St)
- 1833 ...

Charles **Cooper** **(EP)** (K84)
Birmingham (10, Northampton St)
- 1884 ...

Frederick **Cooper** **(EP)** (PC)
Birmingham (41, St. Paul's Sq)
- 1896 ...

George **Cooper** **(OSP)** (B) (SAOR)
Sheffield (Pea Croft/Broad Ln)
1788 - 1800 ...*(See also figure: G.C)*

Henry **Cooper** **(CP/CU)** (WWDB) (WDOB)
Birmingham (97, Bradford St/Ravenhurst St)
- 1835 - 1839 ...

John **Cooper** **(OSP)** (B) (SAOR)
Sheffield (Sandspavers)
1784 ... *(See also figure: I.C)*

John **Cooper** **(OSP)** (WDB) (PDB)
Birmingham (Moland St)
- 1823 - 1825 ...

Joseph W. **Cooper** **(OSP)** (CD) (WTD)
Birmingham (Bromsgrove St)
- 1818 ...

Thomas **Cooper** **(OSP)** (B) (SAOR)
Derby
1802 ... *(See also figure: TC)*

Cooper Brothers **(EP)**
(Don Plate Works)

Cooper Brothers Sheffield

Sheffield (High St/Bridge St/44, Arundel St/ (WDS79) (K80)
Eyre Ln) (NA) (K36)
London (50, Holborn Viaduct)
1866 - 1895 ...
(See also figures: C Bros, CBS) (WDSR) (WDS01)
1895 - 1983 (**& Sons Ltd**.)

Charles **Cooper Chasing** **(EP)** (K78) (K80) (K82)
Birmingham (10, Northampton St)
- 1878 - 1882 ...

Cooper Ludlam

Cooper Ludlam **(EP)**
Sheffield
- 1920 ...

Cope & Culter (Benj. Cutler) **(CP)** (WTDB) (CD)
Birmingham (Edmund St/Ann St/Bartholo-   (WTD) (WDB)
mew Rw)   (PDB)
- 1815 - 1825 ...

Cope & Pinches **(CU)** (CD) (WTD)
Birmingham (Exeter Rw)   (WDB) (PDB)
- 1818 - 1825 ...

COPE

C. G. **Cope** **(OSP)** (B) (M)
Birmingham (Edmond St)
1817 ...

Alfred **Cope** **(EP)** (K03)
Birmingham (107, Carver St)
- 1903 ...

David **Cope** **(MP/CP)**
Birmingham (31, Exeter Rw/7 & 8, New
Bartholomew St)   (WAB)
- 1829 ...   (HTD) (WDOB)
- 1830 - 1880 ... **(& Son)**   (HGD) (CDB) (GS)
(Then: B. S. Spittle)   (K80)

E. **Cope** **(GS)** (MDG)
Birmingham (50, Gt. Charles St)
- 1866 ...

John **Copley & Sons** **(CU)** (WDS79)
(Richmond Works)
Sheffield (123, Creswick St)
- 1879 ... *(See also figure: XX)*

Arthur **Corbell & Co.** **(EP)** (E)
London
1946 - 1950
(Then: moved to United States)

Henry **Corbett** **(EP)** (K36)
Birmingham (146, Hockley Hill)
- 1936 ...

John **Corbett**	**(EP)**	(MDG) (POB)
Birmingham (Hingeston St)		
- 1866 - 1867 ...		

CORN & CO

J. **Corn &** J. **Sheppard**	**(OSP)**	(B) (M)
Birmingham (Exeter Rw)		
1819 ...		

Cornforth & Lavenstein	**(EP)**	(K88)
Birmingham (7, Caroline St)		
- 1888 ...		

CORNFORTH

William **Cornforth**	**(EP)**	(BDB) (GS) (MDG) (POB) (K78) (K80)
Birmingham (6, Northampton St./99, Gt. Hampton St)		
- 1862 - 1880 ...		

Henry **Cornforth**	**(BM/EP)**	(HGD) (CDB) (BDB) (GS) (MDG) (K72) (K78) (K80)
Birmingham (43 & 47, New Hall St)		
- 1850 - 1880		
(Then: Henry Parker & Son)		

CORONA PLATE

Not assigned!	**(EP)**	(E)

George **Cotton**	**(GS)**	(DSRR)
Sheffield (89, Arundel St)		
1841 ...		

William (John) **Cottrell**	**(OSP)**	(SAOR) (DOB) (WWDB)
Birmingham (12, St. Martin's Pl)		
1829 - 1835 ...		

William **Coulthard & Co.**	**(EP)**	
Birmingham (59, Northampton St./2, Regent Pd)		(K03) (K36)
- 1903 ...		
- 1936 ... (**& Son**)		

Cousins & Co.	**(OSP)**	(HDG)
Sheffield (Garden St)		
- 1822 ...		

Isaak **Cousins**	**(OSP)**	(B) (SAOR)
Sheffield (High St)		
1774 ... *(See also figure: I·C)*		

Joseph **Cousins**   **(OSP)** ^(PD)
Sheffield (11, Garden St)
- 1829 ...

A.T. H. **Coward**   **(EP)**
Sheffield
~ 1890 - 1920 *(See also figure: COMA)*

John Y. **Cowlishaw**   **(EP)** ^{(SAOR) (WSD79) (K80) (K93) (SBW) (M)}
Sheffield (Market St/89, Arundel St)
1854 - 1893 ... *(See also figure: J.Y.C)*

Herny **Cox & Co.**   **(GS/CU)** ^(WDS37)
Sheffield
1837 ...

James **Cox &** William **Landers**   **(CU)** ^(SAOR)
Birmingham
1816 ...

Henry John **Cox**   **(EP)** ^{(K72) (K80) (K78)}
Birmingham (7, Warstone Ln/3, Brook St)
- 1872 - 1880 ...

John **Cox**   **(OSP/EP)** ^{(HTD) (CDB) (GS) (MDG) (POB)}
Birmingham (27, Mary St/5, Caroline St)
- 1830 - 1867 ...

John **Cox**   **(CP)** ^{(WTDB) (WAB)}
Birmingham (Islington Rw/Wharf St)
- 1815 - 1829 ...

Thomas **Cox**   **(OSP)** ^{(WTDB) (WDB) (PDB)}
Birmingham (Coleshill St/10, Dean St)
- 1815 - 1825 ...

Walter Charles **Cox**   **(EP)** ^{(K78) (K80) (K82) (K84) (K88) (K92) (K03) (M)}
Birmingham (1, Caroline St/125, Vyse St)
- 1878 - 1903 ... *(See also figure: W.C)*

William **Cox**   **(EP)** ^(GS)
Sheffield (Burgess St)
- 1863 ...

William Henry **Cox**   **(EP)** ^(K80)
Plymouth (28, Whimple St)
- 1880 ...

William & Thomas J. **Cox**	**(OSP/CU)**	(WTDB) (CD) (WTD) (WDB) (PDB)
Birmingham (Gt. Charles St/2, Bromsgrove) - 1815 - 1825 ...		

C.P.WALKER & C͟O.L	*(See also)* C. P. **Walker & Co. Ltd.**	**(CU)**

CP	*(See also)* C. **Proctor &** T. **Beilby**	**(OSP)**

C P	*(See also)* C. **Pickslay & Co.**	**(OSP)**

CR	*(See also)* C. **Roebuck**	**(OSP)**

CRACK NALL	John **Cracknall** Birmingham (42, Staniforth St) 1814 - 1830 ...	**(CP)** (B) (CD) (WTD) (PDB) (WDB) (WAB) (HTD) (M)

Charles & Walter **Cracknell** Birmingham (17, Well St) - 1882 - 1888 ...	**(EP)**	(K82) (K84) (K88)

John **Cracknell** Birmingham (13, St. Paul's Sq/46, Warstone Ln) - 1861 - 1880	**(EP)**	(CDB) (BDB) (GS) (MDG) (K72) (K78) (K80)

E. **Craner** Birmingham (49, Howe St) - 1866 ...	**(EP)**	(MDG)

J. & R. **Crawford** Birmingham (Brearley St) - 1839 ...	**(CP)**	(WDOB)

Thomas Walker **Crawford** Glasgow (296, Argyle St) - 1880 ...	**(EP)**	(K80)

Andrew **Crawshaw** Rotherham (High St) 1826 ... *(See also figure: A.C)*	**(OSP)**	(B) (NGDS) (SAOR)

James **Crawshaw** Sheffield (37/39, High St/61, Solly St) 1816 - 1837 ... *(See also figure: I.C)*	**(CU)**	(B) (SAOR) (HDG) (GDS)(WDS37)

	St. Arnud **Creake** **(EP)** *(See also Hammond, Creake & Co.)* Sheffield (197, Abbeydale Rd/39, Cresent Rd) - 1901 - 1911 ... *(See also figure: S A C)*	(WDS01) (WDSR) (WDS11)
	Joseph **Creed** **(CU/EP)** Birmingham (1, Carver St) - 1849 - 1850 ... - 1839 ... **(& Son)**	(HGDB) (HGD) (WDOB)
CRESWICK & Co SHEFFIELD	**Creswick & Co.** **(EP)** Sheffield (Sycamore St/ Paternoster Rw / 111, Arundel St) - 1851 - 1880 ... *(See also figures: C&Co, IFP C&Co)*	(B) (SAOR) (GE) (K80) (SBW) (W) (M)
	George **Creswick** **(EP)** Sheffield (11, Carver St) - 1936 ...	(K36)
	James **Creswick** **(OSP/CU)** Sheffield (Paternoster Rw) 1828 - 1841 ...	(PD) (GDS) (WDS37) (DSRR)
	Joseph **Creswick** **(OSP)** Sheffield 1777 ... (West Bar Green) 1793 ... (Queen St) *(See also figure: IC)*	(B) (SAOR) (SAOR)
	Thomas & James **Creswick** **(OSP)** Sheffield (Porter St) 1810 ... *(See also figure: TC)*	(B)
	Thomas, James & Nathaniel **Creswick** **(OSP/EP)** Sheffield (Brown St/8/10, Paternoster Rw) - 1818 - 1863 ... *(See also figures: JC NC, TJC&N)*	(B) (SAOR) (CD) (HDG) (PDY) (NGDS) (SDG) (PD) (PDB) (GDS) (HGDY) (GDBS) (WDOS) (GS) (SBW)
	John **Crichton** **(EP)** Edinburgh (12, South East Rose Ln) - 1880 ...	(K80)
CRIS	*(See also)* **(CU/EP)** John **Bednall & Co.**	

Jonathan **Crookes & Son** (CU) ^{(WDS79) (K93)} ^(W)
Sheffield (89, Eldon St)
- 1879 - 1893 ...
(See also figures: A symbol "pistol", symbol "pistol" L)

Crookes, Roberts & Co. (CU) ^{(K93) (W)}
Sheffield (Shoreham St)
- 1893 ... *(See also figure: ARGUS)*

Thomas **Crosbee** (CP/EP)
(Apollo Works)
Birmingham (13, Coleshill St/Moseley St) ^(HGDB) ^(K92)
- 1849 ...
- 1892 ... (**& Sons**)

W. H. **Crosbee** (GS) ^(MDG)
Birmingham (227, Camden St)
- 1866 ...

J. G. **Crouch** (EP) ^(GS)
London (50, Old Compton St)
- 1863 ...

William **Crowley** (CP) ^{(WTDB) (CD)} ^{(WDB) (PDB)} ^{(WAB) (HTD)}
Birmingham (Ludgate Hill/Water St)
- 1815 - 1830 ...

Charles **Croyden & Son** (EP) ^(K80)
Devenport/Devon (20, Fore St)
- 1880 ...

Not assigned! (CU/EP) ^(E)
Sheffield
London
~ 1900 ...

(See also) (EP)
Charles S. **Green & Co. Ltd.**

(See also) (EP)
Charles Truman **Burrows & Sons**

Culf & Kay (EP) [M]
Sheffield (63, Mary St)
~ 1896 ...
1948 - today (**Ltd.**)
(See also figures: C & K, CULFO-NIA)

Arthur **Culf** (BM/EP)
(Rock Works)
Sheffield (34 & 36, Charlotte St/161-167, Howard St)   (K80) (SBW)
- 1880 - 1893   (WDS01)
- 1901 ... (**& Co.**)
(Then: Allcard & Co)

Arthur **Culf**, Junior (BM/EP)   (K80) (SBW)
Sheffield (185, Rockingham St)
- 1880 ...

CULFONIA   *(See also)* (EP)
Culf & Kay

George **Curr** (OSP)   (GDS)
Sheffield (1, Surrey St)
1833 ...

William **Curson** (CP)   (CD) (WTD)
Birmingham (3, New Thomas St)
- 1818 - 1823 ...

Charles **Cusworth** (EP)   (WDS01)
Sheffieldf (16, Steade Rd)
- 1901 ...

Benjamin **Cutler** (CP)   (WTDB) (WTD)
Birmingham (Snowhill/Brearley St)
- 1815 - 1818 ...

Mrs. **Cutler** (CP)   (WDB) (PDB)
Birmingham (Bell St)
- 1823 - 1825 ...

Charles **Cutts** (EP)   (POS) (K54)
(Howard Lane Works)
Sheffield (Howard Ln)
- 1854 ...

George **Cutts** **(CU/BM/EP)**
(Park Britannia Metal & Silver
Plate Works)
Sheffield (Brown Ln/33, Broad St/13, Glenn Rd)
- 1861 - 1880 ...
- 1893 ... (**& Sons**)
(See also figure: G·C S)

(GS) (K72) AD
(K76) (WDS79)
(K80)

(K93)

Jno. Priston **Cutts** **(OSP)**
Sheffield (Division St)
1843 ... *(See also figure: I·P·C)*

(B) (SAOR) (SBW)
(M)

Joseph **Cutts** **(BM/EP)**
(Truro Works)
Sheffield (169, Matilda St)
- 1849 - 1852 ...

(GDBS) (WDOS
AD)

Cutts Brothers **(EP/CU)**
Sheffield (90, Pond St/Harmer Ln/St. Mary's
Rd)
- 1854 - 1863 ...

(POS) (K54) (GS)

Jno. Priston **Cutts, Sutton & Sons (EP/CU)**
Sheffield (51-57, Division St/66 High St)
- 1879 ... *(See also figure:TRY ME)*

(WDS79)

CW **EP** **NS** *(See also)* **(EP)**
Charles **Wilkes**

CWF **S** **EP** *(See also)* **(EP)**
CWF **S** Charles William **Fletcher & Sons Ltd.**
EPNS·A1
ARUNDEL
PLATE

CYCLOPS *(See also)* **(CU)**
CORPORATE MARK. Charles **Cammell & Co. Ltd.**
(Cyclops Steel & Iron Works)

CYCLOPS

D & A **NEVADA SILVER**

D & A

E.P.N.S

(See also) **(EP)**
Thomas H. **Daniel &** Thomas R. **Arter**
(Globe Nevada Silver Works)

D&B

(See also) **(EP)**
Davenport & Bray

D & B

(See also) **(EP)**
Dutten & Benton

D&Co. L ᵀᴰ

(See also) **(EP)**
W. L. **Dickinson & Co. Ltd.**

D&G·HOLY& Co
SHEFFIELD

(See also) **(OSP)**
Daniel & George **Holy & Co.**

D & H
D&H

(See also) **(EP)**
William R. **Deykin &** Walter A. **Harrison**

D & J

(See also) **(EP)**
Frederick **Derry &** Henry **Jones**

D & P

(See also) **(EP)**
Davis & Powers

D & S

(See also) **(BM/EP)**
William **Deykin & Sons**

D&S

(See also) **(OSP)**
James **Dixon & Sons**

D&S G
D & S ✳ G

(See also) **(EP)**
Davis & Sons

D·C

(See also) **(OSP)**
D. **Cadman**

D·HORTON

(See also) **(CP)**
D. **Horton**

D·H&S   **DH&S**   *(See also)*   (EP)
David **Hollander & Sons Ltd.**

D·R   *(See also)*   (OSP)
Dollif **Rollinson**

D.S.C.G.   *(See also)*   (EP)
The **Duchess of Sutherland's Cripples Guild of Handicrafts**

D.W.&C<u>O</u>   *(See also)*   (EP)
Daniel **Welby & Co.**

D❋S   *(See also)*   (OSP)
James **Dixon & Sons**

D❉S   *(See also)*   (OSP)
James **Dixon & Sons**

D ... *(See also)*   (EP)
John **Gilbert & Co. Ltd.**

(See also)   (CP/CU)
Austin & Dodson Ltd.

William **Daffern**   **(GS/EP)**   (MDG) (POB) (K78) (K80) (K82) (K84) (K88) (K92) (SBW) (M)
Birmingham (Wheeler St./11, Vyse St./61, Graham St.)
- 1866 - 1892 ...
(See also figure: RAENO)
(Then: Raeno Silver Plating Co. Ltd.)

Thomas **Dale**   **(EP)**   (K80) (K82) (K84) (K88)
Birmingham (13, Warstone Ln/66, Branston St)
- 1880 - 1888 ...

Richard **Dallyn**   **(EP)**   (WDS01)
Sheffield (136, Harwell Rd)
- 1901 ...

George **Dalton**   **(OSP)**   (B) (SAOR)
Sheffield (Simcroft)
1794 ... *(See also figure: G*D)*

William **Damant**   **(OSP)**   (B) (SAOR)
Sheffield (Smithfield)
1775 ... *(See also figure: W·D)*

J. **Danby**	**(CP)**	(CDB)
Birmingham (49, Brearley St)		
- 1818 ...		

John **Danby**	**(OSP)**	(HDG)
Sheffield (10, Cheney Rw)		
- 1822 ...		

T. **Danby**	**(EP)**	(HGD)
Birmingham (49, Brearley St)		
- 1850 ...		

D

DAN HOLY PARKER & Co *(See also)* **(OSP)**
Daniel **Holy, Parker & Co.**

Thomas H. **Daniel &** Thomas R. **Arter (EP)** (K80) (PC) (K36)
(Globe Nevada Silver Works) (M)
Birmingham (High Gate St) (Rd 674985)
London (98, Hatton Garden)
- 1880 - 1912 ...
1913 - 1936 ... **(Ltd.)**

DANIEL & ARTER

(See also figures: ALUMINIUM SILVER, ARGENLINE, BENGAL SILVER, BRAZILIAN SILVER, BURMAROID, Connought, *INDIAN SILVER, Japanese Silver, LAXEY SILVER, NEVADA SILVER)*

Daniel Manufacturing Co. **(EP)** (K36)
Birmingham (46, Hockley Hill)
- 1936 ...

Thomas **Daniell** **(OSP)** (B)
London
1778 ... *(See also figure: TD)*

DANᴸ HOLY WILKINSON & Co *(See also)* **(OSP)**
Daniel **Holy, Wilkinson & Co.**

John **Darby**	**(CP/EP)**	(WDOB) (HGDB)
Birmingham (Livery St/26, Snowhill/10/		(HGD) (CDB) (GS)
111, Gt. Hampton Rw)		(MDG) (POB)
- 1839 - 1872 ...		(K72)

Samuel **Darby**	**(CP)**	(WTDB) (CD)
Birmingham (Gough St/Snowhill/Peck Ln)		(WTD) (WAB)
- 1815 - 1830 ...		(HTD)

Thomas **Darby** **(EP)** [K92]
(Clyde Works)
Birmingham (Weaman St)
- 1892 ...

William Edward **Darby** **(BM/EP)** [MDG] [K78] [K80]
Birmingham (Wheeler St./109, Gt. Hampton Rw)
- 1866 - 1880 ...

William **Darby** **(OSP)** [B] [SAOR]
Sheffield (Pea Croft)
1785 ... *(See also figure: W·D)*

W. E. **Darlaston** **(GS)** [WDOB]
Birmingham (Brooke St)
- 1839 ...

Frederick H. **Darley** **(EP)** [K80]
Folkestone, Kent (5, Church St)
- 1880 ...

Davenport & Bray **(EP)** [M]
Sheffield
~ 1871 - 1874 ... *(See also figure: D&B)*

George **Davenport** **(BM/EP)** [K80]
Sheffield (57 & 59, Eyre St)
- 1880 ...

Joseph **Davenport** **(EP)** [SD]
Birmingham
- 1850 ...

Joseph **Davenport** **(EP)** [GDBS] [WDOS]
Sheffield (42, Lee Croft/Malinda St)
- 1849 - 1852 ...

A. L. **Davenport Ltd.** **(EP)**
Birmingham
~ 1927 - 1971 *(See also figure: A L D)*
(Then T. Wilkinson & Co. Ltd. in 1932)

Limuel **Davi(d)son** **(OSP)** [B] [SAOR]
Sheffield (Spring Croft)
1787 ... *(See also figure: I·D)*

T. H. **Davies & Co** (EP) (E)
Sheffield

~

(See also figure: T.H.DAVIES &Co*)*

William **Davies & Co.** (EP) (K72)
Birmingham (80, Spencer St)
- 1872 ...

Charles **Davies** (CP/EP) (WDOB) (HGDB)
Birmingham (Mary Ann St/3, Howard St) (HGD)
- 1839 - 1850 ...

W. **Davies** (EP) (MDG)
Birmingham (Peel St)
- 1866 ...

James **Davis & Co.** (EP) (K80)
Bradford (51, Tyrrel St)
- 1880 ...

Davis & Perks (EP) (K36)
Birmingham (64, Spencer St)
- 1936 ...

Davis & Powers (EP)
Birmingham
1939 - 1964 *(See also figure: D&P)*

Davis & Sons (EP) (GS) (Rd 440617)
Glasgow
- 1863 - 1904 ... *(See also figure: D&S G)*

Joseph **Davis** (CP/CU) (B) (WTD) (M)
Birmingham (Great Charles St)
1816 - 1818 ...

Henry Clifford **Davis** (EP)
Birmingham (121, Vyse St/23, Warstone Ln)
~ 1910 - 1933
- 1933 - 1960 ... (**Ltd.**)

Henry **Davis** (EP) (CDB)
Birmingham (Snowhill)
- 1861 ...

John **Davis** (CP) (WDB) (PDB)
Birmingham (6, Lichfield St/30, Newton St) (WAB) (HTD)
- 1823 - 1830 ...

Joseph **Davis** **(EP)** (K82) (K84) (K88) (K92)
Birmingham (Ruby Building, Frederick St)
- 1882 - 1892 ...

Mary **Davis** **(OSP)** (WTD)
Birmingham (Water St)
- 1818 ...

Mrs. Elizabeth **Davis** **(EP)** (K88)
Birmingham (286, Gt. Colemore St)
- 1888 ...

Thomas **Davis** **(CP)** (WTDB)
Birmingham (Water St)
- 1815 ...

William **Davis** **(FP)** (WTDB) (WTD)
Birmingham (Snowhill)
- 1815 - 1818 ...

Davis, Blackham & Co. Ltd. **(EP)**
Birmingham
~ 1900 ...
(See also figure: DB&Co. Ltd.)

Richard **Davis Ltd.** **(EP)** (K36)
Birmingham (66 & 67, Edward St)
- 1936 ...

Stephen **Dawson & Co.** **(EP)** (K88) (K92) (PC) (K03) (M)
Birmingham (252, New John St)
- 1888 - 1903 ...
(See also figures: Dn&Co, SD&Co L^{TD})

Dawson Ltd. **(EP)** (K36)
Birmingham (83, Unett St)
- 1936 ...
(See also figure: SD&Co L^{TD})

H. **Dawson, Wilkinson & Co.** **(OSP)** (B) (SAOR)
Sheffield (Sycamore St)
1833 ... *(See also figure: HDW&Co)*

DB&Cº *(See also)* **(OSP)**
D. **Barnard** J. **Settle & Co.**

D B & Cº.L^{TD} *(See also)* **(EP)**
Davis, Blackham & Co. Ltd.

George **Deakin & Co.** **(EP)** ^{(B) (SAOR) (SBW)}
Sheffield (Eyre St/107, Edward St)
1849 - 1901 ... *(See also figure: GD)*
(Then: Hale Brothers)

James **Deakin &** William Henry **Deakin (EP)** ^(SAOR)
Birmingham
1845 ...

Joseph **Deakin & Sons** **(BM/EP)** ^{(GDBS) (WDOS)}
(Spring Street Works) ^{(GS) (WDS79)}
Sheffield (114, Green Ln/ 51, Bridge St/ ^{(K80) (M)}
59 & 71, Spring St)
- 1849 - 1880 ...
(See also figure: JOSEPH DEA-
KIN & SONS)

Deakin & Staniforth **(EP)** ^{(POS) (K54)}
Sheffield (Green Ln)
- 1854 ...

James **Deakin** **(BM/EP)**
(Sidney Works) (Wm. Pitchford, John &
Albert)
Sheffield (101, Matilda St) ^{(B) (K80)}
1865 - 1880 ^{(K93) (SAOR)}
1878 - 1897 **(& Sons)** ^(WDS01)WDSR)
1897 - 1905 ... **(& Sons Ltd.)**
(See also figures: JD&S, AUTO,
AZTEC, JAMES DEAKIN, symbol
"lamp")

William P. **Deakin** **(EP)** ^(WDS01)
Sheffield (18, Moncrieffe Rd)
- 1901 ...

Samuel **Deakin** A. **Kitchen & Co. (OSP)** ^{(B) (SAOR)}
(S. **Deakin & Co.)**
Sheffield (Holly Croft)
1781 ...
(See also figures: SDK&Co,
SD&Co)

D

	Deakin, Reuss & Co. **(Tiger Works)** Sheffield (Green Ln) - 1879 - 1893 ... *(See also figure: Symbol "tiger")*	**(CU)**	(WDS79) (K93 AD)
DEAKIN SMITH & Co	**Deakin, Smith & Co.** Sheffield (Hawley Croft) 1785 - 1791 ...	**(OSP)**	(B) (GM) (UBD) (M)
	Thomas **Dean & Cheston** Birmingham (Jamaica Rw) - 1818 ...	**(OSP)**	(CD)
	I. S. **Dearden** Sheffield ~ 1910 ... *(See also figure: I.S. DEARDEN)*	**(EP)**	
	William H. **Deeley** Birmingham (37, Gt. Hampton St) - 1823 - 1849 ...	**(CP)**	(WDB) (PDB) (WAB) (HTD) (HGDB)
DEFIANCE	*(See also)* George **Wilkin** **(Palmerston Works)** and Abram **Brooksbank & Co.** **(Malinda Works)**	**(EP)** **(EP/CU)**	
	James **Denison** London (10, Smithfield) - 1808 ...	**(CU)**	(POAD)
	W. **Denning** Sheffield 1786 ...	**(OSP)**	(SAOR)
DENNIS SYKES	Dennis **Sykes** Sheffield (Pinstone St) 1792 ...	**(OSP)**	(B)
	Edward John **Dent & Co.** London 1861 - 1919 *(See also figure: E. Dent)* 1920 ... **(Ltd.)**	**(EP)**	

John **Derby & Sons** (CU) ^{(WDS79) (SBW)} ^(M)
Sheffield (260, St. Philip's Rd/28, Suffolk St)
- 1879 ... *(See also figure: PLENTY)*

Frederick **Derry &** Henry **Jones** (EP) ^{(CDB) (BDB) (GS)} ^{(MDG) (M)}
(Formerly: J. Sheldon & Co)
Birmingham (55, Gt. Hampton St)
- 1861 - 1871 *(See also figure: D&J)*
(Then: Henry Jones & Co)

Frederick **Derry** (BM/EP) ^{(K72) (K78) (K80)}
(Phoenix Works) ^{(K82) (K84) (K88)} ^{(K92) (PC) (SBW)} ^(M)
Birmingham (31 & 32/11 & 13, Hockley St)
- 1872 - 1896 ...
*(See also figures: **FD*, ROYAL STANDARD, STANDARD VICTORIA)*

Dessolle (The) **Electro Plating Co. Ltd.** ^(K03)
(Speedwell Works) (EP)
Birmingham (Chester St)
- 1903 ...

DEVER | **Not assigned!** (OSP) ^(B)
Sheffield

John **Devey** (CU) ^{(WDB) (PDB)} ^{(BDB) (MDG)}
Birmingham (22, Summer St/47, Gt. Hampton St)
- 1823 - 1866 ...

S. **Devey** (CP) ^(DOB)
Birmingham (Loveday St)
- 1833 ...

William **Devy** (CP/CU) ^{(WWDB) (WDOB)}
Birmingham (8, Little Hampton St)
- 1835 - 1839 ...

Charles **Dewsnap** (GS) ^(WDOS)
Sheffield (48, Tripett Ln)
- 1852 ...

Joshua **Dewsnap** **(OSP)** ^(B)

Sheffield

1781 ... (Trinity St) (SAOR)

1803 ... (Arundel St) (SAOR)

(See also figures: ID, I·D, SOUND)

James **Dewsnap** **(CU)** (SAOR)

(Morocco Works) (K82AD)

Sheffield (10, St. Thomas St)

London (Ely Pl, Holborn)

1875 - 1882 ...

Peter **Dewsnap** **(OSP)** (B) (SAOR)

Sheffield (Carver Ln)

1819 ... *(See also figure: P.D)*

W. **Dewsnap** **(OSP)** (B) (SAOR)

Sheffield (Lambert Croft)

1786 ... *(See also figure: W.D)*

James **Deykin & Sons** **(BM/EP)** (MDG) (K72)

(Venetian Works) (K78) (K80) (K82)

(James **Deykin**. **&** William Redfern **Deykin**)

Birmingham (5 & 6, Jennens Rw)

1854 - 1895 *(See also figure: **D&S)*

(Then: Deykin & Harrison)

William R. **Deykin &** Walter A. **Harrison** (PC) (K03) (K36)

(Formerly: J. Deykin & Sons, W.R. Deykin &

Sons)

Birmingham (5 & 6, Jennens Rw) **(EP)**

- 1896 - 1906

1907 - 1936 ... **(Ltd.)**

(See also figures: D & H, VE-
NETIAN SILVER, symbol "gon-
dola")

William R. **Deykin & Sons** **(BM/EP)** (GS) (BDB)

(Formerly: J. Deykin & Sons) (MDG) (POB)

DEYKIN **BIRMINGHAM** Birmingham (5 & 6, Jennens Rw) (K78) (K80) (K84)

- 1862 - 1892 ... (K88) (K92) (M)

(Then: Deykin & Harrison)

DGC
A1

(See also) **(EP)**

Daniel George **Collins Co. Ltd.**

DH **DH&C°**	*(See also)* Daniel **Holy & Co.**	**(OSP)**	(B)
	Joseph **Dickenson** Gainsborough 1780 ... *(See also figure: ID)*	**(OSP)**	(B) (SAOR)
	W. L. **Dickinson & Co. Ltd.** Birmingham 1905 - 1910 *(See also figure: D&Co. Ltd.)*	**(EP)**	
	James **Dingley** Birmingham (Snow Hill) - 1839 ...	**(GS)**	(WDOB)
DIXON&Co	T. **Dixon & Co.** Birmingham 1784 ...	**(OSP)**	(B) (M)
	John **Dixon & Co.** (John **Dixon & Sons**) Sheffield (145, Allen St/40, Smithfield) - 1849 ...	**(BM)**	(GDBS) (WDOS)
	Dixon & Frith Sheffield (Bailey St) - 1828 ...	**(OSP)**	(SDG)
DIXON & SON	James **Dixon & Son** Sheffield (Cornish Pl/Silver St/Green Ln) 1819 - 1835... *(See also figures: D&S, D✲S, JDI-XON)*	**(BM/CU/OSP)**	(B) (PD) (WDG) (M) (SDG) (GDBS) (GDS) (PDB)
DIXON	James **Dixon & Smith** Sheffield 1804 - 1830	**(OSP)**	
DIXON 🎺	James **Dixon & Sons** Sheffield (Cornish Pl/14, St. Andrew St) London (Holborn Circus) - 1837 - 1893 ... - 1936 ... *(See also figures: JD&S, symbol "trumpet")*	**(BM/EP)**	(B) (SAOR) (HGDY) (SBW) (SD) (GS) (POS) (GDBS) (WDOS) (K54) (K72) (WDS79) (K80) (K93) (M) (K36)

Fanshaw **Dixon** (EP) (WDS01)
Sheffield (135, Charlotte Rd)
- 1901 ...

Henry Isaac **Dixon** (EP) (WDOS) (CDB)
Birmingham (Page Hall/110, Pope St) (K78) (K80) (PC)
- 1852 - 1896 ...

Matthew **Dixon** (CP) (SAOR) (WTDB)
Birmingham (Masshouse Ln/137, Snowhill) (CD) (WTD)
1815 - 1850 ... (HGDB) (WDB)
(DOB) (PDB)
(WDOB) (WAB)
(HTD) (HGD)

***Dixon* J**

DIXON'S
IMPERIAL

James **Dixon & Son** (BM/CU/OSP) (B) (PD) (WDG)
Sheffield (Cornish Pl/Silver St/Green Ln) (M) (SDG) (GDBS)
1819 - 1835... (GDS) (PDB)
(See also figures: D&S, D✱S, JDI-XON)

D & J. WELLBY L^{TD}
LONDON

(See also) (EP)
D. & J. **Wellby Ltd.**

DL

(See also) (OSP)
Daniel **Leader**

DN&C^O

(See also) (EP)
S. **Dawson & Co.**

George **Dodd** (OSP) (B) (SAOR)
Sheffield (Portmahon)
1819 ... *(See also figure: GD)*

W. & M. **Dodge** (EP) (B) (SAOR) (M)
Manchester (Market Pl)
1866 ... *(See also figures: WD, W&MD)*

Dolex Brothers (EP) (GS)
Birmingham (8, Luisa St)
- 1863 ...

Doley, White & Dale (EP) (MDG) (POB)
(Doley & White)
Birmingham (102, Mott St)
- 1866 - 1867 ...

	Doley, Wilkes & Doley Birmingham (39, Camden St) - 1849 - 1850 ...	**(EP)**	(HGDB) (HGD)
	Domney & Brown Birmingham (Warstone Pd East) - 1880 ...	**(EP)**	(K80)
	James **Domney** Birmingham (65, Caroline St) 1921 ...	**(EP)**	
DORRIT SILVER	*(See also)* **Hamilton, Laidlaw & Co.**	**(BM/EP)**	(S)
	Mary **Dowler & Son** Birmingham (91, Gt. Charles St) - 1815 - 1818 ...	**(CP)**	(WTDB) (WTD)
	Thomas **Dowler** Birmingham (91, Gt. Charles St) - 1818 - 1835 ...	**(CP/EP)**	(CD) (PDB) (WDB) (WAB) (HTD) (HGD)
	Joseph **Doxey** Sheffield (14, Charles St) - 1871 ...	**(EP)**	(WDS71)
D R & Sons	**Not assigned!**	**(EP)**	(E)
	J. **Drabble & Co.** Sheffield (Eyre St) 1805 ... 1862 ... *(See also figures: I.D&Co., I.DRABBLE)*	**(OSP)**	(B) (SAOR) (MHM) (M)
	Edward Goodrick **Draper & Co.** **(Globe Works)** Sheffield (Penistone Rd/35, Whitham Rd) 1881 - 1901 ... *(See also figure: ED&Co)*	**(EP)**	(SAOR) (K93) (WDS01)
DREW & Co LEADENHALL ST LONDON	**Drew & Co.** London (Leadenhall St) ~ 1900 ...	**(EP)**	(E)
	Drew & Sons London (Picadilly Circus) ~	**(EP)**	(E)

D

DS	*(See also)* Daniel **Smith** **(OSP)**	**(OSP)**
DSK&Co	*(See also)* s. **Deakin** A. **Kitchen & Co.**	**(OSP)**
DS **RS**	*(See also)* Daniel **Smith &** Robert **Sharp**	**(OSP)**
DUCAL PLATE	*(See also)* The **Northern Goldsmiths Company**	**(EP)**
DUCHESS	*(See also)* **Bird & Blake**	**(CU/EP)**

The **Duchess of Sutherland's Cripples Guild of Handicrafts (EP)**
Newcastle
1902 - 1922
(See also figure: D.S.C.G.)

John **Ducker** (GS) (WDOB)
Birmingham (Digbeth)
- 1839 ...

William **Duddle(s)ton** (EP) (CDB) (BDB) (GS)
Birmingham (75, Caroline St)
- 1861 - 1863 ...

Samuel **Duesbury** (EP) (GS)
Sheffield (Blackfields, 24, Devision St)
- 1863 ...

Barnabas **Dugard** (CP) (WWDB) (WDOB)
Birmingham (Bartholomew Rw)
- 1835 - 1839 ...

William **Dugard** (CP) (WDOB)
Birmingham (Upper Priory)
- 1839 ...

Dugard Brothers (EP) (HGDB)
Birmingham (22, Upper Priory)
- 1849 ...

Samuel Richard **Dugmore & Co.** (EP) (K03)
Birmingham (30, Augusta St)
- 1903 ...

	George **Dugmore**	**(EP)**	(PC)
	Birmingham (107, Carver St)		
	- 1896 ...		

	Henry **Duke**	**(GS/CU)**	(B) (SAOR) (WDS37) (DSRR)
	Sheffield (Division St/50, Rockingham Ln/ 9, Gell St)		
	1837 - 1841 ... *(See also figure: HD)*		

	Mrs. Grace **Duke**	**(EP)**	(K80)
	Portsea (49, Hanover St)		
	- 1880 ...		

du Mont Plate

	Not assigned!	**(EP)**	(E)

	William **Duncalf**	**(FP)**	(WTDB) (WTD)
	Birmingham (Coleshill St)		
	- 1815 - 1818 ...		

	G. B. **Dunn**	**(CU/CP)**	(B) (WTDB) (WTD) (CD) (WDB) (PDB) (WAB) (HTD) (M)
	Birmingham (62, New Town Rw)		
	1810 - 1830 ...		

DURATION

(See also) **(CU/EP)**
Frederick **Barnes & Co.**

DURO METAL.

(See also) **(EP)**
(The) **Phosphor Bronze Co.**

	Francis William **Durows**	**(EP)**	(K82) (K84) (K88)
	Birmingham (25, Grosvenor St)		
	- 1882 - 1888 ...		

	John James **Durrant**	**(EP)**	(M)
	London (30, Cheapside)		
	~ 1850 - 1897		
	1897 ...**(& Son)** (William James)		
	(See also figure: JJ Dur rant)		

	John **Dutson**	**(OSP)**	(WDB) (PDB)
	Birmingham (139, Suffolk St)		
	- 1823 - 1825 ...		

	Dutten & Benton	**(EP)**	(GS) (K80)
	Sheffield (13, Norfolk Ln)		
	- 1863 - 1880 ... *(See also figure: D & B)*		

D W T S	**Not assigned!** ~ 1900	**(EP)**	
	<small>William</small> **Dyer** Birmingham (Edmund St) - 1815 - 1830 ...	**(CP)**	<small>(WTDB) (WTD)</small> <small>(WAB) (HTD)</small>
	<small>Abraham</small> **Dyson** Sheffield (12, Charles St) 1835 - 1841 ... *(See also figure: AD)*	**(CU)**	<small>(B) (SAOR)</small> <small>(DSRR)</small>

D

(C) **&** **(C⁰)** **E&C⁰**	*(See also)* **Elkington & Co.**	**(EP)**
E&C⁰ **E& C⁰**	*(See also)* **Elkington & Co.**	**(EP)**
E&C⁰	*(See also)* **Elkington & Co.**	**(EP)**
E & M	*(See also)* **Evans & Matthews**	**(EP)**
E&S **S** **EP**	**Not assigned!** Sheffield	**(EP)** ⁽ᴱ⁾
E·R	*(See also)* E. **Rhodes**	**(OSP)**

E

John **Eades** Birmingham (Lancaster St) - 1815 ...	**(CP)**	(WTDB)
Richard **Eades** Birmingham (23, Paradise St) - 1815 - 1833 ...	**(BM/CP)**	(WTDB) (CD) (WTD) (WDB) (PDB) (WAB) (HTD) (DOB)
G. **Eadon & Co.** Sheffield (Hollis Croft) 1795 ... *(See also figure: GE&Co)*	**(OSP)**	(B) (SAOR)
Eadon, Kibble & Weaver London (3, Amen Corner) - 1791 - 1808 ...	**(T/OSP)**	(UBD) (POAD)
Eagle Plate Co. Ltd. (Egerton Works) Sheffield (Egerton St) - 1936 ...	**(EP)**	(K36)
John **Earl** Sheffield (456, Abbeydale Rd) - 1901 ...	**(EP)**	(WDS01)
John **Eaton** Sheffield (123, Matilda St) - 1863 ...	**(EP)**	(GS)

Thomas Wigfall **Eaton**   **(CU/OSP/EP)**
Sheffield (Radford St/52, New Church St/220, Solly St)
1844 - 1883 ... *(See also figure: T.E)*
1904 - 1911 **(& Co.)**
(See also figure: T.W.EATON)

(B) (SAOR) /SD46)
(WDOS)
(M) (W)

William Charles **Eaton**   **(CU/EP)**
Sheffield (53 & 55, Howard St/65, Thirwell Rd)
1883 - 1905 ...

(SAOR) (K93)
(WDS01) (WDSR)

Mark M. **Eaves**   **(EP)**
Birmingham (10 & 9, Holland St)
- 1882 - 1903 ...

(K82) (K84) (K88)
(K92) (PC) (K03)

E.B.&C<u>o</u>

(See also)   **(EP)**
Edwin **Blyde & Co.**

E.BLYDE & Co.Ltd SHEFFIELD

(See also)   **(EP)**
Edwin **Blyde & Co. Ltd.**

(See also)   **(EP)**
Edwin **Blyde & Co.**

EB

(See also)   **(OSP)**
E. **Bradley**

EB

(See also)   **(OSP)**
Thompson & Barber

E B / **J B**

(See also)   **(EP)**
Edward & John **Barnard**

E.DENT BIG BEN

(See also)   **(EP)**
Edward John **Dent & Co.**

ED & Co

(See also)   **(EP)**
Edward Goodrick **Draper & Co.**

James **Edden**   **(CP)**   (WTDB)
Birmingham (Weaman Rw)
- 1815 ...

Edwin **Edmonds**   **(EP)**   (K36)
Birmingham (31, Warstone Ln)
- 1936 ...

E

	Thomas **Edmonds** Birmingham (28, Ellis St) - 1833	**(CP)**	(DOB)
	George **Edmonds Ltd.** London (118 - 122, Holborn) - 1936 ...	**(EP)**	(K36)
	James **Edward** Birmingham (70, Park St) - 1829 - 1839 ...	**(CP)**	(WAB) (HTD) (WWDB) (WDOB)
	Edwards & Co. Birmingham (209, Newhall St) - 1903 ...	**(EP)**	(K03)
	Henry **Edwards &** Edward Jno. **Ball (CU)** Birmingham (82, High St) 1839 - 1850 ...		(HGDB) (HGD) (SAOR)
EDWARDS&SONS GLASGOW	**Edwards & Sons** Glasgow ~ 1900 ...	**(EP)**	(E)
	Charles **Edwards** Birmingham (116, Hockley St) - 1888 ...	**(EP)**	(K88)
	George **Edwards** Glasgow (Gordon St) 1861 - 1884 *(See also figure: GE)*	**(EP)**	(B) (SBW) (SAOR)
	Mrs. Selina **Edwards** Birmingham (116, Hockley St) - 1892 ...	**(EP)**	(K92)
	William **Edwards** Birmingham 1819 ...	**(CU/OSP)**	(SAOR)
EDWIN BLYDE & Co.LTD	*(See also)* Edwin **Blyde & Co.**	**(EP)**	
E E R J W	*(See also)* Edward, Ed. jun. John & William **Barnard**	**(EP)**	
	William **Eels** Birmingham (147, Granville St/9, Caroline St) - 1884 - 1892 ...	**(EP)**	(K84) (K88) (K92)

E

ℱℱ	*(See also)* Arthur Edward **Furniss**	**(BM/EP)**
𝕰 𝖋 𝕹	**Not assigned!**	**(EP)**
E·GOODWIN	*(See also)* E. **Goodwin**	**(OSP)**
EG	*(See also)* E. **Goodwin**	**(OSP)**
	Samuel **Eg(g)ington** Birmingham (Water St) - 1818 ...	**(OSP)** ^{(WTD) (CD)}
EGLENTINE	Ferdinand **Eglington** Walsall. (38, Park St) - 1880 ...	**(EP)** ^{(K80) (M)}
E H P	*(See also)* E. H. **Parkin & Co.** **(Cornwall Works)**	**(EP)**
E H & S	*(See also)* Edwin **Howard & Son**	**(EP)**
E & J. L	E. & J. **Leek** Birmingham 1923 - 1936	**(EP)**
E.J.BUXTON&Co **SHEFFIELD**	*(See also)* Edwin James **Buxton & Co.**	**(EP)**
E·J·F **E.J.FAIRBAIRNS**	*(See also)* Elisabeth Jane **Fairbairns**	**(EP)**
E.J.H. EP	*(See also)* Edwin Joseph **Houlston Ltd.**	**(EP)**
EJH **NH**	*(See also)* **Haseler Brothers** (Edward Jn. & Noble)	**(EP)**
E J M	*(See also)* Edwin John **Makin**	**(EP)**
E . LECLERE MAKER SHEFFIELD	*(See also)* E. **Leclere**	**(EP)**

	Eldona Manufacturing Co. Ltd. **(EP)** [K36]	
	Birmingham (39, Frederick St)	
	- 1936 ...	
ELECTRO DEP. ELKINGTON & Co.	*(See also)* **Elkington & Co. Ltd.**	**(EP)**
Electro Imperial F.W	*(See also)* Frederick **Whitehouse** **(Lion Works)**	**(CU/EP)**
	(The) **Electrolytic Plating Apparatus** [K03] **Co.** **(EP)**	
	Birmingham (70-74, Victoria St)	
	- 1903 ...	
ELECTROPOTOSI	*(See also)* (The) **Potosi Silver Co.**	**(EP)**
ELKINGTON & Cº	*(See also)* **Elkington & Co.**	**(EP)**
ELKINGTON **H**	*(See also)* **Elkington & Co. Ltd.**	**(EP)**
ELKINGTON PLATE		

The Elkington Company (Elkington, Elkington, Mason & Co. and Elkington & Co.) have used for over 120 years a system of date letters. Because of this it is simple to date when a piece was manufactured.

(E&Cº) (ELEC) (TRO) (PLATE)	1840 Elkington & Co, Birmingham
	From 1841 ... Elkington & Co, Birmingham (Used during: 1841, 1845, 1847, 1848, 1858)
	Between 1842 - 1864 Elkington, Joshua Mason & Co, Birmingham

From 1841 they added an additional date letter. For the first period they used numbers from 1 - 8, with a special reverse 6, placed within a diamond cartouche.

1841   1842   1843   1844   1845   1846   1847   1848

In 1849 they changed the numbers to letters, starting with K - Z also within a diamond cartouche.

For example: 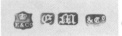   (Elkington, Mason & Co) with a date letter:

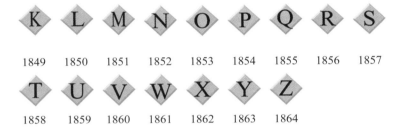

1849   1850   1851   1852   1853   1854   1855   1856   1857

1858   1859   1860   1861   1862   1863   1864

Confusingly the mark E & Co, was officially registered in 1865. But it can be found with a date letter reffering to an earlier date. The fonts used in these earlier marks are plain.

1849   1852   1853   1854   1861

In 1865 the mark      was introduced.

The date letters were placed in a rectangular cartouche with clipped corners.

A	D	E	F	G	H	K	L	M	N	O
1865	1866	1867	1868	1869	1870	1871	1872	1873	1874	1875

P	Q	R	S	T	U	V	W	X	Y	Z
1876	1877	1877	1878	1879	1880	1881	1882	1883	1884	1885

In 1867 first occurrence of: ELKINGTON & Cᵒ

E

In 1886 the clipped rectangular cartouche was replaced with a barrel shaped cartouche:

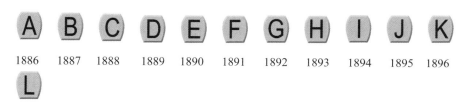

A	B	C	D	E	F	G	H	I	J	K
1886	1887	1888	1889	1890	1891	1892	1893	1894	1895	1896

L

1897

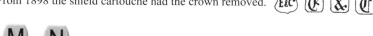 This additional mark was added from 1888.

1897 brought an act of Parliament that banned by law the use of the Sheffield crown within makers' marks on silver plated wares.
From 1898 the shield cartouche had the crown removed.

M N

1898   1899

In 1900 the shield cartouche saw another small modification:

O	P	Q	R	S	T	U	V
1900	1901	1902	1903	1904	1905	1906	1907

In 1908 an additional mark appeared:

1908 1909 1910 1911

1912 saw another change to the date letter cartouche, the barrel shape was replaced with a quatrefoil (four-leaves) cartouche.

1912 1913 1914 1915 1916 1917 1918 1919 1920 1921 1922

1923 1924 1925 1926 1927 1928 1929 1930 1931 1932 1933

1934 1935 1936

1937 brought along another change to the date cartouche, the quatrefoil was replaced with a shield cartouche.

1937 1938 1939 1940 1941 1942 1943 1944 1945 1946 1947

1948 1949 1950 1951 1952 1953 1954 1955 1956 1957 1958

1959 1960

1961 saw the final change of date cartouche to a circular one that should have run until 1970. However production ceased in 1968.

a	b	c	d	e	f	g	h	i	j
1961	1962	1963	1964	1965	1966	1967	1968	1969	1970

Elkington & Johnson **(BM)**   (MDG)
Birmingham (28, Masshouse Ln)
- 1866 ...

Elkington, Mason & Co. (BM/MP/EP)   (B) (HGDB)
Birmingham (136 & 137, New Hall St)   (HGD) (CDB) (GS)
1842 - 1866   (BDB) (MDG)
(See also figure: E M &Co.)

ELL ER BY

w. **Ellerby**   **(OSP)**   (B) (M)
London
1803 ...

Thomas **Ellin & Co.** **(CU)**   (WDS79)
(Sylvester Works)
Sheffield (Arundel St)
- 1879 ... *(See also figure: VULCAN)*

Henry **Elliot & Co.**   **(EP)**
Sheffield
- 1883 ... *(See also figure: Henry Elliot)*

Joseph **Elliot & Sons**   **(EP)**   (W) (M)
Sheffield
~ 1886 ...
(See also figures: C+C,
J.E S, JE&SS, JOSEPH ELLIOT)

Joseph **Elliott**   **(OSP)**   (HDG)
Sheffield (21, Nursery St)
- 1822 ...

Richard **Elliott**   **(CU)**   (SD46)
Sheffield (83, Wellington St)
- 1846 ...

E

Charles **Ellis & Co.**   **(EP)**   (GS) (K80) (SBW) (M)
Sheffield (39 & 57, Norfolk St)
- 1863 - 1880 ...
(See also figure: CE&Co)

Isaac **Ellis & Co.**   **(OSP)**   (B)
Sheffield (Red Hill)
1793 ... *(See also figure: IE&Co)*

Ellis & Co.   **(EP)**   (K36)
Sheffield (190, Rockingham St)
- 1936 ...

Ellis & Co.   **(EP)**   (PC) (K03)
Birmingham (14 & 15, Gt. Hampton St)
- 1896 - 1903 ...

C. **Ellis & Son(s)**   **(GS/EP)**   (MDG)
Birmingham (28, Constitution Hill)
- 1866 ...

Isaac **Ellis & Sons**   **(CU/EP)**   (WDS79) (M) (SBW)
(Portland Works)
Sheffield (55, Arundel St)
- 1879 ... *(See also figures: IE&S,*
ISAAC ELLIS & SONS, PRIMUS)

Charles **Ellis**   **(CP)**   (WAB) (HTD) (WDOB)
Birmingham (Snowhill)
- 1829 - 1839 ...

Christopher **Ellis**   **(OSP)**   (HDG)
Sheffield (Baker's Hill)
- 1822 ...

David **Ellis**   **(OSP)**   (CD) (WDB) (PDB)
Birmingham (Duke St)
- 1818 - 1825 ...

George **Ellis**   **(EP/CU)**   (WDSR)
Sheffield (100a & 102, Charles St/8, Albany
Rd)
- 1905 ...

Thomas **Ellis**   **(EP)**   (B) (SAOR) (K80) (SBW)
Plymouth (65, Old Town St)
1867 - 1880 ... *(See also figure: T.E)*

ELLIS BROS	**Not assigned!** (Appears with HB&H)	**(EP)**	(E)
	George **Ellis Ltd.** Sheffield (100, Charles St) 1920 - 1936 ... *(See also figure: G.ELLIS)*	**(EP)**	(K36)
	John **Ellis,** Peter **Spurr &** Peter **Cadman** Sheffield (Arundel St) 1801 ... *(See also figure: PS)*	**(OSP)**	(B) (SAOR)
	Ellis, Tucker, Marchan & Co. (OSP) Sheffield - 1791 ...		(UBD)
	William **Ellison** Bradford (35, Kirkgate) - 1880 ...	**(EP)**	(K80)
ELL L WARE	**Not assigned!**	**(EP)**	(E)
	J. & A. **Elshaw** Sheffield (83, Rockingham Ln) - 1893 ...	**(GS)**	(K93)
	James **Elshaw** Sheffield (67, Carver St/52, Blackfields) - 1893 ...	**(GS)**	(K93)
	William **Elshaw** Sheffield (107, John St) - 1893 ...	**(GS)**	(K93)
EL T	*(See also)* Edward Landers **Thompson & Co.**	**(EP)**	
EM&Co	*(See also)* **Elkington, Mason & Co.**	**(BM/MP/EP)**	
Embassy	*(See also)* **Gladwin Ltd.** **(Embassy & Montgomery Works)**	**(EP)**	
	George **Embrey** Birmingham (3, Pope St/Albion St) - 1867 - 1880 ...	**(EP)**	(POB) (K72) (K78) (K80)

EM **JM** **EM JM**	*(See also)* **Mappin Brothers**	**(EP)**
EMPIRE	*(See also)* Henry **Barnascone & Son**	**(CU/EP)**
	Empire Plating Co. Birmingham (19, Weaman Rw) - 1882 - 1884 ...	**(EP)** [K82] [K84]
EMPRESS ENCORE	*(See also)* John **Moreton & Co.**	**(EP)**
ENCORE	*(See also)* Thomas **Turner & Co.** **(Suffolk Works)**	**(CU/EP)**
	Thomas **Endsor** Birmingham (New Canal St) - 1839 ...	**(CP)** [WDOB]
ENDURE	*(See also)* J. & J. **Beal** **(Redhill Works)**	**(EP)**
ENGLAND	General term in use from 1890 - 1915	
	Aurelius **Ensell** Birmingham (102, Vyse St) - 1878 ...	**(EP)** [K78]
	Benjamin C. **Enson** Birmingham (Branston St) - 1878 ...	**(EP)** [K78]
	Ensor Manufacturing Co. Birmingham (29 - 33, Victoria St) - 1936 ...	**(EP)** [K36]
E.P.C	General term for: **Electro Plated Copper**	
E.P on B.M	General term for: **Electro Plate on Britannia Metal**	
E.PARKER & SONS SHEFFIELD	*(See also)* **Atkinson Brothers** **(Milton Works)**	**(EP)**

E P ✿✿ N S	*(See also)* **(BM/EP)** **Barker Brothers** **(Unity Works)**
E P B M	General term for: **Electro plated Britannia Metal**
E.P.C	General term for: **Electro plated copper**
E P C A	General term for: **Electro plated copper alloy**
EP = BM	General term for: **Electro plated Britannia Metal**
E P G S	General term for: **Electro plated German silver** Only used till ~ 1914.
E P N S	General term for: **Electro plated Nickel silver** If this stamp appears without any other makers mark, you can assume that the object was propably made in Birmingham.
♔ E P ♔ NS	The crown as a part of marking was banned by an act of parliament in 1897, so if you find a mark with a crown you can assume that the item was made before 1897.
E P on C	General term for: **Electro plated on copper**
E P W M	General term for: **Electro plated White Metal**
E R T R	*(See also)* **(EP)** **Robinson & Co.**
E·S·W	*(See also)* **(EP)** E. S. **Wells**
E.STACEY & SONS	*(See also)* **(BM/EP)** Ebenezer **Stacey & Sons**
E. STACEY SUCCESSORS TO I.VICKERS BRITANNIA PLACE	*(See also)* **(BM)** Ebenezer **Stacey**

E

ES	*(See also)* E. **Smelle**	**(OSP)**	
ES &Cº	*(See also)* E. **Sporle & Co.**	**(OSP)**	
E S & S	*(See also)* Ebenezer **Stacey & Sons**	**(BM/EP)**	
E.THOMASON & Co	*(See also)* E. **Thomason & Dowler**	**(CP)**	
	John M. **Etches** Sheffield (Howard St) 1820 ... *(See also figure: IME)*	**(OSP)**	(B) (SAOR)
EUREKA SILVER	*(See also)* William **Hay**	**(EP)**	
	Charles **Eustace** Birmingham (60, Gt. Charles St/ 13, St. Georges' Pl) - 1833 - 1861 ...	**(CP)**	(DOB) (WDOB) (CDB)
	Evans & Askin Birmingham (George St) - 1839 ...	**(GS)**	(WDOB)
EVANS & MATTHEWS **79 & 80 BULLSTREET** **BIRMINGHAM**	**Evans & Matthews** Birmingham (79 & 80, Bull St) - 1878 - 1880 ... *(See also figure: E&M)*	**(EP)**	(E) (K78) (K80)
	Evans & Robbins Birmingham (86, New John St) - 1936 ...	**(CU)**	(K36)
	J. **Evans & Sons** Birmingham (8, Vyse St) - 1936 ...	**(EP)**	(K36)
	J. W. **Evans & Sons Ltd.** Birmingham (56, Albion St) - 1936 ...	**(EP)**	(K36)
	Frederick Edward **Evans** Birmingham (60, Graham St) - 1882 - 1884 ...	**(EP)**	(K82) (K84)

E

James **Evans** **(CP)** (WTDB) (WDB)
Birmingham (41, Edgbaston St) (PDB)
- 1815 - 1825 ...

Samuel **Evans** **(OSP)**
Birmingham (Church St/32, Lionel St/39, St. (CD) (WTD)
Paul's Sq) (WDB) (PDB)
- 1818 - 1825 ...
1816 - 1839 ... (**& Son**) (B) (HTD) (WAB)
(See also figure: S.EVANS) (DOB) (WWDB)
(WDOB) (M)

Samuel Frederick **Evans** **(EP)** (HGDB) (HGD)
Birmingham (39, St. Paul's Sq/56, Gt. (CDB) (BDB)
Hampton St) (GS) (MDG) (K72)
- 1849 - 1884 ... (K80) (K82) (K84)
- 1878 - 1903 ... (**& Co./Sons**) (K78) (K88) (K92)
(See also figures: SFE&Co, SE&S) (PC) (K03) (M)

E

Stephen **Evans** **(CP)** (WTDB)
Birmingham (New John St)
- 1815 ...

Evans, Lescher & Webb **(EP)** (SBW) (M)
(Evans Sons & Co.)
London
Liverpool
~ 1900 ... *(See also figure: SAVARS.)*

Eve Brothers **(EP)** (K80)
Bristol (39, Nickolas St)
- 1880 ...

𝕰verlasting *(See also)* **(CU)**
Stacey Brothers

Samuel Thomas **Evinson** **(EP)** (K93) (WDS01)
Sheffield (West St/12, Hawksworth Rd)
- 1893 - 1901 ...

William **Ewing** **(CU)** (POAD)
London (Covent Garden)
- 1808 ...

EXCELLENT
FRANCE *(See also)* **(CU)**
VRAI **Brittain, Wilkinson & Brownill**

EXPRESS	*(See also)* John **Clarke & Sons**	**(CU/EP)**	
EXTRA.	*(See also)* John **Sellers & Sons**	**(CU)**	
EYE WITNESS	*(See also)* John **Taylor** and **Needman, Veall & Tyzack** **(Eye Witness Works)**	**(EP)**	
	Isaac **Eyre** Sheffield (38, Arundel St) - 1893 ...	**(EP)**	(K93)
	John **Eyre** Sheffield (Coalpit Ln) 1818 ... 1818 - 1829 ... (**& Co.**) *(See also figure: I·E)*	**(OSP)**	(SAOR) (B) (PD) (NGDS)
	Eyland & Sons Wallsall (11, Lower Rushell St) - 1880 ..	**(EP)**	(K80)

F&A	*(See also)* **Fenton & Anderton**	**(EP)**
F&S ⊠ ♔	*(See also)* A. **Fattorini & Sons**	**(BM/EP)**
F&W **L^TD**	**Not assigned!**	**(EP)** [E]
F.B **E P N S**	*(See also)* **Fenton Brothers (South Moor Works)**	**(EP)**
F.C **&C⁰** **S** ⬥EPNS	*(See also)* Frank **Cobb & Co.**	**(EP)**
F·M	*(See also)* F. **Morton**	**(OSP)**
F **A&C⁰** **S** EP	*(See also)* Frederick Charles **Asman & Co.**	**(EP)**
FABRE	*(See also)* William & John **Birks**	**(CU/OSP)**

Elisabeth Jane **Fairbairns**   **(EP)** [E]
London
~ 1900 *(See also figures: E·J·F, E.J. FAIRBAIRNS)*

C. S. **Farbey**   **(EP)** [K36]
London (Ct. 17, Tottenham Rd)
- 1936 ...

Herny Douglas **Farley**   **(GS)** [WDSR]
Sheffield (Union Ln/21, Glen Rd)
- 1905 ...

Joseph **Farmer**   **(CU)** [POAD]
London (Tavistock St/Covent Garden)
- 1808 ...

James **Farrell** jun.   **(EP)** [K80] [K82] [K84]
Birmingham (30, Lower Essex St)
- 1880 - 1884 ...

Thomas **Farrington**   **(CP)** [WAB] [HTD]
Birmingham (13, Fordrough St)
- 1829 - 1830 ...

FARROW & JACKSON Ltd **LONDON & PARIS.**	**Farrow & Jackson Ltd.** **(EP)** ^{(SBW) (M)} London (91, Mansell St/Aldgate) ~ 1900	

Farrow & Jackson Ltd.   **(EP)** [SBW] [M]
London (91, Mansell St/Aldgate)
~ 1900

FATTORINI & SONS
BRADFORD

FATTORINI & SONS LTD
BRADFORD

A. **Fattorini & Sons**   **(BM/EP)** [M]
(John & Edward)
Bradford (Kirksgate)
~ 1831 - 1909 *(See also figure: F&S)*
1909 - 1984 (**Ltd.**)

T. **Fattorini**   **(CU/EP)** [E]
Bradford/Birmingham
~ 1940 ...
(See also figures: T. FATTORINI,
SKIPTON)

FAUGH-A-BALLAGH

(See also)   **(EP)**
Edwin **Blyde & Co.**

Charles **Favell & Co.**   **(EP)** [S] [SAOR]
Sheffield (111, Arundel St)   [WDS01] [WDSR]
1888 - 1905 ... *(See also figure:*
CF&Co)

Rupert **Favell**, Henry **Elliot & Co. (EP)**
London/Sheffield (13, Norfolk Ln)
1883 - 1893
(See also figure: RF E &Co)
(Then: William Hutton & Sons)

Thomas H. **Fayran**   **(EP)** [K93]
Sheffield (56, Carver St)
- 1893 ...

(See also)   **(EP)**
Fenton Brothers
(South Moor Works)

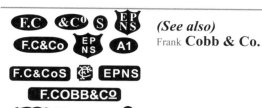

(See also) **(EP)**
Frank **Cobb & Co.**

F D *(See also)* **(BM/EP)**
Frederick **Derry**

Fearn & Gardner **(EP)** (POB)
Birmingham (41, St. Paul's Sq)
- 1867 ...

J. & G. **Fearn** **(OSP)** (B) (SAOR)
London
1823 ... *(See also figure: I.G.F)*

Thomas J. **Fearn** **(EP)** (CDB) (BDB)
Birmingham (4, Warstone Ln/21 & 22, Victoria (GS) (MDG) (AD)
St/300, Camden St) (POB) (K82) (K84)
- 1861 - 1892 ... (K88) (K92)

William **Fearn** **(EP)** (K78) (K80)
Birmingham (Victoria St/Regent St)
- 1878 - 1880 ...

Linder **Fearnley** **(BM)** (WDOS) (M)
Sheffield (58, Bridge St)
- 1849 ...
*(See also figure: LINDER FEARN-
LEY)*

John **Fee** **(EP)** (SAOR) (WDS79)
Sheffield (199, Cementery Rd/171, Eyre St) (K80)
- 1879 - 1880 ...

F E L *(See also)* **(EP)**
Frederick Ewbank **Leefe**

Fell & Williams **(EP)** (K72)
Birmingham (Scotland St)
- 1872 ...

Fenton & Anderton **(EP)** (B) (SAOR) (SBW)
Sheffield (M)
1857 ... *(See also figure: F&A)*

John **Fenton & Co.** **(OSP)** ^{(B) (SAOR)}
Sheffield (Pea Croft)
1799 ... *(See also figure: I.F&Co)*

Fenton & Co. **(EP)** ^(K92)
Birmingham (107, Vyse St)
- 1892 ...

Fenton & Son **(EP)** ^(K72)
Birmingham (28, Northampton St)
- 1872 ...

Joseph **Fenton & Sons** **(CU)** ^(WDS79)
(Sykes Works)
Sheffield (Matilda St/Eyre St)
- 1879 ...
*(See also figure: JOSEPH FEN-
TON & SONS)*

Daniel **Fenton** **(EP)** ^(POB)
Birmingham (20, Regent Pl)
- 1867 ...

Henry **Fenton** **(OSP)** ^(GDS)
Sheffield (Wilkinson St)
- 1833 ...

James **Fenton** **(EP)** ^{(B) (SAOR) (GS)}
^{(SBW) (M)}
Birmingham (74, Gt. Hampton St)
1854 - 1863 ... *(See also figure: JF)*

John Frederick **Fenton** **(EP)** ^{(B) (SAOR) (GS)}
^{(SBW) (M)}
Sheffield (Cadman Ln/Norfolk Ln)
1856 - 1863 ... *(See also figure: J.F.F)*

William James **Fenton** **(EP)** ^{(K78) (K80) (K82)}
^{(K84) (K88) (K92)}
Birmingham (27 & 28, Northampton St/ ^(K03)
121, Vyse St)
- 1878 - 1903 ...

Fenton, Allanson & Machon (OSP) ^{(CD) (HDG)}
(Fenton, Allanson & Co.) ^{(SDG) (NGDS)}
Sheffield (24, Norfolk St) ^{(PDB) (PDY) (B)}
1816 - 1828 ... *(See also figure: IF&Co)* ^(SAOR)

Fenton Brothers   **(EP)**
(John Frederick & Frank)
(South Moor Works)
Sheffield (Norfolk Ln/6, East St/66, Porter St)
1868 - 1893 ...
(See also figures: F.B, F.Brs, JFF   (B) (SAOR) (SBW)
& FF)   (K80) (K93) (M)
~ 1896 - 1899 ... **(Ltd.)**
(See also figures: FF SF, SFD AJF,
SFWS)

Matthew **Fenton**, Richard **Creswick & Co.**   (B) (SAOR)
(**Co.** = William **Watson**)   **(OSP)**
Sheffield (Mulberry St)
1773 - 1789 *(See also figure: MF RC)*
(Then: Fenton, Creswick & Oakes & Co)

Fenton, Creswick, Oakes & Co. (OSP)   (GM)
(Formerly: Fenton, Creswick & Co.)
Sheffield (Mulberry St)
- 1787 - 1795
(Then: Watson & Co.)

Fenton, Russel & Co. Ltd.   **(EP)**
Edinburgh
~ 1900 ... *(See also figure: F.R&Co.*
Ltd)

Fenton, Webster & Danby   **(OSP)**   (B) (SAOR) (PD)
Sheffield (44, Howard St)   (SDG) (NGDS)
1824 - 1829 ... *(See also figure:*
F.W&D)

Fenton Whitehouse   **(EP)**   (K72)
Birmingham (Regent Pl)
- 1872 ...

William Kennedy **Ferguson & Co. (EP)**   (K80)
Leeds (53, Gt. George St)
- 1880 ...

James **Ferrier**   **(EP)**   (K80)
Glasgow (13, South Exchange Pl)
- 1880 ...

FET & Co	*(See also)* Frederick Ellis **Timm & Co.**	**(EP)**	(B) (GS) (K54) (POS) (K80) (SBW) (M)
FF SF	*(See also)* **Fenton Brothers Ltd.**	**(EP)**	(SBW) (M)
F.GREEN & SONS SHEFFIELD	*(See also)* Frederick **Green & Sons** **(London Works)**	**(EP)**	
F G & S	*(See also)* Frederick **Green & Sons** **(London Works)**	**(EP)**	
F H S EP NS FH EP NS MADE IN ENGLAND	*(See also)* Francis **Howard** **(West End/Aberdeen Works)**	**(EP)**	
fh	*(See also)* The **Portland Co. Ltd.** and Francis **Higgins**	**(EP)**	
FIBROLOID	*(See also)* **British Xilonite Co. Ltd.**	**(EP)**	
	William **Fiddian** Birmingham (Luisa St) - 1882 ...	**(EP)**	(K82) (K84)
	Frank **Fidler** **(Advance Works)** Sheffield (Danby St) 1888 - 1893 ...	**(EP)**	(SAOR) (K93)
	Joseph **Fidler** Sheffield (Upper Heeley) - 1852 ...	**(EP)**	(WDOS)
	Alfred **Field & Co.** **(Continental Works)** Sheffield (23, Westfield Terrace) Birmingham - 1893 ...*(See also figure: G * B)*	**(CU/EP)**	(K93) (SBW) (M)

Field & Sons (EP) ^(K80)
Wycombe Bucks (Market Sq/High St)
- 1880 ...

E. W. **Field** (EP) ^(MDG)
Birmingham (70, Newhall St)
- 1866 ...

Henry **Field** (EP) ^(K72)
Birmingham (28, Northwood St)
- 1872 ...

John **Field** (T) ^(POAD)
(Birmingham Warehouse)
London (2, Brownlow St)
- 1808 ...

William **Field** **(CP/OSP)**
Birmingham (Mary Ann St/Brittle St)
- 1818 ...   ^(CD)
- 1823 - 1825 ... **(& Co.)**   ^{(WDB) (PDB)}

Henry **Fielding** **(CU/EP)** ^{(DOB) (CDB)}
(Snape Street Works) ^{(WWDB) (POB)}
Birmingham (123, Livery St/73, Gt. Hamp- ^{(K80) (K80 AD)}
ton St) ^{(PC) (SBW) (M)}
- 1833 - 1861 ...
- 1867 - 1896 ... *(See also figure:* SIL-
VENE*)*

FINNIGANS.L^D Benjamin **Finnigans** (T)
MANCHESTER Manchester (16, Market St)
1875 - 1901
1901 ... **(Ltd.)**

FIRTH *(See also)* (CU)
STAINLESS James **Ryals**

Frank **Fisher** (EP) ^(K92)
(Liberty Mills)
Birmingham (Frankfort St)
- 1892 ...

F

147

Harrison **Fisher** **(EP)**

Sheffield (70, Trafalgar St)

~ 1897 - 1901 ..

(See also figure: HF*S)

1900 - 1925 (**& Co**)

(See also figures: H.F &Co, PEL-HAM PLATE, MADRAS)

(WDS01) (M)

Henry **Fisher** **(EP)**

Sheffield (Piper Ln)

- 1879 ...

(WDS79)

John **Fisher** **(EP/BM)**

Birmingham (Aston/High St/Potters Ln)

- 1850 - 1896 ...

(HGD) (K80)
(K82) (K84) (K88)
(K92) (PC)

Stephen **Fisher** **(CP)**

Birmingham (96, Dale's End)

- 1829 - 1833 ...

(WAB) (HTD)
(DOB)

Fisher, Round & Sons **(EP)**

Birmingham (47, Frederick St)

- 1903 ...

(K03)

Joseph Ruston **Fitter** **(EP)**
(Hall Street Works)

Birmingham (Fordrough St/25, Hall St/
83, Caroline St)

- 1849 - 1888 ...

(HGDB) (HGD)
(CDB) (BDB)
(MDG) (K72)
(K78) (K80) (K82)
(K84) (K88)

Thomas **Fitzer** **(CP)**

Birmingham (Moland St)

- 1829 - 1839 ...

(WAB) (HTD)
(WDOB)

F·J·F

Not assigned! **(EP)**

Sheffield

(E)

John **Flavell** **(EP)**

Birmingham (72, Bath St)

- 1892 ...

(K92)

Charles William **Fletcher & Sons Ltd. (EP)**

Sheffield (76, Arundel St)

1915 - 1952

(See also figures: ARUNDEL PLATE, CWF)

(Then: James Robinson Inc., New York and Robinson Fletcher Ltd.)

(E)

Harry **Fletcher**   **(EP)**   (K36)
Birmingham (3a, Mott St)
- 1936 ...

Flint & Son   **(EP)**   (K82) (K84) (K88)
(Formerly: W. R. Heath & Co)   (K92) (K03)
Birmingham (30 & 32, Victoria St)
- 1882 - 1903 ...

F·MADIN&Cᵒ   *(See also)*   **(OSP)**
F. **Madin & Co.**

F·MOORE   *(See also)*   **(CU/CP)**
Frederick **Moore**

F **M** ✠   **Not assigned!**   **(EP)**   (E)

John **Foden**   **(GS)**   (WDOB)
Birmingham (Windsor St)
- 1839 ...

John **Follows**   **(EP)**   (K72)
Birmingham (2, Mary St/Caroline St)
- 1872 ...

Alfred Henry **Forrester**   **(BM)**   (K88)
(Formely: Pearson & Forrester)
Birmingham (3, King Alfred's Pl)
- 1888 ...

Joseph H. **Forrester**   **(EP)**   (PC) (K03)
Birmingham (39, Parade/1, Summer Hill
Terrace)
- 1896 - 1903 ...

Richard **Forster**   **(OSP)**   (B) (SAOR)
Sheffield (Pond St)
1780 ... *(See also figure: RF)*

Alfred **Foster**   **(EP)**   (K80)
Birmingham (57, Vyse St)
- 1880 ...

Walter **Foster**   **(EP)**   (WDS01)
Sheffield (796, Ecclesall Rd)
- 1901 ...

F

George **Fouch** **(EP)** [(K72)]
Birmingham (Tenby St)
- 1872 ...

James Frederick **Fowler** **(BM/EP)** [(GDS) (GDBS) (WDOS) (K80)]
Sheffield (13, New Church St/17, Copper St)
- 1833 - 1880 ...

Robert **Fowler** **(CU/CP)** [(WAB) (WDOB) (DOB) (CDB) (WWDB) (HGDB) (POB) (HTD)]
Birmingham (23, Cannon St)
- 1829 - 1867

Fox & Biggins **(EP)** [(WDS79) (K80)]
Sheffield (83, Arundel St)
- 1879 - 1880 ...

John **Fox & Co.** **(OSP)** [(CD)]
Birmingham (Lionel St)
- 1818 ...

John **Fox** **(CP)** [(SAOR) (WDB) (PDB)]
Birmingham (31, Lionel St)
1822 - 1825 ...

Samuel & Ann **Fox** **(OSP)** [(B) (SAOR)]
Sheffield (Westbar)
1792 ... *(See also figure: S·F)*

W. **Fox** **(OSP)** [(B) (SAOR)]
Sheffield (West Bar)
1775 ... *(See also figure: W·F)*

FOX PROCTOR
PASMORE & Co

Thomas **Fox & Co.** **(OSP)** [(B) (SAOR) (M)]
(Fox, Proctor, Pasmore & Co)
Sheffield (Holly Croft)
1784 ... *(See also figure: T·F&Co)*

F.R & C^O LD *(See also)* **(EP)**
Fenton, Russel & Co. Ltd.

Henry **Franklin** **(EP)** [(K72) (K78) (K82) (K84) (K88) (K92)]
Birmingham (137, Hampton St)
- 1872 - 1882 ...

FRANK MILLS
HANOVERWORKS . SHEFFIELD

(See also) **(EP)**
Frank **Mills & Co.**
(Hanover Works)

150

C. **Freazer** **(T)** (POAD)
**(Birmingham & Sheffield Ware-
house)**
London (143, Shoreditch)
- 1808 ...

Freeman & Light **(EP)** (PC)
Birmingham (39, St. Paul's Sq)
- 1896 ...

Israel **Freeman & Son Ltd.** **(EP)**
Sheffield
London
~ 1894 - 1910 *(See also figure: I.F.S)*
(Then: Activ in USA)

George **Freeman** **(EP)** (K78) (K80) (K82)
Birmingham (63, 112, Newhall St/ (K84) (K88) (K92)
39 & 41, St. Paul's Sq) (K03)
- 1878 - 1903 ...

Thomas **Freeman** **(OSP/CU)**
Sheffield (50, South St, Moor)
1845 - 1846 ... *(See also figure: TF)* (B) (SD46) (SBW)
Birmingham (SAOR)
1822 ...
(SAOR)

Anne & Elizabeth **Freeth &** William **Jones** (SAOR)
Birmingham
1818 ... **(CU)**

H. **Freeth** **(OSP)** (B) (M)
Birmingham (Upper Priory)
1816 ... *(See also figure: HF)*

Frith & Holmes **(BM)** (GDBS)
Sheffield (3, Burgess St)
- 1849 ...

Henry **Froggatt** **(OSP)** (PDB) (SDG)
Sheffield (30, Eyre St)
- 1825 ...

James **Froggatt** **(BM/OSP)** (PD) (SDG)
Sheffield (30, Eyre St)
- 1828 - 1829 ...

F

FROGATT COLDWELL&LEAN	**Frogatt, Coldwell & Lean (OSP)** (M) (B) Sheffield (Eyre St) 1797 ...
	J. **Froggett** **(EP)** (MDG) Birmingham (2, Unett St) - 1866 ...
	Naylor Thomas **Frost** **(EP)** (K82)(K84) (K88) (K92)(K03) Birmingham (15, Church St/58, Gt. Hampton St) - 1882 - 1903 ...
	Samuel **Frost** **(CU)** (SD46) Sheffield (Broad Ln) - 1846 ...
	John J. **Fryer** **(EP)** (K80) Dumfries /N.B. (99 & 100, English St) - 1880 ...
F.SPILLER LONDON & BRIXTON	*(See also)* **(CU)** F. **Spiller**
FUERTE	*(See also)* **(BM/EP)** Michael **Hunter & Son (Talbot Works)**
	John **Fullerton** **(EP)** (K80) (SAOR) Glasgow (75, Buchanan St) 1878 - 1880 ... *(See also figure: JFG)*
	Arthur Edward **Furniss** **(BM/EP)** (GS) (WDS79) (K80) (K93) (WDS01) (M) Sheffield (Holly St/27, Carver St/Ct. 8, Garden St) - 1863 - 1901 ... *(See figures: AEF, EF)* - 1915 ... **(& Sons)** *(See figure: AEF&S)*
	Frederick Charles **Furniss** **(EP)** (WDS01) Sheffield (44, Bower Rd) - 1901 ...
	Henry **Furniss** **(OSP)** (GDS) (WDS37) Sheffield (Edge House) - 1833 - 1837 ...

F

James **Furniss** **(EP)** ^(K36)
Sheffield (115 & 117, Portobello St)
- 1936 ...

James Edward **Furniss** **(EP)** ^(WDS01)
Sheffield (20, Havelock St)
- 1901 ...

Matthew **Furniss** **(OSP)** ^{(GDS) (WDS37)}
Sheffield (Machon Bank/Low Edge)
- 1833 - 1837 ...

Furniss, Poles & Turner **(OSP)** ^{(B) (SAOR) (CD)}
(Furniss, Poles & Co.) ^{(HDG) (PDY)}
Sheffield (28, Furnival St) ^{(NGDS) (PDB)}
1810 - 1825 ... ^{(PD) (GDS)}
(See also figure: M.F&Co)
(Then: William Briggs)

Furniss, Poles, Turner & Furniss ^{(SDG) (WDS37)}
(Furniss, Poles & Furniss) **(OSP)**
Sheffield (28, Furnival St)
- 1828 - 1837 ...

A. E. **Furniss, Son & Percharde Ltd.** ^(K36)
Sheffield (63, St. Mary's St) **(EP**)
- 1936 ...

F·V·F **Not assigned!** **(EP)** ^(E)

F.W & D *(See also)* **(OSP)**
Fenton, Webster & Danby

F.W.S **Not assigned!** **(EP)** ^(E)

Frederick **Wilson & Co.** **(EP)** ^(K93)
(Formerly: Wilson & Davis)
Sheffield (32, Eyre St/11, Cavendish St)
~ 1882 - 1910

Frederick **Wilson &** William **Davis (EP)** ^{(K80) (M) (SBW)}
(Hattan Works)
London
Sheffield (21, Sycamore St/43, Norfolk St/
32, Eyre St)
1870 - 1882

G & B	**Not assigned!**	**(EP)** [E]
G&B	*(See also)* John **Grinsell &** Henry **Bourne**	**(EP)**
G&C	*(See also)* J. **Green**	**(OSP)**
G & C⁰ **G & C⁰**	*(See also)* **Garrard & Co. Ltd.**	**(EP)**
G&C **G&C** **G**	**Not assigned!** Glasgow ~ 1910 ...	**(EP)** [E]
G & J **B**	*(See also)* G. & J. **Bushell**	**(EP)**
G&S **G&S L**ᵀᴰ	*(See also)* **Gilbert & Spurrier Ltd.**	**(EP)**
G & S EP G & S	*(See also)* **Goodfellow & Sons**	**(EP)**
G&Sᴺˢ	*(See also)* **Goodfellow & Sons**	**(EP)**
G & S C⁰ Lᵀᴰ G & S C⁰ **G&S C⁰**	*(See also)* **Goldsmiths & Silversmiths Co. Ltd.**	**(EP)**
G·A	*(See also)* G. **Addy & Son**	**(OSP)**
G·B	*(See also)* G. **Brittain & Co.**	**(EP)**
G·C	*(See also)* George **Cooper**	**(OSP)**
G.C S EP	*(See also)* George **Cutts** **(Park Britannia Metal & Silver Plate Works)**	**(CU/BM/EP)**
G·H	*(See also)* G. **Hibbert**	**(OSP)**

G·W	*(See also)* G. **Wostenholme**	**(OSP)**
✠ **G B**	*(See also)* Alfred **Field & Co.** and *(See also)* **Brittain, Wilkinson & Brownill**	**(EP)** **(OSP)**
G*D	*(See also)* G. **Dalton**	**(OSP)**
G ⊛ **Gil-bert** ⊛ **PS**	*(See also)* John **Gilbert**	**(CU/CP)**
GA &Cº	*(See also)* G. **Ashforth & Co.**	**(OSP)**
GA	*(See also)* Robert **Gainsford**	**(OSP)** (B)
GAB **NS**	**Not assigned!**	**(EP)** (E)

G

Robert **Gainsford**   **(OSP)** (B) (SAOR) GDS
Sheffield (Eyre St/Totley Hall)
1808 - 1833 ...
(See also figures: GA, RG)

Gainsford, Fenton & Nicholson (CD) (HDG) (PDY)
(Gainsford, Nicholson & Co.) (OSP) (PDB) (NGDS)
Sheffield (Furnival St/90 & 56, Eyre St) (SDG) (PD) (GDS)
- 1818 - 1833 ...

William **Gallimore & Co.**   **(CU/EP)** (SAOR) (K72AD)
(William **Gallimore & Sons)** (K80) (K88AD)
(Electro Plate Works) (K93) (WDSR) (M)
Sheffield (19, Arundel St/Sycamore St/
Arundel Ln)
1867 - 1905 ... *(See also figure: WG & Co.)*

Henry **Gallimore**   **(EP)** (WDS01)
Sheffield (96, Tapton Cresent Rd)
- 1901 ...

John **Gallimore** **(EP/BM)** (WDS79) (SAOR)
(Italian Works) (K93) (K03)
Sheffield (21, Edge Hill Rd/19/35-37, (WDS01) (WDSR)
Matilda St) (WDS11)
- 1879 - 1911 ... *(See also figure: JGS)*

William **Gallimore** **(GS)** (WDS37)
Sheffield (7, Lambert St)
- 1837 ...

William **Gallimore** (jun.) **(EP)** (WDOS)
Sheffield (42, School Croft)
- 1852 ... *(See also figure: W.G)*

S. L. **Gambles & Co.** **(EP)** (WDS01)
Sheffield (92, Division St)
- 1901 ...

Gardner & Priest **(T)** (POAD)
London (382, Strand)
- 1808 ...

James **Gardner** **(CP)** (WDOB)
Birmingham (Barr St)
- 1839 ...

William Henry **Gardner** **(EP)** (K72)
Birmingham (41, St. Paul's Sq)
- 1872 ...

Thomas **Garfitt & Son** **(CU)** (WDS01) (SBW)
(Cross Scythes Works)
Sheffield (66, London Rd)
- 1901 ...

W. **Garnett** **(OSP)** (M) (B)
Sheffield (Bridge Houses)
1803 ...

GARRARD & C̲O̲ L̲T̲D̲

Garrard & Co. Ltd. **(EP)**
London
1909 - 1952
(See also figure: G & Co)

Robert **Garrard** **(OSP/CU)** (POAD)
London (31, Panton St)
1802 - 1818
(Then: R.J. & S. Garrard)

R. J. & S. **Garrard** (Robert, James & Sebastian) London 1818 - 1835 *(Then: R. & S. Garrard)*		**(OSP)**
R. & S. **Garrard** (Robert & Sebastian) London 1835 - 1843		**(OSP)**
William **Gartshore** Glasgow (7, Argyle St) - 1880 ...		**(EP)** ^(K80)

G·B &BRs

(See also)
G. **Battie & Brothers** — **(OSP)**

G.B&S

(See also)
George **Bishop & Sons** — **(EP)**

**G.BUTLER & Co
SHEFFIELDS**

(See also)
George **Butler & Co.**
(Trinity Works) — **(CU/EP)**

GB&Cº

(See also)
G. **Briddock & Co.** — **(OSP)**

G B & Cº S

(See also)
George **Butler & Co.**
(Trinity Works) — **(CU/EP)**

GB&S / G B & S

(See also)
George **Bowen & Son**
(Victoria Works) — **(EP)**

GB & S (Mitra)

(See also)
George **Bishop & Sons** — **(EP)**

GB

Not assigned! — **(EP)**

GBBS

(See also)
G. **Gibbs** — **(OSP)**

GCW
G.C.W.
EPNS

Not assigned!
- 1896 — **(EP)** ^(E)

G

G.DEAKIN.	*(See also)* **Hale Brothers** **(Moorfields Works)**	(CU)	
GD	*(See also)* G. **Deakin & Co.**	(EP)	
GD	*(See also)* G. **Dodd**	(OSP)	
GE	*(See also)* George **Edwards**	(EP)	
GE &Cº	*(See also)* G. **Eaden & Co.**	(OSP)	
GEH●NS EPNS	*(See also)* George Ernst **Hawkins**	(EP)	
	James Frederick **Gellion & Co.** Birmingham (24, Coleshill St/216, Heneage St) - 1882 - 1896 ...	(EP)	(K82) (K84) (K88) (K92) (PC)
G.ELLIS(SILVERSMITHS)LTD EP **MADE IN SHEFFIELD** **ENGLAND**	*(See also)* George **Ellis Ltd.**	(EP)	
	Gem & Co. Birmingham (37, Parade) - 1862 ...	(EP)	(BDB)
GENEVA	Joseph **Nowill** Sheffield (Pea Croft) 1774 ...	(CU)	(B)
GENIUS	*(See also)* John **Blyde** **(Clintock Works)**	(EP)	
	James **George** Birmingham (Newton St/Summer Ln) - 1815 - 1825 ...	(CP)	(WTDB) (WDB) (PDB)
GFW&S EPNS	**Not assigned!**	(EP)	
G. G. HONOUR & SONS LONDON	*(See also)* George Gates **Honour**	(EP)	
G G & S S	*(See also)* George **Gordon & Son** **(Casket Works)**	(EP)	

G

158

G G H L	*(See also)* George Gates **Honour**	**(EP)**
G G H & S	*(See also)* George Gates **Honour**	**(EP)**
G. HAWKSLEY G.H. & Co.S	*(See also)* George **Hawksley**	**(EP)**
GH&Cᵒ	*(See also)* George **Hawksley**	**(EP)**
GH	*(See also)* G. **Harrison**	**(OSP)**
GH	*(See also)* G. **Hawley**	**(OSP)**
GH	*(See also)* G. **Hague**	**(OSP)**
GH	*(See also)* G. **Hardesty**	**(OSP)**
GH **GH** **CH**	*(See also)* George **Hawksley**	**(EP)**
G H W E P N S	*(See also)* George Henry **Whittaker**	**(EP)**
G.I&Co G.I&Co.S EPNS	*(See also)* George **Ibberson & Co.**	**(EP)**

A. **Gibbon & Co.** Birmingham (105, Vyse St) - 1903 ...	**(EP)**	(K03)
Charles **Gibbons** Birmingham (23, Spencer St/41, Frederick St) - 1878 - 1903 ...	**(EP)**	(K78) (K80) (K82) (K84) (K88) (K92) (K03)
Joseph **Gibbs & Co.** Birmingham (Newhall St) - 1815 ...	**(CP/CU)**	(WTDB)
Gibbs & Son Birmingham (14, Easy Rw) - 1823 - 1825 ...	**(CP)**	(WDB) (PDB)

G

Gibbs & Wright (EP) [K03]
Birmingham (140, Hurst St)
- 1903 ...

G. **Gibbs** (OSP) [B] [M]
Birmingham
1808 ... *(See also figure: GBBS)*

H.& J. **Gibbs** (CP) [WWDB] [WDOB]
Birmingham (7 & 8, Gt. Charles St)
- 1835 - 1839 ...

William **Gibbs** (CP) [WAB] [HTD]
Birmingham (Fordrough St)
- 1829 - 1830 ...

GIBSON&CoL.D
BELFAST

William **Gibson & Co. Ltd.** (EP) [M]
Belfast
1896 ...

Gibson & Lord (BM/EP) [K78] [K80] [K82]
Birmingham (79, Newhall St) [K84] [K88] [K92]
- 1878 - 1903 ... [PC] [K03]

Gilbert & Spurrier Ltd. (EP) [SBW] [M]
Birmingham
1886 ...
(See also figures: G & S, G&S Ltd.)

E. **Gilbert** (EP) [MDG]
Birmingham (Ryland St)
- 1866 ...

J. **Gilbert** (EP) [MDG]
Birmingham (1, Little Hill St)
- 1866 ...

John **Gilbert** (CU/CP) [B] [WTDB]
Birmingham (28, Legge St/7 & 8, Bath Rw/ [WTD] [CD]
83-85, Ryland St) [WDB] [PDB]
London (Holborn Dyers Buildings) [WAB] [HTD]
- 1812 - 1884 ... [DOB] [WWDB]
- 1878 - 1888 ... **(& Co. Ltd.)** [HGDB] [SAOR]
- 1894 ... **(& Sons)** [HGD] [CDB]
*(See also figures: G * Gilbert, J.G.* [POB] [MDG]
& S) [K72] [K78] [K82]
[K84] [M]
[K78] [K80] [K82]
[K84] [K88]

	John T. **Gilbert** **(EP)** [K93]	
	(Smith's Wheel)	
	Sheffield (Sidney St)	
	- 1893 ...	

Joseph **Gilbert** **(CP/EP)**	
(Sun Works)	
Birmingham (Ryland St/61, Bissell St/	
Gooch St)	
1841 - 1888 ...	(B) (BDB) (POB)
- 1880 - 1903 ... **(& Sons/& Co.)**	(K72) (K78) (K80)
(See also figures: ALAMADA, AR-	(K82)(K84) (K88)
GENTINA SILVER, J.G)	(K92) (K03)
	(SBW) (M)

Philipp **Gilbert** **(EP)**	(HGDB) (HGD)
Birmingham (34, Bath Rw/44, Islington Rw)	(MDG)
- 1849 - 1866 ...	

G

GILBERT	**Not assigned!** **(EP)** [B]
LONDON	London
	~ 1840

Gilding & Silvering Co. **(EP)**	(W) (SBW) (M)
Middlesex	
~ 1878 ... *(See also figure: ARGOSY)*	

	George M. **Gilson** **(EP)**	[WDS01]
	Sheffield (32, Victoria Rd)	
	- 1901 ...	

G & J W HAWKSLEY	*(See also)* **(EP)**
	George **Hawksley**

G.L&Co.S	*(See also)* **(EP)**
	George **Lee & Co.**

GLADWIN Lᵀᴰ **SHEFFIELD**	**Gladwin Ltd.** **(EP)** [K36) (E]	
	(Embassy & Montgomery Works)	
GLADWIN **ᴸᵀᴰ**	Sheffield	
SHEFFIELD	London (11, Hatton Garden)	
	1921 - 1936 ... *(See also figures: AM-*	
	BASSADOR, EMBASSAY)	

	L. & C. **Glauert** **(Burgess Works & Wallace Works)** Sheffield (11, Cambridge St/34, Furnival St) - 1879 - 1901 ... *(See also figure: PATRIOT)*	**(CU)**	(WDS79) (WDS01) (SBW) (M)
	Joseph **Glave** Sheffield (9, Charles Ln) - 1893 - 1901 ...	**(EP)**	(K93) (WDS01)
	John **Glendall** Birmingham (13, Navigation St) - 1829 - 1839 ...	**(BM)**	(WAB) (DOB) (WDOB)
GLORIOUS	*(See also)* Edwin **Lander & Co.**	**(EP)**	
	Glossop & Nutt Sheffield 1840 ...	**(CU/OSP)**	(SAOR)
	Arthur O. **Glossop** Sheffield (Park Head) - 1879 ...	**(EP)**	(WDS79)
	Gloster & Docker Birmingham (Moseley St) - 1839 - 1842 ...	**(GS)**	(WDOB) (SAOR)
	Henry **Gloster** Birmingham (213, Moseley St) 1848 - 1850 ...	**(EP)**	(SAOR) (HGDB) (HGD)
	William **Gloster** Birmingham (10, King Alfred's Pl) - 1849 - 1861	**(EP)**	(HGDB) (CDB)
	Glover & Cooper Birmingham (Warstone Ln) - 1888 - 1892 ...	**(EP)**	(K88) (K92)
	Lawrence **Glover** Birmingham (2, New Bartholomew St/ 6, Carver St/15, Albion St) - 1862 - 1896 ...	**(EP)**	(BDB) (K78) (K80) (PC)

G

	Robert Frederick **Glover** (EP) (K82) (K84) Birmingham (Warstone Ln) - 1882 - 1884 ...
G.M&SL ᵀᴰ	*(See also)* (EP) George **Maclaurin & Sons Ltd.**
GM "keys" **EP**	**Not assigned!** (EP) (E)
	John **Godfrey** (CU/OSP) (SAOR) Birmingham 1819 ...
	Charles **Godley** (CP) (K82) (K84) (K88) Birmingham (1, Leopold St) - 1882 - 1888 ...
	Gold & Silver Plating Co. Ltd. (EP) (K36) London (53, Westbourne Grove) - 1936 ...
GOLD LINED	*(See also)* (EP) N. C. **Reading & Co.**
GOLDSMITHS & SILVERSMITHS COMPANY 112 REGENT STREET.W.	The **Goldsmiths & Silversmiths Co.** (S) London (112, Regent St) (EP) 1880 - 1898 *(See also figure: M G&S Co)* 1898 ... 1952 (**Ltd.**) *(See also figure: G&S Co)* *(Then: Garrard & Co. Ltd.)*
GOLDSMITHS Cᵒ NEWCASTLE TRIPLE PLATE	**Goldsmiths Company** (EP) (E) Newcastle ~ 1900
	Gomm Manufacturing Co. (EP) (K36) Birmingham (56, Hockley Hill) - 1936 ...
	Jonathan **Gooch & Co.** (EP) (K80) Birmingham (21, Caroline St) - 1880 ...
	Thomas **Goodacre & Sons** (EP) (K80) Birmingham (102, New John St) - 1880 ...

G

Thomas **Goodacre** **(EP)** ^(WDS79)
Sheffield (62, Holly St)
- 1879 ...

Henry Arthur **Goodall** **(EP)** ^{(M) (SBW)}
London
~ *(See also figure: BB)*

Albert Edward **Goodby** **(EP)** ^{(K78) (K80) (K82)}
^{(K84) (K88)}
Sheffield (152, Fitzwilliam St)
Birmingham (102, New John St)
- 1878 - 1888 ...

Thomas **Goode & Co.** **(T)** ^(E)
Sheffield (South Audley St)
~ 1890 ... *(See figure: Thos Goode & Co)*

John **Goode & Sons** **(EP)** ^(SBW)
Birmingham
~ 1890 ...

Goodfellow & Hodd **(EP)**
London
1854 - 1860

George **Goodfellow & Sons** **(EP)**
London
1882 ... *(See also figures: G&S, G&Sns)*

Thomas Hutchinson **Goodfellow (CU/EP)** ^(E)
London (29, Hatton Garden)
1860 - 1916 *(See also figure: TG)*
- 1885 ... **(& Sons)**
(See also figure: TG & S)

Goodfellow, Tilley & Hodd **(EP)**
London
1848 - 1854

William **Goodison** **(BM/EP)** ^{(GS) (WDS79)}
Sheffield (25, Monmouth St/Broomhall St)
- 1863 - 1879 ...

Alexander **Goodman & Co.** **(OSP)** ^{(B) (SAOR)}
Sheffield (Park St)
1801 ... *(See figure: A.G&Co)*

G

Alexander **Goodman**, Robert **Gainsford** (B) (SAOR)
& Co. **(OSP)**
Sheffield (Hawley Croft)
1797 ... 1808 *(See figure: A.G&Co)*

Alexander **Goodman**, Robert **Gainsford**, (POAD)
George **Fairbairn & French** **(OSP)**
London (17, Castle St)
- 1808 ...

Alexander **Goodman**, Robert **Gainsford** (B) (SH)
& George **Fairbairn** **(OSP)**
Sheffield
1800 - July 1808
(See figure: A.Goodman&Co)

E. **Goodwin** **(OSP)** (B) (SAOR)
Sheffield (The Park)
1796 ...
*(See also figures: EG,
E.GOODWIN)*

Roger Brown **Goodwin** **(EP)** (WDSR)
Sheffield (8, Byron Rd)
- 1905 ...

S. **Goodwin** **(CU)** (POAD)
London (57, Haymarket)
- 1808 ...

George **Gordon & Son** **(EP)** (WDS01) (WDSR)
(Casket Works)
Sheffield (129, St. Mary's Rd)
- 1901 - 1905 ... *(See also figure: G G
& S S)*

GORDON SILVER   *(See also)* **(EP)**
Walter **Spurrier & Co.**

Solomon Lewis **Gorer** **(EP)** (W) (SBW) (M)
Middlesex
~ 1878 ... *(See also figure: ARGOSY)*

John **Gosdo & Co.** **(OSP)** (WTD)
Birmingham (Anne St)
- 1818 ...

G

Goss Ltd. **(EP)** (K36)
London (360, Kingsland Pl)
- 1936 ...

Gotscher & Co. **(EP)** (SBW) (M)
Birmingham
~ 1900

W. **Gough &** John Bartlet **Silvester (EP)** (CDB) (GS) (MDG) (POB)
Birmingham (11 & 12, Parade)
- 1861 - 1867 ...

William **Gough** **(EP)** (SAOR) (HGDB) (HGD) (MDG) (M)
Birmingham (11 & 12, Parade)
1840 - 1866 ... *(See also figure: WG)*

John **Gough** **(CP)** (WTDB) (WTD) (CD) (WAB) (HTD)
Birmingham (27, Hurst St/Bristol Rd)
- 1815 - 1830...

John **Gough** (jun) **(EP)** (K72) (K78) (K80) (K82)(K84) (M)
Birmingham (4, James St/12, St. Paul's Pd)
- 1872 - 1884 ... *(See also figure: J.G)*

T. **Gough** **(EP)** (POB)
Birmingham (11, Hill St)
- 1867 ...

Gould & Yerinder **(CU)** (POAD)
London (79, St. Paul's Church Yd)
- 1808 ...

Gourdel, Vales & Co. **(EP)**
London
1865 - 1930
(See also figure: G.V&Co)
1930 - 1939 (**Ltd.**)

Not assigned! **(EP)** (E)

G.R.COLLIS &C<u>o</u>

(See also) **(CU/EP)**
George Richmond **Collis**

F. & R. **Grah** **(EP)** (WDS01)
Sheffield (96, Carver St)
- 1901 ...

Thomas **Graham & Son** **(EP)** (K80)
Hawick, Roxburghshire
- 1880 ...

Not assigned! **(CU/EP)** (E)

John George **Graves** **(EP)**
(Enterprise Works)
Sheffield (Arley St/St. Mary's Rd/Gell St/
169, West St)
- 1901 - 1905 (WDS01)
1905 - 1936 ... (**Ltd.**) (K36)
(See also figures: J.G.GRAVES,
J.G.G.)

Gray & Stanton Manuftg. Co. Ltd. (K36)
(Formerly: Frederick J. Stanton) **(EP)**
Birmingham (28-31, Lower Loveday St)
Manchester (10, New Brown St)
- 1936 ...

Edwin **Gray** **(EP)** (POB)
Harborne
- 1867 ...

John **Grayhurst** **(EP)** (BDB)
Birmingham (56, Mott St)
- 1862 ...

Benjamin **Grayson & Son** **(BM/EP)** (WDS79) (K80)
Sheffield (56, 58 & 60, Holly St/99, Napier St) (WDS01) (SBW)
1872 - 1901 ... (M)
(See also figure: B. GRAYSON)

Charles **Grayson** **(EP)** (K93)
Sheffield (19, Carver Ln)
- 1893 ...

Frederick **Grayson** **(EP)** (WDS01)
Sheffield (61, Sheldon St)
- 1901 ...

G ♛ R *(See also)* **(CU)**
BRADBURY James **Bradbury**

GRC *(See also)* **(CU/EP)**
George Richmond **Collis**

Samuel **Greaves & Co.** **(OSP)** [B] [SAOR]
Sheffield (Norfolk St)
1774 ... *(See also figure: SG&Co)*

Francis **Greaves** **(CU)** [SD46]
Sheffield (41, Radford St)
- 1846 ...

Henry **Greaves** **(EP)** [WDS79] [K80]
Sheffield (47, Chester St)
- 1879 - 1880 ...

John **Greaves** **(EP)** [K93]
Sheffield (13, Devonshire Ln)
- 1893 ...

Joseph **Greaves** **(GS)** [WDOS] [K93]
Sheffield (78 & 105, Arundel St/Ct 4, Sycamore St)
- 1852 - 1893 ...

Thomas **Greaves** **(OSP)** [SAOR] [B]
Sheffield (Gibraltar St)
1774 - 1789 ... *(See also figure: T·G)*

Thomas **Greaves** **(EP)** [K82] [K84]
Birmingham (33, Graham St)
- 1882 - 1884 ...

William **Green & Co.** **(CU/OSP)**
Sheffield
1784 ... (Pinchcroft Ln) [B] [SAOR]
(See also figure: WG & Co)
1787 ... (Eyre St)
(See also figures: SUPER, W. [GM]
GREEN)

Charles S. **Green & Co. Ltd.** **(EP)** [E]
Birmingham (54, St. Paul's Sq)
1905 - 1982 *(See also figures:*
CSG&Co.)

John **Green &** George **Hague** **(OSP)** [SAOR] [B]
Sheffield (Sims Croft)
1792 ... *(See also figure: IG.GH)*

Frederick **Green & Sons**   **(EP)**
(London Works)
Sheffield (76, Bridge St)
1894 ...
(See also figures: F.GREEN
&SONS, FG & S)

J. **Green**   **(CU/CP)**   (B) (POAD)
Birmingham
London (31, Drury Ln)
1807 - 1808 ...

Alfred **Green**   **(EP)**   (POB) (K72) (K78)
Birmingham (10 and then 40, Hylton St)   (K80)
- 1867 - 1880 ...   (K82) (K84) (K88)
- 1882 - 1892 ... (**& Son**)   (K92)

Arthur **Green**   **(EP)**   (WDS79)
Sheffield (89, Pickering Rd)
- 1879 ...

C. **Green**   **(EP)**   (WDB)
Birmingham (16, Vyse St)
- 1866 ...

Francis Hugh **Green**   **(EP)**   (K03)
Birmingham (80, Vyse St)
- 1903 ...

Frederick **Green**   **(EP)**   (K93)
(London Works)
Sheffield (76, Bridge St)
- 1893 ...

James **Green**   **(OSP)**   (B) (SAOR) (SBW)
Sheffield (Fargate)   (M)
1846 ... *(See also figure: G&C)*

James **Green**   **(OSP)**   (SAOR)
Sheffield (Sims Croft)
1785 ... *(See also figure: IG)*

G

John **Green**   **(OSP)**
Sheffield (Market Pl)
1778 ... (Holly Croft)   (B) (SAOR)
(See also figure: IG)   (SAOR)
1783 ... (York Street)   (SAOR)
(See also figure: IG)   (SAOR)
1793 ... **(& Co.)**
(See also figures: I.GREEN & Co,
symbol " keys")

Samuel **Green**   **(EP)**   (WDS79)
Sheffield (91, Arundel St)
- 1879 ...

William F. **Green** jun.   **(GS/EP)**   (MDG) (POB)
Birmingham (10, St. Paul's Sq/50, Augusta St)   (K72) (K78) (K80)
- 1866 - 1880 ...

Green, Bradbury & Firth   (OSP)   (B) (SAOR)
Sheffield (Burgess St)
1828 ... *(See also figure: JB)*

J. **Green, Roberts, Moseley & Co.**   (B)
Sheffield (Market Pl)   **(OSP)**
1793 ... *(See also figure: IG&Co)*

Green, Pickslay & Appleby   (OSP)   (HDG) (NGDS)
Sheffield (14, High St)
- 1822 - 1825 ...

Israel Sigmund **Greenberg**   **(EP)**
Birmingham (44, Frederick St/Vyse St/ 125
& 126, Gt. Hampton St)
1884 - 1888
1889 - 1908 **(& Co.)**
1909 - 1936 ... **(& Co. Ltd.)**   (K36)
(See also figure: I.S.G)

Daniel **Greenfield**   **(GS)**   (WDOB)
Birmingham (Staniforth St)
- 1839 ...

Thomas **Greenfield**   **(GS)**   (WDOB)
Birmingham (A. B. Row)
- 1839 ...

William **Greensill**	**(OSP)**	(CD)
Birmingham (Lower Temple St)		
- 1818 ...		
John **Greer**	**(CU)**	(POAD)
London (8, Creed Ln)		
- 1808 ...		
J. A. **Greetham & Co.**	**(EP)**	(K36)
Sheffield (34, Eyre St)		
- 1936 ...		
J. **Gregory & Co.**	**(OSP)**	(B) (SAOR)
Sheffield (West St)		
1795 ... *(See also figure: JG.&Co)*		
Richard **Gregory & Co.**	**(OSP)**	(B) (SAOR)
Sheffield (Pond Ln)		
1797 ... *(See also figure: RG)*		
S. & J.(T.) **Gregory**	**(CP)**	(WDB) (PDB)
Birmingham (Hurst St)		
- 1823 - 1825 ...		
William **Gregory**	**(CU)**	(SAOR)
Birmingham		
1818 ...		
William Keaton **Gregory**	**(OSP)**	(WDS37)
Sheffield (Wilkinson House)		
- 1837 ...		
William R. **Gregory**	**(OSP)**	(DSRR)
Sheffield (William St)		
- 1841 ...		
Gregory, Wostenholme & Co. (OSP)		(B)
Sheffield (Moor)		
1809 ... *(See also figure: GW&C)*		

G

GRIEL NICKEL SILVER	*(See also)* **Barker Brothers (Unity Works)**	**(BM/EP)**
GRIFFIN "Phoenix"	*(See also)* Arthur **Balfour & Co.**	**(EP)**

Griffin Gilding & Plating Co. (EP) ^{(K82) (K84) (K88)}
Birmingham (15, Caroline St)
- 1882 - 1892 ...

(K82) (K84) (K88) (K92)

Griffiths & Browett (EP) (M)
Birmingham
1862 ...

John **Griffiths (EP)** (K80)
Birmingham (19, Regent Pl)
- 1880 ...

John **Grinsell &** Henry **Bourne (EP)** (CDB) (BDB) (GS) (MDG) (POB)
Birmingham (19, Ludgate Hill)
- 1861 - 1867 ... *(See also figure: G&B)*

John **Grinsell & Sons (EP)** (K80) (PC) (M)
(Victoria Works)
Birmingham (Tower St/St. George's Pd)
- 1880 - 1896 ... *(See also figures: J.G&S, J.G&Sons, symbol: "cupi-do")*

Abel **Grove (BM)** (DOB)
Birmingham (107, Dale's End)
- 1833 ...

John **Grove (EP)** (K80) (K93)
Birmingham (10, Hylton St/53, Carver St)
- 1880 - 1893 ...

William **Grove (CP)** (WDB)
Birmingham
- 1823 ...

Alfred **Groves & Co. (EP)** (K92)
Birmingham (46, Vyse St)
- 1892 ...

Richard **Groves & Sons (CU/EP)**
(Beehive Works)
Sheffield (Snow Ln/Allen St/Egerton St)
- 1879 ...
1927 - 1942 (**Ltd.**)
(See also figures: R.G & S, USE)

(WDS79)

G

	John **Groves** Birmingham (Broad St) - 1818 ...	**(OSP W)**	(CD)
	Samuel **Groves** Birmingham (Cheapside/28, Moor St/28/ 69, Broad St) - 1829 - 1903 ...	**(BM/EP)**	(WAB) (DOB) (HGD) (MDG) (POB) (K72) (K78) (K80) (K82) (K84) (K88) (K92) (PC) (K03)
GS	*(See also)* G. **Stokes**	**(OSP)**	
	General term for: **German Silver**	**(GS)**	
	General term for: **German silver electro plated**	**(EP)**	
	(See also) George Shadford **Lee**	**(EP)**	
	(See also) William jun. & George **Sissons**	**(EP)**	
	(See also) George **Travis & Co.** **(Clarence Works)**	**(BM/EP)**	
G. TURNER & Co	*(See also)* Samuel **Biggin**	**(EP)**	
	(See also) George **Travis & Co.** **(Clarence Works)**	**(BM/EP)**	
GT	*(See also)* G. **Teasdell**	**(EP)**	
GU	*(See also)* George **Unite** Birmingham	**(EP)**	

	I. **Guide & Co.** **(Helm Works)** Sheffield (Ct. 1, Arundel Ln) - 1901 ... *(See also figures: IG&Co.,* *I.GUIDE)*	**(CU/EP)**
	J. Thomas **Gun** **(Sheffield Warehouse)** London (Ct 136, Salisbury St) - 1808 ...	**(T)** ^(POAD)
	Gunston Sons & Co. Liverpool ~ 1892 ... *(See also figure: ADELANTE)*	**(EP)** ^{(W) (M)}
G.V&Cº	*(See also)* **Gourdel, Vales & Co.**	**(EP)**
G.W.HARRIS & Cº **SHEFFIELD**	*(See also)* G. W. **Harris & Co.**	**(BM/CU)**
GW&C	*(See also)* Gregory **Wostenholme & Co.**	**(OSP)**
GW	*(See also)* George **Ward**	**(OSP/EP)**
G W S	*(See also)* George **Wish** **(Denmark Works)**	**(EP)**

G

H & A	*(See also)* **Harrold & Ashwin**	**(EP)**
H&B	*(See also)* **Hardy, Bell & Co.**	**(OSP)**
H & Cº	Not assigned!	**(EP)** [E]
H&F	*(See also)* **Hukin & Fenton**	**(EP)**
H&H	*(See also)* **Howard & Hawksworth**	**(OSP)**
H & H **H & H** EP	*(See also)* Jonathan W. **Hukin &** John Th. **Heath**	**(EP)**
H&I B ⋈ ⊕	*(See also)* **Hamilton & Inches**	**(EP)**
H&L ✿ C ⊕ ♔	*(See also)* Richard **Hodd &** William **Linley**	**(EP)**
H & L G **H & L S**	*(See also)* **Hamilton & Laidlaw**	**(BM/EP)**
H&N **H&N EPNS**	*(See also)* **Holman & Norton**	**(EP)**
H&P	*(See also)* Joseph **Hirons &** Henry Hodson **Plante**	**(EP)**
H & S ♔ ⊕	*(See also)* Thomas **Hands & Son**	**(BM/EP)**
H&S E P N S H & S MANUFACTURE	*(See also)* William C. **Hutton & Sons**	**(CP)**
H & S Ω	*(See also)* William Carr **Hutton**	**(BM/GS/CU/CP)**
H&T	*(See also)* M. **Hunter &** J. **Twig**	**(OSP)**

H

Marks	Description	Type
H.A	*(See also)* Henry **Atkin**	(BM/EP)
H·B	*(See also)* H. **Blake**	(OSP)
H.B	*(See also)* Herny H. **Bourne**	(EP)
H.F **EPNS A1** **&Cᵒ·S**	*(See also)* Harrison **Fisher**	(EP)
H·H **H·H** ❀ **EP** **A1**	*(See also)* **Harrison Brothers & Howson**	(EP)
H·R	*(See also)* Henry **Rock**	(OSP)
H·R	*(See also)* H. **Hewitt &** H. **Rock**	(OSP)
H.S **Lᴰ** **S** **EP**	*(See also)* Henry **Stratford Ltd.**	(EP)
H.S **S** **EP** **H.S** **S** 👑	*(See also)* Henry **Stratford**	(EP)
H·W	*(See also)* Hannah **Watkinson**	(OSP)
H 🍍	*(See also)* Daniel & George **Holy & Co.**	(OSP)
H 🖐 H	*(See also)* Henry **Harrison & Co.** **(Atwell Works)**	(BM/EP)
H	*(See also)* **Harrods Stores Ltd.**	(EP)
H **A** **&** **S** **EP**	Not assigned!	(EP) ^(E)
H **A** **∞** **S**	*(See also)* Henry **Atkin & Co.**	(OSP/BM/EP)
HA **H** **A**	*(See also)* **Archer, Machin & Marsh** **(Archer & Co.)**	(EP)

Haddon Brothers   **(EP)**   (K80) (K82) (K84)
Birmingham (82, Vyse St/5, Key Hill)
- 1880 - 1884 ...

William **Hadfield**   **(OSP)**   (HDG)
Sheffield (18, Gell St)
- 1822 ...

Benjamin **Hadley**   **(OSP)**   (WTDB) (WTD)
Birmingham (Cottage Ln/Crescent Rd)   (CD)
- 1815 - 1818 ...

(See also)   **(BM/EP)**
Atkin Brothers
(Truro Works)

George **Hague**   **(OSP)**   (B) (SAOR)
Sheffield (Sims Croft)
1798 ... *(See also figure: GH)*

Hague & Nowill   **(OSP)**   (SAOR)
Sheffield
1786 ...

Hale Brothers   **(CU)**   (WDS01) (SBW)
(Moorfields Works)
Sheffield (Snow Ln)
- 1901 ... *(See also figures:*
G.DEAKIN., symbol "horse head")

William **Haley**   **(OSP)**   (DOB) (WWDB)
Birmingham (60, Loveday St)
- 1833 - 1835 ...

John **Hall & Co.**   **(EP)**
Manchester (68, King St)
~ 1860 ... *(See also figure:*
J.HALL&Co)

Hall & Walker   **(EP)**   (POS) (K54)
Sheffield (8, Howard St)
- 1854 ...

W. **Hall**   **(CP)**   (B) (M)
Birmingham
1820 ...

Henry **Hall** **(CP)** (B) (WAB) (HTD) (DOB) (WWDB) (M)
Birmingham (51, Shadwell St/105, Gt. Hampton St)
- 1829 - 1835 ... *(See also figure: ℋℋ)*

James **Hall** **(CP)** (WWDB)
Birmingham (30, Lancaster St)
- 1835 ...

Joseph **Hall** **(EP)** (WDS71)
Sheffield (18, Talbot St)
- 1871 ...

William **Hall** **(OSP)** (GDS)
Sheffield (6, Mulburry St)
- 1833 ...

Hall Street Metal Rolling Co. (GS) (K88)
Birmingham (25, Hall St)
- 1888 ...

John **Hallam** **(CU)** (W)
Sheffield
1787 ... *(See also figure: ASAY)*

William Henry **Hallam** **(EP)** (K82) (K84)
Birmingham (316, Brearley St)
- 1882 - 1884 ...

William Artur **Hallett** **(EP)** (K03)
Birmingham (8, Newhall Hill)
- 1903 ..

Hamilton & Co. **(EP)**
London (Strand)
~ 1900 ...

John **Hamilton & Co.** **(EP)** (K82) (K84)
Birmingham (98, Pritchett St)
- 1882 - 1884 ...

Hamilton & Inches **(EP)** (S)
Edinburgh (Princess St/87, George St)
London (52, Beauchamp Pl)
1895 - 1897 ... *(See also figure: H&I)*

Hamilton & Laidlaw **(BM/EP)**
Glasgow (Queen St/84, Miller St)
1891 - 1893 ...
(See also figures: H&L G, H&L & ^(S)
Co, DORRIT SILVER)
- 1893 - 1939
(See also figure: HL & Co G)

Charles **Hammond** **(OSP)** (B) (SAOR)
Sheffield (Church Ln)
1824 ... *(See also figure C.H.S)*

Hammond, St. Arnaud **Creake & Co.**
Sheffield (63, St. Mary's Rd) **(EP)** (M) (K93)
1886 - 1920 (WDS01) (WDSR)
1920 - 1935 (**Ltd**.) *(See also figure:* (WDS11)
HC&Co)

Hammond Turner Ltd. **(EP)** (K36)
Birmingham
- 1936 ...

W. **Hancock &** J. **Rowbotham (OSP)** (B) (SAOR)
Sheffield (Norfolk St)
1773 ...
(See also figures: W·H I·R,
WHIR&Co)

Samuel **Hancock & Sons** **(CU)** (WDS79) (WDS01)
(Mazeppa Works) (SBW) (M)
Sheffield (12, Sycamore St/Charlotte St)
- 1879 - 1901 ...
(See also figure: MAZEPPA)

Ernest **Hancock** **(EP)** (WDS01)
Sheffield (87, Brunswick St)
- 1901 ...

James **Hancock** **(EP)** (WDS79) (K80)
Sheffield (42, Holly St) (K93)
- 1879 - 1893 ...

Joseph **Hancock** **(OSP)** (B) (M)
Sheffield (Union St/High St)
1755 ...
(See also figures: I·H, IOS HAN-
COCK)

William C. **Hancock** **(BM)** (K80)

Sheffield (32, Upper St. Philip's Road)
- 1880 ...

Edwin H. **Hancocks** **(EP)** (K80)

Sheffield (38, Arundel Ln)
- 1880 ...

J. H. **Hands & Co.** **(EP)** (PC)
(Colonial Plate Works)

Birmingham (54, 56, & 58, Lombard St)
- 1896 ...

Hands & Dore **(GS/EP)** (HGDB) (HGD)

Birmingham (11, Edmund St)
- 1849 - 1850 ...

John **Hands** **(CP)** (WAB)

Birmingham (Bruton's Walk/Prospect Rw)
- 1829 ...

Thomas **Hands** **(BM/EP)** (CDB) (BDB)
(GS) (MDG)(POB)

Birmingham (8, New Hall St/138, Suffolk St)
~ 1850 ...
(K72) (K78) (K80)
- 1861 - 1892 ... **(& Son)** (K82) (K84) (K88)
(See also figures: H&S, PERUVI- (K92) (SBW) (M)
AN, symbol "coat of arms")

Matthias **Hanson** **(CU)** (B) (WTDB)
(WTD) (WDB)

Birmingham (25, New Meeting St)
(PDB) (M)
1810 - 1825 ...

George **Hardcastle** **(EP)** (K72) (K80)

Birmingham (5/2, Augusta St)
- 1872 - 1880 ...

George **Harde(i)sty** **(CU)** (NGDS) (B)
(SAOR) (GDS)

Sheffield (Rockingham St/Norfolk Ln/190,
(WDS37) (DSRR)
Broad Ln/15, Eyre St)
(SD46)
1825 - 1846 ... *(See also figure: GH)*

Frederick **Harding** **(EP)**

Birmingham (83/58, Spencer St)
- 1892 - 1903 ... (K92) (K03)
- 1882 - 1888 ... **(& Co.)** (K82) (K84) (K88)

John **Hardman & Co.**　　**(EP)**　(SAOR) (M)
Birmingham
1845 - 1875 *(See also figure: JH.&Co)*

John **Hardman,** William **Powell & Co.**　(SAOR) (M)
Birmingham　　**(EP)**
1883 ... *(See also figure: H.P.&Co)*

Joseph **Hardy & Co.**　　**(CP)**　(CD) (WTD)
Birmingham (Mary Ann St/31/176, Gt.　(WWDB)(HTD)
Hampton Rw)　　(WDB) (WAB)
- 1818 - 1835　　(PDB) (DOB)

Hardy & Whiteley　　**(EP)**　(WDS01)
Sheffield (20, Cambridge St)
- 1901 ...

Francis Henry **Hardy**　　**(EP)**　(K93)
Sheffield (57, Trafalgar St)
- 1893 ...

James A. **Hardy**　　**(CP/CU)**
Birmingham (Summer Hill Terrace/Sand　(WAB) (HTD)
Pits)　　(DOB) (WWDB)
- 1829 - 1839 ...　　(WDOB) (SAOR)
1824 ... **(& Co.)**　　(SAOR)

James H. **Hardy**　　**(EP)**　(K80)
Birmingham (St. Philips Road)
- 1880 ...

John **Hardy**　　**(CP)**　(WAB) (HTD)
Birmingham (Caroline St/Gt. Hampton Rw)　(DOB)
- 1829 - 1833 ...

Joseph **Hardy**　　**(OSP)**　(WTDB)
Birmingham (Mary Ann St)
- 1815 ...

Joseph **Hardy**　　**(OSP)**　(B) (SAOR)
Sheffield (Wicker)
1799 ... *(See also figure: I·H)*

Thomas **Hardy**　　**(OSP)**　(B) (SAOR)
Sheffield (Union Ln)
1836 ... *(See also figure: TH)*

H

Hardy, Bell & Co. **(OSP)** (B) (SAOR)
Sheffield (Union Ln)
1831 ... *(See also figure: H&B)*

Daniel **Hargreaves** **(EP)** (K80)
Lancs/Bacup
- 1880 ...

J. **Harlow & Co.** **(EP)** (GS) (MDG)
Birmingham (4, Warstone Ln)
- 1863 - 1866 ...

Henry **Harlow** **(EP)** (K72)
Birmingham (54, Gt. Hampton St)
- 1872 ...

Albert **Harper** **(EP)** (K80)
Manchester (87, Bridge St)
- 1880 ...

J. **Harper** **(EP)** (CDB)
Birmingham (10, Frederick St)
- 1861 ...

G. W. **Harris & Co.** **(BM/CU)** (HGD) (M)
Sheffield (83, Arundel St)
- 1850 ...
~ 1858 ... **(EP)**
(See also figure: G.W.HARRIS)

Harris & Co. **(EP)** (K78) (K80)
Birmingham (34, Parade)
- 1878 - 1880 ...

Harris & Hancock **(EP)** (POS) (K54)
Sheffield (45, Nursery St)
- 1854 ...

Harris & Son **(EP)** (GS)
Sheffield (Orchard St)
- 1863 ...

Benjamin **Harris** **(EP)** (K92)
Birmingham (50, Albion St)
- 1892 ...

Henry **Harris** **(EP)** (K80)
Bristol (9, Pearson St)
- 1880 ...

James **Harris** **(CP)** ^{(WWDB) (WDOB)}
Birmingham (54, Gt. Charles St)
- 1835 - 1839 ...

John **Harris** **(EP)** ^(K80)
Walsall (72, Wednesbury Rd)
- 1880 ...

Joseph **Harris** **(CU)** ^{(CD) (WDB)}
Birmingham (Lionel St/19, Prinsep St) ^(PDB)
- 1818 - 1825 ...

Harris Plating Works Ltd. **(EP)** ^(K36)
London (13 & 15, Goswell Rd/10-13, Glass-house Yd)
- 1936 ...

Harrison & Acton **(BM)** ^{(WDB) (PDB)}
Birmingham (49, Bull St)
- 1823 - 1825 ...

Henry **Harrison & Co.** **(BM/EP)** ^{(WDS79) (K80)}
(Atwell Works)
Sheffield (Pond Hill)
- 1879 - 1880 ...
(See also figure: H symbol "hand" H)

William Wheatcroft **Harrison & Co. (EP)**
(Montgomery Works) ^{(B) (GS) (K80)}
Sheffield (Fargate/Pepper Alley/230, Ro- ^{(K93) (SBW)}
ckingham)
London (3, St. Andrew St)
- 1863 - 1893 ... ^(SAOR)
(See also figure: WWHS)
1861 ... *(See also figure: W.W.H&Co)*
1866 ... *(See also figure: WWH)*
1898 ... *(See also figure:*
W.W.HARRISON)

Harrison & Hipwood **(EP)** ^(K36)
Birmingham (6, Warstone Parade)
- 1936 ...

HARRISON & SON'S
OLD SHEFFIELD PLATE
REPRODUCTIONS

Harrison & Sons **(EP)**
Sheffield
~ 1880 ...

	J. **Harrison** **(CU)** Sheffield 1809 ...	(B) (M)

HARRISON
NORFOLK WORKS
SHEFFIELD

John **Harrison**   **(BM/CU/OSP/EP)**
(Norfolk Works)
Sheffield (Holly Croft/Norfolk Ln/
116, Scotland St)
1778 - 1863 ...
(See also figures: I.H, IH S)
- 1833 - 1883 **(& Co.)**
*(See also figures: I.H&Co,
JH&Co)*
- 1879 - 1883 ... **(& Co. Ltd.)**
(Then: Richard Richardson)

(SAOR) (WDG)
(GDS) (POS)
(WDS37) (DSRR)
(SD46) (M)
(WDOS) (GDBS)
(K54) (B) (SBW)
(GS)
(B) (GDS) (SBW)
(SAOR)
(WDS79) (K80)
(SAOR)

Edmund **Harrison**   **(EP)**
Sheffield (123, Charlotte Rd)
- 1901 ...

(WDS01)

George **Harrison**   **(OSP)**
Birmingham (Summerhill Terrace)
1823 - 1825 ... *(See also figure: GH)*

(WDB) (PDB) (B)

Joseph **Harrison**   **(CU/OSP)**
Birmingham
1813 ...

(SAOR)

Joseph **Harrison**   **(EP)**
Birmingham (58, Gt. Hampton St)
- 1903 ...

(K03)

HARRISON BROS
& HOWSON
SHEFFIELD

Harrison Brothers & Howson
(Rockingham Plate Works &
Shoreham Works)   **(CU/EP)**
(James William Harrison, Henry Harrison & James
William Howson)
Sheffield (67, Norfolk St/Rockingham Ln/
St. Mary's Rd/Carver St)
London (Hatton Garden/Holborn Viaduct)
1847 - 1936 ...
(See also figures: Alpha, H·H)
*(In 1925 they sold the Trademark "ALPHA" to
Viners)*

(B) (SAOR) (K80)
(K93) (WDS01)
(K36) (SBW) (M)

HARRODS LONDON S.W.	**Harrods Stores Ltd.** **(EP)** London 1889 - 1897 *(See also figures: H, H Ld)*	

Harrold & Ashwin **(EP)** (M) (POB)
Birmingham (136, Suffolk St)
- 1867 ... *(See also figure: H&A)*

William **Harrold** **(EP)** (K72)
Birmingham (136, Suffolk St)
- 1872 ...

John **Hart** **(EP)** (CDB) (BDB)
Birmingham (124, Vyse St/48, Warstone Ln/ (GS) (MDG)(POB)
44, Augusta St) (K72) (K78) (K80)
- 1861 - 1884 ... (K84) (K78) (K80)
- 1878 - 1902 ... (**& Co./& Son**) (K88) (K92) (K03)

John **Hartill** **(EP)** (K82) (K84)
Birmingham (38, Lionel St)
- 1882 - 1884 ...

Hartley & Baxter **(EP)**
Sheffield (7, Eyre Ln/40, Matilda St)
1905 - 1940

J. E. **Hartley & Co.** **(EP)** (K82) (K84) (K88)
Birmingham (13, St. Paul's Sq) (K92)
- 1882 - 1892 ...

Hartley, Baxter & Co. **(EP)** (WDS01)
Sheffield (82, Tender St)
- 1901 ... *(See also figure: HB&Co)*

Henry Millington **Harwood & Sons** **(EP)** (M)
Birmingham (Newhall St)
1892 - 1894

H. M. **Harwood &** Herny H. **Plante** **(EP)** (K88) (K92) (M)
(Formerly: Harwood, Plante & Harrison)
Birmingham (185 & 187, Newhall St)
- 1888 - 1892 ...
(See also figure: HMH HHP)

William **Harwood & Sons** **(CP)** (B) (SAOR) (HDG)
(Harwood & Co.)
Sheffield (Howard St/44, Norfolk St)
1801 - 1822 ...
(See also figure: W·H&Co)

Thomas **Harwood** **(CP/EP)**
Birmingham (Bread St/Mott St/Bath St/
13, Mount St/185 & 187, Newhall St)
London (3, Duke St)
- 1815 - 1850 ...
(See also figure: TH)
- 1861 - 1880 ... **(& Son)**
(See also figure: TH&S)

(B) (SAOR)
(WTD) (WWDB)
(HGDB) (WDOB)
(HTD) (M) (WAB)
(WDB) (DOB)
(PDB) (CD) (HGD)
(CDB) (BDB) (GS)
(MDG)(POB)
(K72) (K78) (K80)

R. **Harwood** **(CU)** (HGDB) (HGD)
Birmingham (16, Bromsgrove St)
- 1849 - 1850 ...

Samuel **Harwood** **(CU)**
Sheffield (Highfield/3, Union St/99, Norfolk St)
1835 ... *(See also figure: SH)*
- 1837 - 1846 ... **(& Co.)**

(B) (SAOR)

(WDS37) (SD46)

H. M. **Harwood, Plante & Harrison**
Birmingham (185 & 187, Newhall St) **(EP)**
London (12, Hatton Garden)
- 1882 - 1884 ...
(See also figure: HP&H)
(Then: Harwood & Plante)

(K82) (K84) (M)

Harwood, Sons & Harrison **(EP)**
Birmingham
1883 - 1886 *(See also figure: HS&H)*

Maxwell **Haseler** **(EP)** (K78)
Birmingham (71, Gt. Hampton St)
- 1878 ...

Haseler Brothers (Edward Jn. & Noble)
Birmingham (Branston St) **(EP)**
- 1882 - 1905
(See also figures: EJH NH, H.Brs)

(K82) (K84) (K88)
(M)

W. H. **Hastelow** **(GS)** (MDG)
Birmingham (32, Gt. Charles St)
- 1866 ...

Aaron **Hatfield**   **(CP/OSP)**   (B) (SAOR)
Sheffield (7, Pepper Alley)   (NGDS) (GDS)
1808 - 1818 ...   (PD) (WDS37) (S)
1823 - 1846 ... **(& Sons)**   (DSRR) (SD46)
(See figures: A.H., AH JH)   (B) (S)

Edward **Hatfield**   **(OSP)**   (GDS) (DSRR)
(Western Bank Works)
Sheffield (Sutton Cottage)
- 1833 - 1841 ...

Hattersley & Falding   **(BM)**   (K80)
(Snider Works)
Sheffield (Napier St)
- 1880 ...

Charles Henry **Hattersley**   **(EP)**   (K93) (WDS01)
(Snider Works)   (WDSR) (WDS11)
Sheffield (109, Napier St/17 & 19, Matilda   (K36)
St/38, Dover Rd)
- 1893 - 1936 ... *(See also figure: CHH S)*

Frank **Hawker & Co. Ltd.**   **(EP)**   (K36)
(Carpathian Silver Company)
Birmingham (44 - 54, Spencer St)
London (Fulwood Pl)
- 1936 ...
*(See also figure: CARPATHIAN
SILVER)*

George Ernst **Hawkins**   **(EP)**   (K88) (K92) (PC)
Birmingham (15 & 16, Legge Ln)   (K03)
- 1888 - 1903 ... *(See also figure:
GEH**)*

Thomas **Hawkins**   **(EP)**
Birmingham (9 & 73, Mark St)   (K78) (K80) (K82)
- 1878 - 1892 ...   (K84) (K88) (K92)
- 1903 ... **(& Sons)**   (K03)

William **Hawkins**   **(CP)**   (WDOB) (HGDB)
Birmingham (William St/70, Buckingham St)
- 1839 - 1849 ...

George **Hawksley** **(EP)**

Sheffield (32, Charlotte St)

1858 - 1863 ...

(See also figures: GH,
G.HAWKSLEY

- 1849 - 1889 ... **(& Co.)**

(See also figures: CCCo, GH CH,
GH&Co, G&JW HAWKSLEY)

(Then: Until 1946 Edwin John Makin)

(B) (GS) (SBW)

(B) (GDBS)
(WDOS) (POS)
(K54) (SAOR)
(SBW) (M)

Hawksworth **(EP)** (M)

Sheffield

~ 1873 - 1892 *(See also figure: I·K·B)*

Charles **Hawksworth** **(OPS)** (DSRR)

Sheffield (Nursery St)

- 1841 ...

John Smith **Hawksworth** **(OSP)** (GDS) (DSRR)

Sheffield (9, Orchard Ln/238, Brook Hill)

- 1833 - 1841 ...

Thomas **Hawksworth** **(EP)** (WDS79) (K80)
(K93)

Sheffield (27, Chester St/52, Charlotte St)

- 1879 - 1893 ...

Charles **Hawksworth,** John **Eyre & Co.**

Sheffield (White Rails/ **(OSP/EP)**
68, Nursery St/62/124, Rockingham St)

1833 - 1871 ...

(See also figures: CH JE, JKB TH
GW)

1873 - 1905 ... **(& Co. Ltd.)**

(See also figures: HE & Co. Ltd,
SIBERIAN SILVER, trademark
"Capital")

(SAOR) (B)
(HGDY) (DSRR)
(SD46) (GDBS)
(WDOS) (K54)
(POS) (GS)
(WDS71) (SBW)
(M) (SAOR)
(WDS79) (K80)
(K93) (WDS01)
(WDSR) (M)

Daniel **Hawley** **(OSP)** (HDG)

Sheffield (11, New Church St)

- 1822 ...

George **Hawley** **(OSP)** (B) (SAOR)

Sheffield (Hollys Croft)

1784 ... *(See also figure: GH)*

Willian **Hay**	**(CU)**	(M)
Birmingham		
~ 1890 ..		
(See also figure: EUREKA SIL-VER)		

Haynes Brothers	**(EP)**	(K80)
Maidstone (Week St/King St)		
- 1880 ...		

Joseph **Haywood & Co.**	**(CP/CU)**	(SAOR) (M) (K72)
(Glamorgan Works)		(K80AD) (WDS01)
Sheffield (45-61, Pond St)		
1872 - 1880 ...		
(See also figure: JOSEPH HAY-WOOD)		

George **Haywood**	**(EP)**	(CDB)
Birmingham (26, Carver St)		
- 1861 ...		

John **Haywood**	**(OSP)**	(DSRR)
Sheffield (Screwsbury Rd)		
- 1841 ...		

H

H.B.B. E.P.N.S	**Not assigned!**	**(EP)**

H.BARNASCONE SHEFFIELD	*(See also)* Henry **Barnascone**	**(CU/EP)**

H.BRˢ	*(See also)* **Haseler Brothers** (Edward jun. & Noble)	**(EP)**

HB & C° S	**Not assigned!** Sheffield	**(EP)** (E)

H B & Co	*(See also)* **Hartley, Baxter & Co.**	**(EP)**

H

(See also) **(CU/EP)** **Harrison Brothers & Howson** **(Rockingham Plate Works/Shore-** **ham Works)**	

(See also)   **(OSP)**
Battie, Howard & Hawksworth

(See also)   **(CU)**
Henry **Barnascone & Son**

Not assigned!   **(EP)** [E]
Sheffield
~

(See also)   **(EP)**
H.C & Co.. S   **Hammond, Creake & Co.**

(See also)   **(OSP)**
Henry **Coar**

Not assigned!   **(EP)** [E]
London
~ 1895 ...

(See also)   **(OSP)**
H. **Duke**

(See also)   **(OSP)**
H. **Dawson, Wilkinson & Co.**

(See also)   **(EP)**
Hawksworth, Eyre & Co.

Headley, Birch & Co.   **(GS)** [K88] [K92]
(Cumberland Works)
Birmingham (71 & 73, Vittoria St)
- 1888 - 1892 ...

	Heath & Harrison (EP)	(K88) (K92)
	Birmingham (58, Gt. Hampton St) - 1888 - 1892 ...	

	Elisa **Heath** (EP)	(K92) (K03)
	Birmingham (39, Frederick St) - 1892 - 1903 ...	

	John **Heath** (CP)	(DOB)
	Birmingham (Ct. 6, Kenion St) - 1833 ...	

	William Richard **Heath** (EP)	(MDG) (POB) (K72) (K78) (K80)
	Birmingham (22, Hall St/67, Victoria St) - 1866 - 1880 ... *(Then: Flint & Son)*	

HECWORTH REPRODUCTION OLD SHEFFIELD	**Hecworth** (EP) ~ 1900 ...	(E)

	Arthur Egerton **Heckford** (EP)	(K88) (SBW) (M)
	Birmingham (53, St. Paul's Square) - 1888 ... *(See also figure: SILVERMINI-MUM)*	

	Cecil Frederick **Heckford** (EP)	(K03)
	Bingham (26, Frederick St) - 1903 ...	

	Edmund **Heeley & Co.** (CU)	(K70AD)
	Birmingham (25, Union St) - 1870 ...	

	James **Heeley & Sons** (GS/CP)	(DOB) (HGD)
	Birmingham (146 & 147, Gt. Charles St/ Mount St/Graham St) - 1833 - 1850 ...	

	Henry **Hemming** (CU)	(K72) (K80) (PC)
	Birmingham (47, Northwood St/20, George St) - 1872 - 1896 ...	

	Thomas **Hemming** (EP)	(K78)
	Birmingham (21, Caroline St) - 1878 ...	

H

James **Hems & Co.** **(EP)** (K88)
Birmingham (6, Augusta St)
- 1888 ...

George **Hendren & Co.** **(EP)** (K72)
Birmingham (13, Vittoria St)
- 1872 ...

John **Henfrey & Son** **(OSP)** (B) (SAOR)
Sheffield (Spring St)
1775 ... *(See also figure: I&SH)*

Henley Silver Rolling **(EP)** (W)
& Wire Mills Ltd.
Sheffield
~ 1892 ...
(See also figure: ABOYEUR)

Samuel **Hennell** **(OSP)** (B) (SAOR)
London (5, Snowhill)
1828 ... *(See also figure: S·H)*

James T. **Henry** **(CU/CP/EP)** (GS) (K72) AD
(Lincoln Electro Plate Works) (K80)
Sheffield (Howard Ln/38, Arundel St)
- 1863 - 1880 ...

HENRY BARNASCONE &SON | *(See also)* | **(EP)**
SHEFFIELD.ENGLAND | Henry **Barnascone & Son**

HENRY | *(See also)* | **(BM/EP)**
BIGGIN & Co | Henry **Biggin & Co.**
SHEFFIELD | **(Matilda Works)**

Henry Elliot & Co | *(See also)* | **(EP)**
Sheffield | Henry **Elliot & Co.**

HENRY ROGERS, SONS & Co | *(See also)* | **(CU/EP)**
CUTLERS SHEFFIELD | Henry **Rogers, Son & Co.**

HENRY ROSSELL & Co | *(See also)* | **(EP)**
SHEFFIELD | Henry **Rossell & Co.**

Edmund A. **Henson** **(EP)** (POB) (K72) (K78)
Birmingham (61, Constitution Hill) (K80)
- 1867 - 1880 ...

	Thomas W. **Hepton** Scarborough, Yorkshire - 1880 ...	**(EP)**	(K80)
HERALD TRUMPETER	**(See also)** C. A. E. **Speyer & Co.**	**(CU/EP)**	
HERBERT MACLAURIN SHEFFIELD	**(See also)** Herbert **Maclaurin (Matilda Works)**	**(EP)**	
	Mrs. Gertrude **Herold** Birmingham (49, Albion St) - 1892 ...	**(EP)**	(K92)
HERRIOTT **SHEFFIELD**	E. **Herriott & Sons** Sheffield -1901 - 1923 ...	**(CU/EP)**	(WDS01) (Rd)
	W. W. **Hervey** Birmingham (16, Bull Ring/1 & 2, Moor St) - 1862 ...	**(EP)**	(BDB)
	Esther **Hesketh** Birmingham (Navigation St) - 1818 ...	**(OSP)**	(WTD)
	Samuel **Hesketh** Birmingham (Navigation St) - 1815 ...	**(CP)**	(WTDB)
HESSIN	**(See also)** Andrew **Charles**	**(EP)**	
	Hewitt & Co. Birmingham (26, Victoria St) - 1903 ...	**(EP)**	(K03)
	Henry **Hewitt &** Henry **Rock** Sheffield (Norfolk St) 1799 ... **(See also figure: H.R)**	**(OSP)**	(B) (SAOR)
	Francis **Hewitt** Birmingham (Warstone Ln) - 1903 ...	**(EP)**	(K03)
	Herny William **Hewitt** Birmingham (9 & 10, Hingeston St) - 1866 - 1878 ...	**(EP)**	(MDG) (K78)

H

Hewitt, Anstay & Wilson (EP)	(K03)
Birmingham (43 & 44, Kenyon St) - 1903 ...	

James **Hewlett** (CU/CP)	(SAOR) (WDB) (PDB) (WAB) (HTD) (HGDB) (HGD)
Birmingham (131, Gt. Charles St) 1819 - 1850 ...	

A. **Hewlett Ltd.** (EP)	(K36)
Birmingham (44, Hockley Hill) - 1936 ...	

Hewson Brothers (EP)	(K36)
Birmingham (18, Albion St) - 1936 ...	

H

🅷 🅵 & 🅒🅞 🆂 🄰🄸	*(See also)* (EP) Harrison **Fisher**
🅷 🅵 ✪ 🆂 🄰🄸 🄴🄿🄽🄢	*(See also)* (EP) Harrison **Fisher**
HF	*(See also)* (OSP) H. **Freeth**
HG&C⁰	*(See also)* (OSP) J. **Jones**, H. **Greenway & Co.**
🅷 🅶 🅻 & 🅒🅞	*(See also)* (EP) H. G. **Long & Co.**
H . H & S	*(See also)* (BM/EP) Henry **Hobson & Sons**
H.HARROP	*(See also)* (CP/EP) George **Barnsley & Sons**
🕮🔱🕮🔱	*(See also)* (CP) Henry **Hall**

HH& JEB	**Walker & Hall** (EP) **(Electro Works)**	(B) (K54) (POS) (GS) (K93) (SBW) (M)
	Sheffield (9 & 15, Howard St/10-18, Eyre St) - 1854 - 1893 ...	

🅷🅷 & 🆂	*(See also)* (BM/EP) Henry **Hobson & Sons**

(See also) **(EP)**
Henry Hodson **Plante & Co.**
(Frederick Street Works)

(See also) **(CU/EP)**
William **Marples & Sons Ltd.**

George **Hibbert** **(OSP)** (B) (SAOR)
Sheffield (Mulberry St)
1834 ... *(See also figure: G.H)*

George **Hides & Son** **(CU)** (WDSR)
Sheffield (14, Hollis Croft)
- 1905 ...

Francis **Higgins** **(EP)**
(The **Portland Co. Ltd.**)
London (Riding House St)
1859 - 1869
1868 - 1909 **(& Son)**
1909 - 1940 **(Ltd.)** *(See also figure: fh)*

H

HIGGINSON ROBINSON   **Higginson Robinson** **(EP)** (M)
Liverpool
~ 1900

J. H. **Higgs & Co.** **(EP)** (K72) (K80)
Birmingham (45, Augusta St/103, Vyse St)
- 1872 - 1880 ...

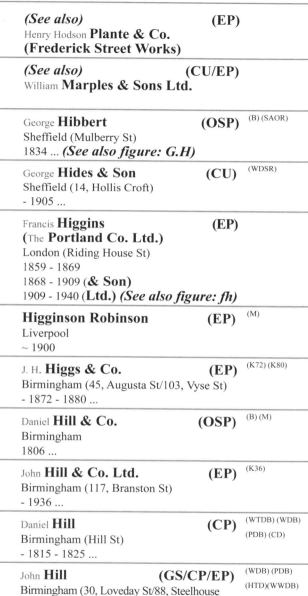

Daniel **Hill & Co.** **(OSP)** (B) (M)
Birmingham
1806 ...

John **Hill & Co. Ltd.** **(EP)** (K36)
Birmingham (117, Branston St)
- 1936 ...

Daniel **Hill** **(CP)** (WTDB) (WDB)
Birmingham (Hill St) (PDB) (CD)
- 1815 - 1825 ...

John **Hill** **(GS/CP/EP)** (WDB) (PDB)
Birmingham (30, Loveday St/88, Steelhouse (HTD)(WWDB)
Ln/40, Bennett St) (WDOB) (DOB)
- 1823 - 1871 ... (WAB) (HGDB)
(HGD) (WDS71)

William R. **Hill** **(CU/EP)** ^{(HGD) (MDG)}
^(POB)
Birmingham (54, Union St/50, Newhall Hill)
- 1850 - 1867 ...

Hill Brothers **(EP)** ^(K36)
Sheffield (23, Eyre St)
- 1936 ...

Charles **Hillcox** **(EP)** ^(K80)
Birmingham (59 & 60, Gt. Hampton St)
- 1880 ...

J. H. **Hillcox** **(EP)** ^(PC)
Birmingham (196, New John St)
- 1896 ...

Samuel **Hillcox** **(EP)** ^(K72)
Birmingham (59, Gt. Hampton St)
- 1872 ...

George Edwin **Hillier** **(EP)** ^{(K82) (K84) (K03)}
Birmingham (9, Harford St/183, Hockley St)
- 1882 - 1903 ...

Hills, Menke & Co. **(EP)** ^{(W) (M) (SBW)}
Birmingham
~ 1892 ...
(See also figure: AFRICAN SIL-VER)

David **Hilton** **(BM)**
Sheffield (66, Trinity St/St. Philip's Road)
- 1852 ... ^(WDOS)
- 1863 ... (**& Son**) ^(GS)

Joseph **Hinchcliffe** **(OSP)** ^{(B) (SAOR)}
Sheffield (Campo Ln)
1799 ... *(See also figure: I.H)*

John **Hines** **(EP)** ^(K03)
Birmingham (66 & 67, Caroline St)
- 1903 ...

J. **Hinks** **(CU)** ^{(B) (M)}
Birmingham
1812 ...

William R. **Hill** **(CU/EP)** [HGD] [MDG] [POB]
Birmingham (54, Union St/50, Newhall Hill)
- 1850 - 1867 ...

Hill Brothers **(EP)** [K36]
Sheffield (23, Eyre St)
- 1936 ...

Charles **Hillcox** **(EP)** [K80]
Birmingham (59 & 60, Gt. Hampton St)
- 1880 ...

J. H. **Hillcox** **(EP)** [PC]
Birmingham (196, New John St)
- 1896 ...

Samuel **Hillcox** **(EP)** [K72]
Birmingham (59, Gt. Hampton St)
- 1872 ...

George Edwin **Hillier** **(EP)** [K82] [K84] [K03]
Birmingham (9, Harford St/183, Hockley St)
- 1882 - 1903 ...

Hills, Menke & Co. **(EP)** [W] [M] [SBW]
Birmingham
~ 1892 ...
(See also figure: AFRICAN SIL-VER)

David **Hilton** **(BM)**
Sheffield (66, Trinity St/St. Philip's Road)
- 1852 ... [WDOS]
- 1863 ... (**& Son**) [GS]

Joseph **Hinchcliffe** **(OSP)** [B] [SAOR]
Sheffield (Campo Ln)
1799 ... *(See also figure: I.H)*

John **Hines** **(EP)** [K03]
Birmingham (66 & 67, Caroline St)
- 1903 ...

HINKS

J. **Hinks** **(CU)** [B] [M]
Birmingham
1812 ...

James **Hinton**   **(EP)** ^(K03)
Birmingham (25, Price St)
- 1903 ...

Thomas **Hinton**   **(CU/EP)** (K72) (K92) (PC)
Birmingham (Ct. 30, Lionel St./46, Hylton St)
- 1872 - 1896 ...

Hinton Brothers   **(EP)** (K03)
Birmingham (46, Hylton St)
- 1903 ...

James **Hipkins**   **(BM)** (WDB) (WAB)
Birmingham (33 & 34, Ward St/6, Wood- (DOB)
cock St)
- 1823 - 1833 ...

J. **Hipkiss**   **(OSP)** (B) (M)
Birmingham
1808 ...

HIPKISS

William **Hipwood**   **(CP)** (B) (WTDB) (CD)
Birmingham (4, Prospect Rw) (WDB) (PDB)
1809 - 1830 ... (WAB) (HTD)
(See also figure: W.HIPWOOD)

Joseph **Hirons &** Henry Hodson **Plante (EP)**
Birmingham (55 & 56, Frederick St)
London (12, Hatton Garden) (B) (BDB)
1860 - 1862 ... *(See also figure: H&P)* (GS) (MDG) (K72)
(Hiron, Plante & Bourne) (K78) (K80) (M)
- 1863 - 1880 ... **(& Co.)**
(See also figure: H.P&Co)

Charles F. **Hirons**   **(EP)** (K82) (K84) (K88)
Birmingham (107, Charlotte St/18, Barr St)
- 1882 - 1888 ...

Alexander **Hitson**   **(EP)** (K80)
Birmingham (15, Spencer St)
- 1880 ...

(See also)   **(EP)**
James **Howard**
(Broom Spring Works)

H J R   *(See also)*   **(EP)**
Higginson Robinson

Mark	Name / Details	Type	Ref
HJA B (shield)	**Not assigned!** Birmingham ~	(EP)	
H J J C & Co	**Not assigned!**	(EP)	
H.L & Co	*(See also)* **Hamilton, Laidlaw & Co.**	(BM/EP)	
H L & Co / HL & Co	*(See also)* **Hamilton, Laidlaw & Co.**	(BM/EP)	
H L^D EP. / H L^D (crown)	*(See also)* **Harrods Stores Ltd.**	(EP)	
H.M & C^O	*(See also)* Henry **Mackanzie & Co.**	(EP)	
HMH HHP	*(See also)* H. M. **Harwood &** H. H. **Plante**	(EP)	
Hob day	John **Hobday** Birmingham (11, Legge St./32, Digby St./ 33, Marshall St.) - 1829 - 1862 ...	(CP)	(WAB) (B) (HTD) (WDOB) (WWDB) (HGDB) (HGD) (M) (BDB)
	John **Hobday** Birmingham (42, Cheapside) - 1892 ...	(EP)	(K92)
	William **Hobday** Birmingham (28, Mary St/12, Kenyon St/ 28, Tower St) - 1880 - 1892 ...	(EP)	(K80) (K82) (K84) (K88) (K92)
	Hobson & Cousins Sheffield - 1825 ...	(OSP)	(PDB)
	Henry **Hobson & Sons** **(Queen Street Factory)** Sheffield (23, Carver St/Eyre Ln) - 1845 - 1901 ... *(See also figures: HH&S, EXPRESS)*	(CU/EP)	(E) (WDS01)
	George **Hobson & Sons** Sheffield ~ 1870 ...	(EP)	(SBW)

Charles **Hobson**   **(OSP)**   (GDS)
Sheffield (108, Duke St)
- 1833 ...

Edward **Hobson**   **(BM)**   (MDG)
Birmingham (108, Barr St)
- 1866 ...

William Henry **Hobson**   **(BM/EP)**   (MDG) (K80)
Birmingham (32, Essex St /Luisa St)
- 1866 - 1880 ...

William **Hockley**   **(CP)**   (DOB)
Birmingham (Dean St)
- 1833 ...

Richard **Hodd &** William **Linley**   **(EP)**   (AD72)
London
1849 - 1872 ... *(See also figure: H&L)*
(Then: R. Hodd & Son)

Richard **Hodd & Son**   **(EP)**   (K80) (K82) (K84)
(Minerva Works)   (K88) (K92) (K93)
(Formerly: Hodd & Liney)   (K36) (SBW) (M)
London (30 & 31, Hatton Garden)
- 1878 - 1936 ... *(See also figure: RH RH)*

C. **Hodgetts & Son**   **(CP/EP)**   (WDOB) (HGDB)
Birmingham (60, Loveday St)   (HGD)
- 1839 - 1850 ...

Frederick **Hodgetts**   **(EP)**   (K82) (K84) (K92)
Birmingham (12, Warstone Pd/6, Hylton St)   (PC)
- 1882 - 1896 ...

J. **Hodgetts**   **(EP)**   (PC)
Birmingham (56, Branston St)
- 1896 ...

William **Hodgetts**   **(EP)**   (K72)
Birmingham (11, Caroline St)
- 1872 ...

Hodgetts Brothers   **(EP)**   (K78) (K80)
Birmingham (150, Tenby St North)
- 1878 - 1880 ...

H

	Thomas **Hodgkins** **(EP)** Birmingham (10, Gough St) - 1849 ...	(HGDB)
	James H. **Hodgkinson** **(EP)** Birmingham (31, Victoria St) - 1880 ...	(K80)
	John Trippet **Holden** **(EP)** Birmingham (111, Vyse St/63, Newhall St/ 21, Caroline St) - 1866 - 1878 ...	(MDG) (K72) (K78)
HOLDSWORTH & SONS	Henry **Holdsworth** **(CU/BM/EP)** Sheffield (Arundel St/ 176, Bramall Ln) - 1863 ... ~ 1864 - 1893 ... **(& Sons)**	(GS) (K80) (K93) (M)
HOLDSWORTH	William **Holdsworth** **(BM/OSP)** Sheffield (14, Angel St) - 1828 - 1829 ...	(SDG) (PD)
HOLLAND&C⁰	H. **Holland & Co.** **(OSP)** Birmingham 1784 ...	(B) (M)
	Thomas **Holland** **(OSP)** London (21, Bell Yard/Temple Bar) - 1808 ...	(POAD)
	David **Hollander & Sons** **(EP)** Birmingham (124-128, Barr St) - 1936 ... ~ 1950 ... **(Ltd.)** *(See also figure: D.H&S)*	(K36)
	Samuel **Hollely** **(EP)** Sheffield (106, Ecclesall New Rd) - 1854 ...	(POS) (K54)
	R. N. **Hollings & Co.** **(EP)** Birmingham (18, Branston St) - 1936 ...	(K36)
	Christopher **Hollis & Son** **(EP)** (Ch. **Hollis & Co)** Birmingham (3, Mary Ann St) - 1850 - 1892 ...	(HGD) (CDB) (BDB) (GS) (MDG) (K72) (K78) (K80) (K82) (K84) (K88) (K92)

H

John **Hollis** (CP) ^(WTDB)
(Formerly: John Johnson & Co)
Birmingham (Livery St/Gt. Hampton St)
- 1815 ...

Holman & Norton (EP) ^{(Rd 333737) (K36)}
Birmingham (43, Howard St)
- 1899 - 1936 ... *(See also figure: H&N)*

Holmes Plating Co.Ltd. (EP) ^(K36)
London (8, Myron Pl)
- 1936 ...

Samuel **Holt** (EP) ^(K80)
Birmingham (20, Northampton St)
- 1880 ...

Daniel & George **Holy & Co.** (OSP) ^{(B) (CD) (PDY) (PDB) (NGDS) (SDG) (PD) (HDG) (M)}
(Daniel & George **Holy**)

Sheffield (Mulberry St)
1817 - 1830 ... *(See also figures: H symbol "pineaple", D & G. Holy & Co.)*

H

Daniel **Holy & Co.** (OSP) ^{(B) (SAOR)}
Sheffield (Norfolk St)
1776 - 1778 ...
(See also figures: DH, DH&Co)

Thomas **Holy &** William **Newbold (OSP)** ^{(B) (SAOR)}
Sheffield (West Bar)
1774 ... *(See also figure: THWN)*

Daniel **Holy** (OSP) ^(PD)
Sheffield (Mulberry St)
- 1828 ...

George **Holy** (OSP) ^(PD)
Sheffield (Mulberry St)
- 1828 ...

Daniel **Holy, Parker & Co.** (OSP) ^(B)
Sheffield (Mulberry St)
- 1787 ... *(See also figure: DAN HOLY PARKER & Co.)*

Daniel **Holy, Wilkinson & Co. (OSP)** (B) (GM)
Sheffield (Mulberry St)
1784 - 1791 ... *(See also figure: DANL HOLY WILKINSON & Co.)*

HOMELAND

(See also) **(EP)** (SBW)
George **Waterhouse & Co.**

Charles **Homer** **(EP)** (K82) (K84) (K88) (K92)
Birmingham (88, Vauxhall Rd)
- 1882 - 1892 ...

George **Homer** **(CP/EP)** (K82) (K84) (K88) (K92)
Birmingham (33, New John St)
- 1882 - 1892 ...

James **Homer** **(BM/EP)** (K78) (K80) (K82) (K84) (K88) (PC)
(Reliance Works)
Birmingham (97, Sycamore Rd/Cecil St)
- 1878 - 1896 ...

William **Homer** **(GS/CP)** (WDOB)
Birmingham (Bromsgrove St)
- 1839 ...

George Gates **Honour** **(EP)** (S)
London
~ 1900 ... *(See also figure: GGHL)*
~ 1900 ... *(See also figures: GGH&S, G.G.HONOUR)*

R. & J. **Hoole** **(OSP)** (POAD)
London (16, Bridge Ln)
- 1808 ...

HOOLE,
STANIFORTH & Co

(See also) **(CU)**
Edgar **Allen & Co.**
(Well Meadow Steel Works)

T. & W. **Hooper** **(CU)** (WDB) (PDB)
Birmingham (Duke St)
- 1823 - 1825 ...

G. & T. **Hooper** **(CU)** (HGDB)
Birmingham (31, Lancaster St)
- 1849 ...

	William **Hooper** (CP) Birmingham (Bartholomew St/Duddeston Rw) - 1833 - 1839 ...	(WWDB) (WDOB)
	J. V. **Hope &** G. F. W. **Hope** (EP) **(Atlantic Works)** London (Wednesbury) ~ 1890 ...	(SBW)
	Samuel **Hope & Son** (EP) Walsall (64, Long St) - 1880 ...	(K80)
HOPE	*(See also)* (CU/EP) W. H. **Brittain** **(Alma Works)**	
	George Joseph **Hope** (EP) Birmingham (13 & 14, Hylton St) - 1878 - 1880 ...	(K78) (K80)
	E. E. **Hopkins & Co.** (EP) Birmingham (40, Northampton St) - 1872 ...	(K72)
	John **Hopkins** (EP) Birmingham (40, St. Paul's Sq) - 1882 - 1892 ...	(K82) (K84) (K88) (K92)
	Joseph **Hopkins** (BM/EP) Birmingham (23, Augusta St/15, Regent Pd) - 1878 - 1880 ... - 1882 - 1903 ... (**& Son**)	(K78) (K80) (K82) (K84) (K88) (K92) (PC) (K03)
	Joseph **Hopkins** jun. (EP) Birmingham (103, High St/Aston) - 1878 - 1892 ...	(K78) (K80) (K82) (K84) (K88) (K92)
	Thomas **Hopwood** (EP) Birmingham (30, Snape St) - 1862 ...	(BDB)
	A. **Horn** (OSP) London (11, Gt. Queen St) - 1808 ...	(POAD)
	Horten & Bushell (EP) Birmingham (106, Ashton Rd) - 1862 - 1863 ...	(BDB) (GS)

H

Horton & Whitehouse (CP) ^(WTDB)
Birmingham (Paradise St)
- 1815 ...

John **Horton** (CP/CU) ^{(B) (WTDB)}
^(WTD) /CD)
Birmingham (Foredrough St)
1809 - 1832 ... ^{(SAOR) (M)}

Charles **Horton** (GS) ^(K93)
Sheffield (43, Union Ln)
- 1893 ...

D. **Horton** (CP) ^(B)
Birmingham
1808 ... *(See also figure: D.HORTON)*

J. **Horton** (EP) ^(GS)
Birmingham (77, Caroline St)
- 1863 ...

Samuel **Horton** (CU/OSP) ^(SAOR)
Birmingham
1814 ...

Thomas **Horton** (GS) ^(WDOB)
Birmingham (Lench St)
- 1839 ...

William **Horton** (CP) ^(WTDB)
Birmingham (Cross St/Hill St)
- 1815 ...

Horton Brothers (EP) ^(K80)
Liverpool (56, Bold St)
- 1880 ...

Francis **Horwood** (EP) ^(K93)
Sheffield (99, Division St)
- 1893 ...

John **Houlden** (OSP) ^{(B) (SDG)}
Sheffield (Pea Croft/Solly St)
1825 ... *(See also figure: IH)*

Albert **Houlston** (EP) ^(K72)
Birmingham (61, Pershore St)
- 1872 ...

F. A. **Houlston** **(EP)** (K88)
Birmingham (45, Spencer St)
- 1888 ...

Edwin Joseph **Houlston Ltd.** **(EP)** (K36)
Birmingham (11, Caroline St)
- 1936 ...

Bartholomew **Hounsfield** **(OSP)** (B) (SAOR)
Sheffield (Pond Ln)
1831 ... *(See also figure: B H)*

Howard & Hawksworth **(OSP)** (SAOR) (WDS37)
Sheffield (Hartshead/6 & 9, Orchard Ln) (SD46) (DSRR)
1835 - 1854 ... *(See also figure: H&H)* (HGDY) (POS)
(GDBS) (WDOS)
(B)

Edwin **Howard & Son** **(EP)** (SI) (E)
Sheffield (90, Pond St/5, Bridge St)
~ 1870 - 1878 ... *(See also figure: EH&S)*

H

HOWARD SHEFFIELD

Francis **Howard** **(CU/EP)** (SAOR) (K80)
(West End/Aberdeen Works) (Rd 79622) (K93)
Sheffield (68, West St/Trafalgar St/ (WDS01) (WDSR)
99, Division St) (WDS11) (SBW)
1878 - 1922 (M)
1923 - 1974 **(Ltd.)**
*(See also figures: FH * S, WELL DONE, symbol "target")*

S. & T. **Howard** **(CU/CP)** (B) (M)
London
1809 ... *(See also figure: SH&Co)*

James **Howard** **(CU)**
(Broom Spring Works)
Sheffield (124, Fitzwilliam St/Bath St)
- 1851 - 1862 *(See also figure: HJ)* (WDOS) (GS)
- 1863 - 1901 ... **(& Sons/& Co.)** (SBW) (M)
(See also figure: HJ & Co.) (WDS01)

William **Howard** **(OSP)** (DSRR)
Sheffield (Orchard Ln)
- 1841 ...

Howard, Battie & Hawksworth (OSP)
Sheffield (Charles St/Watson's Walk/Harts-
head)
- 1822 - 1833

(PDY) (PD) (GDS)
(HDG) (SDG)
(NGDS) (PDB)

Jonathan **Howe**   **(EP)**
Birmingham (26, Key Hill)
- 1867 ...

(POB)

Martha **Howe**   **(BM/EP)**
(Gatefield Works)
Sheffield (Corporation St/48, Robert St)
- 1863 - 1880 ...

(GS) (K80)

William **Howe**   **(EP)**
Sheffield (17, Corporation St/8, Lambert St/
Wollen St/48, Robert St)
- 1879 ...
~ 1858 - 1880 ... **(& Co.)**
(See also figure: WH&Co)

(WDS79)
(K80)

Howes & Browett   **(EP)**
Birmingham (13, Dean St)
- 1862 - 1866 ...

(BDB) (GS)
(MDG)

Joseph **Howes & Son**   **(BM/EP)**
(Standard Works)
Birmingham (Macdonald St)
- 1878 - 1880 ...

(K78) (K80)

Joseph **Howes**   **(BM/EP)**
Birmingham (66, Bromsgrove St/19,
Blucher St/12, Dean St)
- 1833 - 1861 ...

(DOB) (WDOB)
(HGD) (CDB)

John **Howlden**   **(OSP)**
Sheffield (Solly St)
1825 - 1829 ...

(SAOR) (PD)
(SDG)

John **Hoyland & Co.**   **(OSP/CP)**
Sheffield
1764 - 1779 *(See also figure: JH&Co)*

(B) (SAOR)

J. **Hoyland & Co.**   **(OSP)**
Sheffield (Union St)
1773 - 1779 *(See also figure: IH&Co)*
(Then: Younge, Greaves & Hoyland)

(B)

	W. **Hoyland & Co.** **(OSP)** [B] [SAOR]	

W. **Hoyland & Co.** **(OSP)** [B] [SAOR]
Sheffield (Burgess St)
1777 ...
(See also figures: W·H, WH&Co)

Thomas **Hoyland** **(OSP)** [B] [SAOR]
Sheffield (Pond St)
1776 ... *(See also figure: T·H)*

Hoyland, Clarbour & Barnard (CU) [B]
Sheffield (Hillfoot)
1787 ... *(See also figure: CLARBOUR)*

" THREE CROWNS "
H P
& H

Not assigned! **(EP)** [E]

H·P.&Cᵒ

(See also) **(EP)**
Hardman, Powell & Co.

H·P &Cᵒ

(See also) **(EP)**
Joseph **Hirons &** Henry Hodson **Plante &**
Co. (Hiron, Plante & Bourne)

HP &H

(See also) **(EP)**
Harwood, Plante & Harrison

Not assigned! **(EP)** [E]

HRS&Cᵒ

(See also) **(CU/EP)**
Henry **Rogers, Sons & Co.**

HS &H

(See also) **(EP)**
Harwood, Sons & Harrison

H SAMUEL

(See also) **(EP)**
H. **Samuel & Sons**

H SAMUEL
WARRANTED
SHEFFIELD

(See also) **(EP)**
Harriett **Samuel**

H·T T·L

(See also) **(OSP)**
Henry **Tudor &** Thomas **Leader**
(Sycamore Works)

ℋℐ&𝒸ᵒ
𝔥𝔱 𝔥𝔱 𝔥𝔱

(See also) **(OSP)**
Henry **Tudor &** Thomas **Leader**
(Sycamore Works)

HT&Cᵒ

(See also) **(OSP)**
Henry **Tudor &** S. **Nicholson**

H

G. (C.) **Hubbard** **(EP)** ^{(GS) (WDS71)}
Sheffield (South St/7, Screwsbury Terrace)
- 1863 - 1871 ...

Harvey A. **Hudson** **(EP)** ^(K78)
Birmingham (283, Broad St)
- 1878 ...

Daniel **Hughes** **(EP)** ^(SDC)
Coventry (31, Widdrington Rd)
- 1912 ...

Edward **Hughes** **(CU/CP)** ^{(WTDB) (WDB) (PDB) (WAB) (HTD)}
Birmingham (34, Paradise St)
- 1818 - 1830 ...

Joseph **Hughes** **(CP)** ^{(WAB) (HTD) (DOB)}
Birmingham (18, Ann St/Ct. 5, Water St)
- 1829 - 1833 ...

William **Hughes** **(CU)** ^(WWDB)
Birmingham (Park St)
- 1835 ...

Hukin & Fenton **(EP)** ^{(B) (SAOR) (SBW) (M)}
Birmingham (Cadman Ln)
1856 ... *(See also figure: H&F)*

Jonathan W. **Hukin &** John Th. **Heath** **(EP)** ^{(GS) (K72) (K78) (K80) (K82) (K84) (K88) (K92) (PC) (K03) (SBW) (M)}
Birmingham (70 & 71, Newhall St/129 and then 138 & 139, Gt. Charles St)
- 1863 - 1903 ...
- 1904 - 1953 (**Ltd.**)
(See also figure: H&H)

J. W. **Hukin** **(EP)** ^{(CDB) (MDG)}
Birmingham (70 & 71, New Hall St)
- 1861 - 1866 ...

George Henry **Hulley** **(EP)** ^{(SAOR) (WDS01) (K36)}
(Ecclesall Works)
Sheffield (17 - 19, Cambridge St./245, Rocking-ham St.)
1887 - 1936 ...

William R. **Humphreys & Co. (CU/EP)** (WDS01) (SBW)
(Haddon Works/Eyre Street Works) (M) (E)
Sheffield (76, Eyre St)
- 1901 - 1904
1904 - 1925 (**Ltd**.)
(See also figures: W.R.H&Co S,
RADIANT)

C. **Humphreys** (EP) (CDB)
Birmingham (117, New John St)
- 1861 ...

James Henry **Hunt & Co.** (EP) (K92) (M)
Birmingham (2, Regent Pd)
- 1892 ...
(See also figure: J.H.H&Co)

Alexander **Hunt** (OSP) (B) (SAOR)
Sheffield (Bailey Ln)
1822 ... *(See figure: A.H.)*

Charles **Hunt** (GS) (WDOB)
Birmingham (Livery St)
- 1839 ...

Harold **Hunt** (EP) (K36)
Sheffield (82, Backfields)
- 1936 ...

James Henry **Hunt** (EP) (K80) (K82) (K84)
Birmingham (55, Hockley Hill/3, Regent Pd) (M)
- 1880 - 1884 ... *(See also figures:*
J.H.H, SIBERIAN SILVER)

Matthew **Hunt** (EP) (K92) (PC) (K03)
Birmingham (237 & 298, Icknield St)
- 1892 - 1903 ...

Michael **Hunter &** Josiah **Twig(g) (OSP)** (B) (SAOR)
Sheffield (Cheney Square)
1781 ...
(See also figures: WATCH HUM-
BLE, H&T, MH&Co)

HUNTER
SHEFFIELD

Michael **Hunter & Son** (BM/EP) (SBW) (K80) (M)
(Talbot Works)
Sheffield (Saville St)
- 1880 ... *(See also figure: FUERTE)*

Benjamin **Huntsmann** **(CP)** (K88AD) (K93 AD) (WDS01) (W)
Attercliffe (Workshop Rd/Tinsley Park Rd)
- 1888 - 1901 ... *(See also figures: AJAX, B.HUNTSMAN)*

Alfred **Hutchinson** **(EP)** (K80)
Birmingham (Warstone Ln)
- 1880 ...

William & Henry **Hutchinson** **(OSP)** (B) (SAOR)
Sheffield (Norfolk St)
1837 ... *(See also figure: W&H.H)*

Herbert **Hutton** **(EP)** (WDS79) (WDS01)
Sheffield (Ranmoor Park/19, Tapton House Rd)
- 1879 - 1901 ...

T. **Hutton** **(EP)** (MDG)
Birmingham (194, Warstone Ln)
- 1866 ...

William **Hutton** **(CU/CP)** (B) (SAOR) (WDB) (PDB)
Birmingham (4, Fleet St)
1807 - 1842

HUTTON·SHEFFIELD

(See also) **(CP)**
William C. **Hutton & Sons**

Hutton & Houghton **(OSP)** (CD)
Birmingham (30, Paradise St)
- 1818 ...

William Carr **Hutton & Son** **(GS/CP)** (WAB) (HTD) (WWDB) (WDOB)
Birmingham (Gt. Charles St)
- 1829 - 1839 ...

H

William C. **Hutton & Sons**   **(CP/EP)**
Sheffield (10, Surrey St/27, High St/27,
Market St/146, West St)
London (Holborn Circus)
1841 ...
1849 ... *(See also figure: WH&S)*
1857 ...*(See also figure: RH, WH)*
1875 ... *(See also figure: W^M H&S)*
1893 ...
1893 - 1930
- 1906 ... (**Ltd.**)
(See also figures: ANGLE PLATE,
Argentine Plate)
(Then: Absorbed into James Dixon & Sons)

(B) (SAOR)
(DSRR) (SD46)
(GS) (K80) (K93)
(M)

(WDOS AD)
(B) (GDBS)

(B) (K88AD)

(B)

William Carr **Hutton** **(BM/GS/CU/CP)**
(Hanover Square Works)
Sheffield (35, Pinstone St/27, High St/
Surrey St)
~ 1830 - 1841 ...
(See also figures: WH, H&S, AN-
GLE PLATE)

(B) (GDS) (DSRR)
(SBW) (M)

H

H·W&C⁰   *(See also)*   **(OSP)**
H. **Whitelock & Co.**

(B)

H·W&C⁰   *(See also)*   **(OSP)**
Hannah **Watkinson &** William **Watson**

(B)

H.W&C⁰   *(See also)*   **(EP)**
Horace **Woodward & Co.**
(Atlas Works)

(K78) (K80) (Rd)
(M)

H.W. L^TD
HW LTD   *(See also)*   **(EP)**
Henry **Wilkinson & Co. Ltd.**

H.W L^TD WEAR

HW &Co   *(See also)*   **(CU/OSP/EP)**
Herny **Wilkinson & Co.**

HW &Co **M** **S** **EP** **⚔**

HW &Co **M** **S** **EP**

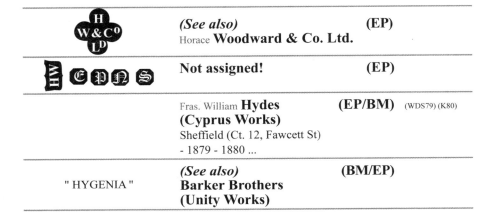

	(See also) ₕₒᵣₐcₑ **Woodward & Co. Ltd.**	**(EP)**
	Not assigned!	**(EP)**
	Fras. William **Hydes** **(Cyprus Works)** Sheffield (Ct. 12, Fawcett St) - 1879 - 1880 ...	**(EP/BM)** (WDS79) (K80)
" HYGENIA "	*(See also)* **Barker Brothers** **(Unity Works)**	**(BM/EP)**

┼ ┼ I E	*(See also)* _{Samuel} **Ashforth**	(OSP)
┼ I . XL	*(See also)* _{George} **Wostenholm & Sons Ltd.** **(Washington Works)**	(CU)
I·B	*(See also)* _{J.} **Barraclough &** _{J.} **Rowbotham**	(OSP)
I·B	*(See also)* _{J.} **Borwick**	(OSP)
I·B	*(See also)* _{John} **Burdekin**	(OSP)
I·C	*(See also)* _{J.} **Cawton**	(OSP)
I·C	*(See also)* _{John} **Cooper**	(OSP)
I·C	*(See also)* _{Isaak} **Cosins**	(OSP)
I·C	*(See also)* _{James} **Crawshaw**	(OSP)
I·D	*(See also)* _{I.} **Davidson**	(OSP)
I·D	*(See also)* _{J.} **Dewsnap**	(OSP)
I·E	*(See also)* _{John} **Eyre & Co.**	(OSP)
I·F **S** **E.P.N.S**	*(See also)* _{Israel} **Freeman & Son Ltd.**	(EP)
I·G	*(See also)* _{J.} **Green**	(OSP)
I·H	*(See also)* _{Joseph} **Hancock**	(OSP)
I·H	*(See also)* _{Joseph} **Hardy**	(OSP)
I·H	*(See also)* _{John} **Harrison** **(Norfolk Works)**	(BM/CU/OSP/EP)

I

I·H	*(See also)* J. **Hinchcliffe**	(OSP)
I·K	*(See also)* J. **Kay**	(OSP)
I·K	*(See also)* J. **Kirkby**	(OSP)
I·L	*(See also)* John **Law**	(OSP)
I·L	*(See also)* Joseph **Law**	(OSP)
I·L	*(See also)* John **Littlewood**	(OSP)
I·M	*(See also)* J. **Mappin**	(OSP)
I·M	*(See also)* J. **Marsh**	(OSP)
I·M	*(See also)* J. **Micklethwaite &** J. **Hounsfield**	(OSP)
I.M.	General term for: **Imperial Measure** 1826 ...	(OSP)
I·N	*(See also)* J. **Newton & Son**	(OSP)
I · O	*(See also)* John **Oxley**	(OSP)
I·R	*(See also)* Joseph **Rodgers & Son**	(OSP)
I·R	*(See also)* J. **Rowbotham**	(OSP)
I·S	*(See also)* J. & S. **Saynor**	(OSP)
I·S	*(See also)* J. **Seynor**	(OSP)
I.S	*(See also)* J. **Sponner**	(OSP)

I·S	*(See also)* J. **Staniforth & Co.**	**(OSP)**
I·S	*(See also)* J. **Staniforth**	**(OSP)**
I·W	*(See also)* J. **Watkinson**	**(OSP)**
I.W	*(See also)* John **Watson & Son**	**(OSP)**
I.W	*(See also)* John **Watson**	**(OSP)**
I·W	*(See also)* J. **Wilkinson**	**(OSP)**
I·W	*(See also)* John **Winter**	**(OSP)**
IANTHE	**Ian Heath Ltd.** Birmingham ~ 1960 ...	**(EP)**
I B **& Cº**	*(See also)* J. **Briggs & Co.**	**(OSP)**
IB	*(See also)* J. **Bailey**	**(OSP)**
I B	*(See also)* Joseph **Barnes**	**(OSP)**
IB	*(See also)* John **Bell**	**(OSP)**

I

George **Ibberson & Co.** **(CU/EP)** ^{(WDS01)(E)} **(Central Works)** Sheffield (102, West St) - 1901 - 1954 *(See also figures:* *G.I&Co., symbol "violine")*	
John **Ibberson** **(OSP)** ^{(B)(SAOR)} Sheffield (Gibraltar St) 1774 ... *(See also figure: J.I)*	
William **Ibbitt** **(OSP)** ^(DSRR) Sheffield (152, Broad Ln) - 1841 ...	

	Ibbotson & Saville Sheffield (Paternoster Rw) - 1829 ...	**(OSP)** ^(PD)
	Charles **Ibbotson** Sheffileld (224, Albany Rd) - 1901 ...	**(CU)** ^(WDS01)
IC	*(See also)* Joseph **Creswick**	**(OSP)**
I.D&Cᵒ **I.DRABBLE** **& Co**	*(See also)* J. **Drabble & Co.**	**(OSP)**
ID	*(See also)* J. **Dewsnap**	**(OSP)**
ID	*(See also)* J. **Dickenson**	**(OSP)**
IE&Cᵒ	*(See also)* Isaac **Ellis & Co.**	**(OSP)**
I E & S	*(See also)* Isaac **Ellis & Sons**	**(EP)**
+ + I E	*(See also)* Samuel **Ashforth**	**(OSP)**
I·F&Cᵒ	*(See also)* John **Fenton & Co.**	**(OSP)**
I.F.S	*(See also)* Israel **Freeman & Son Ltd.**	**(EP)**
I F&Cᵒ	*(See also)* **Fenton, Allanson & Machon** **Fenton, Allanson & Co**	**(OSP)**
IFP **C&Cᵒ**	*(See also)* **Creswick & Co.**	**(EP)**
I·G&SONS	*(See also)* John **Grinsell & Sons** **(Victoria Works)**	**(EP)**
I.G.F **II**	*(See also)* J. & G. **Fearn**	**(OSP)**

I·GREEN&Cº	*(See also)* J. **Green & Co.**	**(OSP)**
I. GUIDE & Co **SHEFFIELD**	*(See also)* I. **Guide & Co.**	**(EP)**
IG&Cº	*(See also)* J. **Green, Roberts, Moseley & Co.**	**(OSP)**
I G & C S	*(See also)* I. **Guide & Co.**	**(EP)**
IG·GH	*(See also)* J. **Green &** G. **Hague**	**(OSP)**
IG	*(See also)* J. **Green**	**(OSP)**
I GUIDE	*(See also)* Frank **Wood**	**(EP)**
I . H & Co	*(See also)* **(BM/CU/OSP/EP)** John **Harrison** **(Norfolk Works)**	
I. & H. SORBY.	*(See also)* **Lockwood Brothers** **(Spital Hill Works)**	**(CU/EP)**
IH&Cº **I H** **C º** *I H & C*	*(See also)* J. **Hoyland & Co.**	**(OSP)**
IH	*(See also)* John **Houlden**	**(OSP)**
J H N W **J H**	*(See also)* John **Harrison** **(Norfolk Works)**	**(OSP/EP)**
I&IW **&Cº** **I. & I. W** **& Co**	*(See also)* I. & I. **Waterhouse & Co.**	**(OSP)**
I&I WATERHOUSE & Cº	*(See also)* I. & I. **Waterhouse & Co.**	**(OSP)**
▮▮▮	*(See also)* George **Lees**	**(CU)**

Mark	(See also)	Code
I·K &Cº	*(See also)* J. **Kirkby, Gregory & Co.**	(OSP)
I·K·B	*(See also)* **Hawksworth**	(EP)
I·KAY & Cº	*(See also)* J. **Kay & Co.**	(OSP)
I K &S	*(See also)* J. **Knowles & Son**	(EP)
IK·IW & Co	*(See also)* J. **Kirkby,** J. **Waterhouse & Co.**	(OSP)
IK	*(See also)* J. **Kirkby**	(OSP)
I·L&Cº	*(See also)* J. **Linley & Co.**	(OSP)
I·LOVE & Cº	*(See also)* J. **Love & Co.** **(Love, Silverside, Darby & Co)**	(OSP)
IL&Cº	*(See also)* J. **Love & Co.** **(Love, Silverside, Darby & Co)**	(OSP)
I LIN WOOD	*(See also)* John **Linwood**	(CU)
I·M &Cº	*(See also)* J. **Makin & Co.**	(OSP)
I.M&Cº	*(See also)* J. **Mappin & Co.**	(OSP)
IM &Cº	*(See also)* J. **Margrave & Co.**	(OSP)
IME	*(See also)* J. M. **Etches**	(OSP)
IMPERIAL	*(See also)* Edgar **Allen & Co.** **(Well Meadow Steel Works)**	(CU)
Imperial F.W.	*(See also)* Frederick **Whitehouse** **(Lion Works)**	(CU/EP)

Mark	(See also)	Type	Refs
I·N·K	*(See also)* J. **Kemp**	**(OSP)**	
IN	*(See also)* Joseph **Nowill**	**(OSP/CU)**	
IN BILBO	*(See also)* Nathaniel **Travis**	**(CU)**	
INDIAN SAND GOLD	*(See also)* N. C. **Reading & Co.**	**(EP)**	
INDIAN SILVER	*(See also)* Thomas H. **Daniel &** Thomas R. **Arter** **(Globe Nevada Silver Works)**	**(EP)**	
INDUSTRIA A C M E	*(See also)* John **Bedford & Sons**	**(CU)**	
	John **Ingram** Birmingham (28 & 126, Suffolk S) - 1878 - 1884 ... *(See also figure: SILVERODE)*	**(EP)**	(K78) (K80) (K82) (K84) (SBW)
J N M **C⁰**	*(See also)* John Newton **Mappin &** George **Webb** **(Royal Plate Works)**	**(EP)**	
IN MIND.	*(See also)* **Atkinson Brothers** **(Milton Works)**	**(EP)**	
INSIGNIA PLATE	*(See also)* Georg Shadford **Lee &** Henry **Wigfull Ltd.** **(John Street Works)**	**(BM/EP)**	
Invisible Action	*(See also)* **Perry & Co. Ltd.**	**(EP)**	
IOSᴴ HANCOCK SHEFFIELD	*(See also)* Joseph **Hancock**	**(OSP)**	
I·P	*(See also)* J. **Parkin &** A. **Wigham**	**(OSP)**	
I P&C⁰	*(See also)* J. **Parsons & Co.**	**(OSP)**	
I P	*(See also)* J. **Peacock &** G. **Austin**	**(OSP)**	

Mark	Reference	Classification	
I·R&Cᵒ	*(See also)* **Roberts, Clayton & Emery** **(Roberts, Clayton & Co)**	(OSP)	
I·R&Cᵒ	*(See also)* J. **Roberts**, S. **Moseley &** J. **Settle**	(OSP)	
I R·Co ⏢	*(See also)* John **Rowbotham & Co.**	(OSP)	
I R	*(See also)* John **Roberts**	(OSP)	
I R	*(See also)* J. **Rotherham**	(OSP)	
I R	*(See also)* John **Rowbotham**	(OSP)	
	Nathaniel **Irving** Sheffield (Screwsbury Rd) - 1852 ...	(EP)	(WDOS)
I & S. ROBERTS	*(See also)* J. & S. **Roberts**	(OSP)	
I&SH	*(See also)* J. & S. **Henfrey**	(OSP)	
I·S&Cᵒ	*(See also)* J. **Shore & Co.**	(OSP)	
I·S &Cᵒ	*(See also)* John **Sykes & Co.**	(CU/OSP)	
I.S.DEARDEN **SHEFFIELD** **ENGLAND**	*(See also)* I. S. **Dearden**	(EP)	
🜲 🜲 I.S.G B 🜲 🜲	*(See also)* Israel Sigmund **Greenberg**	(EP)	
I·S Cᵒ	*(See also)* J. **Shemeld & Co.**	(OSP)	
I S&Cᵒ	*(See also)* J. **Sharrow & Co.**	(OSP)	
IS	*(See also)* Isaac **Sampson**	(OSP)	
IS	*(See also)* John **Settle &** W. **Hatfield**	(OSP)	

IS	*(See also)* J. **Simmons**	(OSP)
IS	*(See also)* J. **Smith**	(OSP)
ISAAC ELLIS & SONS **SHEFFIELD**	*(See also)* Isaac **Ellis & Sons**	(EP)
I S E R V E	*(See also)* Walter J. **Ramsbottom** **(Vine Works)**	(CU)
	E. **Issacs & Co.** Birmingham (16, James St) - 1903 ...	(EP) (K03)
I S **T S**	*(See also)* John & Thomas **Settle, Gunn & Co.**	(OSP)
I&T·S	*(See also)* John & Thomas **Settle**	(OSP)
I.TYLER	*(See also)* John **Tyler**	(BM/OSP)
I·T	*(See also)* J. **Taylor**	(OSP)
ITY **&Cᵒ**	*(See also)* J. T. **Younge & Co.**	(OSP)
ITY&Cᵒ	*(See also)* J. **Younge & Sons**	(OSP)
I. VICKERS	*(See also)* James **Vickers**	(BM)
I· VICKERS	*(See also)* John **Vickers** **(Britannia Place)**	(CU/BM)
I·W **&Cᵒ**	*(See also)* Joseph **Wilson & Co.**	(OSP)
I.WOLSTENHOLME	*(See also)* Joseph **Wolstenholme**	(BM)
IW&Cᵒ	*(See also)* John **Winter & Co.**	(OSP)

I

IW 👑	*(See also)* John **Winter & Co.**	(OSP)
I W	*(See also)* J. **Wilson**	(OSP)
I W	*(See also)* J. **Wright**	(OSP)
IW EPNS	**Not assigned!**	(CU/EP)
I W **I R**	*(See also)* J. **Whip &** J. **Rose**	(OSP)
+ **I . XL**	*(See also)* George **Wostenholm & Sons Ltd.** **(Washington Works)**	(CU)
IXION	*(See also)* G. E. **Walton & Co. Ltd.**	(EP)
IY &S	*(See also)* John **Yates & Sons**	(CU/EP)
IY **IY** **Co**	*(See also)* John **Younge & Co.**	(OSP)

J&CT	*(See also)* James & Charles **Tidmarsh**	**(EP)**
J&D	**Not assigned!**	**(EP)**
J.B	*(See also)* J. **Burburry**	**(OSP)**
J.B	*(See also)* Thomas **Bradbury & Sons** (Joseph **Bradbury**)	**(EP)**
J·B	*(See also)* John **Biggin**	**(EP)**
J·B S GENIUS	*(See also)* John **Blyde** **(Clintock Works)**	**(EP)**
J.G J.G	*(See also)* Joseph **Gilbert** **(Sun Works)**	**(CP/EP)**
J.G	*(See also)* John **Gough** (jun)	**(EP)**
J.H	**Not assigned!**	**(EP)**
J·I	*(See also)* J. **Ibberson**	**(OSP)**
J·J	*(See also)* J. **Jervis**	**(OSP)**
J·M	*(See also)* Joseph **Mappin & Co.** (Joseph **Mappin & Son**)	**(EP)**
J ⚜ M ✳	*(See also)* Joseph **Mappin & Brothers** **(Queen's Cutlery Works)**	**(EP)**
J·N J·N ♔ PS	*(See also)* John **Neal &Co.**	**(EP)**
J·N	*(See also)* J. & W. **Nowill**	**(OSP)**

J

J·R	*(See also)* John **Rodgers & Co.**	(OSP)
J·R	*(See also)* Joseph **Rodgers & Sons** (George)	(EP)
J.S	*(See also)* Josephus **Smith**	(OSP)
J.T **J.T**	*(See also)* J. **Thompson**	(EP)
J·T	*(See also)* J. **Tibbitts**	(OSP)
J.W	*(See also)* Joseph **Wolstenholme**	(EP/BM)
J. ALLAN&CO. SHEFFIELD	*(See also)* James **Allan & Co.**	(EP)
J A. S.	*(See also)* Joseph **Ashworth**	(EP)
	William **Jackson & Co.** **(Sheaf Island Works)** Sheffield (Pond Hill) - 1879 - 1901 ... *(See also figures:* *Symbol "circle", R. VERNON &* *SONS)*	(CU) (WDS79) (WDS01) (SBW)
	Wilfried **Jackson** Sheffield (75 & 77, Hollis Croft/17, Broom- field Rd) - 1879 - 1901 ...	(BM/EP) (WDS79) (K80) (K93) (WDS01)
	James & Gibbs Birmingham (6, Newhall St) - 1818 ...	(CU/CP)
	John **James & Sons** **(Victoria Works)** Redditch ~ 1880 ... *(See also figure: LEVIANTHAN)*	(EP)
JAMES ALLAN & Co. SHEFFIELD	*(See also)* James **Allan & Co.**	(EP)

JAMES ALLAN SHEFFIELD	*(See also)* James **Allan**	**(CU/EP)**
JAMES BARBER SHEFFIELD	*(See also)* I. & James **Barber**	**(EP)**
JAMES DEAKIN&SONS **CUTLERS** **SHEFFIELD**	*(See also)* James **Deakin** **(Sidney Works)**	**(BM/EP)**
JAMES DIXON & SONS BRITANNIA METAL	*(See also)* James **Dixon & Sons**	**(BM/EP)**
JAMES HARDY&CoL^{TD} **ABERDEEN** **ADELPHI QUALITY**	*(See also)* James **Hardy & Co. Ltd.**	**(EP)**
JAPANESE SILVER	*(See also)* Thomas H. **Daniel &** Thomas R. **Arter** **(Globe Nevada Silver Works)**	**(EP)**

	(See also) Jehoiad Alsop **Rhodes**	**(EP)**
	William **Jarratt** Birmingham (Suffolk St) - 1818 ...	**(OSP)** ^(WTD)
	Charles **Jarvis** Birmingham (29, Sheep St) - 1833 - 1839 ...	**(CP)** ^{(DOB) (WDOB)}
	Harry **Jarvis** Birmingham (3, Brearly St) - 1903 ...	**(EP)** ^(K03)
	Henry **Jarvis** Birmingham (3, Fisher St) - 1849 ...	**(EP)** ^(HGDB)
	George **Jarvis** Birmingham (31, Burbury St/113/256, Unett St/3, Brearley St) - 1861 - 1880 ... - 1882 - 1936 ... **(& Son)**	**(EP)** ^{(CDB) (K72) (K78) (K80) (K82) (K84) (K88) (K92) (K36)}
	Thomas **Jarvis** Birmingham (149, Well St/New John St) - 1862 - 1863 ...	**(EP)** ^{(BDB) (GS)}

J

JAY JAYS	James **Jay** London (Essex Rd/Oxford St) 1867 - 1897 *(See also figure: MAJESTIC)*	**(EP)**
J.B **&** **G.B**	*(See also)* Jonas & George **Bowen**	**(EP)**
J.B & S EP	*(See also)* John **Baker & Sons**	**(EP)**
J.B.C&S.Lᴰ	*(See also)* John Bishop **Chatterley & Sons Ltd.** **(Albert Works)**	**(EP)**
J·B·C	*(See also)* John Bodman **Carrington**	**(EP)**
J·B **S** GENIUS	*(See also)* John **Blyde** **(Clintock Works)**	**(EP)**
J. BROWN **SHEFFIELD**	*(See also)* Joseph **Brown**	**(EP)**
J·B **TB**	*(See also)* Thomas **Bradbury & Sons**	**(EP)**
J B & Cº	*(See also)* John **Bednall & Co.**	**(EP)**
J B & Cº Lᵀᴰ	*(See also)* John **Batt**	**(EP)**
J B & S EPB	*(See also)* James **Ballantyne & Son**	**(EP)**
JB & S	*(See also)* Jonathan **Bell & Sons**	**(EP)**
JB&S	*(See also)* Jonas **Bowen & Sons**	**(EP)**
JB & S EP	**Not assigned!**	**(EP)**
JB	*(See also)* Jonathan **Bell**	**(EP)**

J

JB	*(See also)* John **Biggin**	**(EP)**
JB	*(See also)* **Green, Bradbury & Firth**	**(OSP)**
J B **E B**	*(See also)* Thomas **Bradbury & Sons**	**(EP)**
JBS	*(See also)* J. B. **Silvester**	**(EP)**
j.C&CºLD	*(See also)* John **Collyer & Co. Ltd.**	**(EP)**
J.C.LᴰP E.P.N.S	**Not assigned!**	**(EP)**
J C &Cº	*(See also)* James **Chesterman & Co.** **(Bow Works)**	**(EP)**
J C & Cº Lᵀ **J&C CºLᴰ** &CºLTD	*(See also)* John **Collyer & Co. Ltd.**	**(EP)**
J C &S	*(See also)* John **Clarke & Sons**	**(EP)**
J&C SONS	*(See also)* John **Clarke & Sons Ltd.**	**(EP)**
J C N C	*(See also)* Thomas, James & Nathaniel **Creswick**	**(OSP/EP)**
J.D&CºLD	*(See also)* **Johnson, Durban & Co. Ltd.** **(Crown Works)**	**(EP)**
J·D & S EP	*(See also)* **James Deakin** **(Sidney Works)**	**(BM/EP)**
J·D&S	*(See also)* James **Dixon & Sons**	**(BM/EP)**

J

227

Logo	Company	Category
J D & Co LTD	*(See also)* **Johnson, Durban & Co. Ltd. (Crown Works)**	(EP)
JD & S EP NS	*(See also)* **James Deakin (Sidney Works)**	(BM/EP)
J D & S PN S	*(See also)* James **Dixon & Sons**	(BM/EP)
J D F	**Not assigned!**	(EP) (E) (Dia)
JDIXON	*(See also)* James **Dixon & Son**	(CU/OSP)
J.E.B	*(See also)* Joseph Edward **Bushell**	(EP)
J·E S	*(See also)* Joseph **Elliot & Sons**	(EP)
J E & S S	*(See also)* Joseph **Elliot & Sons**	(EP)
	David **Jee** Coventry 1819 ...	(CU/OSP) (SAOR)
	J. H. **Jefferies** Birmingham (42, Newhall St) - 1866 ...	(EP) (MDG)
	Jenkins & Ringrose (Granville Works) Sheffield (Granville St) - 1936 ...	(EP) (K36)

Jenkins & Timm (EP)
(Pensilvia Works)
Sheffield (23, Orchard Ln/188 - 196,
Solly St/34, Eyre St)
1889 - 1914   (SAOR) (WDS01)
1915 - 1930 (**Ltd.**)   (WDSR)
(See also figures: J&T S, symbol
"swords")

David **Jenkins**   (CU)   (SAOR)
Birmingham
1812 ...

A. **Jennings**   (EP)   (CDB)
Birmingham (31, Whittall St)
- 1861 ...

George **Jenns**   (CU/CP)   (WDB) (PDB)
Birmingham (Aston Rd)
- 1823 - 1825 ...

James **Jerbis**   (EP)   (MDG)
Biurmingham (31, Banburry St)
- 1866 ...

John **Jervis**   (OSP)   (B) (SAOR)
Sheffield (Pea Croft)
1775 ... *(See also figure: J.J)*

William **Jervis**   (OSP)   (B) (SAOR)
Sheffield (White Croft)
1789 ...*(See also figures: W·J,*
W.JER VIS)

William **Jessop & Sons Ltd.** (CU)   (WDS79) (K93)
(Brightside Works)   (K93 AD)
Sheffield (Brightside Ln)
London (76, Cannon St)
- 1878 - 1893 ...
(See figure: AEROPLANE)

William **Jessop**   (OSP)   (B) (SAOR)
Sheffield (Howard St)
1796 ... *(See also figure: WJ)*

Richard **Jewesson**   (OSP)   (B) (SAOR)
Sheffield (Milk St)
1800 ... *(See also figure: R·J)*

	Richard **Jewesson, Midleton & Co. (OSP)** [B] Sheffield ~ 1798 ... *(See also figure: R^D JE-WESSON)*	
J·F·F	*(See also)* John Frederick **Fenton**	**(EP)**
JF	*(See also)* James **Fenton**	**(EP)**
JFF &FF	*(See also)* **Fenton Brothers (South Moor Works)**	**(EP)**
J F G	*(See also)* John **Fullerton**	**(EP)**
J & G B	*(See also)* Jonas & George **Bowen**	**(EP)**
J.G&S	*(See also)* John **Grinsell & Sons (Victoria Works)**	**(EP)**
J.G. &S **C P N S**	*(See also)* John **Gilbert & Sons**	**(EP)**
J.G.G ✹ S J.G.GRAVES E P N S	*(See also)* John George **Graves (Enterprise Works)**	**(EP)**
JG&SONS	*(See also)* John **Grinsell & Sons (Victoria Works)**	**(EP)**
J G.&Cᵒ	*(See also)* J. **Gregory & Co.**	**(OSP)**
J G & S S	*(See also)* John **Grinsell & Sons (Victoria Works)**	**(EP)**
JG **♀ ⚜ ❀** **J G E P**	*(See also)* Joseph **Gilbert (Sun Works)**	**(CP/EP)**
J G ❀ 2 EP	**Not assigned!**	**(EP)**

230

JG S	*(See also)* John **Gallimore** (Italian Works)	(EP)
J. H & S	*(See also)* John **Slater & Son**	(EP)
J·H·H	*(See also)* James Henry **Hunt**	(EP)
J.H.P	*(See also)* John Henry **Potter**	(EP)
J.H.POTTER SUPERIOR SILVER PLATE SHEFFIELD / **J.H.POTTER SHEFFIELD**	*(See also)* John Henry **Potter** (Rockingham Works)	(CU/EP)
J.H.S	*(See also)* John **Slater & Son**	(EP)
J.HALL& Co MANCHESTER	*(See also)* John **Hall & Co.**	(EP)
J·HH&Cº	*(See also)* James Henry **Hunt & Co.**	(EP)
JH&Cº	John **Harrison** (Norfolk Works)	(BM/CU/OSP/EP)
J H & C	*(See also)* John **Hoyland & Co.**	(OSP)
J H.&Cº	*(See also)* John **Hardman & Co.**	(EP)
JH	*(See also)* Thomas, James & Nathaniel **Creswick**	(OSP/EP)
JHM EPNS	Not assigned!	(EP) [E]
J H S EP	Not assigned! - 1902 ...	(EP) [E]
J&JB	*(See also)* John & Jonathan **Bell**	(OSP)

J

J & JM (mark)	J. & J. **Maxfield** **(EP)** ^(K93) Sheffield (42, Eyre St/169, Arundel St) - 1893 - 1908 *(Then: Maxfield & Sons, Silversmiths Ltd.)*	
J & J W / **J & J W ST** (marks)	*(See also)* **(EP)** James & Josiah **Williams**	
J J Dur rant (mark)	*(See also)* **(EP)** John James **Durrant**	
J.K & C<u>o</u>	**Not assigned!** **(EP)** ^(E)	
J K&C° (mark)	*(See also)* **(OSP)** J. **Kirkby**, J. **Waterhouse** & J. **Hodgson**	
JKB TH GW	*(See also)* **(OSP/EP)** **Hawksworth, Eyre & Co.**	
J L & S (mark)	*(See also)* **(EP)** James **Lewis & Sons**	
JL (mark)	*(See also)* **(OSP)** John (Jonathan) **Littlewood**	
J L L™ (mark)	**Not assigned!** **(EP)**	
J. MARSDEN SHEFFIELD	*(See also)* **(CU)** J. **Marsden**	
J M & B (mark)	*(See also)* **(EP)** Joseph **Mappin & Brothers** **(Queen's Cutlery Works)**	
J M&C° (mark)	*(See also)* **(OSP)** **Middleton, Jewesson & Co.**	
J M & C° (mark)	*(See also)* **(EP)** John **Morton & Co.**	
JM (mark)	*(See also)* **(OSP)** J. **Makin**	
JM (mark)	*(See also)* **(EP)** Joseph **Mappin & Son**	
JM (mark)	*(See also)* **(EP)** J. **Moore**	

J

JMC **EP NS**	**Not assigned!**	**(EP)**
J·NICHOLDS	*(See also)* James **Nicholds**	**(OSP)**
🄹 🄽 & 🅂	*(See also)* John **Nowill & Sons** **(Nowill's Cutlery & Plate Works)**	**(EP)**
JN	*(See also)* John **Needham**	**(EP)**
JN	*(See also)* J. **North**	**(EP)**
🄹 🄽 🄼 🄲o	*(See also)* John Newton **Mappin &** George **Webb** **(Royal Plate Works)**	**(BM/EP/CU)**
J┼N S	*(See also)* John **Nodder & Sons** **(Devenport Works/Taranaki** **Works)**	**(EP)**
JOHN ADWICK PONDS WORKS	*(See also)* **Marsh Bros. & Co.**	**(EP)**
JOHN ASKHAM SHEFFIELD **OBOGGAN**	*(See also)* John **Askham**	**(CU/EP)**
JOHN BAKER	*(See also)* John **Baker**	**(OSP)**
JOHN BARNETT	*(See also)* John **Barnett**	**(EP)**
JOHN BATT & Co.Lᴅ SHEFFIELD	*(See also)* John **Batt**	**(EP)**
JOHN NODDER & SONS SHEFFIELD	*(See also)* John **Nodder & Sons** **(Devenport Works/Taranaki** **Works)**	**(EP)**
JOHNPARSONS&Cᴼ	*(See also)* John **Parsons & Co.**	**(OSP)**
JOHN PERRY **NOTTINGHAM**	*(See also)* John **Perry**	**(T)** [E]

J

JOHN YATES & SONS *(See also)*   **(CU/EP)**
John **Yates & Son(s)**

Christopher **Johnson & Co.** **(CU/EP)**
(Western Works & Western Steel Works)
Sheffield (207 - 223, Portobello St)
- 1879 - 1938
(See also figures: CJ&Co, C.JOHNSON & Co.)
1938 - 1952 (**Ltd.**)

(WDS79) (M)

Johnson & Co.   **(EP)**
(Johnson, Durban & Co. Ltd.)
(Crown Electro Plate Works)
Birmingham (81, Lichfield St/Aston Rd/ Hubert St)
- 1872 - 1896 ...
~ 1897 - 1903 ... *(See also figure: J.D&Co Ld)*

(K72) (K78) (K80)
(K82) (K84) (K88)
(K92) (PC)

(M) (K03)

John **Johnson**   **(CP)**
Sheffield (New Inkleys/Aston Rd)
~ 1812 - 1818 ...

(M) (WTDB) (CD)

JOHN SON

J

George W. **Johnson** **(BM/EP)**
Liverpool (21, Brownlow Hill)
- 1880 ...

(K80)

Joseph **Johnson**   **(OSP)**
Sheffield (Aston Rd)
- 1818 ...

(CD)

Robinson M. **Johnson**   **(EP)**
(Shoreham Plate Works)
Sheffield (1, Montgomery Rd)
- 1879 ...
1875 - 1879 ... (**& Co.**)
(See also figure: R M J & Co)

(WDS79)
(SAOR) (SBW)
(WDS79)

William **Johnson**   **(CU)**
Birmingham
1819 ...

(SAOR)

W. F. **Johnson** (EP) (E)
Leicester
~ 1890-1910
(See also figure: W. F. JOHNSON)

William J. **Johnston** (EP) (K80)
Carlisle (Brown Ln)
- 1880 ...

William F. **Johnstone** (EP) (GS) (MDG) (POB)
Birmingham (98, Gt. Hampton St)
- 1863 - 1867 ...

JOHN SYKES &C⁰

(See also) (CU/OSP)
John **Sykes & Co.**

Charles **Jones & Co.** (EP) (K80)
Ipswich (19 & 21, Nickolas St)
- 1880 ...

Henry **Jones & Co.** (CU/EP) (K72) (K78) (K80)
(Formerly: Derry & Jones) (K82) (K84) (K88)
Birmingham (55, Gt. Hampton St)
- 1872 - 1888 ...

Jones & Lempke (EP) (K36)
London (27, New Charles St)
- 1936 ...

Robert **Jones & Son** (EP) (PC)
Birmingham (105, Cheapside)
- 1896 ...

JONES

Charles **Jones** (CP) (B) (SAOR)
Birmingham (23, New St) (WDB) (PDB) (M)
- 1823 - 1828 ...

Arthur **Jones** (EP) (CDB)
Birmingham (Kenyon St)
- 1861 ...

C. **Jones** (EP) (SBW) (M)
Liverpool
~ 1880 *(See also figure: PILOT)*

Charles **Jones** (GS) (K93)
Sheffield (Boden Ln)
- 1893 ...

J

	Frederick **Jones** Sheffield (Ct. 5, St. Thomas St) - 1893 ...	**(GS)**	(K93)
	Henry **Jones** Birmingham (28, Northwood St) - 1849 - 1850 ...	**(EP)**	(HGDB) (HGD)
	Jonathan **Jones** Birmingham (56, Snowhill) - 1892 ...	**(EP)**	(K92)
	Richard **Jones** Birmingham (25, Ludgate Hill) - 1878 ...	**(EP)**	(K78)
	S. J. **Jones** Birmingham (29, Summer Rw/29, Gt. Charles St/20, George St) - 1861 - 1866 ...	**(EP)**	(GS) (CDB) (MDG)
	Thomas Charles **Jones** Birmingham (37, Branston St) - 1888 - 1903 ...	**(EP)**	(K88) (K92) (K03)
	J. **Jones**, H. **Greenway & Co.** **(OSP)** Sheffield (Holly's Croft) 1783 ... *(See also figure: HG&Co)*		(B) (SAOR)
JOR DAN	Thomas **Jordan** Sheffield 1814 ...	**(CP)**	(M) (B)
	Thomas J. **Jordan** Birmingham (Bordesley St/48, Whittall St) - 1818 - 1839 ...	**(CP)**	(WTD) (HTD) (WDB) (PDB) (WAB) (CD) (DOB) (WDOB)
	Joseph & Sons Birmingham (49, St. Paul's Sq) - 1863 ...	**(EP)**	(GS)
JOSEPH ASHFORTH & CO.	*(See also)* John James **Saville & Co.**	**(EP)**	
JOSEPH DEAKIN & SONS SHEFFIELD	*(See also)* Joseph **Deakin & Sons** **(Spring Street Works)**	**(EP)**	

JOSEPH ELLIOT & SONS CUTLERS, SHEFFIELD	*(See also)* Joseph **Elliot & Sons**	**(EP)**
JOSEPH FENTON&SONS SHEFFIELD	*(See also)* Joseph **Fenton & Sons** **(Sykes Works)**	**(EP)**
JOSEPH HAYWOOD&COMPY MANUFACTURES.SHEFFIELD	*(See also)* Joseph **Haywood & Co.** **gan Works)**	**(CU/EP)**
JOSEPH RIDGE & Co SHEFFIELD	*(See also)* Joseph **Ridge & Co.** **(Ridge, Allcard & Co)** **(Lion Works)**	**(EP)**
JOSEPH ROGERS & SONS SHEFFIELD E·P	*(See also)* Joseph **Rodgers & Sons** (George)	**(CU/CP/EP)**
JOSEPHUS SMITH	*(See also)* Josephus **Smith**	**(OSP)**
JOS ᴴ BEAL & SONS SHEFFIELD	*(See also)* Joseph **Beal & Sons**	**(CU/EP)**
JOS ᴴ LILLY	*(See also)* Joseph **Lilly**	**(CU)**
J.P & S	**Not assigned!**	**(EP)**
J. PETFIELD WICKER SHEFFIELD	*(See also)* Jackson **Petfield**	**(EP)**
J P & C⁰ J.P Paragon Metal &C⁰	*(See also)* James **Pinder & Co.** **(Colonial Plate Works)**	**(EP)**
J·Q&C⁰	*(See also)* J. **Quixall & Co.**	**(OSP)**
J.R&S ✷ ✠	*(See also)* Joseph **Rodgers & Sons** (George)	**(EP)**
J.R & S	*(See also)* John **Round &Son** **(Tudor Works & Arundel Works)**	**(EP)**

J

J. R. McC.	*(See also)* James Robert **McClelland**	**(EP)**
  J.R & C<u>o</u> 	*(See also)* Joseph **Ridge & Co.** **(Ridge, Allcard & Co)** **(Lion Works)**	**(EP)**
     	(See also) John **Round &Son** **(Tudor Works & Arundel Works)**	**(EP)**
	(See also) John **Rogers & Sons** (George)	**(CP/CU)**
	(See also) John **Roberts**	**(OSP)**
	(See also) Joseph **Rodgers & Sons** (George)	**(EP)**
	(See also) John **Round & Son** **(Truro Works/Arundel Works)**	**(EP)**
	(See also) James Rankine **Laing &** William **Laing**	**(EP)**
	(See also Jacob & Samuel **Roberts & Co.**	**(OSP/CU)**
J.S.&S.	*(See also)* John **Shaw & Sons Ltd.**	**(EP/CU)**
	(See also) Jacob & Samuel **Roberts & Co.**	**(OSP/CU)**
	Not assigned!	**(EP)**
	(See also) John **Askham**	**(CU/EP)**
	(See also) John **Sherwood & Sons** **(Regent Works)**	**(EP)**

J S ✳ S JS*S SHEFFIELD ENGLAND	*(See also)* John **Sanderson**	(EP)
J.S *J.S*	*(See also)* John **Smallwood**	(CP)
J S H & Co	**Not assigned!**	(EP)
JSMITH **EXTRA**	*(See also)* J. **Smith & Son**	(CU)
J S S EP NS	**Not assigned!**	(EP)
J & T S	*(See also)* John **Jenkins &** Herbert **Timm** **(Pensilvia Works)**	(EP)
J.T **T.T**	*(See also)* **Towndrow Brothers**	(EP)
J T & Co S J.T&CoLᴰS **J T & Co LD**	*(See also)* John **Turton & Co.**	(EP)
J T & S	*(See also)* John **Townroe & Sons**	(EP)
JT	**Not assigned!**	(EP)
JT S ✗ EP	*(See also)* John **Turton & Co.**	(EP)
J T M L 𝕄𝕋	*(See also)* James **Tidmarsh**	(EP)
	Judd & Co. London *~ (See also figure: THE CYPRUS)*	(EP) (M) (SBW)
	John W. **Judge** Sheffield (55, Trippet Ln/50, Highton St) - 1905 ...	(EP) (WDSR)
	John **Jukes** sen. Birmingham (New St) - 1818 ...	(CU/CP) (WTD)

J

	Paris **Justice**	**(OSP)** [B] [SAOR]
	Sheffield (Spring Croft)	
	1774 ... *(See also figure: P·J)*	

J.W.Benson Scan	*(See also)* J. W. **Benson Ltd.** **(Empire Plate)**	**(EP)**
J·W·T	*(See also)* James Walter **Tiptaft**	**(EP)**
J·W **E·H**	*(See also)* John **Waterhouse, Hatfield & Co.**	**(OSP)**
J·WOLSTENHOLME SHEFFIELD	*(See also)* Joseph **Wolstenholme**	**(BM)**
⚓ **J** **W** ⚓	*(See also)* Joseph **Willmore**	**(OSP)**
J ⚓ **W** **S** **EP** **J** **W** ✷ ✷	Not assigned!	**(EP)**
J·Y·C	*(See also)* John Y. **Cowlishaw**	**(EP)**
J. YATES & SONS	*(See also)* John **Yates & Son(s)**	**(CU/EP)**
J **Y** **&** **S** **YS** **J** **Y** **&** **S** **A** **J Y & S** **J** **YATES** **&SONS**	*(See also)* John **Yates & Son(s)**	**(CU/EP)**

J

K & Cº EP	Not assigned! ~ 1867 ...	**(EP)**	(Diamond)
K & M	Not assigned!	**(EP)**	(E)
K&P 🌼 G **K&P G EP**	*(See also)* Alfred **Kleinwort &** Percy **Peerless**	**(EP)**	(M)
K & W	*(See also)* **Kitchen & Walker**	**(OSP)**	
K·B	Not assigned!	**(EP)**	
K 9	*(See also)* Edgar **Allen & Co.** **(Well Meadow Steel Works)**	**(CU)**	
	Mrs. Sarah **Kain** Birmingham (55, Clement St) - 1892 ...	**(EP)**	(K92)
	H. **Kalckhoff** Birmingham (69, Warstone Ln) - 1936 ...	**(EP)**	(K36)
KANGAROO	*(See also)* Robert **Sorby & Sons Ltd.**	**(EP)**	
" KARANTI SILVER "	*(See also)* **Levetus Brothers**	**(EP)**	
	John **Kay** Sheffield (Meadow St) 1804 ... *(See also figure: I.K)* 1795 ... *(See also figure: I.KAY&Co)*	**(OSP)**	(B) (SAOR) (B) (SAOR)
	Kayser, Ellison & Co. **(Carlisle Works)** *(Formerly: Wilson, Hawksworth, Ellison & Co.)* Sheffield (Carlisle St/Sutherland St) - 1893 ... - 1901 (**Ltd.**) *(See also figures:* *AQUA, symbol "padlock")*	**(CU)**	(W) (K93 AD) (WDS01)

K

Ann **Keeling** **(EP)** (K78) (K80) (K82) (K84)
Birmingham (6, Richard St/103, Spencer St)
- 1878 - 1884 ...

Keep Brothers **(EP)** (SBW)
Birmingham
~ *(See also figure: STERLING L BRAND)*

KELK

Charles **Kelk** **(OSP)** (B)
Sheffield (Spring St)
1775 ...

Charles **Kelk** **(OSP)** (WTDB)
Birmingham (Pinfold St)
- 1815 ...

Albert & Azariah **Kelly** **(EP)** (K80) (K82)
Birmingham (87, New John St)
- 1880 - 1884 ...

Abraham **Kemisch** **(EP)** (K72)
Birmingham (38, Longmore St)
- 1872 ...

Edward **Kemish** **(BM)** (WDOB) (GS) (MDG)
Birmingham (Shallow St/68, Graham St/
Clement St)
- 1839 - 1866 ...

James Henry **Kemish** **(BM/EP)** (BDB) (MDG) (K72) (K80) (K82) (K84) (K88) (K92) (PC) (K03)
Birmingham (174, Newhall St/Mount St/
69 and then 5, Graham St)
- 1862 - 1903 ...

Abraham **Kemp** **(EP)**
Birmingham (Tenby St North/Warstone Ln)
1842 - 1854 ...
- 1882 - 1888 ... **(& Son)** (SAOR) (SI)
(See also figure: A K) (K82AD) (K88 AD)

Charles **Kemp** **(BM/GS)** (HGD)
Birmingham (111, Hampton St)
- 1850 ...

Josiah **Kemp** **(OSP)** (B) (SAOR)
Sheffield (Norfolk St)
1779 ... *(See also figure: I·N·K)*

KEMP BRO<u>S</u> UNION S<u>T</u> BRISTOL	**Kemp Brothers** (EP) [E] Bristol (Union St) ~ 1890 ... *(See also figure: K^p Bros)*	

Peter **Kempson** (CU/OSP) [SAOR]
Birmingham
1820 ...

KENDAL & DENT CHEAPSIDE	**Kendal & Dent** (EP) London (106, Cheapside) ~ 1883 ...	

John **Kendall & Co.** (EP) [PC]
Birmingham (18, Albion St)
- 1896 ...

William **Kendrick** (CP/EP)
Birmingham (40, Blucher St/16, Bull Ring)
1828 - 1849 ...   [SAOR] [HGDB]
- 1829 - 1830 ... (**& Co.**)   [WAB] [HTD]

Kennedy & Asprey (CU/CP)
London
1841 - 1843
(Then: Charles Asprey)

Arthur **Kennerley** (EP) [WDS01]
Sheffield (20, Clarke St)
- 1901 ...

Kent Brothers Ltd. (EP) [K36]
Sheffield (168, Broad Ln)
- 1936 ...

KENTPLATE	**Not assigned!** (EP) [E] ~ 1959 ...	

Thomas **Kettle** (OSP) [SAOR] [CD]
Birmingham (22 and then 99, Suffolk St)   [PDB]
- 1818 - 1825 ...

Kidd & Bensly (EP) [K80] [K82]
Birmingham (Alfred St/Warstone Ln)
- 1880 - 1882 ...

Kidd & Elmer (EP) [K84] [K88]
Birmingham (Alfred St/Warstone Ln)
- 1884 - 1888 ...

K

Edward **Kidd** Birmingham (4, Bath Rw) - 1861 - 1878 - 1880 ... (**& Co.**)	**(EP)**	(CDB) (BDB) (MDG) (POB) (K72) (K78) (K80)
William **Kilminster** Sheffieldf (1, New George St) - 1841 ...	**(OSP)**	(DSRR)
John **King & Co.** Birmingham (286 and then 45, Icknield St) - 1882 - 1896 ...	**(EP)**	(K82) (K84) (K88) (K92) (PC)
KINGSLEY PLATE *(See also)* Walter **Belk & Son** (**Kingsley Works**)	**(EP)**	
KINGSWAY PLATE *(See also)* William **Suckling Ltd.**	**(EP)**	
KINGTONS METAL *(See also)* **Levetus Brothers**	**(EP)**	
Robert **Kippax & Co.** Sheffield (High St) 1774 ... *(See also figures: R·K, R·K&CO)*	**(OSP)**	(B) (SAOR)
Kippax & Nowill Sheffield (High St) 1813 ...	**(T)**	(B)
KIRBY.BEARD&C\underline{o}L\underline{p} **Kirby, Beard & Co. Ltd.** Birmingham/Redditch ~ 1897 ...	**(OSP)**	(M)
Gregory **Kirbys & Co.** Sheffield (18, Carver St) - 1825 - 1833 ...	**(OSP)**	(NGDS) (SDG) (PD) (GDS)
Samuel **Kirkby & Co.** Sheffield (Pond St/Blackfield) 1794 ... *(See also figure: S·K)* 1796 ... *(See also figure: SK&Co)* 1812 ... *(See also figure: S.K&Co)*	**(OSP)**	(B) (SAOR) (SAOR)
Joseph **Kirkby & Son** Sheffield (124, Rockingham St) - 1846 ...	**(CP/CU)**	(SD46)

K

Arthur **Kirkby** **(EP)** (WDS01)
Sheffield (77, Harcourt Rw)
- 1901 ...

James **Kirkby** **(OSP)**
Sheffield
1800 ... (Lambert St) (B) (SAOR)
(See also figure: IK) (SAOR)
1809 ... (Moor) *(See also figure:I·K)* (SAOR)
1808 ... **(& Co.)**

Mary **Kirkby** **(OSP)** (B) (SAOR)
Sheffield (Brinsworth Orchard)
1780 .. *(See also figure: M·K)*

Samuel & W. **Kirkby** **(CU/OSP)** (B) (SAOR)
Sheffield (High St/Duke Ln/Eyre St) (NGDS) (GDS)
1821 - 1837 ... *(See also figure: SK)* (WDS37)

KIRKBY
FOR·USE

Samuel **Kirkby** **(OSP)** (B) (M)
Sheffield (Carver Ln)
1812 ...

J. **Kirkby, Gregory & Co.** **(OSP)** (B) (SAOR)
Sheffield (Carver St)
1822 ... *(See also figure: I·K&Co)*

J. **Kirkby,** J. **Waterhouse & Co. (OSP)** (B) (SAOR) (CD)
Sheffield (Backfields/Carver St) (HDG) (PDY)
1793 - 1822 ...
(See also figures: IK·IW&Co,
KW&Co)

K

J. **Kirkby,** J. **Waterhouse &** J. **Hodgson** (B)
Sheffield (Carver St) **(OSP)**
1808 ... *(See also figure: JK&Co)*

Thomas (Theophilus) **Kirkham** **(CP)** (SAOR) (WAB)
Birmingham (31, Cannon St/13, Cherry St) (HTD) (WWDB)
1828 - 1839 ... (WDOB)

Kitchen & Co. **(BM)** (GDS)
Sheffield (Green Ln)
- 1833 ...

Kitchen & Walker **(OSP)** (B) (SAOR)
Sheffield (Burgess St)
1835 ... *(See also figure: K&W)*

George **Kitchen** **(OSP)** (NGDS)
Sheffield (5, Gell St)
- 1825 ...

Thomas **Kitchen** **(OSP)** (B) (SAOR)
Chesterfield (Dog Hole)
1810 ... *(See also figure: T.H*)

Kitchen, Walker & Curr **(OSP)** (B) (SAOR) (GDS)
Sheffield (Union St/18 & 25, Burgess St)
1832 - 1833 ... *(See also figure: KW&C)*

Samuel & J. **Kitchin** **(CU)** (K72AD) (K88AD)
(Soho Cutlery Works) (WDS01)
(Formerly: Samuel Kitchin)
Sheffield (Summerfield St)
- 1872 - 1901 ...
(See also figure: Samuel Kitchin)

George **Kitching** **(OSP)** (GDS)
Sheffield (18, Gell St)
- 1833 ...

Alfred **Kleinwort &** Percy **Peerless (EP)** (M)
London
1895 ... *(See also figure: K&P)*

George **Knight** **(EP)** (K80)
Somerset/Yeovil (Middle St)
- 1880 ...

Walter F. **Knight** **(EP)** (K36)
Wellingborough (Stanley Rd)
- 1936 ...

Knight Brothers **(EP)** (K80)
Sheffield (28, Burgess St)
- 1880 ...

William **Knott** **(EP)**
(Arundel Works) (WDS01) (WDSR)
Sheffield (108, Brown Ln/108, Arundel Ln/ (WDS11)
85, Woodland St)
- 1901 - 1911 ...

John **Knowles & Son** **(EP)** (B) (M) (SAOR)
Sheffield (Burgess St)
1860 ... *(See also figure: IK&S)*

George **Knowles** (EP) ^{(POS) (K54)}
Sheffield (29, South St)
- 1854 ...

William **Knowles** (OSP) ^(GDS)
Sheffield (39, Howard St)
- 1833 ...

K^P BRO^S A1 *(See also)* (EP)
Kemp Brothers

Samuel **Krinks** (EP) ^{(K82) (K84)}
Birmingham (1, Alfred St/Warstone Ln)
- 1882 - 1884 ...

KW &C *(See also)* (OSP)
Kitchen, Walker & Curr

KW&C^O *(See also)* (OSP)
J. **Kirkby,** J. **Waterhouse & Co**

◇ 🔫 ⌐	*(See also)* Jonathan **Crookes & Son**	**(CU)**
L&B	*(See also)* **Larder & Burgess**	**(EP)**
𝕷&𝕭 **L**&**B**	*(See also)* **Lingard & Baker**	**(EP)**
✠ L & Co	*(See also)* Thomas **Law & Co.**	**(CU)**
L&CO **L & Cᵒ**	Arthur Lasemby **Liberty & Co.** London 1875 -1894 1894 - 1920 ... (**Ltd.**)	**(EP)**
L&J **S**	**Not assigned!**	**(EP)**
L&M	*(See also)* **Lee & Middleton**	**(CU)**
L **W** **&** **S** L&W E.P.N.S A.I. **L&W** **S** ⚓ **EP** **L** & **W** **S** L & W . S E.P.B.M. **L** & **W** **Lᴰ**	*(See also)* George Shadford **Lee &** Henry **Wigfull Ltd.** **(John Street Works)**	**(BM/EP)**
L·M	*(See also)* L. **Marriott**	**(OSP)**
	James Rankine **Laing &** William **Laing (EP)** Glasgow 1900 - 1914 (**See also figure: JR WL**)	
	Lamb & Steeley **(EP)** Birmingham (2, Mary Ann St) - 1866 - 1872 ...	(MDG) (K72)

L

Thomas **Lamborn**   **(OSP)**   (B) (SAOR)
Sheffield (Milk St)
1776 ... *(See also figure: TL)*

Land & Oxley   **(EP)**   (K93)
(Nimrod Works)
Sheffield (Eldon St)
- 1893 ...

Thomas **Land**   **(EP)**
(Colonial Works)
Sheffield (13, Cheney Rw /107, Trafalgar St/
Queens Rd)
- 1879 ...   (WDS79)
1901 - 1908 (**& Sons**)   (WDS01)
1909 - 1952 (**Ltd.**)   (K36) (M) (W)
(See also figures: CIVIC, TL&SS)
(Then: E.H. Parkin)

Edwin **Lander & Co.**   **(EP)**   (SBW) (M)
Birmingham
~ *(See also figure: GLORIUS)*

James **Lander**   **(CP)**   (WTDB) (WTD)
Birmingham (Bartholomew Rw)   (CD)
- 1815 - 1818 ...

Richard **Lander**   **(CP)**   (WTDB)
Birmingham (Slaney St)
- 1815 ...

William **Lander**   **(CU)**   (SAOR)
Birmingham
1815 ...

Joyce **Lane**   **(CP)**   (WAB)
Birmingham (14, Bell St)
- 1829 ...

William **Lane**   **(CP)**   (CD) (WDB)
Birmingham (17, Bell St)   (PDB)
- 1818 - 1825 ...

William **Langford & Sons**   **(EP)**   (K80)
Bristol (40, College Green)
- 1880 ...

L

John **Langford**	**(BM)**	(MDG) (K80) (K82) (K84) (K88) (K92)
Birmingham (24, Coleshill)		
- 1866 - 1892 ...		

Samuel Edwin **Lang(s)ton**	**(EP)**	(CDB) (BDB) (MDG) (K72)
Birmingham (54 and then 46, Buckingham St/ 15, Vittoria St)		
- 1861 - 1872 ...		

Lanson Ltd.	**(EP)**	(S)
(St. Dunstan Works)		
Birmingham (Pemberton St)		
1933 - 1961 *(See also figure: L. Ltd.)*		

(LA P)	**Not assigned!**	**(EP/CU)**	(E) (Fishcutlery)

Larder & Burgess	**(EP)**	(WDS01) (K36)
Sheffield (90, Mary St/144, Eyre St/Matilda St/ Regent St)		
- 1901 - 1936 ...		
(See figures: ADMIRAL, L&B)		

Walter **Latham & Co.**	**(EP)**	(WDSR)
(Walter **Latham & Son**)		
(Brocco Works)		
Sheffield (71, Rustling Rd/186, Solly St)		
- 1905 ...		

Thomas **Latham &** Ernest **Morton (EP)**		(K72) (K78) (K80) (K82) (K84) (K88) (K92) (Rd 200567) (PC)
Birmingham (83/115, Caroline St/115 & 116, Vyse St)		
- 1872 - 1896 ...		
1915 ... **(Ltd.)**		
(See also figure: TL&EM)		

Thomas **Latham**	**(CU/OSP)**	(SAOR)
Birmingham		
1821 ...		

James **Laughton**	**(CP)**	(DOB) (WWDB) (WDOB)
Birmingham (119, Up. Tower St/8, St. Paul's Sq)		
- 1833 - 1839 ...		

Lauterbach & Wilding	**(EP)**	(K03)
Birmingham (113, Branston St)		
- 1903 ...		

L

✠ LAW	Thomas **Law & Co.** (CU) Sheffield (Norfolk St) 1774 - 1791 ... *(See also figures: ARGENT LAX, L&Co)*	(B) (GM) (UBD)
LAW&SON	John **Law & Son** (OSP) Sheffield 1807 - 1824 *(Then: J. Law, Atkid & Oxley)*	(M) (B) (NGDS)
	George **Law** (EP) Birmingham (Ct 9, Tower St) - 1866 - 1878 ...	(MDG) (K72) (K78)
	James **Law** (FP) Birmingham (274, Cheapside) - 1829 - 1833 ...	(WAB) (HTD) (DOB)
	John **Law** (FP) Birmingham (23, Navigation St) - 1829 - 1833 ...	(WAB) (DOB)
	John **Law** (OSP) Sheffield (Howard St) 1790 ... *(See also figure: I·L)*	(B) (SAOR)
	Joseph **Law** (OSP) Sheffield (Church Ln) 1824 ... *(See also figure: I·L)*	(B) (SAOR)
	R. **Law** (OSP) Sheffield 1807 ... *(See also figure: R.LAW.)*	(M) (B)
	Thomas **Law** (OSP) Sheffield 1758 - 1773 ...*(See also figure: TL LAW)*	(B) (SAOR) (M)
	J. **Law, Atkid & Oxley** (CU/OSP) *(Formerly: John Law & Son)* Sheffield (100, Eyre St) 1824 - 1829 ... *(See also figure: LL)*	(B) (PD) (SAOR) (NGDS)
	Sambrook **Lawley** (EP) Birmingham (197, Aston Rd) - 1872 - 1880 ...	(K72) (K80)

L

	Samuel **Lawley**	**(EP)**	(CDB) (POB)
	Birmingham (197, Aston Rd)		
	- 1861 - 1867 ..		
	John **Lawrence & Co.**	**(CU/OSP)**	(SAOR)
	Birmingham		
	1813 ...		
	Lawrence & Son	**(EP)**	(K72) (K78)
	Birmingham (8, Luisa St)		
	- 1872 - 1878 ...		
	Lawson & Holden	**(EP)**	(HGDB)
	Birmingham (147, Gt. Charles St)		
	- 1849 ...		
	Lawson, Rankin & Co.	**(EP)**	(K80)
	Glasgow (85, Buchanan St)		
	- 1880 ...		
LAXEY SILVER	*(See also)*	**(EP)**	
	Thomas H. **Daniel &** Thomas R. **Arter**		
	(Globe Nevada Silver Works)		
	Laycock Brothers	**(EP/CU)**	(WDS79)
	Sheffield (17, New Church St)		
	- 1879 ... *(See also figure: T.W.)*		
L.B.S.Cº	*(See also)*	**(EP)**	
	Lawrence B. **Smith & Co.**		
🅛 🅑&🅛 ✠ 🅢	*(See also)*	**(EP)**	
	Levesley Brothers & Lloyd		
⬤🅑 ✠ 🅢	*(See also)*	**(EP)**	
	Levesley Brothers		
	(Central Works)		
LB	*(See also)*	**(OSP)**	
	L. **Brownell**		
LB	*(See also)*	**(EP)**	
	Levesley Brothers		
	(Central Works)		
LB	*(See also)*	**(EP)**	
	Lockwood Brothers		

L

252

L BRS

(See also)
Levesley Brothers
(Central Works)
(EP)

A.C. **Lea** (OSP) (B) (M)
Birmingham
1808 ... *(See also figure: AC LEA)*

Thomas **Leadbeater** (CU/CP) (WDB) (PDB)
Birmingham (40, Barford St)
- 1823 - 1825 ...

Daniel **Leader** (OSP) (B) (SAOR)
Sheffield (Surrey St)
1797 ... *(See also figure: DL)*

Thomas & Daniel **Leader** (OSP) (B) (SAOR)
Sheffield (Surrey St)
1798 ... *(See also figure: TLDL)*

John **Leather** (CP) (WWDB) (WDOB)
Birmingham (Cardigan St/Howe St)
- 1835 - 1839 ...

E. **Leclere** (EP)
Sheffield (56, Howard St)
~ 1870 ...
(See also figure: E.LECLERE)

Ledsam & Vale (CU) (SAOR)
Birmingham
1818 ...

Daniel **Ledsam** (BM) (WAB)
Birmingham (Edmund St)
- 1829 ...

John **Ledward** (CP) (WAB) (HTD) (DOB)
Birmingham (Mount St/33, Mott St)
- 1829 - 1833 ...

R. **Ledward** (OSP) (WWDB)
Birmingham (33, Mott St)
- 1835 ...

George **Lee & Co.** (BM/EP) (K93) (WDS01) (WDSR) (M)
Sheffield (87, Eldon St)
- 1893 - 1905 ... *(See also figure:*
G.L.&Co)

L

	Henry **Lee & Co.** (CU)	(SD46)
	Sheffield (21, New Church St)	
	- 1846 ...	
	James **Lee & Co.** (BM/EP)	(WDS79) (K80)
	Sheffield (87, Eldon St)	
	- 1879 - 1880 ...	
LEE & COMPY ELECTRO PLATE SHEFFIELD	*(See also)* (EP) **Lee, White & Co.**	
	Lee & Middleton (CU)	(B) (SAOR) (DSRR) (SBW) (M)
	Sheffield (12, Mulberry St)	
	1840 - 1841 ... *(See also figure: L&M)*	
LEE & WIGFULL (SHEFFIELD) L^{TD} MADE IN SHEFFIELD	George Shadford **Lee &** Henry **Wigfull Ltd. (John Street Works)** (CU/BM/EP)	(SAOR) (K80) (K93) (WDS01) (WDSR) (SBW) (M) (Rd 225792)
	Sheffield (John St)	
	London (Holborn Viaduct)	
	1879 - 1968	
	(See also figures: ALBION, L & W, INSIGNIA)	
	George Shadford **Lee** (EP)	(M)
	Sheffield	
	~ 1864 ... *(See also figure: GSL *)*	
	James Thomas **Lee** (EP)	(K80)
	Birmingham (169, Hockley Hill)	
	- 1880 ...	
	William **Lee (Shrewsbury Works)** (EP)	(K82) (K84)
	Birmingham (Vittoria St)	
	- 1882 - 1884 ...	
	Lee, White & Co. (EP)	(M)
	Sheffield	
	~ 1886 ... *(See also figure: LEE & COMPY)*	
	Leeds & Birmingham Plating Co. (EP)	(K93)
	Leeds (32, Gt. George St)	
	- 1893 ...	
	(See also) (EP)	
	Frederick Ewbank **Leefe**	

L

	E. & J. **Leek Ltd.** (EP) London (12 & 13, Hatton Garden) - 1936 ...	(K36)
	Lees & Patrick (BM) Birmingham (85, Hospital St) - 1850 ...	(HGD)
	Samuel **Lees & Son** (EP) Birmingham (108 and then 61, Barr St) - 1872 - 1892 ...	(K72) (K82) (K84) (K88) (K92)
	William **Lees & Son** (EP) Birmingham (108 and then 61, Barr St) - 1878 - 1936 ...	(K78) (K80) (PC) (K36)
LEES	George **Lees** (CP) Birmingham (45, Park St) 1811 - 1825 ... *(See also figure: I I I)*	(WDB) (PDB) (M) (B)
	George Philip **Lempriere** (EP) Birmingham (42, Spencer St) - 1882 - 1884 ...	(K82) (K84)
	Patrick **Leonard** (OSP) Manchester (Salford) 1835 ... *(See also figure: PL)*	(B) (SAOR)
L' ÉSPAGNE	*(See also)* (CU/OSP) **Ashforth, Ellis & Co.**	
	Levesley Brothers (EP) **(Levesley Brothers & Lloyd)** **(Central Works)** Sheffield (West St/76 then 62, Mary St/ 203, Arundel St) 1863 - 1936 ... *(See also figures: LB, CLTL, LB*S, L Brs)*	(B) (K80) (K93) (WDS01) (K36) (SBW)
	Levesley Brothers & Lloyd (EP) Sheffield ~ 1895 ... *(See also figure: LB& L)*	

L

	Levetus Brothers **(EP)**	(K80AD) (K88) (K92) (PC) (M)
	(Canada Works)	
	Birmingham (68 & 70/47, Vittoria St)	
	- 1880 - 1896 ... *(See also figures: KA-RANTI, KINGTONS METAL)*	

	S. J. **Levi & Co.** **(EP)**	
	(Squirrel Works)	
	Birmingham (23, Regent Pl)	
	- 1897 - 1935 ...	(E) (K36)
	1936 ... **(Ltd.)**	
	(See also figures: S.J.L & Co., LEVIATHAN PLATE, symbol "squirrel")	

Levi & Salaman	**(EP)**
Birmingham	
- 1878	
(Then: Potosi Co)	

LEVIANTHAN.	*(See also)* **(EP)**
	John **James & Sons**
	(Victoria Works)

LEVIATHAN PLATE	*(See also)* **(EP)**
	S. J. **Levi & Co.**
	(Squirrel Works)

	James **Lewis & Sons** **(EP)**
	Sheffield (149, London Rd)
	1894 - 1909
	(See also figure: J L & S)

	Lewis, Rose & Co. Ltd. **(EP)**	(K36)
	Sheffield (Norfolk St)	
	- 1936 ...	
	(See also figures: LR, symbol "rose")	

LIBERTY **MADE IN ENGLAND**	Arthur Lasemby **Liberty & Co.** **(EP)**
	London
	1875 -1894 *(See also figure: L&Co)*
	1894 - 1920 ... **(Ltd.)**

LIFE	*(See also)* **(EP)**
	John Francis **Townsend**

	John **Lilly & Son** **(CP)**	(SAOR) (WDB) (PDB) (WAB)
	(John **Lilly &** William B. **Lilly)**	
	Birmingham (23, St. Paul's Sq)	
	- 1823 - 1829 ...	

LILLY	Joseph **Lilly (Lilley)** **(CP/CU)**	(WTDB) (WTD) (WDB) (PDB) (CD)
	Birmingham (32, Fordrough St)	
	- 1815 - 1825 ...	
	(See also figure: JOSH LILLY)	

LILLY	John **Lilly** jun. **(CP)**	(SAOR) (WTD) (WWDB) (DOB) (CD) (B) (WDOB)
	Birmingham (St. Paul's Sq)	
	1815 - 1839 ...	

	R. & J. **Linacre** **(CU)**	(K88) (AD)
	(Cobnar Works)	
	Sheffield	
	- 1888 ...	

LINDER FEARNLEY SHEFFIELD	*(See also)* **(EP)**	
	Linder **Fearnley**	

	John **Lindley & Co.** **(OSP)**	(SAOR)
	Sheffield	
	1788 ...	

	Alfred **Lindley** **(BM/EP)**	(K93)
	(Richmond Works)	
	Sheffield (99, Napier St/25-27, Eyre St)	
	1881 - 1893 ...	
	(See also figures: Alfred Lindley, AL*S)	

	W. **Lindrop & Sons** **(EP)**	(K36)
	Stoke-on-Trent (Trafalgar St)	
	- 1936 ...	

LINDSAY & PAISLEY L<u>D</u> GLASGOW	**Lindsay & Paisley Ltd.** **(EP)**	
	Glasgow (Gordan St)	
	1898 - 1936	
	(See also figure: LUNAR PLATE)	

	John **Linegar** **(EP)**	(CDB) (BDB) (GS) (POB) (K80) (K82) (K84) (K88) (K92) (PC)
	Birmingham (62, Constitution Hill /71/107, Vyse St/63 & 64, Spencer St)	
	- 1861 - 1896 ...	

Benjamin **Lines & Son**　　**(GS)**　^(K92)
Birmingham (71 & 73, Vittoria St)
- 1892 ...

Lines, Bunn & Mason　　**(EP)**　^(PC)
Birmingham (62, Hockley St)
- 1896 ...

Lingard & Baker　　**(EP)**　(MDG) (K72)
(K78) (K80) (K82)
Birmingham (52, Gt. Hampton St/33, Powell St)　(K84) (K88) (K92)
- 1866 - 1896 ... *(See also figure: L&B)*　(M) (PC)

Lingard & Hackwood　　**(EP)**　(K92) (PC)
Birmingham (Tenby St North/47, Vyse St)
- 1892 - 1896 ...

George **Lingard**　　**(EP)**　^(K88)
Birmingham (Tenby St North)
- 1888 ...

John **Lingard**　　**(EP)**　(K82) (K84)
Birmingham (188, Gt. Hampton Rw)
- 1882 - 1884 ...

Thomas **Ling(h)en**　　**(CP)**　(WDB) (PDB)
(DOB)
Birmingham (38, Newhall St)
- 1823 - 1833 ...

J. **Linley & Co.**　　**(OSP)**　^(B)
Sheffield (Spring Croft)
1788 ... *(See also figure: I·L&Co)*

James **Linley**　　**(OSP)**　^(PD)
Sheffield (Workhouse Croft)
- 1829 ...

John **Linley**　　**(EP)**　^(MDG)
Birmingham (107, Vyse St)
- 1866 ...

S. & R. **Linley**　　**(CU)**　(K88) (AD)
(Clough Works)
Sheffield
1772 - 1888 ... *(See also figure: OLD O)*

William **Linley**　　**(OSP)**　(B) (SAOR)
Sheffield (Lambert St)
1797 ... *(See also figure: W·L)*

LIN WOOD	William **Linsley** Birmingham 1817 ...	**(CU)**	(SAOR)
	Matthew **Linwood & Sons** Birmingham (Edmund St) 1808 - 1815 ...	**(CP)**	(B) (SAOR) (WTDB)
	John **Linwood** Birmingham (57, St. Paul's Sq) 1807 - 1833 ... *(See also figure: I LIN WOOD)*	**(CP)**	(WTD) (WTDB) (WDB) (PDB) (M) (CD) (B) (DOB)
	Matthew **Linwood** Birmingham (New Hall St) - 1818 ...	**(OSP)**	(WTD) (CD)
	W. **Linwood** Birmingham 1807 ... *(See also figure: W.LINWOOD)*	**(CP)**	(M) (B)
	Lion Works Ltd. *(Formerly: Hammond Turner Ltd.)* Birmingham (Summerhill) - 1936 ...	**(EP)**	(K36)
	Lister & Knowles **(Progress Works)** Sheffield (Matilda St) - 1872 ...	**(CU)**	(K72) AD
	J. **Litchfield** Birmingham (29, Watery Ln) - 1866 ...	**(EP)**	(MDG)
	Litherland & Newbold Birmingham (18, Smallbrook St) - 1829 - 1830 ...	**(CP)**	(WAB) (HTD)
	John Alfred **Little & Sons** Liverpool (12, Bold St) - 1880 ...	**(EP)**	(K80)
	Jonathan **Littlewood** Sheffield (Westbar Green) 1773 ... *(See also figures: I·L, JL)*	**(OSP)**	(B) (M) (SAOR)

L

L . L ᵀᴰ	*(See also)* **Lanson Ltd. (St. Dunstan Works)**	**(EP)**
LL	*(See also)* J. **Law, Atkid & Oxley**	**(OSP)**
	Llewelyn & Ryland Birmingham (Prospect Rw) - 1823 - 1839 ...	**(BM)** (WDB) (PDB) (WAB) (DOB) (WDOB)
LLOYD DAVIES German Steel	*(See also)* **Spear & Jackson**	**(CP)**
	William **Lock** Birmingham (12, Whittall St/141, Hockley Hill) - 1863 - 1880 ...	**(EP)** (GS) (K80)
LOCKHART & READING	**Not assigned!**	**(EP)**
LOCKWOOD BROTHERS	**Lockwood Brothers (Spital Hill Works)** Sheffield (74, Arundel St/Spital Hill) 1855 - 1880 ... - 1881 - 1901 ... **(Ltd.)** *(See also figures: LB, +CX +, Pampa, Monkey , REAL PAMPA KNIFE, ROBT. BAXTER & Co., I. & H. SORBY)*	**(CU/EP)** (B) (SAOR) (K72) AD (K80) (SBW) (M) (WDS01)
	James **Lodge (Cambridge Works)** Sheffield (216, Solly St) - 1936 ...	**(EP)** (K36)
	H. G. **Long & Co.** Sheffield ~ 1890 ... *(See also figure: HGL&Co)*	**(EP)** (M)
	Jno. **Longford** Birmingham (24, Coleshill St) - 1850 ...	**(BM)** (HGD)
	Edmund **Lonsdale (Victoria Works)** Sheffield (Portobello St) - 1880 ...	**(EP)** (K80)

L

Londsdale Silver Plate	***(See also)*** A. E. **Posten & Co. Ltd.**	**(EP)**	
	M. & S. **Lotheim** Birmingham (35, Vittoria St) - 1896 ...	**(EP)**	(PC)
	Morton **Love & Co.** Sheffield - 1791 ...	**(OSP)**	(UBD)
	J. **Love & Darby & Co.** Sheffield (Pea Croft) - 1787 ... ***(See also figure: I.LOVE & Co)***	**(OSP)**	(GM) (M)
LOVE ←NER	***(See also)*** Thomas **Barnes & Sons**	**(CU)**	(W)
LOVE SILVERSIDE DARBY & Cº	J. **Love & Co.** **(Love, Silverside, Darby & Co)** Sheffield (Pea Croft) 1783 - 1805 ... ***(See also figures: IL&Co., OVE, SILVERSIDE&Co, I.LOVE&Co)***	**(OSP)**	(SAOR) (GM) (M) (B)
	Samuel **Lowbridge** Birmingham (Old Summer St/9, Unett St) - 1839 - 1849 ...	**(EP)**	(WDOB) (HGDB)
	George **Lowe** Birmingham (61, Graham St) - 1880 ...	**(EP)**	(K80)
	Isaac **Lowe** Birmingham (21, Lower Priory) - 1833 - 1839 ...	**(CU)**	(DOB) (WWDB) (WDOB)
	J. & H. **Lowe** Birmingham (34, Fordrough St) - 1849 - 1850 ...	**(CU/EP)**	(HGDB) (HGD)
	Richard **Lowe** Birmingham - 1823 ...	**(CP)**	(WDB)
	Thomas **Lowe** Birmingham (21, Gt. Charles St/Church St) - 1825 - 1839 ...	**(CP)**	(PDB) (DOB) (WWDB) (WDOB)

T. P. **Lowe**	**(OSP)**	(SAOR) (SBW) (B)

T. P. **Lowe**   **(OSP)**   (SAOR) (SBW) (B)
Sheffield (Charles St)
1840 ... *(See also figure: TPL)*

William **Lowe**   **(Coach/CP)**   (WTDB) (WDB) (PDB) (WDOB)
Birmingham (Bartholomew St/15, Castle St)
- 1815 - 1839 ...

William **Lowe** jun.   **(CP)**   (WDB)
Birmingham
- 1823 ...

Robert **Loxley**   **(EP)**   (WDS71)
Sheffield (Nottingham Rd)
- 1871 ...

Richard **Loy**   **(OSP/CU)**   (B) (SAOR)
Sheffield
1792 ...*(See also figures: ALVA, R·L, R.LOY)*

L·P &C⁰   *(See also)*   **(OSP)**
L. **Proctor & Co.**

LR&C⁰   **Not assigned!**   **(EP)**
Sheffield

L R.S.EPNS   **Not assigned!**   **(EP)**

LR   *(See also)*   **(EP)**
Lewis, Rose & Co. Ltd.

⟨£ s d⟩   *(See also)*   **(CU)**
Edgar **Allen & Co.**
(Well Meadow Steel Works)

𝕷 𝕿 𝕮⁰   **Not assigned!**   **(EP)**

Lucas & Tyzak   **(EP)**   (CDB)
Birmingham (124, Gt. Hampton St)
- 1861 ...

L. **Lucas**   **(EP)**   (K36)
Birmingham (53, Northampton St)
- 1936 ...

	Thomas **Lucas** Birmingham (66, Caroline St) - 1862 - 1866 ...	**(EP)** ^{(BDB) (MDG)}
	William **Lucas** Birmingham (18, Buckingham St) - 1849 - 1850 ...	**(EP)** ^{(HGDB) (HGD)}
LUNAR PLATE	*(See also)* **Lindsay & Paisley Ltd.**	**(EP)**
L&W.S	**Not assigned!**	**(EP)**

Thomas **Lucas** (EP) (BDB) (MDG)
Birmingham (66, Caroline St)
- 1862 - 1866 ...

William **Lucas** (EP) (HGDB) (HGD)
Birmingham (18, Buckingham St)
- 1849 - 1850 ...

LUNAR PLATE   *(See also)* (EP)
Lindsay & Paisley Ltd.

L&W.S   **Not assigned!** (EP)

William Henry **Lyde** **(CU/EP)** (K78) (K80) (K82)
(K84) (K88) (K92)
Birmingham (Warstone Ln/26, Constitution (PC) (M)
Hill/26/50, Newhall St)
- 1878 - 1896 ... *(See also figure: W.H.L)*

Walter A. **Lyndon** **(CU)** (W)
Birmingham
~ 1878 ... *(See also figure: ATHENA)*

Alfred **Lyne** **(EP)** (K80)
Bristol (27, Victoria St)
- 1880 ...

John **Lyne** **(CP)** (WDOB)
Birmingham (Price St)
- 1839 ...

L

(See also) Joseph **Mappin & Brothers** (Queen's Cutlery Works)	**(EP)**
(See also) **Mackay & Chisholm**	**(EP)**
(See also) **Marples & Co.**	**(EP)** (E) (S)
(See also) Robert Fead **Mosley & Co.** (Portland Works)	**(EP)**
(See also) **Martin & Naylor**	**(OSP)**
(See also) **Maxfield & Sons** (Enterprise Works)	**(EP)**
Not assigned!	**(EP)**
(See also) **Madin & Tricket**	**(CU)**
(See also) John Newton **Mappin &** George **Webb** (Royal Plate Works)	**(BM/EP/CU)**
(See also) **Maleham & Yeomans**	**(EP)** (S)
(See also) Alfred **Beckett & Sons**	**(CU)**
(See also) Mary **Kirkby**	**(OSP)**
(See also) M. **Rogers**	**(OSP)**

M

Macaulay & Oxley (EP) ^(WDS01)
Sheffield (48, Carver St)
- 1901 ...

John **Macefield** (CP) ^{(WTDB) (WTD)}
Birmingham (Navigation St)
- 1815 - 1818 ...

Joseph & William **Machon & Co. (OSP)** ^{(HGDY) (DSRR)}
Sheffield (19/49, Norfolk St) ^(SD46)
London (31, Castle St)
- 1837 - 1846 ...

Godfrey **Machon** (OSP) ^{(NGDS) (GDS)}
Sheffield (16, Gell St)
- 1825 - 1833 ...

Joseph **Machon** (OSP) ^{(WDS37) (DSRR)}
Sheffield (Mount Pisgah/Glossop Rd)
- 1837 - 1841 ...

William **Machon** (OSP) ^{(WDS37) (SDRR)}
Sheffield (24, Norfolk St/Broomspring Ln)
- 1837 - 1841 ...

Henry **Mackanzie** (EP) ^{(K78) (K80)}
Birmingham (11, Moreton St/263, Icknield
St/170, Pitsford St) ^{(K82) (K84)}
- 1878 - 1880 ... ^{(K88) (K92) (PC)}
- 1882 - 1903 ...**(& Co.)** ^(K03)
(See also figure: H.M. & Co.)

MACKAY & CHRISHOLM	**Mackay & Chisholm** (EP) ^{(SAOR) (B)} Edinburgh (49, New Buildings/57 & 59, ^{(SBW) (M)} Princes St/ North Bridge) 1861 ... *(See also figure: M&C)*

Samuel **Maclaurin & Son** (EP) ^(WDS01)
Sheffield (229, Wellington St)
- 1901 ...

MACLAURIN.BROS SHEFFIELD	**Maclaurin Brothers** (EP) ^{(K80) (K93)} **(Sidney Works)** Sheffield (16, 18 & 20, Sidney St) - 1880 - 1893 ...

M

Herbert **Maclaurin** **(EP)** (WDS01) (M)
(Matilda Works)
Sheffield (Sylvester St/107, Matilda St)
1894 - 1923
(See also figure: HERBERT MA-
CLAURIN)

George **Maclaurin** **(EP)**
Sheffield (66, Cecil Rd/117, Matilda St)
- 1879 ...
- 1893 ... (**& Son**) (WDS79)
(See also figure: G.M&S Ltd) (K93)

James **Maclaurin** **(EP)**
(Boston Works)
Sheffield (70, Bowden St/16, Sidney St)
~ 1860 ... (**& Sons**)
- 1901 ... (WDS01)

F. **Madin & Co.** **(OSP)** (B) (M)
Sheffield (Farfield)
1788 ... *(See also figure: F.MADIN*
& Co.)

Philip **Madin &** Robert **Trickett (OSP/CU)**
Sheffield (Farfield)
1779 ... *(See also figure: M&T)* (B) (SAOR)
1781 ... *(See also figure: PM RT)* (SAOR)

MADRAS SILVER *(See also)* **(EP)**
Harrison **Fisher**

John **Magenis** **(CP)** (WTDB) (WAB)
Birmingham (Branstone St/41, Birchall St) (DOB)
- 1815 - 1833 ...

Thomas **Magenis** **(OSP)** (WTD) (CD)
Birmingham (Lionel St)
- 1818 ...

MAJESTIC PLATE *(See also)* **(EP)**
James **Jay**

Joseph **Makin & Co.** **(OSP)** (B) (SAOR)
Sheffield (Hollis Croft)
1798 ... *(See also figure: I·M&Co)*

Edwin John **Makin** **(EP)** *(Formerly: George Hawksley & Co)* Sheffield (32, Charlotte St) 1867 ... *(See also figure: E J M)*		(B) (SBW) (M)
Joseph **Makin** **(OSP)** Sheffield (Pickle) 1786 ... *(See also figure: JM)*		(B) (SAOR)
Maleham & Yeomans **(EP)** Sheffield 1901 - 1931 *(See also figure: M&Y)*		(S)
George **Mallander** **(EP)** Sheffield (70, Bowdon St) - 1880 ...		(K80)
James **Mallol** **(EP)** Birmingham (176, Warstone Ln) - 1882 - 1903 ...		(K82) (K84) (K88) (K92) (PC) (K03)
William **Mammatt** **(EP)** **(Albion Works/Portland Works)** Sheffield (82, Devision St/121, Arundel St/ Hill St) 1876 - 1879 ... 1885 - 1901 ... **(& Sons)** *(See also figure: W M)* *(Then: Maxfield & Sons Ltd.)*		(SAOR) (WDS79) (SAOR) (K93) (WDS01) (M)
William **Mammatt,** George A. **Buxton & Co.** **(Arundel Plate Works)** **(EP)** Sheffield (32, Eyre St) 1865 ... *(See also figure: MB&Co)*		(SAOR) (B) (M)
MANCO REGd ELECTRO PLATE MADE IN ENGLAND	**Not assigned!** **(EP)** - 1920 ...	
MANDARIN	*(See also)* **(CU)** Adolphe **Arbenz**	
MANOR PLATE	*(See also)* **(EP)** Thomas **Wilkinson & Co. Ltd.**	
Charles **Manton** **(EP)** Birmingham (34, Gt. Hampton St) - 1880 - 1903 ...		(K80) (K82) (K84) (K03)

M

267

	Henry **Manton** (CU/OSP) Birmingham 1832 - 1849 ...	(SAOR)
	Henry J. **Manton** (CU/EP) **(Union Works)** Birmingham (108 - 110, Gt. Charles St) - 1872 - 1903 ...	(K72) (K78) (WDS79) (K80) (K82) (K84) (PC) (WDS01) (K03)
	William **Manton** (EP) Birmingham (103, Vyse St) 1882 - 1896 ...	(SAOR) (PC)
	Manwaring, Hutchfuson & Co. (EP) Birmingham (45, Warstone Ln) - 1903 ...	(K03)
MAPLE & C⁰ LONDON **MAPLES &C⁰ LONDON** MAPLE & C⁰.LIMᴰ LONDON	J. **Maple & Co.** (T) London ~ 1860 - 1916 ... - 1891 ... **(Ltd.)**	(Rd 658962)
	J. **Mappin & Co.** (OSP) Sheffield (Fargate) 1775 ... *(See also figure: I.M&Co)*	(B) (SAOR)
	Joseph **Mappin & Co.** (CU) (Joseph **Mappin & Son(s))** Sheffield (52, Norfolk St) 1833 - 1848 *(See also figure: J.M)* *(Then: Amalgamated with William Sansom & Co)*	(B) (SAOR) (WDS37) (DSRR) (SD46) (WDOS) (M)
MAPPIN & WEBB **S&L** **MAPPIN & WEBB** **MAPPIN PLATE**	John Newton **Mappin &** George **Webb** **(Royal Plate Works) (BM/EP/CU)** London (158 - 162, Oxford St) Sheffield (Pond Hill/179 & 181, Norfolk St) Birmingham (19, New St) - 1866 - 1898 ... *(See also figures: J N M & CO,* *M&W, PRINCE'S PLATE,* *TRUSTWORTHY, symbol "sun"')*	(B) (MDG) (SAOR) (K80) (K93) (M)

M

MAPPIN&WEBB L^{TD}	**Mappin & Webb Ltd.** (EP) **(The Royal Works)** *(In 1902 amalgamated with Mappin Brothers)* London (156-162, Oxford St/2, Queen Victoria St/18 & 22, Poultry/Regent St) Sheffield (179 & 181, Norfolk St/161-167, Howard St) 1898 - 1936 (WDS01) (M) (K36)
	Frederick **Mappin** (EP) (WDS01) Sheffield (239, Ann's Rd) - 1901 ...
	Jonathan **Mappin** (OSP) (B) (SAOR) Sheffield (Fargate) 1775 ... *(See also figure: I·M)*
	Joseph **Mappin** (CU) Sheffield (Fargate) 1810 - 1841
Mappin Biarritz	*(See also)* (BM/CU/EP) John Newton **Mappin &** George **Webb** **(Royal Plate Works)**
MAP PIN BROS **MAPPIN BROTHERS** **MAP PIN BROT HERS**	Joseph **Mappin Brothers** (EP/CU) (SAOR) (POS) (K80) (B) (M) (K54) (WDS79) (K93) (WDS01) **(Queen's Cutlery Works)** Sheffield (6 - 10, Baker's Hill/66 & 67, Cheapside) London (220, Regent St) 1850 - 1901 ... *(See also figures: EM JM, MB, M&B, JM&B, J*M, M.BROS, symbol "sun")* *(Then: Mappin & Webb Ltd.)*
	Mappin, Webb & Co. (EP) (SAOR) (B) (M) Sheffield (Eyre St) 1864 - 1872 *(See also figure: MW & Co.)*
	Mapplebeck & Lowe (EP) (HGD) Birmingham (6 & 7, Bull Ring) - 1850 ...
	J. **Marchant** (EP) (GS) Birmingham (71, Caroline St) - 1863 ...

M

P. **Marchant** **(EP)** (CDB)
Birmingham (71, Caroline St)
- 1861 ...

James **Margrave & Co.** **(OSP)** (B) (SAOR)
Sheffield (Townhead Cross)
1773 ... ***(See also figure: IM&Co)***

John **Marigold** **(CP)** (WAB) (WDOB)
Birmingham (Charles St/Newton St)
- 1829 - 1839 ...

William **Markland** **(CU/OSP)**
Birmingham (Sand St)
- 1818 - 1823 ... ***(See also figure: W·MARKLAND)*** (CD) (WDB) (M) (WTD)
- 1818 ... (**& Co.**)

Mrs. L. **Marks** **(EP)** (MDG)
Birmingham (145, Hockley Hill)
- 1866 ...

Philip **Marks** **(EP)**
Sheffield
~ ***(See also figure: P.M)***

Marples & Co. **(CU/EP)** (WDS01) (K03)
Sheffield (Napier St)
Birmingham (52, Touby St)
- 1901 - 1903 ... ***(See also figure: M & Co.)***
(A subsidiary of Martin, Hall & Co)
(Then: Marples, Wingfield & Wilkins)

M

Robert **Marples & Son (Hermitage Works)** **(CU)** (K72) AD
Sheffield (Hermitage St)
- 1872 ...

William **Marples & Sons (Hibernia Works)** **(CU/EP)**
Sheffield (Westfield Terrace)
~ 1885 ... (SBW) (M)
- 1901 ... (***Ltd.***) (WDS01)
(See also figures: HIBERNIA, WM*)

Robert **Marples** (CP) (GE) (K72AD)
Sheffield
1828 - 1851 ...

Thomas **Marples** (EP) (SAOR) (SBW)
Sheffield (Arundel St) (B)
1855 ... *(See also figure: TM)*

Marples, Wingfield & Wilkins (EP) (K36)
(Sykes Works & Portland Works)
(Formerly: Marples & Co.)
Sheffield (148, Eyre St/75-77, Hill St)
1908 - 1936 ...
(See also figure: RELIABLE)

Francis **Marrian &** John B. **Gransby** (EP) (SAOR) (HGD)
Birmingham (9, Cannon St)
1849 - 1850 ...

Marrian & Tye (EP) (CDB) (GS)
Birmingham (14, Cannon St) (MDG)
- 1861 - 1866 ...

Francis **Marrian** (CU) (SAOR)
Birmingham
1839 ...

Francis Thomas **Marrian** (EP) (K82) (K84) (K88)
Birmingham (123, Gt. Hampton St)
- 1882 - 1888 ...

Marrian, Bocock & Co. (EP) (K72) (K78) (K80)
(Francis **Marrian & Co**)
Birmingham (14, Cannon St)
- 1872 - 1880 ...

M

Luke **Marriott** (OSP) (B) (SAOR)
Sheffield (Coalpit Ln)
1787 ... *(See also figure: L.M)*

MARS *(See also)* (CU)
Thomas **Beely**

George Rayner **Mardsen & Son (CU/GS)** (WDS79) (K93)
(Argyle Works)
Sheffield (18, Hollis Croft/53, Blackfields)
- 1879 - 1893 ...
(See also figure: PROLIFIC)

J. **Marsden**   **(CU)** ^(E)
Sheffield
~ 1930 ...
(See also figure: J. MARSDEN)

William **Marsden**   **(OSP)**
Sheffield (Waingate/ Norfolk St)
1774 ... *(See also figure: W·M)*
1773 ... *(See also figure: WM&Co)*   (B) (SAOR)
                               (B) (SAOR)

John **Marsfield**   **(CP)** ^(WDB)
Birmingham
- 1823 ...

Benjamin **Marsh & Sons**   **(EP)** ^(K72)
Birmingham (83, Coleshill St)
- 1872 ...

Arthur **Marsh**   **(CU)**
Sheffield
1845 - 1868 ... *(See also figure: A M)*

Benjamin **Marsh**   **(EP)** ^(K78)
Birmingham (83, Coleshill St)
- 1878 ...

James **Marsh**   **(OSP)** ^{(B) (SAOR)}
Sheffield (Park)
1793 ... *(See also figure: I·M)*

James Henry **Marsh**   **(EP)** ^(WDS01)
Sheffield (55, Vincent Rd)
- 1901 ...

Marsh Bros. & Co.   **(EP)**
Sheffield
1853 - 1920 *(See also figure: JOHN ADWICK)*

Alfred George **Marshall**   **(EP)** ^(K72)
Birmingham (80, Wyse St)
- 1872 ...

Mary **Marshall**   **(FP)** ^(WTDB)
Birmingham (Loveday St)
- 1815 ...

Martin & Naylor   **(OSP)**
Sheffield (Fargate)
- 1852 *(See also figure: M&N)*
(Then: Roberts & Hall)

(See also)   **(EP)**
Allen & Martin

Benjamin **Martin**   **(CU)**   (B) (SAOR)
Sheffield (Ladies Walk Moor/13/12, South St)   (NGDS)(GDS)
1820 - 1837 ... *(See also figure: B·M)*   (WDS37)

William **Martin**   **(EP)**   (K72)
Birmingham (131, Latimer St)
- 1872 ...

Martin Brothers & Co.   **(EP)**   (B) (SAOR)
Sheffield (Division St)   (SBW) (M)
1846 ... *(See figure: A.H)*

Richard **Martin**, Ebenezer **Hall & Co.**   (B) (SAOR) (K54)
(Shrewsbury Works)   **(GS/EP)**   (POS) (GS) (K80)
(Formerly: Roberts & Hall)   (WDSR) (nicht
Sheffield (47-55, Broad St)   K36) (SBW) (M)
London (15, Fleet St)
1854 - 1905 ...
1854 - 1935 (**& Co. Ltd.**)   (B) (WDS71)
(See also figures: MH&Co, RM   (WDS01)
EH, MARTINOID PAT.)

Francis Richard **Martino**   **(GS/EP)**   (K84) (K88) (K92)
(Formerly: Sir Joshua Mason)   (K93) (SBW) (M)
Sheffield (199 & 201 Arundel St)
Birmingham (4, Gt. Charles St/37 & 38,
Princip St)
- 1884 - 1893 ...
(See also figures: New Caledonian
Silver, PLATINOID)

MARTINOID PAT.   *(See also)*   **(EP)**
Richard **Martin**, Ebenezer **Hall & Co. Ltd.**
(Shrewsbury Works)

John **Masefield**   **(CP)**   (WAB)
Birmingham (6, St. Martin's Place)
- 1829 ...

	Mason & Simmons Birmingham (New Canal St) - 1839 ...	**(GS)**	(WDOB)
	George **Mason** Birmingham (86, Vyse St) - 1892 - 1903 ...	**(EP)**	(K92) (K03)
	Mason, Shepherd & Co. Sheffield (Victoria St) - 1863 ...	**(EP)**	(GS)
	John **Massey** Birmingham (331, Icknield St./402, Monument Rd) - 1872 - 1903 ...	**(EP)**	(K72) (K78) (K80) (K82) (K84) (K88)(K03)
" MATADOR " SILVERPRIDE PLATE	**Not assigned!**	**(EP)**	
	Robert A. **Mathers** Coventry 1818 ...	**(CU)**	(SAOR)
MATTHEW WILSON WHITECHAPEL LIVERPOOL	*(See also)* Matthew **Wilson**	**(EP)**	
	Matthews & Silver Birmingham (142, Conybere St) - 1892 ...	**(CP)**	(K92)
	William **Matthews** Birmingham (70, Parade St) - 1861 ...	**(EP)**	(CDB)
MATTHIAS SPENCER & SONS	*(See also)* Matthias **Spencer & Sons** **(Albion Steel Works)**	**(CU/EP)**	
MAURICE BAUM	*(See also)* Maurice **Baum** **(Albert Works)**	**(EP)**	
	Maxfield & Sons **(Enterprise Works)** Sheffield (42, Eyre St/169, Arundel St) London (47, Beak St/Regent St) 1855 - 1901 *(See also figure: M&S)* *(Then: J. & J. Maxfield Ltd.)*	**(EP)**	(M) (K93)

M

J. & J. **Maxfield**   **(CU/EP)**

Sheffield (42, Eyre St/169, Arundel St)

- 1893 - 1901 ...

(See also figures: J&JM, M&S)   (K93) (WDS01)

1901 - 1908 (**Ltd.**)

(See also figure: J&JM, M&S)

1908 ... (**& Sons Ltd.**)

(Acquisition of W. Mammatt & Sons)

(See also figure: M&S)

(Then: J. & J. Maxfield Ltd.)

MAZEPPA

(See also)   **(EP)**

Samuel **Hancock & Sons**
(**Mazeppa Works**)

(See also)   **(EP)**

Joseph **Mappin & Brothers**
(**Queen's Cutlery Works**)

Not assigned!   **(EP)**   (Rd 266155)

- 1895 ...

(See also)   **(EP)**

Maurice **Baum**
(**Albert Works**)

(See also)   **(EP)**

W. **Mammatt,** George A. **Buxton & Co.**
(**Arundel Plate Works**)

(See also)   **(EP)**

M. **Beal**

(See also)   **(EP)**

Joseph **Mappin & Brothers**
(**Queen's Cutlery Works**)

(See also)   **(EP)**

McLean Brothers & Rigg Ltd.

Joseph **Mappin Brothers**   **(EP/CU)**
(**Queen's Cutlery Works**)

John **McCarty**   **(EP)**   (K03)

Birmingham (7, Vyse St)

- 1903 ...

James Robert **McClelland** (EP) ^{(M) (SBW)}
Sheffield
~ *(See also figures: BRENADA SILVER, J.R.MCC)*

Jane **McGregor** (EP) ^{(K72) (K78)}
Birmingham (68, Hockley Hill)
- 1872 - 1878 ...

Joseph **McGregor** (EP) ^{(GS) (CDB) (MDG)}
Birmingham (68, Hockley Hill)
- 1861 - 1866 ...

M. **McHale** (EP) ^(MDG)
Birmingham (60, Ludgate Hill)
- 1866 ...

R. & W. **McKenzie** (EP) ^{(PC) (K03)}
Birmingham (97, Upper Trinity St)
- 1896 - 1903 ...

McLean Brothers & Rigg Ltd. (EP) ^{(W) (M)}
London
- 1896 *(See also figure: M B R)*

John **McLeaownan McMurtie** (EP) ^(M)
Glasgow
~ 1900
(See also figure: NICKELINE)

(See also) (EP) ^(E)
T. **McLellan Ltd.**
Belfast
~ *(See also figure: T.McLELLAN Ltd.)*

M

William **Meadows** (EP) ^(K92)
Birmingham (17, Hingeston St)
- 1892 ...

Samuel **Mearbeck** (OSP) ^{(B) (SAOR)}
Sheffield (Angel St)
1812 ... *(See also figure: SM)*

𝔐𝔢𝔡𝔞𝔩𝔩𝔦𝔬𝔫 | *(See also)* (EP)
William **Tay & Son Ltd.**

	Meeson & Green (Orchard Works) Sheffield (7, Orchard Ln) - 1879 - 1880 ...	**(BM/EP)**	(WDS79) (K80)
	James **Meeson** Sheffield (91, Pickering Rd) - 1879 ...	**(EP)**	(WDS79)
	Arthur Joseph **Memmott** Sheffield (211, Shirebrook Rd) - 1901 ...	**(EP)**	(WDS01)
	Walter George **Memmott** Sheffield (32, Kersley Rd/22, Charles St) - 1879 - 1880 ...	**(EP)**	(WDS79) (K80)
	P. **Merchant** Birmingham (71, Caroline St) - 1866 ...	**(EP)**	(MDG)
	Meredith & Co. (Libety Mills) Birmingham (Frankfort St) - 1892 ...	**(EP)**	(K92)
MERE DITH	H. **Meredith** Birmingham 1807 ...	**(CP)**	(B) (M)
MERIT	John **Baker** **(Wheeldon Works)**	**(EP)**	
	H. & T. **Merry** Birmingham (Cherry St) - 1839 ...	**(GS)**	(WDOB)
MEXICAN SILVER	*(See also)* James **Tidmarch**	**(GS)**	
M.F&Cᵒ MF& Cᵒ	*(See also)* **Furniss, Poles & Turner**	**(OSP)**	
MF RC	*(See also)* M. **Fenton**, R. **Creswick & Co.**	**(OSP)**	
M G&S Cᵒ	*(See also)* The **Goldsmiths & Silversmiths Co.**	**(EP)**	

M

(See also)   **(OSP)**
M. **Hunter** & J. **Twig**

(See also)   **(EP)**
Richard **Martin,** Ebenezer **Hall & Co.**
(Shrewsbury Works)

John **Micklethwaite** & John **Hounsfield**   (B) (SAOR)
Sheffield (Pond Hill)   **(OSP)**
1786 ... *(See also figure: I.M)*

Middleton & Eaves   **(EP)**   (K78)
Birmingham (9, George St)
- 1878 ...

Albert Rupert **Middleton**   **(EP)**   (K88) (K92) (PC)
Birmingham (6, Legge Ln)   (K03)
- 1888 - 1903 ...

John **Middleton**   **(EP)**   (K72) (K80) (K82)
Birmingham (Parade/ 9, George St/   (K84)(PC) (K03)
18, Gt. Charles St)
- 1872 ... **(& Co)**
- 1880 - 1903 ...

John **Middleton** jun.   **(EP)**   (K03)
Birmingham (48, Hall St)
- 1903 ...

Mrs. Harriet A. **Middleton**   **(EP)**   (K88)
Birmingham (102, Broad St)
- 1888 ...

Middleton, Jewesson & Co. (OSP)   (B) (SAOR)
Sheffield (Campo Ln)
1798 ... *(See also figure: JM&Co)*

Charles **Miles**   **(EP)**   (K80)
Bristol (2, Narrow Wine St)
- 1880 ...

M

Thomas Henry **Millard** (EP) (K80)
Bristol (12, Nicholas St)
- 1880 ...

John **Miller & Co.** (EP) (K80)
Glasgow (153, Greendyke St)
- 1880 ...

Thomas **Miller** (EP) (MDG) (K80)
Birmingham (28, Northwood St/12/25, (K82) (K84)
Victoria St) (K88) (K92) (PC)
- 1866 - 1903 ... (K03)

Miller, Chartres & Co. Ltd. (EP) (K36)
London (35, Old St)
- 1936 ...

Millichamp & Co. (BM/EP) (K82) (K84)
Birmingham (10, Brook St)
- 1882 - 1884 ...

Frank **Mills & Co.** (EP)
(Hanover Works)
Sheffield (63, Division St)
1894 - 1906
(See also figure: FRANK MILLS)

Mills & Patten (CP) (WTD)
Birmingham
- 1818 ...

Mills & Wiley (EP) (K92)
Birmingham (277a, Coventry Rd)
- 1892 ...

Thomas **Mills** (EP) (PC) (K03)
Birmingham (244/246, Icknield St)
- 1888 - 1903 ...

Thomas & Walter **Mills** (EP) (K72) (K78) (K80)
Birmingham (22, Key Hill/244, Icknield St/ (K82) (K84)
9 & 11, Park Rd)
- 1872 - 1884 ...

Walter **Mills** (EP) (K88) (K92)
Birmingham (3, Ford St, Hockley)
- 1888 - 1892 ...

M

Arthur **Millward**	**(EP)**	
Sheffield (39, Eyre St/Clifford Lodge)		(WDS01)
- 1901 ...		(K80) (K93)
- 1879 - 1893 ... (**& Son**)		
William **Millward**	**(EP)**	(K72) (K78)
Birmingham (37, St. Paul's Sq)		(WDS79) (K80)
Sheffield (45, Wostenholm Rd)		(K82) (K84) (K88)
- 1872 - 1903 ...		(K92) (K03)
William & Arthur **Millward**	**(EP)**	(GS) (MDG)
Birmingham (37, St. Paul's Sq)		
- 1863 - 1866 ...		
Minshull & Bayley	**(OSP)**	(CD)
(Minshall & Bayley)		
Birmingham (Edmund St)		
- 1818 ...		
Charles **Minshull**	**(CP)**	(WDOB)
Birmingham (Tyndall St)		
- 1839 ...		
Robert **Mitchell & Co.**	**(CP/CU)**	(SAOR)
Birmingham		
1812 ...		
Albert Henry **Mitchell**	**(EP)**	(K80) (K82) (K84)
Birmingham (26, Warstone Ln)		(K88)
- 1880 - 1888 ...		
Frank **Mitchell**	**(EP)**	(K78) (K88)
Birmingham (20, Northampton St./23, Augusta St.)		
- 1878 - 1888 ...		
Henry **Mitchell**	**(EP)**	(CDB) (GS)
Birmingham (16, Augusta St)		(MDG)
- 1861 - 1866 ...		
William Frederick **Mitchell**	**(EP)**	(K36)
Birmingham (18, Northampton St)		
- 1936 ...		
MIXITINE	*(See also)* **Swann & Adams** **(Canada Works)**	**(EP)**

M

J. & L. **Mole**	**(EP)**	(K80)
Birmingham (87, High Street)		
- 1880 ...		

MONARCHY PLATE

(See also) **(EP)**
The **Northern Goldsmiths Company**
&
Elkington & Co.

MONKEY

(See also) **(EP)**
Lockwood & Brothers

MONTANA SILVER

(See also) **(EP)**
Collins & Wallis

MOORE

John **Moore** **(OSP/CU)** (B) (SAOR)
Birmingham (Gt. Charles St) (WTD) (CD) (M)
1784 - 1818 ...

Christian **Moore** **(OSP)** (DSRR)
Sheffield (Glossop Rd)
- 1841 ...

Frederick **Moore** **(CU/CP)** (B) (SAOR)
Birmingham (William St/Suffolk St) (WDB) (M)
1820 - 1829 ... *(See also figure:* (WAB)
F.MOORE)

James **Moore** **(OSP)** (B) (SAOR)
Derby
1795 ... *(See also figure: JM)*

Joseph **Moore** **(EP)** (K80)
Darlington/Durham (16, Priestgate)
- 1880 ...

Victor **Moore** **(EP)** (K03)
Birmingham (35, Hylton St)
- 1903 ...

William **Moore** **(CP)** (WTDB)
Birmingham (Brichole St)
- 1815 ...

Frederick Alfred **Moreton & Co.** **(EP)** (K88)
Smethwick (48a, New St)
- 1888 ...

M

John **Moreton & Co.**   **(CU/EP)**   (WDS79) (WDS01) (M)
Sheffield (96, Carver St)
London
Wolverhampton
- 1879 - 1901 ...*(See also figures:*
JM&Co, EMPRESS, ENCORE,
symbol "butterfly")

Morewood & Co. Ltd.   **(CU)**   (W)
Birmingham
~ 1890 ... *(See also figure: AURICH-*
ALCUM)

George **Morgan**   **(Coach)**   (WTDB) (WTD) (CD) (WAB) (DOB)
Birmingham (126, Lionel St)
- 1815 - 1833 ...

R. F. **Morley & Co.**   **(EP)**   (SAOR)
Sheffield
1886 ...

Edward **Morley**   **(EP)**   (K80)
Norwich (7, Haymarket)
- 1880 ...

Timothy **Morris**   **(EP)**   (K80)
Birmingham (3 & 4, Market St)
- 1880 ...

Morrison & Thomas   **(EP)**   (K03)
Birmingham (4 & 5, Blumsbury St)
- 1903 ...

M   MORTON&Cᴼ   *(See also)*   **(OSP)**
Richard **Morton**

Morton & Perks   **(EP)**
Birmingham (7/9, New Spring St)
- 1892 - 1903 ...   (K92) (PC) (K03)
- 1936 ... (**Ltd.**)   (K36)

J. **Morton & Son**   **(EP)**   (K03)
Birmingham (8, Luisa St)
- 1903 ...

Charles **Morton & Sons**   **(EP)**   (MDG)
Birmingham (3, Nelson St)
- 1866 ...

Charles **Morton** **(EP)** (K72) (K78) (K80)
Birmingham (78, Spencer St)
- 1872 - 1880 ...

Francis **Morton** **(OSP)** (B) (SAOR)
Sheffield (White Rails)
1820 ... *(See also figure: F·M)*

George **Morton** **(OSP)** (DSRR)
Sheffield (Broomhill)
- 1841 ...

George **Morton** **(EP)** (GS) (MDG)
Birmingham (47, St. Paul's Sq) (K72) (K78) (K80)
- 1863 - 1884 ... (K82) (K84)

Henry **Morton** **(EP)** (K78)
Birmingham (8, Kenion St)
- 1878 ...

Joshua **Morton** **(EP)**
Birmingham (13, New Spring St)
- 1882 - 1884 ... **(& Co.)** (K82) (K84)
- 1888 ... (K88)

William **Morton** **(EP)** (B) (K80) (SAOR)
Sheffield (Commercial St/20, Sycamore St/ (WDS01)
Ct. 26, Norwich St)
1869 - 1901 ... *(See also figure: W·M)*

Morton, Handley, Sykes & Co. (OSP) (UBD)
Sheffield
- 1791 ...

A. **Morton Ltd.** **(EP)** (K36)
Birmingham (5 - 7, Tenby St North)
- 1936 ...

M

Morton, Warris & Co. **(OSP)** (B) (GM)
Sheffield (Brinsworth's Orchard)
1780 - 1787 ...

Richard **Morton** **(OSP)**
Sheffield (Fargate/Brinsworth Orchard)
1773 ... *(See also figure: R·M)*
1780 ... *(See also figure: R·M)* (B) (SAOR)
1773 - 1781 ... **(& Co.)** (SAOR)
(See also figures: R·M, R·M&Co, (SAOR)
MORTON & CO.)

MORTONS
PATENT

	Edward Charles **Moseley** (EP) ^(WDSR) Sheffield (98, Vincent Rd) - 1905 ...	

Edward Charles **Moseley** (EP) (WDSR)
Sheffield (98, Vincent Rd)
- 1905 ...

MOSES EADON

Moses Eaden & Sons (EP)
Sheffield (Monmore Green)
~ 1880

MOSLEY'S **A1** **EPNS**

Robert Fead **Mosley** (CU/EP)
(Portland Works)
Sheffield (Randall St)
- 1880 ...   (SI)
1883 ... **(& Co)**
(See also figures: M&Co, R F M)   (SAOR)
- 1905 - 1947 ... **(& Co. Ltd.)**
(See also figures: M&Co.L^{TD}*,*   (WDSR)
RFM*S)

Moss & Gamble Brothers (CU) (K93) (WDS01)
(Franklin Works & Wadsley Bridge (W)
Works)
Sheffield (1, Russel St/Wadsley Br)
- 1893 - 1901 ... *(See figure: A.H)*

Frank **Moss** (EP) (K03)
Birmingham (24, Spencer St)
- 1903 ...

Mottram & Hawkins (CU) (WDOS AD)
Sheffield (15, Carr Ln/Rockingham St)
- 1852 ...

M

Motteram & Hawthorn (BM) (WAB)
Birmingham (Edmund St)
- 1829 ...

Charles **Motteram** (CP) (WTD)
Birmingham
- 1818 ...

William **Mottram** (EP) (CDB)
Birmingham (Singer's Hill)
- 1861 ...

Moule & Bridgens (BM) (WDB)
Birmingham
- 1823 ...

	T. **Moulson** Birmingham (91, Hill St) - 1861 ...	(EP)	(CDB)
	William **Mounsey** Sheffield (9, School Croft) - 1837 ...	(GS)	(WDS37)
	Mousley & Co. Birmingham (55, Albion St) - 1878 ...	(EP)	(K78)
	Thomas **Mousley** Birmingham (53, Howard St) - 1850 ...	(EP)	(HGD)
	Mousley Brothers & Wood Birmingham (235, Icknield St) - 1872 ...	(EP)	(K72)
	(See also) Thomas **Prime & Son**	(EP)	
	(See also) Thomas **Turner & Co.** **(Suffolk Works)**	(EP)	
	Not assigned!	(EP)	
M.S.Jʀ & Cᵒ	*(See also)* **Selig, Sonnenthal & Co.**	(EP)	
	(See also) **Barker & Ellis** - 1912	(EP)	
	John R. **Muggeridge** Birmingham (15, Upper Tower St) - 1861 - 1884 ...	(EP)	(CDB) (GS) (MDG) (K72) (K78) (K80) (K82) (K84)
	Mrs. Ellen **Muggeridge** Birmingham (25, Ludgate Hill) - 1888 ...	(EP)	(K88)
MUIRHEAD & ARTHUR GLASGOW	James **Muirhead & Arthur** **(Muirhead & Co.)** Glasgow (Argyle St) 1877 ...	(T)	(S) (SAOR) (M)

M

MULBERRY CUTLERY & Co **SHEFFIELD**	*(See also)* Lewis **Barnascone**	**(CU)**
	Fred J. **Munroe** Hull (9, Pearson St) - 1880 ...	**(EP)** ^(K80)
	Murrle, J. B. **Bennett & Co.** London (Charterhouse St) 1901 - 1905	**(EP)**
	Ethelbert W. H. **Mutlow** Birmingham (36a, Unett St) - 1936 ...	**(EP)** ^(K36)
M.W & W *Coffer* *dam* TRADE MARK " Reliable "	**Not assigned!** (Possibly Mark Willis & Son (William))	**(EP)** ^(E)
	(See also) **Mappin, Webb & Co.**	**(EP)**
	(See also) Mark **Willis & Son**	**(EP)**
	Not assigned! (Possibly Mark Willis & Son (William))	**(EP)** ^(E)
	(See also) Mark **Willis** **(Exchange Works)**	**(EP)**
	William James **Myatt & Co.** Birmingham ~ 1900 ... *(See also figure:* *WJM&Co)*	**(EP)** ^(M)
	E. **Myring** Birmingham (Ct. 13, Inge St) - 1833 ...	**(CP)** ^(DOB)

M

N & H — **Nathan & Hayes** (EP) [PC]
Birmingham (285, Icknield St)
- 1896 ...
(Then: S. Blanckensee & Sons Ltd.)

N&W   **N&W** — *(See also)* (EP)
Norton & White

N·S — *(See also)* (OSP)
Naylor & Settle

N·T — *(See also)* (OSP/CU)
Nathaniel **Travis**

N.W — *(See also)* (EP)
Norton & White

NACZI
TRADE MARK — *(See also)* (CU/BM/EP)
Philip **Ashberry**

William **Naylor & Co. (BM/CP/GS/EP)** [K80] [K82] [K84]
(Caledonian Works)
(Formerly: Naylor, Clark & Co)
Birmingham (14, Victoria St/29-31, Vittoria St)
- 1880 - 1884 ...
(See also figures: AUSTRALIAN
SILVER, WN&Co)

Naylor & Settle (OSP) [B] [SAOR]
Sheffield (Coalpit Ln)
1778 ... *(See also figure: N·S)*

Naylor, Clark & Co. (EP) [K72] [K80]
Birmingham (14, Vittoria St)
- 1872 - 1880 ...
(See also figure: NC&Co)
(Then: William Naylor & Co)

N&B S — Not assigned! (EP)

N C & Cᵒ
NC &CO — *(See also)* (EP)
Naylor, Clark & Co.

NC — *(See also)* (OSP/EP)
Thomas, James & Nathaniel **Creswick**

N

N.E.V.A.	*(See also)* **(CU/EP)** John **Clarke & Sons**	

	Albert C. **Neal** **(EP)** Birmingham (153, Ashted Rw) - 1866 ...	(MDG)

NEAL'S PYRO SILVER	John **Neal & Co.** **(EP)** London (Edgeware Rd) ~ 1852 - 1880 *(See also figures: J.N, NJ, PYRO GOLD)*	(SBW) (M)

	Charles **Needham** **(OSP/CP)** Sheffield (Wicker 56/7, Willey St) 1810 - 1852 ... *(See also figure: C·N)*	(B) (SAOR) (CD) (PDY) (SDG) (M) (HGDY) (DSRR) (GDBS) (WDOS)

	Edward **Needham** **(CP)** Birmingham (16, Coleshill St) - 1829 - 1839 ...	(WAB) (DOB) (WDOB)

	John **Needham** **(EP)** Sheffield (Jehu Lane/53, Arundel St) ~ 1848 - 1881 ... *(See also figure: JN)*	(GS) (POS) (K54) (B) (SAOR) (SBW) (M)

	Needman, Veall & Tyzack **(EP)** **(Eye Witness Works & Nimrod Works)** *(Formerly: John Taylor)* Sheffield (Pond St/Milton St/111, Eldon St) 1889 - 1897... - 1901 - 1925 ... **(Ltd.)** *(See also figures: EYE WITNESS, NVT, TAYLOR)*	(SBW) (M) (WDS01)

NEILL	*(See also)* **(CU/OSP/EP)** Herny **Wilkinson & Co.**	

N

	John **Neill** **(EP)** Birmingham (154, Broad St/21, Gough St/28, Ellis St) - 1872 ...	(MDG) (K72)

	Sharman Dermott **Neill** **(EP)** Belfast 1888 ... *(See also figure: AX1)*	(SAOR) (SBW)

	Neville & Lowe (CP)	(WTDB) (CD)
	Birmingham (Gt. Charles St)	
	London (16, King St)	
	- 1815 - 1818 ...	

NEVADA SILVER

(See also) (EP)
Thomas H. **Daniel &** Thomas R. **Arter**
(Globe Nevada Silver Works)

Thomas **Newbold** (CU) ^(SAOR)
Birmingham
1820 ...

William **Newbould & Sons** (OSP) ^(B)
Sheffield
1804 ... *(See also figure: W^M NEW-BOULD)*

NEW CALEDONIAN SILVER

(See also) (GS/EP)
Francis Richard **Martino**

E. **Newell & Co.** (EP) ^(WDS01)
Sheffield (58, Holly St)
- 1901 ...

Thomas **Newell** (EP) ^(WDS01)
Sheffield (161, Monmouth St)
- 1901 ...

NEWHALL

Not assigned! (EP) ^(E)

W. **Newmann & Son** (EP) ^(CDB)
Birmingham (Bristol St)
- 1861 ...

Marcus **Newmark &** Barnett H. **Abrahams**
London (EP)
1866 - 1871
1871 - 1884 (Newmark, Abrahams & Goldsmiths)
(Then: Barnett Henry Abrahams)

Frederick **Newton & Co.** (EP) ^(SBW)
London
~

N

John **Newton & Son**	**(CU)**	(B) (SAOR) (GDS)
Sheffield (Sharrow Moor)		
1829 - 1833 ... *(See also figure: I·N)*		

Francis **Newton & Sons** **(Portobello Works)**	**(CU)**	(WDS79) (SBW)
Sheffield (127, Portobello St)		
- 1879 ...		

Ellis **Newton**	**(EP)**	(SBW) (M)
Birmingham		
~ *(See also figure: AX1)*		

Rupert Edward **Newton**	**(EP)**	(K72) (K78) (K80) (K82) (K84) (PC) (K03)
Birmingham (8, Caroline St/45, Northampton St/65, Victoria St)		
- 1872 - 1903 ...		

S. **Newton**	**(EP)**	(CDB)
Birmingham (Harford St)		
- 1861 ...		

Not assigned!	**(EP)**	

James **Nicholds**	**(OSP)**	(B) (M) (WTDB) (WTD) (CD) (WDB)
Birmingham (13, Fordrough St)		
1808 - 1823 ...		
(See also figure: J.NICHOLDS)		

John **Nicholls**	**(EP)**	(GS)
Birmingham (81, Spencer St)		
- 1863 ...		

Robert George **Nicholls**	**(EP)**	(K82) (K84) (K88)
Birmingham (7, Regent Parade)		
- 1882 - 1888 ...		

N

Nicholson & White **(North Street Works)**	**(EP)**	(POS) (K54)
Sheffield (53, North St)		
- 1854 ...		

Nicholson, Fidler & White **(Nicholson & Co.)** **(North Street Works)**	**(EP)**	(WDOS)
Sheffield (53, North St)		
- 1852 ...		

NICKELINE	*(See also)* John **McLeaownan McMurtie**	**(EP)**
NIMROD	*(See also)* Matthias **Spencer & Sons** **(Albion Steel Works)**	**(EP)**
	Thomas **Nixon & Co.** Sheffield (Norfolk Ln) 1808 ... *(See also figure: TN&Co)*	**(OSP)** (B) (SAOR)
	Charles Edward **Nixon** **(Street Wolfram's Works)** Sheffield (185, Rockingham St/ 226, Brookhill/103, Napier St) 1880 - 1893 ... *(See also figure: C.E N)*	**(EP)** (SAOR) (S) (K80) (K93) (M)
	J. **Nixon** Handsworth (Church Rd) - 1863 ...	**(EP)** (GS)
	John & Thomas **Nixon** Birmingham (22, Gt. Hampton Rd) - 1861 ...	**(EP)** (CDB)
	John **Nixon** Birmingham (Upper Priory) - 1815 ...	**(OSP)** (WTDB)
	Thomas **Nixon** Birmingham (168, New John St) - 1863 ...	**(EP)** (GS)
NJ	*(See also)* John **Neal &Co.**	**(EP)**
N Ltd.	*(See also)* John **Nowill & Sons Ltd.** **(Nowill's Cutlery & Plate Works)**	**(EP)**
NODDER NODDERS SILVER	John **Nodder & Sons** **(Devenport Works/Taranaki Works)** Sheffield (188, Rockingham St/226, Brook- hill/Edward St) 1863 - 1901 1901 - 1904 (**Ltd.**) *(See also figures: JOHN NOD- DER, OSMINIUM, JNS)*	**(EP)** (GS) (SBW) (K80) (K93) (WDS01) (M)

N

J. **North** (EP)   (B) (SAOR) (SBW) (M)
Sheffield (South St Moor)
1858 ... *(See also figure: JN)*

Northern Goldsmiths Company (EP)   (K80) (Rd.334132)
Newcastle-Upon-Tyne
~ 1880 - 1899 ...
(See also figures: DUCAL PLATE, Monarchy Plate, Cardinal Plate)
(Then: Elkington & Co, Birmingham)

NORTHERN GOLDSMITHS
COMPANY
DUCAL PLATE
NEWCASTLE UPON TYNE

Norton & White (EP)   (K72) (K78) (K80) (K82) (K84) (K88) (K92) (PC) (M)
Birmingham (91, Gt. Charles St/185 & 187, Newhall St)
- 1872 - 1896 ... *(See also figure: N & W)*

John **Nowill & Sons** (EP)   (SD46) (SAOR) (WDS79) (SBW) (K93) (K36)
(Nowill's Cutlery & Plate Works)
Sheffield (Meadow St/135, Scotland St)
- 1846 - 1936
1937 - 1950 (**Ltd.**)
(See also figures: J N & S, N.Ltd.)

John & William **Nowill** (OSP)   (B) (SAOR)
Sheffield (Meadow St)
1825 ... *(See also figure: J.N)*

Joseph **Nowill** (OSP/CU)
Sheffield
1774 ... (Pea Croft)
(See also figure: GENEVA)   (B)
1783 ...(Copper St) *(See also figure: IN)*   (SAOR)
1813 ... (High St) *(See also figure: IN)*   (SAOR)

Sidney **Nowill** (EP)   (WDS01)
Sheffield (94, Ivy Park Rd)
- 1901 ...

Thomas **Nowill** (CU)
Sheffield
1786 ... (Meadow St)
1790 ... (Norfolk St)   (B) (SAOR)
1800 ... (High St)   (SAOR)
- 1825 ... (7, Meadow St) (**& Co.**)   (SAOR) (NGDS)
(See also figure: T·N)

N

NS&C⁰
N S
N SMITH & C⁰
" hand "

(See also)   **(CU)**
Nathaniel **Smith**

N SPENCER
SHEFFIELD

(See also)   **(CU)**
J. R. **Spencer & Son**
(Albion Steel Works)

William Rufus **Nutt**   **(EP)** ^{(K80) (M)}
(Wentworth Works)
Sheffield (23, Burgess St)
- 1880 ...
~ 1894 ... **(& Co.)**
(See also figure: WR.N & Co.)

N.V.T. **S** ℭ 𝔓 𝔅 𝔐
N V & T

(See also)   **(EP)**
Needman, Veall & Tyzack
(Eye Witness Works)

N

	(See also) **Oliver & Bower Ltd.**	**(EP)**
O&E	*(See also)* **Osborn & Elliot**	**(OSP)**
	(See also) **Owen & Wild**	**(EP)**
	William **Oakes** Birmingham (6, Exeter Rw) - 1866 ...	**(EP)** (MDG)
	Albert **Oates** **(Atlantic Works)** Sheffield (18/64 & 66, Upper St/Philip's Rd) ~ 1872 - 1901 ... *(See also figure: A O T)*	**(CU)** (W) (K93) (WDS01)
	(See also) **Owen Brothers**	**(EP)**
OIO	Shirley **Clarke & Co.** **(Boston Works)**	**(CU)**
	James **Oldham** Sheffield (69, Arundel St) - 1879 - 1893 ...	**(EP)** (WDS79) (K80) (K93)
	T. **Oldham** Sheffield (69, Arundel St) 1860 ... *(See also figure: T.OLDHAM)*	**(EP)** (M) (B)
OLD ○	*(See also)* William. J. **Bingham** **(Clough Works)** and S. & R. **Linley** **(Conbar Works & Clough Works)** Sheffield - 1886 - 1888 ...	**(CU)** **(CU)**
	The **Old Park Silver Mills Co. Ltd.** **(Old Park Mills)** **(GS/BM/CU)** Sheffield - 1893 ...	(K93)

	Oliver & Bower Ltd.	**(EP)**	(K36)
	Sheffield (Howard St)		
	London (Hatton Garden)		
	- 1936 ... *(See also figure: O&B Ld S)*		

	George **Oliver**	**(EP)**	(GS) (CDB)
	Birmingham (24, Summer Rw)		(MDG)
	- 1861 - 1866 ...		

	Walter **Oliver**	**(EP)**	(K88)
	Birmingham (17, Hingeston St)		
	- 1888 ...		

OLLIVANT & BOTSFORD	**Ollivant & Botsford**	**(EP)**	(K80)
	Manchester (2, Exchange St)		
	- 1880 ...		

	Stephen G. **Onion**	**(BM/GS)**	(HGD)
	Birmingham (10, Brook St)		
	- 1850 ...		

	Stephen G. **Onion &** Mark **Perkins (CU)**		(SAOR)
	Birmingham		
	1818 ...		

	Onion & Son	**(GS)**	(WDOB)
	Birmingham (Brook St)		
	- 1839 ...		

	Henry **Onions & Co.**	**(EP)**	(K80)
	Birmingham (21, Caroline St)		
	- 1880 ...		

O N W A R D	*(See also)* **Slack & Grinold (Bath Works)**	**(EP)**

	Openshaw & Co.	**(EP)**
	Birmingham/London	
	~ 1900 ... *(See also figure: RAIN-BOW)*	

OPOBA	*(See also)* **Boswell, Hatfield & Co. (Hope Works)**	**(EP)**

O P U S	*(See also)* **Tricket, Haslehurst, Whiteley & Pryor**	**(EP)**

	Joseph **Orchard**	**(EP)**	(K78) (K80)
	Birmingham (20, Upper Hospital St)		
	- 1878 - 1880 ...		
ORIENT PLATE	**Not assigned!**	**(EP)**	
	Thomas Sellars **Ortley**	**(EP)**	(WDS79)
	Sheffield (71, Roebuck Rd)		
	- 1879 ...		
	Samuel **Osborn & Co.**	**(CU/EP)**	
	(Clyde Steel Works & Iron Works)		
	Sheffield (207, Rockingham St/184, Brook Hill)		(WDS79) (WDS01)
	- 1879 - 1901 ...		(W)
	- 1936 ... **(Ltd.)** *(See also figures: ABBEY, symbol " hand")*		(K36)
	Osborn & Elliot	**(OSP)**	(SAOR) (SBW)
	Sheffield (South St Moor)		(B) (M)
	1843 ... *(See also figure: O&E)*		
	Osborn & Hyndman	**(EP)**	(K80)
	Birmingham (62, Edgbaston St)		
	- 1880 ...		
	Osborn & Sons	**(CU/EP)**	(HGD) (CDB)
	Birmingham (16, Bennett's Hill/54, New St)		
	- 1850 - 1861 ...		
OSMINIUM SILVER	*(See also)*	**(EP)**	
	John **Nodder & Sons**		
	(Devenport Works/Taranaki Works)		
	John **Oswin**	**(CU)**	(SAOR)
	Coventry		
	1815 ...		
OSYRIS / OSIRIS	*(See also)*	**(EP)**	
	H. **Schü(ue)rhoff & Co.**		

O

Thomas **Otley & Co.** **(EP/BM)**
(Meadow Works)
Sheffield (48, Lambert St/33, Meadow St)
- 1849 - 1852 ...
(See figures: Thomas Otley, T.
OTLEY)
- 1879 - 1905 ... **(& Sons)**
(See also figures: T. OTLEY , T.O
& S)
- 1900 ... (**Ltd**.)
(See also figure: T.O & S Ltd)

(GDBS) (WDOS)
(M)

(SAOR) (K80)
(WDSR)

William **Otley & Co.** **(EP)**
Sheffield (69, Henry St)
- 1893 ...

(K93)

John **Otley** **(EP)**
Sheffield (14, Hoole Rd)
- 1901 ...

(WDS01)

Richard & Thomas **Otley** **(BM)**
Sheffield (Union Pl)
- 1833 ...

(GDS)

Samuel **Oughton &** Thomas **Smith (CU)**
Birmingham
1818 ...

(SAOR)

Oughton & Son **(EP)**
Birmingham (2, Caroline St)
- 1882 - 1884...

(K82) (K84)

⚜
O V A

(See also) **(CU)**
Tricket, Haslehurst, Whiteley
& Pryor

William **Overton** **(OSP)**
Birmingham (Gt. Brook St/Coleshill St)
- 1815 - 1818 ...

(WTDB) (WTD)
(CD)

Owen & Levick **(BM)**
Sheffield (92, Wellington St)
- 1852 ...

(WDOS)

R. **Owen & Son** **(OSP)**
Sheffield (West Bar)
1788 ... *(See also figure: R·O)*

(B) (SAOR)

Owen & Wild (EP)

Owen & Wild (EP) (E) (K93) (WDS01)
Sheffield (34 & 36, Holly St)
- 1893 - 1901 ... *(See also figure: O & W)*

Charles **Owen** (EP)
(Wellington Works)
Sheffield (92, Wellington St/130, West St)
- 1854 - 1863 ...
(See also figure: CHAR^{S}OWEN)
1863 - 1877 (**& Co.**) (POS) (K54) (GS)
(See also figure: CHAR^{S}OWEN & Co)
(Then: Owen Brothers)

Denison **Owen** (BM/EP) (WDS79)
Sheffield (37, Corporation St)
- 1879 ...

Joseph **Owen** (OSP) (DSRR)
Sheffield (Broomhall Field St)
- 1841 ...

Lewis Thomas **Owen** (EP) (K80)
Sheffield (17, Figtree Ln)
- 1880 ...

Owen Brothers (EP) (K80) (Rd)
(Formerly: Charles Owen & Co.)
Sheffield (12, Baker Hill)
- 1880 - 1903 ... *(See also figure: O Bros)*

John **Oxley** (CU) (GDS) (SAOR)
Sheffield (43, Howard St/12, Charles St/ (SBW) (M) (B)
21, Eyre St) (DSRR) (SD46)
- 1833 - 1846 ... *(See also figure: I · O)*

Walter **Oxley** (EP) (K36)
Sheffield (318, Queens Rd)
- 1936 ...

O

	(See also) **Pinder Brothers**	**(EP)**
P&D	*(See also)* **Pembrook & Dingley**	**(EP)**
P D &	*(See also)* **Pembrook & Dickins**	**(EP)**
& P M	*(See also)* **Priestley & Moore Ltd.**	**(EP)**
P&M	*(See also)* <small>William</small> **Parkin & Marshall** **(Telegraph Works)**	**(CU/EP)**
P.D	*(See also)* <small>P.</small> **Dewsnap**	**(OSP)**
P.G	**Not assigned!**	**(EP)**
P.J	*(See also)* <small>P.</small> **Justice**	**(OSP)**
P.M	*(See also)* <small>Philip</small> **Marks**	**(EP)**
P·S	<small>P.</small> **Spur & Son** Sheffield (Church Ln) 1788 ...	**(OSP)** <small>(B)</small>
P.A&S	*(See also)* <small>Philip</small> **Ashberry & Sons**	**(BM/EP)**
<small>P</small> **A** <small>C</small> <small>L</small>	*(See also)* **Asprey & Co. Ltd.**	**(EP)**
	<small>William</small> **Padley** Sheffield (Crescent Rd/8/10 & 12, Howard St/ Meadow St) - 1879 ... - 1878 - 1893 ... **(& Sons)** - 1905 ... **(Ltd.)** *(See also figures: WP&S, symbol "hand")*	**(EP)** <small>(WDS79)</small> <small>(Dia) (K93)</small> <small>(WDSR)</small>

P

Padley, Parkin & Co. (OSP) ^{(SAOR) (GDBS)}
Sheffield (Watson Walk)
1846 - 1849 ... *(See also figures:*
PP&Co., symbol "hand")

(SAOR) (GDBS) (SBW) (B) (M)

Padley, Parkin & Staniforth (EP) (WDOS) (M) (K54)
Sheffield (1, Watson Walk)
- 1852 - 1854 ...
(See also figure: PP&S)

Padley, Staniforth & Co. (EP) (SAOR) (SBW) (B) (M)
Sheffield (Harthead)
1857 ... *(See also figure: PS&Co)*

Augustus **Padmore** (EP) (K88) (K92)
Birmingham (245, Icknield St)
- 1888 - 1892 ...

William **Page & Co.** (EP)
Birmingham (Cranemore St/Cattle's Grove/
55, Albion St)
- 1880 - 1903 ...
- 1936 ... (**Ltd.**)
(See also figures: WP , BOLI-
VIAN SILVER, SILVERITE,
W^MPAGE&Co, WP&Co)

(K80) (K82) (K84) (K88) (K92) (PC) (K03) (SBW) (M)

(K36)

William **Page** (GS/CP) (WAB) (HTD) (DOB) (WWDB) (WDOB)
Birmingham (Belmont Rw/74, Dale's End/
Lawley St/Curzon St)
- 1829 - 1839 ...

PAGE.KEEN&PAGE
PLYMOUTH

Page, Keen & Page (EP)
Plymouth (17, George St)
~ 1860 - 1880 ...

George **Painter** (CP) (WAB)
Birmingham (Ellis St)
- 1829 ...

John **Painter** (CP) (WTDB) (WTD) (WDB)
Birmingham (Ellis St/Exeter Rw)
- 1815 - 1823 ...

W. **Pairpoint & Sons Ltd.** (EP) (K36)
London (41, Gerrard St)
- 1936 ...

PALATINE PLATE	*(See also)* **Stephenson & Sons**	**(EP)**	
	Joseph **Palmer** Birmingham (Inge St) - 1829 - 1830 ...	**(CU)**	(WAB) (HTD)
PAMPA REAL KNIFE	*(See also)* **Lockwood Brothers**	**(CU/EP)**	
✠ PAPA	*(See also)* Jacob & Samuel **Roberts**	**(CU/OSP)**	
	Alfred **Pardoe** Birmingham (33, Victoria St) - 1888 - 1892 ...	**(EP)**	(K88) (K92)
	Pare & Greasley Birmingham (13 & 4, Gt. Hampton St) - 1866 - 1867 ...	**(EP)**	(MDG) (POB)
	Parker & Brown Sheffield (38, Garden St) - 1880 - 1893 ... *(In 1893 they took over: John Brown)*	**(EP)**	(K80) (K93)
	Henry **Parker & Co.** **(Parker & Sons)** **(Lozells Works)** *(Formerly: Henry Cornforth)* Birmingham (85 & 87, Clifford St/10, Brook St) - 1878 - 1896 ...	**(BM/EP)**	(K78) (K80) (K82) (K84) (K88) (PC)
	Parker & Fereday Birmingham (Slaney St) - 1815 ...	**(OSP)**	(WTDB)
	Joseph **Parker & Sons** Sheffield (58 & 60, Trinity St) - 1936 ...	**(EP)**	(K36)
	Henry Thomas **Parker** Birmingham (1, Bromsgrove St) - 1829 ...	**(CP)**	(WAB)
	John **Parker** Birmingham (Slaney St) - 1818 - 1823 ...	**(OSP)**	(WTD) (CD) (WDB)

P

John **Parker**	**(CU/ CP/EP)**	(WAB) (HTD) (DOB) (WWDB) (SAOR)(WDOB) (HGDB) (HGD)
Birmingham (23, Summer Rw) - 1829 - 1836 ... - 1839 - 1850 ... **(& Sons)**		
John Frederick **Parker**	**(CP)**	(SAOR) (WAB) (HTD) (DOB) (WWDB) (WDOB) (HGDB) (HGD)
Birmingham (72, High St/Parade) 1826 - 1850 ...		
Joseph **Parker**	**(EP)**	(GS) (WDS01)
Sheffield (3, Burgess St/58 & 60, Trinity St) - 1863 ... - 1901 ... **(& Sons)**		
William **Parker**	**(EP)**	(K80)
(Formerly: Henry Cornforth) Manchester (14, Grove Chambers) - 1880 ...		
Isaak **Parkes**	**(CU)**	(SAOR)
Birmingham 1819 ...		
John **Parkes**	**(CU)**	(SAOR)
Birmingham 1813 ...		
Joseph **Parkes**	**(CU)**	(WAB) (HTD) (DOB)
Birmingham (Queen St) - 1829 - 1833 ...		
William **Parkes**	**(CP)**	(WAB) (HTD) (SAOR)
Birmingham (Church St) - 1829 - 1840 ...		
William **Parkes**	**(EP)**	(CDB) (GS) (MDG) (POB) (K72) (K78) (K80) (K82) (K84)
Birmingham (13, New Summer St/ 28, Upper Tower St) - 1861 - 1884 ...		
E.H. **Parkin & Co.** **(Cornwall Works)**	**(EP)**	(K36)
Sheffield (212, Brookhill St/122, Scotland St) - 1919 - 1940 1940 - 1952 (**Ltd**.) *(See also figures: E H P, Cameo, PSL)* *(Then: Thomas Land)*		

P

PARKIN & MARSHALL SHEFFIELD	William **Parkin & Marshall (CU/EP) (Telegraph Works)** Sheffield (Furnival Street 23/Sylvester St/ Milton St) 1861 ... 1866 ... *(See also figure: WP)* - 1879 - 1901 ... *(See also figures: P&M S, XL ALL)*	(K80) (K93) (SBW) (B) (M) (B) (SAOR) (WDS79) (WDS01) (SAOR)
	John **Parkin &** Abraham **Wigham (OSP)** Sheffield (Carver St) 1792 ... *(See also figure: I·P)*	(B) (SAOR)
PARKIN	William **Parkin** **(BM/CP)** Sheffield (Flat St/Lee Croft/Thomas St/ Broomhall Ln/42, Campo Ln) 1817 - 1833 ... *(See also figure: WP)*	(B) (SAOR) (CD) (NGDS) (PD) (SDG) (PDY) (PDB) (GDS)
	Charles **Parkin** **(EP)** Manchester (85, Princess St) - 1880 ...	(K80)
	George **Parkin** **(EP)** Sheffield (Ecclesall New Rd) - 1854 ...	(POS) (K54)
	Richard **Parkin** **(BM)** Sheffield (40, Campo Ln/Spring St) - 1849 - 1852 ... *(See also figure: RICHARD PAR- KIN)* - 1863 ... (**& Son**) *(See also figure: RICHARD PARKIN & SON)*	(GDBS) (WDOS) (GS) (M)
	Thomas **Parkin** **(BM/EP)** Sheffield (45/15, Sycamore St) - 1849 - 1863 ... *(See also figure: THOS PARKIN)*	(GDBS) (WDOS) (POS) (K54)(GS) (M)
	Thomas **Parkin** **(OSP)** Sheffield (Cooper St) 1791 ... *(See also figure: T·P)*	(B) (SAOR)
	G. **Parrott** **(BM)** Birmingham (84, Woodcock St) - 1866 ...	(MDG)

P

Charles **Parsons & Co.**   **(EP)**   (K82) (K84) (K88)
Birmingham (Ct. 14, Barr St)
- 1882 - 1888 ...

John **Parsons & Co.**   **(OSP)**   (B) (SAOR) (GM)
(Formerly: Winter, Parsons & Hall)
Sheffield (Market Pl)
1783 - 1787 ... *(See also figures:*
IP&Co, JOHN PARSON & Co,
symbol "keys")

Thomas **Parsons**   **(BM/CP)**   (WAB) (HTD)
                               (DOB) (HGD)
Birmingham (15, Kenion St/130, Gt. Hampton St)
- 1829 - 1850 ...

William **Parsons**   **(EP)**   (K80)
Birmingham (10, Hylton St)
- 1880 ...

Martin **Partridge & Co.**   **(EP)**   (PC)
Birmingham (61, Graham St)
- 1896 ...

C. B. **Partridge**   **(CP/EP)**
Birmingham (11 & 12, New Bond St./115,
Northwood St)
- 1903 ...   (K03)
- 1882 - 1892 ... **(& Sons)**   (K82) (K84) (K88)
                                     (K92)

Ebenezer Joseph **Partridge**   **(EP)**   (K03)
Birmingham (61, Graham St)
- 1903 ...

Elizabeth **Partridge**   **(OSP)**   (WTDB)
Birmingham (Charlotte St)
- 1815 ...

Frederick **Partridge**   **(EP)**   (K80)
Birmingham (15, Tenby St)
- 1880 ...

William **Partridge**   **(CP)**   (WDB)
Birmingham
- 1823 ...

P

	George **Parton** Birmingham (82, Caroline St) - 1833 ...	**(CP)** [DOB]

(See also)
 Philip **Ashberry & Sons**   **(BM/EP)**

	Alfred S. **Paterson** **(Colonial Works)** Birmingham (14, Victoria St) - 1861 - 1863 ...	**(EP)** [GS] [CDB]
	Paterson Brothers Birmingham (14, Victoria St) - 1861 - 1866 ...	**(EP)** [CDB] [MDG]
	Benjamin **Patrick & Co.** Birmingham (46, Augusta St) - 1880 ...	**(EP)** [K80]
" PATRIOT "	L. & C. **Glauert** Sheffield ~ 1895 ...	**(EP)**
	William **Patten** Birmingham - 1823 ...	**(CP)** [WDB]
	William **Patten** Sheffield (Silver St) 1780 ... *(See also figure: W·P)*	**(OSP)** [B] [SAOR]
	Payton & Co. Birmingham (Scotland St) - 1880 ...	**(EP)** [SBW] [K80]
P.BROS.(S)LTD	*(See also)* **Pinder Brothers**	**(EP)**
P.B **PINRO** **EP/NS**	*(See also)* **Pinder Brothers**	**(EP)**
PB	*(See also)* **Proctor & Beilby**	**(OSP)**

P

	(See also) **Pinder Brothers**	(EP)	
	Not assigned!	(EP)	
	Joseph **Peace & Co.** Sheffield ~ 1865 - 1892 *(See figure: AIGO)*	(EP)	(W)
	J. **Peacock &** G. **Austin** Sheffield (Pond St) 1798 ... *(See also figure: IP)*	(OSP)	(B) (SAOR)
PEAKE	Michael **Peake** Birmingham (Cannon St) 1807 - 1815 ...	(Coach)	(B) (M) (WTDB)
	Pearce & Buxton (Naga Works) Sheffield (Eyre Ln) - 1893 ...	(EP)	(K93)
Pearce & Sons	**Pearce & Sons Ltd.** Leicester (34, Gallowtree Gate) Leeds (Bond St) York (Lendal) ~ 1900 - 1930 ...	(CU/EP)	(E)
	John **Pearce** Sheffield (38, Angel St) - 1849 - 1852 ...	(BM)	(GDBS) (WDOS)
	A. & F. **Pears** London - 1900 *(See figure: A & F Pears)*	(EP)	(M)
	William **Pearsall** Birmingham (29, High St) - 1880 ...	(EP)	(K80)
	Pearson & Co. Birmingham (23, George St) - 1888 ...	(EP)	(K88)

P

Pearson & Forrester (BM) (K82) (K84)
Birmingham (3, King Alfred's Pl)
- 1882 - 1884 ...
(Then: Pearson and Forrester became two separate companies)

Alfred Henry **Pearson** (BM) (K88)
(Formerly: Pearson & Forrester)
Birmingham (3, King Alfred's Pl)
- 1888 ...

PEAR SON

Richard **Pearson** (CP/Coach) (B) (WTDB) (WTD) (WDB) (M)
Birmingham (Princes St)
1811 - 1823 ...

William **Pearson** (EP) (PC) (K92)
Birmingham (206, Camden St)
- 1892 - 1896 ...

Frederick **Peat** (EP) (WDSR)
Sheffield (4, Springhouse Rd)
- 1905 ...

Pegler Brothers (EP) (K80)
Norwich (41 & 43, London St)
- 1880 ...

PELHAM **PLATE**

(See also) (EP)
Harrison **Fisher**

PEM ..BER..TON

Pemberton & Mitchell (OSP) (B) (SAOR) (M)
Birmingham (Edmond St)
1816 - 1817 ...

Pemberton & Son (CU) (SAOR)
Birmingham
1821 ...

Samuel **Pemberton** (CU) (SAOR)
Birmingham
1813 ...

Pembrook & Dickins (EP) (PC) (K03)
Birmingham (43, Hall St)
- 1896 - 1903 ... *(See also figure: P&D)*

Pembrook & Dingley (EP) (K72) (K78) (K80) (K82) (K84) (K88) (K92) (M)
Birmingham (43, Hall St)
- 1872 - 1892 ... *(See also figure: P&D)*

P

Charles **Pembrook** Birmingham (43, Hall St) - 1861 - 1867 ...	**(EP)**	(CDB) (GS) (MDG) (POB)
Pendleton & Dix Sheffield (5, Holly St) - 1901 ...	**(EP)**	(WDS01)
Pendleton & Merrill Sheffield (5, Holly St) - 1880 - 1893 ...	**(EP)**	(K80) (K93)
Edwin **Pendleton** Sheffield (6, Sharrow Ln) - 1879 ...	**(EP)**	(WDS79)
Samuel **Pendleton** Birmingham (Dean St) - 1861 ...	**(EP)**	(CDB)
Arthur **Pepper & Co. Ltd.** London (67 & 68, Hatton Garden) - 1936 ...	**(EP)**	(K36)
Mrs. Mary Ann **Perkins** Birmingham (19, Regent Pl) - 1866 ...	**(EP)**	(MDG)
Henry **Perks** Manchester (24, Corn Exchange Chambers) - 1880 ...	**(EP)**	(K80)
Perry & Co. Ltd. Birmingham ~ 1900 ... *(See also figures: AMERICAN SILVER ALLOY, Invisible Action - W.E.W.)*	**(EP)**	(SBW) (M)
Charles **Perry** Birmingham (Congreve St) - 1823 - 1829 ...	**(CP)**	(WDB) (WAB)
John **Perry** Nottingham ~ 1900 ...	**(T)**	(E)
PERUVIAN SILVER	*(See also)* Thomas **Hands & Son**	**(BM/EP)**

P

308

Jackson **Petfield**	**(EP)**	(M)
Sheffield		
~ 1876 ... *(See also figure: J.PETFIELD)*		

David **Pettifer**	**(EP)**	(SAOR) (K78)
Birmingham (11, Unett St)		(K80) (K82) (K84)
1847 - 1903 ...		(K88) (K92) (K03)

Generic Mark - Plated German Silver **(GS)**
- 1897

R. & G. **Phelps**	**(EP)**	(GS)
Birmingham (73, Spencer St)		
- 1863 ...		

PHILIP
ASHBERRY & SONS
SHEFFIELD

PHILIP ASHBERRY & SONS
BEST ELECTRO PLATE
SHEFFIELD

PHILIP ASHBERRY & SONS
SHEFFIELD

(See also) **(BM/EP)**
Philip **Ashberry & Sons**

James **Philips & Co.**	**(EP)**	(K03)
Birmingham (244, Icknield St)		
- 1903 ...		

Philips & Perry	**(CP)**	(WTDB)
Birmingham (St. Mary's Rw)		
- 1815 ...		

John **Phillips & Son**	**(OSP)**	(CD) (WDB)
Birmingham (Brook St)		
- 1818 - 1823 ...		

Frederick Richard **Phillips**	**(CU/EP)**	(K80) (K82) (K84)
Birmingham (37, Tenby St)		(K88) (K92) (PC)
- 1880 - 1896 ...		

G. **Phillips**	**(GS)**	(MDG)
Birmingham (4, Bordesley St)		
- 1866 ...		

	Thomas **Phillips** Birmingham (90, Gt. Charles St) - 1872 ...	**(EP)**	(K72)
	Joseph W. **Phipson** Birmingham (New St) - 1829 - 1830 ...	**(CP)**	(WAB) (HTD)
P.H.V & C<u>o</u>	P. H. **Vogel & Co.** Birmingham (Warstone Parade) ~ 1920 ...	**(EP)**	(S)
PHOSPHOR.	(The) **Phosphor Bronze Co.** Southwark Surrey ~ 1890 ... *(See also figure: DURO METAL)*	**(EP)**	(SBW) (M)
	Charles **Pickslay & Co.** Sheffield (High St) 1828 ... *(See also figure: CP)*	**(OSP)**	(B) (SAOR)
	Picksley, Appleby & Bertram (OSP) Sheffield (High St) - 1829 ...		(PD)
PILOT	*(See also)* C. **Jones**	**(EP)**	
Pim ley	Samuel **Pimley** Birmingham (21, Steelhouse Ln) - 1815 - 1835 ...	**(CP)**	(WTDB) (WTD) (HTD) (CD) (WDB) (WAB) (M) (WWDB) (DOB)
	Henry **Pimm** Birmingham (61, Lionel St) - 1872 ...	**(EP)**	(K72)
	Pinches & Laughton Birmingham (92, Gt. Charles St) 1829 - 1830 ...	**(CP)**	(SAOR) (WAB) (HTD)
	William **Pinches** Birmingham - 1823 ...	**(CP)**	(WDB)

P

James **Pinder & Co.** **(CU/EP)**
(Colonial Plate Works)
Sheffield (12 & 14, Carver St/14 & 16, Furnival St)
- 1880 - 1901 ...
(See also figure: JP&Co)

(K80) (K93)
(WDS01) (M)
(SBW)

John **Pinder & Co.** **(EP)**
Sheffield
1874 ...

(SAOR)

PINDER
BROS
SHEFFIELD

Pinder Brothers **(EP)**
(John Thomas & Charles Edward)
Sheffield
1877 - 1882 (Ct. 2, Headford St)
1882 - 1888 (2, Fitzwilliam Ln)
1888 - 1895 (142, Rockingham Ln)
1895 - 1939 (176, Broomhall Ln/Ct. 4, 48, Garden St)
1939 - today (**Ltd.**)
(See also figures: P, P.B, P Bros, PINRO, ALPIN)

(PI)

(SAOR)

(WDS01)

PINRO

(See also) **(EP)**
Pinder Brothers

James **Piper** **(CP)**
Birmingham (Tower Hill)
- 1815 ...

(WTDB)

Joseph **Pitt** **(CP)**
Birmingham
- 1823 ...

(WDB)

P J B

Not assigned! **(EP)**

PL

(See also) **(OSP)**
P. **Leonard**

Henry Hodson **Plante & Co.** **(EP)**
(Frederick Street Works)
Birmingham (55, Frederick St)
~ 1882 - 1896 ...
(See also figure: HHP&Co)

(PC) (M) (SBW)

P

	G. **Plating & Co.** (EP)	(K36)
	Birmingham (49-52, Tenby St North)	
	- 1936 ...	
	The **Plating Company Ltd.** (EP)	(K72) (K80) (K82) (K84) (K88) (K93) (WDS01)
	Sheffield (82, Lichfield St/239, Solly St/ Henrietta St/24, Wheeldon St)	
	- 1872 - 1901 ...	
PLATINOID	*(See also)* (GS/EP)	
	Francis Richard **Martino**	
PLATO	**Not assigned!** (EP)	(E)
	~ 1920 ...	
	William **Platt** (OSP)	(CD) (SAOR)
	Birmingham (Caroline St)	
	- 1818 - 1823 ...	
PLENTY	*(See also)* (EP)	
	John **Derby & Sons**	
PLUTUS	*(See also)* (CU)	
	Beldon, Hoyland & Co.	
🄿 🄼 🄲ᵈ	**Not assigned!** (EP)	
PM RT	*(See also)* (OSP)	
	P. **Madin &** R. **Trickett**	
🄿 🄾 & 🅂 EP	**Not assigned!** (EP)	
	Benjamin **Polack** (OSP)	(B) (SAOR)
	Sheffield (High St)	
	1807 ... *(See also figure: BP)*	
	William **Poles** (CU)	(GDS) (WDS37)
	Sheffield (Glossop Rd)	
	- 1833 - 1837 ...	
	Maurice **Pollack** (EP)	(POB)
	Birmingham (78, Spencer St)	
	- 1867 ...	
	Christopher **Poller** (FP)	(WTDB) (WWDB)
	Birmingham (Duddeston St/4, Bartholomew St)	
	- 1815 - 1835 ...	

P

Richard **Poller** (FP) ^(WAB)
Birmingham (Steelhouse Ln)
- 1829 ...

J. **Poncia & Son** (BM/GS) ^(HGD)
Birmingham (50, Pershore St)
- 1850 ...

Poole & Jackson (EP) ^(K80)
Birmingham (22, Branston St)
- 1880 ...

James **Pool(e)** (EP) ^{(K72) (K78) (K82)}
^{(K84) (K88)}
Birmingham (30/73, Northwood St/
4, Ingleby St)
- 1872 - 1888 ...

John Vonder **Poppenburg** (EP) ^(K72)
Birmingham (25, Branston St)
- 1872 ...

William **Poplur** (EP) ^{(K78) (K80) (K82)}
^{(K84) (K88) (K92)}
Birmingham (18, Wynn St/13, Bell Barn Rd) ^(K03)
- 1878 - 1903 ...

Thomas Reeves **Porter** (CP) ^{(WTDB) (WTD)}
^(CD)
Birmingham (Bristol St)
- 1815 - 1818 ...

The **Portland Co. Ltd.** (EP)
(Francis **Higgins**)
London (Riding House St)
1859 - 1869
1868 - 1909 (Francis **Higgins & Son**)
1909 - 1940 (Francis **Higgins & Son Ltd.**)
(See also figure: fh)

William **Postans &** George **Tyl** (CU) ^(SAOR)
Birmingham
1819 ...

A. E. **Poston & Co. Ltd.** (EP)

POSTON PRODUCTS
LTD
*Lonsdale
Silver Plate*

Birmingham
London
~ 1930 - 1960
*(See figures: LONSDALE,
A. E. POSTON)*

P

Ahner **Potler** **(EP)** (K03)
Birmingham (35, Unett St)
- 1903 ...

(The) **Potosi Silver Co.** **(EP)** (K80) (K82) (K84)
(Formerly: Levi & Salaman) (K88) (K92) (PC)
Birmingham (21, Barr St/St. George St/ (K03) (SBW) (M)

POTOSI **SILVER**

143, Newhall St)
- 1880 - 1903 ...
*(See also figures: ELECTRO PO-
TOSI, PS&Co., symbol "bird")*

Abner **Potter** **(EP)** (K92)
Birmingham (258, New John St)
- 1892 ...

POTTER-SHEFLD **SILVA**

John Henry **Potter** **(CU/EP)** (SAOR) (E) (W)
(Rockingham Works) (K93) (WDSR)
Sheffield (65, Division St/11, Marlborough Rd) (SBW) (M)
1885 - 1938 ...

POTTER

POTTER **S** **A1**

*(See also figures: J.H.P,
J.H.POTTER, ARARA, SUPERIOR)*

Samuel **Potter** **(EP)** (K80)
Birmingham (27, Mary St/Caroline St)
- 1880 ...

Pourer Top Manufacturing Co. Ltd. (K36)
Birmingham (24, Mary St) **(EP)**
- 1936 ...

Richard **Povey** **(CP)** (DOB)
Birmingham (Loveday St)
- 1833 ...

Charles **Powell** **(CP)** (WTDB) (CD)
Birmingham (Colmore St)
- 1815 - 1818 ...

Elizabeth **Powell** **(CP)** (WAB)
Birmingham (10, Carr's Ln)
- 1829 ...

George **Powell** **(EP)** (K88) (K92)
Birmingham (Ct. 1, New Summer St)
- 1888 - 1892 ...

P

James **Powell**   **(CP)** ^(WDB)
Birmingham
- 1823 ...

Samuel **Power**   **(EP)** ^(K03)
Birmingham (115, Northwood St)
- 1903 ...

John **Poynton & Co.**   **(OSP)** ^{(B) (SAOR)}
Sheffield (Scotland St)
1804 ... *(See also figure: I·P &CO)*

Thomas **Poynton &** R. **Flower**   **(OSP)** ^{(B) (SAOR)}
Sheffield (Pond St)
1801 ... *(See also figure: TP)*

PP
&C⁰

(See also)   **(OSP)**
Padley, Parkin & Co.

ℙ ℙ & 𝕊

(See also)   **(EP)**
Padley, Parkin & Staniforth

PRACTICAL CUTLERY C⁰
SHEFFIELD

(See also)   **(CU/EP)**
Walter **Birch**

Price & Phillips   **(EP)** ^(K88)
Birmingham (115, Spencer St)
- 1888 ...

Cornelius **Price**   **(EP)** ^{(K78) (K78)}
Birmingham (5, Hylton St)
- 1878 - 1880 ...

Edward **Price**   **(EP)** ^{(K92) (K03)}
Birmingham (115, Spencer St/134, Branston St)
- 1903 ...

Joseph **Price**   **(EP)** ^{(GS) (K93)}
^(SAOR)
Sheffield (66, Wicker/8, Hermitage St)
- 1863 - 1893 ...

Walter **Price**   **(EP)** ^(K03)
Birmingham (35, Northampton St)
- 1903 ...

William **Price**   **(CP)** ^{(WTDB) (CD)}
Birmingham (Moor St)
- 1815 - 1818 ...

P

	Arthur **Priestley & Co.** **(EP)**	(SAOR) (K93) (WDS01)
	(Priestley & Shaw) Sheffield (4, Carver Ln) 1889 - 1901 ...	

PRIESTLEY&MOORE E.P.N.S.A.I.

Priestley & Moore Ltd. **(EP)**
Sheffield
~ 1910 ... *(See also figures: P &M, VALIANT PLATE)*

John **Prime** **(CP)** (M)
Birmingham
- 1823 - 1839 ...

Thomas **Prime** **(MP/CP/EP)**
Birmingham (18 & 19, Northwood St/107, Ryland St)
- 1829 - 1850 ...
- 1861 - 1892 ... **(& Son)**
(See also figure: MP Prime)

(WAB) (SAOR) (HTD) (DOB) (WWDB) (HGDB) (HGD) (CDB) (GS) (MDG) (POB) (K72) (SAOR) (K78) (K80) (K82) (K84) (K88) (K92) (SBW) (M)

Charles **Primer** **(BM/GS)** (HGD)
Birmingham (Hanley St)
- 1850 ...

PRIMUS

(See also) **(CU/EP)**
Isaac **Ellis & Sons**
(Portland Works)

PRINCE'S PLATE
RD 71552

(See also) **(BM/EP/CU)** (Rd 71552)
John Newton **Mappin &** George **Webb**
(Royal Plate Works)

Robert **Pringle** **(BM/EP)**
(Wilderness Works)
London (Wilderness Rw/ 40 & 42, Clerkenwell Rd)
- 1881
- 1882 ... **(& Co.)**
- 1892 ... **(& Sons)**
- 1931 - 1936 ... **(& Sons Ltd.)**

(SBW) (M)

(K36)

P

Thomas **Prior** (OSP) (B) (SAOR)
Sheffield (Gibraltar St)
1778 ... *(See also figure: T·P)*

Charles **Proctor &** Thomas **Beilby (OSP)**
Sheffield (Milk St/New Market St)
1792 ... *(See also figure: PB)* (B) (SAOR)
1795 ... *(See also figure: CP)* (SAOR)

Luke **Proctor & Co.** (OSP) (B) (SAOR)
Sheffield (Milk St)
1785 ... *(See also figure: L.P&Co)*

Charles & L. **Proctor** (OSP) (B) (SAOR)
Sheffield (Milk St)
1773 ... *(See also figure C·L P)*

W. **Proctor** (OSP) (B) (SAOR)
Sheffield (Fruit Market)
1817 ... *(See also figure: WP)*

PROLIFIC

(See also) (CU/GS)
George Rayner **Mardsen & Son**
(Argyle Works)

Phineas **Proud** (CP) (DOB)
Birmingham (39, Aston St)
- 1833 ...

Pryor & Tyzack (EP) (B) (GS) (SBW)
Sheffield (80, Devision St/Granville St) (M)
- 1863 ... *(See also figures: PT)*

Pryor, Tyzack & Co. (EP) (B) (SAOR) (GS)
Sheffield (80, Devision St/Granville St) (SBW) (M)
1861 - 1863
(See also figure: PT&Co)
(Then: Pryor & Tyzack)

PS
(See also) (OSP)
J. **Ellis,** P. **Spurr &** P. **Cadman** jun.

PS &C⁰
(See also) (EP)
Padley, Staniforth & Co.

PS " symbols "
(See also) (EP)
John **Gilbert**

P

317

ⓟ ⓢ Ⓒ⁰ 🄴🄿 ⓟ 🅂 Ⓒ⁰ 🄴🄿 ◆	*(See also)* (The) **Potosi Silver Co.**	**(EP)**
ⓟ ⓢ ⓛ	*(See also)* E.H. **Parkin & Co.** **(Cornwall Works)**	**(EP)**
ⓟ ⓣ & Ⓒ⁰ ⓢ	*(See also)* **Pryor Tzack & Co.**	**(EP)**
🄿🄣	*(See also)* **Pryor & Tyzack**	**(EP)**
	Richard **Puller** Birmingham (Steelhouse Ln) - 1830 ...	**(FP)** (HTD)
	John **Pursall** Birmingham (24, Gt. Hampton St/109, Vyse St/ 34, Vittoria St) - 1861 - 1884 ...	**(EP)** (CDB) (K78) (K80) (K82) (K84)
	Mrs. Catherine **Pursall** Birmingham (63, Gt. Hampton St.) - 1888 ...	**(EP)** (K88)
	Charles **Putrell** (jun) Sheffield (77, Monmouth St) - 1901 ...	**(EP)** (WDS01)
	Thomas **Pye** Birmingham (22, Duddeston Rw) - 1850 ...	**(EP)** (HGD)
PYRO PYRO GOLD	*(See also)* John **Neal &Co.**	**(EP)**
	Quibell & Sons Birmingham (19a, Pitsford St) - 1936 ...	**(EP)** (K36)
	Joseph **Quixall & Co.** Sheffield (Pond St) 1803 ... *(See also figure: J.Q&Co)*	**(OSP)** (B) (SAOR)

P

R&B	*(See also)* **Rose & Brough**	**(EP)**
R & B / **R&B** **S** **EP** / **R&B** **S** **EP** ✿	*(See also)* Samuel **Roberts &** Charles **Belk** **(Furnival Works)**	**(EP)**
R&B / **R & B**	*(See also)* Samuel **Roberts &** William **Briggs** **(Furnival Works)**	**(EP)**
R&C ✻ **S**	*(See also)* Benjamin W. **Ramsden & Co.**	**(EP)**
R&D **S&L** / **R&D** **L&S** / **R&D** **S&L**	*(See also)* **Roberts & Dore**	**(EP)**
R&D	**Not assigned!** ~ 1910 ...	**(EP)** [E]
R&E **S**	**Not assigned!** Sheffield	**(EP)** [E]
R&H	*(See also)* **Roberts & Hall**	**(EP)**
R & S **M P**	*(See also)* **Roberts, Smith & Co.**	**(OSP)**
R&S / **R & S**	*(See also)* Samuel **Roberts &** Joseph **Slater**	**(EP)**
R·B	*(See also)* R. **Barnard &** W. **Hadfield**	**(OSP)**
R·J	*(See also)* R. **Jewesson**	**(OSP)**
R·K	*(See also)* R. **Kippax & Co.**	**(OSP)**
R·L	*(See also)* Richard **Loy**	**(OSP/CU)**

R

R·M	*(See also)* Richard **Morton & Co.**	**(OSP)**
R·M **R·M**	*(See also)* Richard **Morton**	**(OSP)**
R·O	*(See also)* R. **Owen & Son**	**(OSP)**
R·T	*(See also)* Robert **Tricket & Co.**	**(OSP)**
R·T	*(See also)* Robert **Tricket**	**(OSP/CU)**
R A	*(See also)* Richard **Atkinson**	**(OSP)**
RABONE RABONE BROTHERS & C̲o̲	**Rabone Brothers & Co.** Birmingham ~	**(EP)**
" RADIANT "	*(See also)* William R. **Humphreys & Co.** **(Haddon Works & Eyre Street Works)**	**(EP)**
	William **Rae & Co.** Liverpool ~ 1900 ... *(See also figure: W.R.SILVERO & Co)*	**(EP)**
RAENO SILVER	*(See also)* William **Daffern** and **Raeno Silver Plating Co. Ltd. (EP)**	**(EP)**
	Raeno Silver Plating Co. Ltd. (EP) *(Formerly: William Daffern)* Birmingham 1910 - 1935 ... *(See also figure: RSP&Co)*	

RAINBOW

(See also)   **(CU/EP)**
John **Ridal**
(Paxton Works)
Sheffield
and
Openshaw & Co.   **(EP)**
Birmingham/London
~

Walter J. **Ramsbottom**   **(CU)**   (SBW) (M)
(Vine Works)
Sheffield
~ (See also figure: ISERVE)

Benjamin W. **Ramsden**   **(EP)**   (SAOR)
Sheffield
1875 ... *(See also figure: R&Co)*

Thomas **Ramsey**   **(CU)**   (GDS) (WDS37)
Sheffield (Crooks Moor)
- 1833 - 1837 ...

G. **Randle**   **(EP)**   (PC)
Birmingham (30, Augusta St)
- 1896 ...

John **Ratcliff**   **(CP)**   (WTDB)
Birmingham (Lower Temple St)
- 1815 ...

John & Charles **Ratcliffe & Co.**   **(EP)**   (HGD) (GS) (POS)
(Suffolk Street Works)   (WDOS) (K54)
Birmingham (140 and then 136, Suffolk St)
Sheffield (67, Arundel St)
- 1850 - 1863 ...

Thomas **Ratcliffe**   **(OSP)**   (B) (SAOR)
Sheffield (Red Croft)
1778 ... *(See also figure: T·R)*

Charles **Ratherham & Son**   **(OSP)**   (WTDB) (WTD)
(Charles & Edward **Ratherham**)   (CD) (SAOR)
Birmingham (45, Gt. Charles St)
- 1815 - 1820 ...

Charles **Ratherham**   **(CP)**   (SAOR) (WDB)
Birmingham (133, Gt. Charles St)   (WAB) (DOB)
- 1823 - 1833 ...

R

	Edward **Rather(h)am** Birmingham (133, Gt. Charles St) 1847 - 1863 ...	**(EP)**	(SAOR) (HGD) (GS) (CDB)
	Richard **Ratherham** Coventry 1816 ...	**(OSP)**	(SAOR)
	Ravault & Lawton Birmingham (Harford St) - 1903 ...	**(EP)**	(K03)
	Rawson Brothers **(Globe Curtlery Works)** Sheffield (19 & 21, Carver St) - 1901 ...	**(EP/CU)**	(WDS01)
R.BROADHEAD & CO **SHEFFIELD**	*(See also)* Roger **Broadhead & Co.** **(Britannia Works)**	**(BM/EP)**	
RB	*(See also)* R. **Barnard**	**(OSP)**	
R B	*(See also)* **Rhodes Brothers**	**(EP)**	
R·C·& Co **R·C·& Co** **PATENT**	*(See also)* S. **Roberts,** G. **Cadman & Co.**	**(OSP)**	
RᴰJEWESSON **MIDLETON&Cᵒ**	*(See also)* Richard **Jewesson, Midleton & Co.**	**(OSP)**	
	Charles C. **Read** Birmingham (55, Buckingham St) - 1882 - 1888 ...	**(BM/EP)**	(K82) (K84) (K88)
	Jefferson **Read** **(Arcanum Plating Works)** Birmingham (Luisa St/17, Augusta St) - 1878 - 1903 ...	**(CP/CU/EP)**	(K78) (K82) (K84) (K88) (K92) (K03)
	Rachel **Read** Birmingham (42, Spencer St) - 1880 ...	**(EP)**	(K80)

R

N. C. **Reading & Co.** **(EP)** ^{(K78) (K80) (K82)}
(K84) (K88) (K92)
(Formerly: Walter Reading)
(K03) (SBW) (M)
Birmingham (186 & 187, Warstone Ln/33-35,
Hall St)
- 1878 - 1903 ...
(See also figures: GOLD LINED,
INDIAN SAND GOLD, VENETIA
GOLDPLATE)

John **Reading & Sons** **(EP)** (PC)
Birmingham (17, Vyse St)
- 1896 ...

John **Reading** **(CP)** (WTDB) (WTD)
(WDB) (WAB)
Birmingham (Prospect Rw)
- 1815 - 1829 ...

Walter **Reading** **(EP)** (K72) (K78)
Birmingham (186, Warstone Ln)
- 1872 - 1878 ...
(Then: N. C. Reading & Co)

Reading Brothers **(EP)** (K78) (K80)
Birmingham (6 - 8, Spencer St)
- 1878 - 1880 ...

REAL   KNIFE   *(See also)* **(CU/EP)**
PAMPA   **Lockwood Brothers**

William **Reay & Son** **(EP)** (K80)
Birmingham (70 & 71, Mott St)
- 1880 ...

RECTO   *(See also)* **(CU/EP)**
Frederick **Barnes & Co.**

George **Redding** **(CP)** (DOB)
Birmingham (73, Kenion St)
- 1833 ...

T. **Redfern** **(EP)** (MDG)
Birmingham (133, Gt. Charles St)
- 1866 ...

Reed & Lucas **(OSP)** (CD)
Sheffield (Royds Mill)
- 1818 ...

R

	Jefferson **Reed** ouisa St) - 1878 ...	(K78)
☐**REGENT PLATE**	*(See also)* **(EP)** **Garrard & Co. Ltd.**	
REGENT SILVER	*(See also)* **(EP)** John **Sherwood & Son** (Richard & John jun.)	
REGIS PLATE	*(See also)* **(EP)** William **Suckling Ltd.**	
	James **Reid** **(CP)** ^(CD) Biurmingham (5, Hall St) - 1818 ...	
	(See also) **(EP)** **Bramwell & Co.** **(Bramwell Brownhil & Co. Ltd.)** and William **Ryland** **(EP)** **(Gatefield Works)** and **Marples, Wingfield & Wilkins (EP)** **(Sykes Works/Portland Works)**	
Reliance Plate	**Oneida Community** **(EP)**	
	Thomas **Renshaw & Co.** **(CU)** (WDS79)(WDS01) (Thomas **Renshaw & Sons)** **(Stand Works & Sylvester Works)** Sheffield (Corporation St) - 1879 - 1901 ... *(See also figure: STAND)*	
	William **Renshaw** **(CP)** (WTDB)(WTD) Birmingham (38, Cherry St) (CD)(WDB) - 1815 - 1839 ... (WAB)(DOB) (WDOB)	
	Restall & Gellion **(BM/EP)** (K80) Birmingham (24, Coleshill St) - 1880 ...	
	Reynolds & Westwood **(EP)** (K88)(K92)(K03) Birmingham (10/44, Vyse St) - 1888 - 1903 ...	

R

	John **Reynolds** **(CP/EP)** (WTDB) (K72) (K78) Birmingham (Edmund St/Ct. 17, Price St) - 1815 - 1878 ...	

RF

(See also) **(OSP)**
Richard **Forster**

RF E & Co

(See also) **(EP)**
Rupert **Favell**, Henry **Elliot & Co.**

R F M EP
R F M ☆ S
R F M ☆ S

(See also) **(EP)**
Robert Fead **Mosley**

R.G &S USE

(See also) **(CU/EP)**
Richard **Groves & Sons**
(Beehive Works)

RG

(See also) **(OSP)**
Robert **Gainsford**

RG

(See also) **(OSP)**
R. **Gregory & Co.**

R GRC

Not assigned! **(EP)** (B)
~ 1850 ...

R.H
R.H ✝ C P ♔

(See also) **(EP)**
Richard **Hodd & Son**
(Minerva Works)

RH

(See also) **(EP)**
William C. **Hutton & Sons**

Jehoiad Alsop **Rhodes & Barber** **(EP)**
(Britain Works)
(Formerly: J. A. Rhodes)
Sheffield (58, Howard St)   (SAOR(WDS79)
1870 - 1880 ... *(See also figure: ^{A}JR)*   (K80) (SBW) (M)

Ebenezer **Rhodes** **(OSP)** (B) (SAOR)
Sheffield (Wicker)
1791 ... *(See also figure: E·R)*

Ebenezer **Rhodes** **(OSP)** (AB)
Sheffield
- 1812 ...

R

	Jehoiad Alsop **Rhodes** (EP) Sheffield - 1869 *(See also figure: $A^J R$)* *(Then: Rhodes & Barber)*	(SAOR) (K80) (SBW) (M)
	John **Rhodes** (EP) Sheffield (13, Howard St) - 1849 - 1852 ...	(GDBS) (WDOS)
	Thomas & John **Rhodes** (OSP) Sheffield (13, Howard St) - 1846 ...	(SD46)
	Rhodes Brothers (EP) Sheffield (12, Mulberry St) 1854 - 1863 ... *(See also figure: RB)*	(SAOR) (GS) (POS) (K54) (B) (SBW)
RICHARD ELLIOTT	*(See also)* (CU) John **Sellers & Sons**	
RICHARD PARKIN & SON SHEFFIELD	*(See also)* (EP) Richard **Parkin & Son**	
	Richards & Co. (CP) Birmingham (Mary St) - 1839 ...	(WDOB)
	Theophilus **Richards & Co.** (EP) Birmingham ~ 1900 ... *(See also figures: VALOR, THEOPHILUS RICHARDS)*	(M) (SBW)
	Thomas Spendelow **Richards & Co.** (EP) Birmingham (54, Tenby St) - 1872 ... *(See also figure: CHAMPION)*	(K72) (SBW)
	Richards & Walsh (EP) Wexford ~ *(See also figure: R&WW)*	
	Henry **Richards** (CP) Sheffield (42, Arundel Ln) - 1880 ...	(K80)
R	Josiah & G. **Richards** (CU) Birmingham 1812 ...	(SAOR)

Richard **Richards** (CP) (WDB)
Birmingham
- 1823 ...

Thomas **Richards** (CP) (WAB) (SAOR)
Birmingham (Caroline St)
- 1829 - 1836 ...

Thomas **Richards** (EP) (K92)
Birmingham (Regent Rw)
- 1892 ...

William **Richards** (CP) (WAB)
Birmingham (James St/Navigation St)
- 1829 ...

Richardson & Binney Ltd. (EP) (K36)
Sheffield (16-20, Bowdon St)
- 1936 ...

Richard **Richardson** (BM/CU/EP) (SBW) (WDS79)
(Cornwall Works) (K80) (SAOR)
Sheffield (Norfolk St/Scotland St) (K93) (WDS01)
London (13, Hatton Garden) (WDSR)
Glasgow (15, Renfield St)
- 1879 - 1905 ...
(See also figure: RR S)

Richer & Son (EP) (K80)
Bristol (6, Frogmore St)
- 1880 ...

John **Ridal** (CU/EP) (SBW) (M)
(Paxton Works)
Sheffield
~ 1900 ...
(See also figure: RAINBOW)

Charles **Rider** (CP) (DOB)
Birmingham (Holt St)
- 1833 ...

Joseph **Ridge & Co.**   **(EP)** ^(SAOR)
(Ridge, Allcard & Co)
(Lion Works)
(Formerly: Ridge, Woodcock & Hardy)
Sheffield (47, Eyre St)
1881 - 1886
(See also figures: JOSEPH RIDGE&Co, JR&Co.)
(Then: John Round & Sons Ltd.)

Joseph **Ridge**   **(EP)** ^(WDS79)
Sheffield (241, Cementery Rd)
- 1879 ...

Ridge, Woodcock & Hardy (BM/EP) ^{(WDS79) (K80)}
Sheffield (Eldon St) ^(M)
~ 1872 - 1880 ...
(See also figure: RW&HS)
(Then: Joseph Ridge & Co)

RJS   **Not assigned!**   **(EP)** ^(E)
- 1896

R·K &C⁰   *(See also)*   **(OSP)**
R. **Kippax & Co.**

R. LAW.   *(See also)*   **(OSP)**
R. **Law**

R.LOY   *(See also)*   **(OSP/CU)**
Richard **Loy**

R·M &C⁰   *(See also)*   **(OSP)**
Richard **Morton & Co.**

R M E H   *(See also)*   **(EP)**
Richard **Martin,** Ebenezer **Hall & Co. Ltd.**
(Shrewsbury Works)

R M J & Co   *(See also)*   **(EP)**
Robinson M. **Johnson**
RMJ & C⁰   **(Shoreham Plate Works)**

Rachel **Road**   **(EP)** ^(K78)
Birmingham (42, Spencer St)
- 1878 ...

R

John & Thomas **Robathan(m)** **(CP)** (WTDB) (WTD)
(CD) (WDB)
Birmingham (11, Hall St)
- 1815 - 1823 ...

John **Robathan** **(CP)** (WDOB)
Birmingham (Victoria St)
- 1839 ...

Thomas **Robathan** **(CP)** (WDOB)
Birmingham (Hall St)
- 1839 ...

Samuel **Roberts &** Charles **Belk (CU/EP)**
(Furnival Works)
(Formerly: Roberts & Briggs)
Sheffield (38, Furnival St)
London (24, Holborn Viaduct)

1864 - 1901 ...
(B) (SAOR) (K80)
- 1901 - 1920 ... **(Ltd.)**
(Rd 244543) (K93)
(See also figures: R&B, SR CB,
(SBW) (M) (Rd
symbol "lamp", ROMNEY PLATE)
609013) (WDS01)
(WDSR)

Samuel **Roberts &** William **Briggs (EP)** (B) (SAOR) (GS)
(Furnival Works) (SBW) (M)
(Formerly: William Briggs)
Sheffield (38, Furnival St)
London
1859 - 1863 ... *(See also figure: R&B)*
(Then: Roberts & Belk)

Roberts & Cadman **(OSP)**
(S. **Roberts,** G. **Cadman & Co.)**
Sheffield (Norfolk St/Eyre St)
1786 ...

(See also figures: R.C&Co,
(B)
SRGC&Co, symbol " bell ")
1798 ...
(See also figures: R.C&Co. PA-
TENT,
(CD) (PDY)
symbol " bell ")
- 1818 - 1822 ...

R

Jacob & Samuel **Roberts & Co. (OSP/CU)** (M) (B)
Sheffield (Pond Hill/Arundel St)
~ 1765 - 1781 ...
(See also figure: J.S.R)

Samuel **Roberts & Co.** **(OSP)** (B) (SAOR) (M)
Sheffield (Brinsworth Orchard/Arundel St)
1773 - 1781 ...
(See also figure: S·R&Co)

Roberts & Co. **(EP)** (GS)
(Shoreham Works)
Sheffield (Shoreham St)
- 1863 ...

Roberts & Dore **(EP)** (K36)
Sheffield (115-117, Portobello St)
London
~ 1916 - 1936 ...
(See also figure: R & D S&L)

Roberts & Hall **(EP)** (SAOR) (GDBS)
(*Formerly: John Roberts*) (WDOS) (SBW)
Sheffield (Low St Park/51, Broad St) (B)
1847 - 1852 ... *(See also figure: R&H)*
(In 1852 amalgamated with Martin & Naylor)

Samuel **Roberts &** Joseph **Slater** **(EP)** (E) (SAOR) (SD46)
Sheffield (38, Furnival St) (GDBS) (WDOS)
1845 - 1854 ... *(See also figure: R&S)* (K54) (POS)
(SBW)

Roberts & Staniforth **(EP/CU)** (WDSR)
Sheffield (25a, Wellington St)
- 1905 ...

Roberts & Timm **(EP)** (WDS79) (K80)
Sheffield (23, Orchard Ln)
- 1879 - 1880 ...

Henry **Roberts** **(OSP)** (DSRR)
Sheffield (37, Furnival St)
- 1841 ...

Jacob & Samuel **Roberts** **(CU/OSP)** (SAOR) (B)
Sheffield (Union St)
1781 ...
(See also figures: ABBA, I&S.
ROBERTS, PAPA)

R

John **Roberts** **(OSP)** (HGDY) (GDS)
(B) (WDSR)(SBW)
Sheffield (Low St Park/Shrewsbury Rd) (DSRR) (SD46)
- 1833 - 1846 ... *(See also figure: JR)* (SAOR)
(Then: Roberts & Hall)

John **Roberts** **(OSP)** (B) (SAOR)
Sheffield (Sykes Sq)
1786 ... *(See also figure: IR)*

Robert **Roberts** **(CP)** (WDOB)
Birmingham (Mott St)
- 1839 ...

S. **Roberts** **(OSP)** (B) (SAOR)
Sheffield (Cheney Sq)
1773 ... *(See also figure: SR)*

Samuel **Roberts** **(OSP)** (GDS)
Sheffield (Park Grange)
- 1833 ...

Samuel jun. **Roberts** **(OSP)** (DSRR) (WDS79)
Sheffield (Park Grange/Eyre St/Psalter Ln)
- 1841 - 1879 ...

Sarah **Roberts** **(CU)** (PD)
Sheffield (20, Arundel St)
- 1829 ...

Sidney **Roberts** **(OSP)** (GDS)
Sheffield (17, Gell St)
- 1833 ...

Roberts, Clayton & Emery (OSP) (B) (SAOR) (CD)
(Roberts, Clayton & Co)
Sheffield (Solly St)
1813 - 1818 ... *(See also figure: I·R&Co)*

J. **Roberts**, S. **Moseley** & J. **Settle (OSP)** (B) (SAOR)
Sheffield (Market Pl)
1805 ... *(See also figure: I·R&Co)*

Roberts, Samuel **Smith & Co. (OSP)** (SAOR) (SDG)
(PD) (HGDY)
Sheffield (5/9, Eyre St) (WDS37) (DSRR)
1828 - 1846 ... *(See also figures: R&S* (SD46)
MP, S·R&Co, symbol " bell ")

331

Robinson & Allport	**(CP)**	(WTD) (SAOR) (CD) (WDB) (WAB)
Birmingham (Loveday St/12, Weaman Rw) - 1818 - 1829 ...		

Robinson & Co.	**(EP)**	(B) (SAOR) (M) (SBW)
Sheffield (Eyre St) 1864 ... *(See also figure: ER TR)*		

Edward **Robinson & Co.**	**(EP)**	(K80)
Sheffield (32, Pinestone St) - 1880 ...		

Robinson & Kitching	**(OSP)**	(PDB) (PD) (SDG)
Sheffield (South St) - 1825 - 1829 ...		

William **Robinson**	**(EP)**	(MDG) (K72) (K78) (K80)
Birmingham (6, Newhall Hill/260, Icknield St/87, Prescott St) - 1866 - 1880 ...		

ROBᵀ BAXTER & Cᵒ SHEFFIELD	*(See also)* Robert **Baxter & Co.**	**(CU/OSP)**

Rock & Cooper	**(CP)**	(WDB)
Birmingham - 1823 ...		

Henry **Rock**	**(OSP)**	(B) (SAOR)
Sheffield (Broad Ln) 1798 ... *(See also figure: H.R)*		

Joseph **Rock**	**(OSP)**	(SAOR)
Walsall 1813 ...		

R O D	*(See also)* Robert **Bateman** **(Don Works)**	**(CU/CP)**

Samuel **Roden**	**(EP)**	(K92) (PC)
Birmingham (111, Icknield St) - 1892 - 1896 ...		

George **Rodgers & Co.**	**(CU)**	(WDOS AD)
Sheffield (13, Norfolk Ln) - 1852 ...		

R

John **Rodgers & Co.**　　　**(OSP)**　(B) (SAOR) (M)
Sheffield (Pond St)
1805 ... *(See also figure: J.R)*

Joseph **Rodgers & Sons** (George)
Sheffield (6, Norfolk St)　　**(CU/CP/EP)**
London (4, Cullum St/60, Holborn Viaduct)
1812 - 1890 ...
(See also figures: I·R, JR GR,
JOSEPH ROGERS, J.R, JR&S,
3436)
Sheffield (2/6, Norfolk St/28 & 44, Eyre Ln/
Pond Hill)
- 1879 - 1970 **(& Sons Ltd.)**
(See also figure: Maltese cross)

(B) (SAOR)
(WDS37) (DSRR)
(PD) (SD46)
(GDBS) (WDOS)
(GS) (K72) AD
(WDS79) (SBW)
(M)
(WDS79) (K80)
(K93) (WDS01)
(K36)

RODGERS
RODGERSINE

C. W. **Rodgers**　　　　**(CU)**　(WDOS AD)
Sheffield (52, Lambert St)
- 1852 ...

Thomas **Rodgers**　　　**(OSP)**
Sheffield　　　　　　　　　　(B)
1790 ... (Brinsworth Orchard)　(SAOR)
1802 ... (Coalpit Ln) *(See also figure: TR)*

Charles **Roebuck**　　　**(OSP)**　(B) (SAOR)
Sheffield (Lambert Croft)
1786 ... *(See also figure: CR)*

John **Rogers & Co.**　　　**(CP)**　(WDB)
Birmingham
- 1823 ...

J. **Rogers**　　　　　　**(CU)**　(B) (M)
Birmingham (New St)
1819 ...

Henry **Rogers**　　　　　**(EP)**　(K80)
Birmingham (126, Balsall Heath Rd)
- 1880 ...

Maurice **Rogers**　　　**(OSP)**　(B) (SAOR)
Sheffield (Holly Croft)
1776 .... *(See also figure: M·R)*

William **Rogers** **(GS/CP/EP)** ^{(HGD) (MDG)}
Birmingham (149, Gt. Hampton Rw/ ^{(K72) (K78) (K80)}
3, Augusta St)
- 1850 - 1880 ...

Henry **Rogers, Sons & Co.** **(CU/EP)** ^{(WDS01) (E) (M)}
Sheffield (80 & 82, Eyre St)
- 1901 ... *(See also figures: HENRY*
ROGERS, HRS & Co)

A. **Rollason & Sons** **(GS)** ^(K93)
Sheffield (70, Surrey St)
- 1893 ...

Dollif **Rollinson** **(OSP)** ^{(GM) (B)}
Sheffield (Spring St/Market Pl)
1787 - 1790 ... *(See also figure: D.R)*

" ROMNEY PLATE "
Trademark

(See also) **(EP)**
Samuel **Roberts &** Charles **Belk**
(Furnival Works)

Benjamin **Rooke & Sons** **(OSP)** ^{(SAOR) (CD) (B)}
Sheffield (Sycamore St/Pond Hill) ^(PDY)
1818 - 1822 ... *(See also figure: B·R)*

Thomas **Rooke** **(CU)** ^{(SDG) (GDS)}
Sheffield (Tudor St/23, Sycamore St)
- 1828 - 1833 ...

Herbert **Room** **(EP)** ^(HGD)
Birmingham (16, Bull Ring)
- 1850 ...

Roper & Edwards **(EP)** ^{(K78) (K82) (K84)}
Birmingham (45, Augusta St) ^(K88)
- 1878 - 1888 ...

Henry **Roper** **(EP)** ^(K72)
Birmingham (6, Moreton St)
- 1872 ...

Rose & Brough **(EP)** ^{(K92) (PC) (M)}
Birmingham (20, Hockley St)
- 1892 - 1896 ... *(See also figure: R & B)*

Charles E. **Rose & Co.** **(EP)** ^{(K80) (K82) (K84)}
Birmingham (17, Augusta St) ^{(K88) (K92)}
- 1880 - 1892 ...

R

Rosing Brothers & Co. (EP) ^{(SBW) (M)}
London
~ 1850 - 1860 ...
(See also figure: AMAZONE)

Jeremiah **Ross** **(CU/OSP)** ^(SAOR)
Walsall
1815 ...

Thomas **Ross** **(EP)** ^(CDB)
Birmingham (76, Pope St)
- 1861 ...

Henry **Rossell & Co.** **(EP)** ^{(WDS79) (SBW)}
(Wallace Works) ^(M)
Sheffield (Furnival St)
- 1879 ...
(See also figures: HENRY ROSSEL&Co, VICTORY)

William **Rostill** **(CP)** ^{(WDB) (WAB)}
Birmingham
- 1823 - 1829 ...

James **Rotherham** **(OSP)** ^{(B) (SAOR)}
Sheffield (Spring St)
1792 ... *(See also figure: IR)*

Edwin **Round & Son Ltd.** **(EP)** ^{(WDS79) (K80)}
Sheffield (7, Orchard Ln/36, Holly St)
- 1879 - 1880 ...

Benjamin J. **Round** **(EP)**
Birmingham (9, & 10 Northampton St/
65, Albion St/Frederick St) ^{(K80) (K82) (K84)}
- 1880 - 1903 ... ^{(K88) (K92) (K03)}
- 1880 - 1903 ... (**& Sons**) ^{(K80) (K03)(M)}
(See also figure: B.J.R&S.)

Edward **Round** **(OSP)** ^{(POS) (K54)}
Sheffield (3, Broome Close)
- 1854 ...

John **Round**   (CU/MP/EP)
(Tudor Works & Arundel Plate Works)
(In 1886 acquisition of Joseph Ridge & Co)
Sheffield (6, Tudor St/34, Eyre St)
- 1849 - 1854 ...
- 1872 - 1880 ... **(& Son)** (Edwin)
(See figures: JR ER, JR&S)
1874 - 1957 ... (**Ltd.**)
*(See also figures: ALL, ALLTHE-
ROUND, AMINTO, ÆNEAS,
ARATOR, ARENAM, AVENA,
BALAZO, BANDOLA, BEBARA,
BURVIS, JR&S)*

(GDBS) (WDOS)
(K54) (POS)

(B) (K72) (SAOR)
(K80AD) (SBW)
(M)

(B) (SAOR)
(WDS79) (K80)
(K93) (WDS01)
(W) (SBW) (M)

Joseph **Rowan & Son**   (EP)
Sheffield (33, Club St)
- 1905 ...

(WDSR)

Henry **Rowan**   (EP)
Sheffield (Wellington St)
- 1863 ...

(GS)

John **Rowbotham & Co.**   (OSP)
Sheffield (Norfolk St)
1773 - 1774 ...
(See also figure: IR·Co)

(SAOR) (B)

John **Rowbotham**   (OSP)
Sheffield
1776 ... (Norfolk St) *(See also figure: IR)*
1793 ... (Whitecroft) *(See also figure: IR)*

(B)
(SAOR)

Benjamin **Rowlings**   (OSP)
Sheffield
1823 ... *(See also figure: B.R)*

(B) (SAOR)

Rowlinson & Co.   (EP)
Birmingham (41, Northwood St)
- 1866 ...

(MDG)

ROYAL COUNTY PLATE   *(See also)*   (EP)
Bracher & Sydenham

R   " ROYAL STANDARD "   *(See also)*   (BM/EP)
Frederick **Derry**

336

Thomas **Royle**   **(EP)**   [SAOR]
Sheffield (Union Ln)
1851 ... *(See also figure: TR)*

R P X L [illustration]   *(See also)*   **(EP)**
                                     Robert **Pringle & Co.**
R P ✪ L [illustration]

R.RICHARDSON
CORNWALL WORKS   *(See also)*   **(BM/EP)**
SHEFFIELD   Richard **Richardson**
                            (Cornwall Works)
[R.R SHEFFIELD E.P.N.S / ESTᵈ 1796]
RR **S** **R** **EP**

R.S & Cº   *(See also)*   **(EP)**
                      Robert **Stevenson & Co.**

R S &Cº   *(See also)*   **(OSP)**
                     R. **Sutcliffe &** A. **Sporle**

RS   Robert **Sutcliffe**   **(CU)**   [B]
                Sheffield
                1781 ...

RS   **Not assigned!**   **(CU/EP)**

R S P Cº   *(See also)*   **(EP)**
                      Raeno Silver Plating Co. Ltd.

RT & Cº   *(See also)*   **(OSP)**
                     Robert **Tricket & Co.**

RT   *(See also)*   **(OSP/CU)**
                Robert **Tricket**

Richard **Rutledge**   **(BM/EP)**   [K80]
Birmingham (55, Buckingham St)
- 1880 ...

Edward **Russell**   **(EP)**   [K78] [K80] [K82]
Birmingham (46, Northampton St)   [K84]
- 1878 - 1884 ...

337

	Matthias Allen **Russell** Birmingham (69, Mott St/126, Vyse St) - 1861 - 1872 ...	**(EP)**	(CDB) (GS) (MDG) (K72)
	Samuel **Russel** **(Eyrestreet Works)** Sheffield (188, West St/Eyre St) - 1849 - 1863 ...	**(BM/EP)**	(GDBS) (GS)
	William **Rutherford** Sheffield (28, Norfolk St) - 1854 - 1871 ...	**(GS/EP)**	(POS) (K54) (WDS71)
R.VERNON & SONS.	*(See also)* Alfred **Beckett & Sons**	**(CU)**	
R. VERNON & SONS IMPERIAL	*(See also)* William **Jackson & Co.** **(Sheaf Island Works)**	**(CU)**	
R & W. SORLEY GLASGOW	*(See also)* R. & W. **Sorley**	**(EP)**	
R&WW	*(See also)* **Richards & Walsh**	**(EP)**	
R W & H S	*(See also)* **Ridge, Woodcock & Hardy**	**(BM/EP)**	
RW&W	**Not assigned!** ~1850	**(EP)**	(B)
RW	*(See also)* R. **Wass**	**(OSP)**	
RYALS	James **Ryals** Sheffield ~ 1900 ... *(See also figure: FIRTH)*	**(CU)**	(E)
	Charles **Ryder** Birmingham (Hollo Way/New John St) - 1829 - 1839 ...	**(CP)**	(WAB) (WDOB)
	C. E. **Ryder** Birmingham (345, Pershore Rd) - 1866 ...	**(EP)**	(MDG)
	Thomas **Ryland & Son** (William) Birmingham (40, Newhall St) 1803 - 1833 ...	**(CP)**	(SAOR) (DOB)

R

RYLAND

William **Ryland & Sons** **(CP/Coach)**
Birmingham (Lw Temple St/Exeter Rw/
28, Gt. Charles St)
1807 - 1839 ...

(B) (CD) (WDB)
(WAB) (DOB)
(SAOR)

C. **Ryland** **(EP)**
Birmingham (5, Newhall St)
- 1866 ...

(MDG)

John **Ryland** **(EP)**
Birmingham (30, Harford St/166, Gt. Hampton Rw)
- 1863 - 1903 ...

(GS) (MDG) (K72)
(K78) (K80) (K82)
(K84) (K88) (K92)
(K03)

William **Ryland** **(GS/CP)**
Birmingham (Temple St/Gt. Charles St)
- 1818 - 1839 ...

(WTD) (WDOB)

William **Ryland** **(EP)**
(Gatefield Works)
Sheffield (Rockingham St)
- 1863 ...
(See also figure: RELIABLE)

(GS)

Rylands' Electro Plating Co. Ltd. **(EP)**
Sheffield (68-72, Eyre St)
- 1879 - 1901 ...

(WDS79) (K80)
(K93) (WDS01)

	Not assigned! (In combination with J. Maple & Co.)	**(EP)**
	(See also) **Sanders & Blackband**	**(EP)**
	(See also) **Slack & Barlow Ltd.**	**(EP)**
	(See also) **Sansom & Creswick**	**(EP)**
	(See also) Albert **Skinner & Co.**	**(EP)**
	(See also) Arthur Elwell **Spurrier & Co.**	**(EP)**
	(See also) **Sansom & Davenport**	**(EP)**
	(See also) **Sansom & Harwood**	**(OSP)**
	(See also) **Slater, Son & Horton**	**(EP)**
	(See also) Henry **Stacey & Horton**	**(EP)**
	(See also) **Sutherland & Horne**	**(CU/EP)**
	(See also) Alexander **Spear &** Sam **Jackson**	**(EP)**
	(See also) **Stevenson & Law**	**(EP)**
	(See also) **Stafford & Newton**	**(OSP)**

S

S&P (oval) / **S&P**	*(See also)* Sampson **Sanders &** Bernard A. **Pedlinham** Birmingham (Gt. Hampton St) 1920 ...	**(EP)** (SI)
S&S	*(See also)* J. **Smith & Son**	**(CU/OSP)**
S&S EP NS	*(See also)* **Stephenson & Sons**	**(EP)**
S&W	*(See also)* **Stower & Wragg**	**(EP)**
S·B	*(See also)* S. **Bennett &** P. **Spurr**	**(OSP)**
S·F	*(See also)* Samuel & Ann **Fox**	**(OSP)**
S·H	*(See also)* Samuel **Hennell**	**(OSP)**
S·K	*(See also)* Samuel **Kirkby & Co.**	**(OSP)**
S·T	*(See also)* S. **Tinker**	**(OSP)**
S·W	*(See also)* S. **Warburton & Co.**	**(OSP)**
S (hand symbol)	**Not assigned!**	**(EP)**
SAC	*(See also)* Saint Arnoud **Creake**	**(OSP)**
	Frederick **Salaman** Birmingham (48, Warstone Ln) - 1880 - 1884 ...	**(EP)** (K80) (K82) (K84)
SALT	John **Salt** Birmingham (35, Hall St) - 1896 ...	**(CU/EP)** (PC) (B)
	Frederick **Saltfleet** Sheffield (2, Dawson St) - 1880 ...	**(EP)** (K80)

S

Isaac **Sampson** **(OSP)** [(B) (SAOR)]
Sheffield (Burgess St)
1795 ... *(See also figure: IS)*

Sampson Mordan & Co. **(EP)**
(City Road Factory)
London
~ 1900 ...*(See also figure: SM&Co)*
~ 1910 ... **(Ltd.)**
(See also figure: SM&Co.L^{TD})

Henry **Samson** **(OSP)** [(SDG)]
Sheffield (22, Orchard St)
- 1828 ...

H. **Samuel & Sons** **(EP)** [(M)]
Manchester
~ *(See also figure: H SAMUEL)*

Harriett **Samuel** **(EP)** [(M)]
Sheffield
~ 1880 ...
(See also figure: H SAMUEL)

SAMUEL KITCHIN
SHEFFIELD
(See also) **(CU)**
Samuel & J. **Kitchin**
(Soho Cutlery Works)

Sanders & Blackband **(EP)** [(K36)]
Birmingham (70-76, Northwood St)
- 1936 ... *(See also figure: S&B)*

Sampson **Sanders &** Bernard Albert **Ped-** [(SI)]
linham **(EP)**
Birmingham (Gt. Hampton St)
1920 ...

George **Sanders** **(CU/OSP)** [(SAOR)]
Coventry
1814 ...

John **Sanders** **(CP)** [(WAB) (HTD)]
Birmingham (Gt. Charles St)
- 1829 - 1830 ...

John **Sanders** **(EP)** [(K80) (K82) (K84)]
Birmingham (83, Newhall St) [(K88)]
- 1880 - 1888 ...

S

Joseph **Sanders** (GS/EP)
Birmingham (Gt. Charles St/30, Newhall St)
- 1839 - 1878 ...

(WDOB) (HGDB)
(HGD) (CDB)
(BDB) (GS)
(MDG)(K72) (K78)

Sanderson & Roe (EP)
Sheffield (34 & 36, Holly St)
- 1893 ...

(K93)

John **Sanderson** (EP)
Sheffield (36, Holly St)
1880 - 1901 ... *(See also figures: JS*S, ARGYLE PLATE)*

(SAOR) (WDS01)

Edward **Sankey** (EP)
Birmingham (89, Pershore St)
- 1880 ...

(K80)

Sansom & Creswick (EP)
(Formerly: Sansom & Davenport)
Sheffield (Rockingham St)
1856 - 1857 ... *(See also figure: S & C)*

(SAOR) (B) (SBW)
(M)

Sansom & Davenport (EP)
Sheffield (114, Rockingham St)
1853 - 1854 ... *(See also figure: S&D)*
(Then: Sansom & Creswick)

(SAOR) (POS)
(K54) (SBW)
(B) (M)

Sansom & Harwood (OSP)
Sheffield (Norfolk Ln)
1833 ... *(See also figure: S&H)*

(B) (SAOR)

Thomas **Sansom & Sons** (CP/CU)
(Abraham, John & William)
Sheffield (45, Norfolk St)
1821 - 1846 ...

(B) (DSRR)
(SD46) (M)

Thomas **Sansom** (OSP/CU)
Sheffield (Norfolk St)
1808 ... *(See also figure: TS)*

(SAOR) (B)

William **Sansom** (CP/CU)
Sheffield (Union St/36 & 105, Norfolk St)
1835 ...
- 1837 - 1846 ... *(& Co.)*
(See also figure: WS)

(B) (SAOR)

(WDS37) (DSRR)
(SD46)

SAN
SOM

S

Edward **Sault** (EP) [K92]
Birmingham (40, Caroline St)
- 1892 ...

Joseph **Sault** (EP) [CDB] [BDB] [GS]
Birmingham (37, Church St/Lodge Rd)
- 1861 - 1863 ...

Sault Brothers (EP) [MDG] [POB]
Birmingham (Lodge Rd)
- 1866 - 1867 ...

W. J. **Saunders** (EP) [K80]
Birmingham (Gt. Hampton Rw/
121, Wheeler St)
- 1880 ...

W. S. **Savage & Co.** (CU/EP) [K80] [K93]
(**W. Savage, Smith & Co**) [WDS01] [WDSR]
Sheffield (173, Pond St) [SBW] [W]
- 1880 - 1905 ...
(See also figures: ARIZONA, The NATIONAL)

Walter S. **Savage** (EP) [WDS79]
Sheffield (433, Shoreham St)
- 1879 ...

SAVARS. *(See also)* (EP) [SBW] [M]
Evans, Lescher & Webb
(Evans Sons & Co.)

John James **Saville & Co.** (CU) [K93] [WDS01]
Sheffield (Shoreham St) [W]
- 1893 - 1901 ... *(See also figures: AKROS, JOSEPH ASHFORT & CO.)*

C. W. **Saville** (CU) [WDOS AD]
Sheffield (37, Townhead St)
- 1852 ...

SAV ORY **LON DON** Adey Bellamy **Savory & Sons** (EP) [M]
London
~ 1854 - 1866 ...

SAVOY *(See also)* (BM/EP)
Philip **Ashberry & Sons**

S

George **Sawyer** **(CU/CP)** ^{(DOB) (WDOB)} ^(HGD)
Birmingham (Ct. 20, Constitution Hill/16, Henrietta St)
- 1833 - 1850 ...

J. & S. **Saynor** **(OSP)** ^{(B) (SAOR)}
Sheffield (Bank St)
1792 ... *(See also figure: I·S)*

S.B&S L^D *(See also)* **(EP)**
Solomon **Blanckensee & Sons Ltd.**

S B & Co *(See also)* **(EP)**
S. **Bright & Co.**

S B & M *(See also)* **(EP)**
Sturges, Bladon & Middleton

SB *(See also)* **(EP)**
Slack Brothers
(Leicester Works)

S B L W *(See also)* **(EP)**
Slack Brothers
(Leicester Works)

S B M *(See also)* **(EP)**
Sturges, Bladon & Middleton

S BROS *(See also)* **(EP)**
Slater Brothers
(Leicester Works)

S.C.YOUNGE & Co *(See also)* **(OSP)**
S. & C. **Younge & Co.**

SC *(See also)* **(OSP)**
S. **Colmore**
(OSP)

Scanlan & Co. **(BM)** ^(K78)
(Unity Works)
Birmingham (Kensington St)
- 1878 ...

H. **Schürhoff & Co.** **(EP)** ^{(SBW) (M)}
Birmingham
~ 1900
(See also figures: ADELANTE, OSYRIS)

S

Alexander **Scott &** George **Randle (EP)** [(E) (S)]
Sheffield/Birmingham
1922 - 1931 *(See also figure: A.S & G.R.)*

Alexander **Scott** **(EP)** [(S)]
Glasgow
1922 - 1937
(See also figure: Alexander Scott)

James **Scott** **(EP)** [(K82) (K84)]
Birmingham (125a, Branston St)
- 1882 - 1884 ...

W. **Scott** **(CP)** [(M)]
Birmingham
1807 ...

Scottish Nickel Plating Co. Ltd. (EP) [(K80)]
Glasgow (106, Stirling St)
- 1880 ...

Scragg & Co. **(BM/EP)** [(K78) (K80) (K82)]
Birmingham (62, Tenby St North)
- 1878 - 1882 ...

William **Scragg & Co.** **(BM/EP)** [(BDB) (MDG) (POB) (K72)]
Birmingham (Scotland St)
- 1862 - 1872 ...

William **Screeton** **(CU)** [(WDB) (PDB)]
Birmingham (119, Pritchett St)
- 1823 - 1825 ...

SCY &Co | *(See also)* **(OSP)**
S. & C. **Younge & Co.**

SD&Co | *(See also)* **(OSP)**
S. **Deakin** A. **Kitchen & Co.**

S·D &Co LTD | *(See also)* **(EP)**
Steward **Dawson & Co.**

SDK&Co | *(See also)* **(OSP)**
S. **Deakin** A. **Kitchen & Co.**

S·EVANS | *(See also)* **(OSP)**
Samuel **Evans**

S

346

SE &S	*(See also)* Samuel Frederick **Evans & Co.** **(Evans & Sons)**	**(EP)**
	W. S. **Searls & Co.** Birmingham (46, Worcester St) - 1872 - 1880 ...	**(EP)** (K72) (K78) (K80)
	William J. **Sears** **(Alpha Works)** Sheffield (88a, Trafalgar St) 1889 - 1936 ...	**(EP)** (SAOR) (K36)
" SELECT "	*(See also)* **Bingham & Ogden**	**(CU)**
SELFRIDGE & C<u>º</u> **LONDON**	**Selfridge & Co. Ltd.** London (Oxford St) ~ 1900 ...	**(T)**
	Selig, Sonnenthal & Co. London Sheffield *~ (See also figures: S.S.&Co, M.S.Jr.&Co.)*	**(EP)** (SBW)
	William **Selkirk** Birmingham (Aston Rd) - 1815 - 1818 ...	**(CP)** (WTDB) (WTD CD)
	John **Sellers & Sons** Sheffield (151, Arundel St) - 1901 ... *(See also figure: EXTRA)*	**(CU)** (WDS01)
	Senior & Farquharson Sheffield (117, Fitzwilliam St) - 1936 ...	**(EP)** (K36)
SENRAB	*(See also)* Frederick **Barnes & Co.**	**(CU/EP)**
✠ SET	Thomas **Settle & Co.** (Thomas Warris) Sheffield (Brinsworth Orchard) 1780 ... *(See also figure: T·S&Co)* 1787 - 1788 ...	**(CP)** (B) (SAOR) (B) (SAOR)
	John **Settle &** W. **Hatfield** Sheffield (Scotland St) 1802 ... *(See also figure: IS)*	**(OSP)** (B) (SAOR)

S

347

John & Thomas **Settle**	**(OSP)**	(SAOR) (CD) (PDY) (PDB) (NGDS) (B)
Sheffield (Norfolk St)		
1815 - 1825 ...		
(See also figures: I&T·S, T&I.S, T&S·S)		

Thomas **Settle**	**(OSP)**	(SAOR) (B) (HDG)
Sheffield (Norfolk St)		
1781 - 1822 ... *(See also figure: T·S)*		

John & Thomas **Settle, Gunn & Co.**	**(OSP)**	(SAOR) (PD) (SDG) (NGDS) (B)
Sheffield (Norfolk St)		
1825 - 1829 ... *(See also figure: IS TS)*		

John **Seynor**	**(OSP)**	(B) (SAOR)
Sheffield (Pea Croft)		
1785 ... *(See also figure: I·S)*		

S x F	*(See also)*	**(BM/EP)**
	James **Shaw & Fisher**	
	(Crossed arrows only on White Metal)	

S F AJF	*(See also)* **Fenton Brothers Ltd.**	**(EP)**

SFE&Cº	*(See also)* Samuel Frederick **Evans & Co.** **(Evans & Sons)**	**(EP)**

S F WS	*(See also)* **Fenton Brothers Ltd.**	**(EP)**

SG&Cº	*(See also)* S. **Greaves & Co.**	**(OSP)**

S H & Cº	*(See also)* S. & T. **Howard**	**(CU/CP)**

S H &Cº (crown EP) **S H &Cº EP**	Frederick **Sibray**, J. F. **Hall & Co.** **(EP)** **(Fitzwalter Works)** Sheffield (111-115, Mary's Rd) - 1893 - 1897 1898 ...	(K93)

SH	*(See also)* Samuel **Harwood**	**(OSP)**

	Joseph **Shakesheave**	**(EP)** (K80) (K82) (K84) (K88) (K92)
	Birmingham (40, St. Paul's Sq)	
	- 1880 - 1892 ...	

S

Davy **Shale**   **(EP)**   (HGDB) (HGD)
Birmingham (9, Bath St)
- 1849 - 1850 ...

William **Shallcross**   **(OSP)**   (SD46)
Sheffield (Trinity St)
- 1846 ...

Sharman & Hydes   **(BM/EP)**   (K80)
(Cyprus Works)
Sheffield (Fawcett St)
- 1880 ...

Frederick **Sharp**   **(CP)**   (WTDB)
Birmingham (Pritchett St)
- 1815 ...

James **Sharrow & Co.**   **(OSP)**   (B) (SAOR)
Sheffield (Eyre St)
1793 ... *(See also figure: IS&Co)*

George **Shaw & Co.**   **(OSP)**   (PDB) (WDOS)
(George **Shaw & Sons)**
Sheffield (147, Allen St/Love St)
- 1825 - 1852 ...

SHAW&FISHER
SHEFFIELD

SHAW&FISHER
43 SUFFOLKROAD
SHEFFIELD

James **Shaw & Fisher**   **(BM/EP)**   (SAOR) (GDS)
(Norfolk Works)   (WDS37) (SD46)
Sheffield (Howard Pl/Eyre Ln/Kelham   (GDBS) (WDOS)
Island/39 - 43, Suffolk Rd)   (POS) (K54) (GS)
- 1833 - 1893 ...   (K80) (K88AD)
(See also figure: S x F)   (K93) (M)
(Then: James Deakin)   (K93 AD) (SBW)

Shaw & Hewitt   **(EP)**   (GS)
Sheffield (Campo Ln)
- 1863 ...

John **Shaw & Sons Ltd.**   **(EP/CU)**   (K93) (W) (SBW)
Wolverhampton ( )   (M)
Sheffield (8, Copper St)
- 1893 ... *(See also figures: AURO-*
RA, Common Sense, *J.S.&S.)*

George **Shaw**   **(BM)**   (GDS)
Sheffield (28, Allen St)
- 1833 ...

S

James & George **Shaw** **(BM/CU)** (SDG)
Sheffield (Kilham's Wheel)
- 1828 ...

John **Shaw** **(OSP)**
Sheffield (Chapel Walk/Fargate)
1820 - 1822 ... (SAOR) (HDG)
- 1822 ... **(& Sons)** (HDG)

T. **Shaw** **(OSP)** (B) (SAOR)
Sheffield (Fig St)
1780 ... *(See also figure: T·S)*

Thomas **Shaw** **(GS)** (SAOR) (WDOB)
Birmingham (Caroline St)
1822 - 1839 ...

William **Shaw** **(CP)** (WTDB) (WTD)
Birmingham (Edmond St)
- 1815 - 1818 ...

Sheffield Goods Supply Co. **(EP)** (K93)
Sheffield (39, Leadmill Rd)
- 1893 ...

Sheffield Nickel & Silver Plating (SAOR) (K80) (M)
Co. Ltd. **(EP)**
(Globe Works)
Sheffield (Penistone Rd)
1873 - 1886 ... *(See also figures:*
SPMC, SSP Ltd.)

SHEFFIELD PLATE | General term used for electroplated items
OLD STYLE | during the Old Sheffield Plate revival between 1890 - 1910.

John **Sheldon** **(EP)**
Birmingham
1841 ...
- 1863 ... **(& Co.)** (SAOR)
(Then: Derry & Jones) (GS)

William H. **Sheldon** **(BM/EP)**
Sheffield (150, Rockingham Ln/188, Solly St) (WDS01)
- 1901 ... (K36)
- 1936 ... **(& Son)**

S

J. **Shemeld & Co.**   **(OSP)**   (B) (SAOR)
Sheffield (Arundel St)
1777 ... *(See also figure: I·S Co)*

Shemeld, Parkin & Co.   **(OSP)**   (B) (SAOR)
Sheffield (Union St)
1781 ... *(See also figure: S·P&Co)*

SHEP-HARD

Joseph **Shephard**   **(OSP)**   (WTD) (WDB) (PDB) (CD) (M)
Birmingham (Cross St/Hill St/Vauxhall St)
- 1818 - 1825 ...

Sheppard & Corn   **(OSP)**   (WTD) (CD)
Birmingham (Exeter Rw)
- 1818 ...

Sheppard & Devey   **(EP)**   (K72)
Birmingham (4, Newton St)
- 1872 ...

Sheppard & Son   **(BM/EP)**   (K78) (K80)
Birmingham (62, Caroline St)
- 1878 - 1880 ...

John **Sheppard**   **(CP)**   (PDB) (WAB) (DOB) (WWDB) (WDOB)
Birmingham (Suffolk St/Ryland Rd)
- 1825 - 1839 ...

Joseph **Sheppard**   **(CP)**   (WAB) (HTD)
Birmingham (Aston St)
- 1829 - 1830 ...

Mrs. Selina **Sheppard**   **(BM)**   (K88) (K92)
Birmingham (30, Northwood St)
- 1888 - 1892 ..

William **Sheppard**   **(BM/EP)**   (K82) (K84)
Birmingham (28, Mary St)
- 1882 - 1884 ...

Thomas **Sherwin**   **(CU)**   (WWDB)
Birmingham (Witton St)
- 1835 ...

Sherwood & Barratt   **(EP)**   (CDB)
Birmingham (52, Gt. Hampton St)
- 1861 ...

S

Sherwood & Bourne   **(EP)**   (CDB) (BDB) (GS) (MDG) (POB)
Birmingham (71 & 72, Spencer St)
- 1861 - 1867 ...

John **Sherwood & Son(s)**   **(EP/CP)**   (SAOR) (HGDB) (HGD) (CDB)
(Richard & John jun.) **(Regent Works)**   (BDB) (MDG)
Birmingham (76/94 - 96, Lichfield St/   (POB) (K72) (K78)
Regent St)   (K80) (K82) (K84)
- 1839 - 1903 ...   (K88) (K92) (PC)
(See also figures: REGENT SIL-   (K03) (M)
VER, JS&S)

Albert **Sherwood**   **(EP)**   (BDB) (GS)
Birmingham (52, Gt. Hampton St)
- 1862 - 1863 ...

John **Sherwood**   **(CP)**   (SAOR) (WTDB) (WTD) (WDB)
Birmingham (11, Upper Priory)   (PDB) (CD)
- 1815 - 1825 ...

John B. (R). **Sherwood**   **(CP)**   (WAB) (HTD) (DOB) (WWDB)
Birmingham (94/76, Lichfield St)
- 1829 - 1835 ...

E. **Shillito & Co.**   **(EP)**   (WDSR)
Sheffield (60, Cambridge St)
- 1905 ...

George Badensack **Shillito**   **(EP)**   (K80)
Sheffield (30, Charlotte St)
- 1880 ...

William **Shirtcliffe & Sons**   **(EP)**
Sheffield
1921 - 1931 *(See also figure: W.S&S)*
1921 - 1931 (**& Son Ltd.**)
(Then: Garrard London)

Charles & Matthew **Shirtcliffe**   **(CU)**   (NGDS) (SD46)
Sheffield (102, Broad Ln/Garden St)
- 1825 - 1846 ...

Frederick **Shirtcliffe**   **(EP)**   (K80)
(Havelock Works)
Sheffield (Leadmill)
- 1880 ...

S

	John **Shore & Co.** **(OSP)** [(B) (SAOR)] Sheffield (Sycamore St) 1799 ... *(See also figure: I·S&Co)*	
SIBERIAN SILVER Siberian Silver	*(See also)* **(EP)** James Henry **Hunt** and **Hawksworth, Eyre & Co. Ltd. (EP)**	
	Frederick **Sibray**, J. F. **Hall & Co.** **(EP)** [(K93) (WDS01)] **(Fitzwalter Works)** Sheffield (111-115, Mary's Rd) - 1893 - 1901 ... *(See also figure: SH&Co)*	
𝕊𝕀𝕃𝕂	R. **Silk** **(CP)** [(B) (M)] Birmingham 1809 ...	
Sil-kirk	W. **Silkirk** **(CP)** [(B) (M)] Birmingham 1807 ...	
SILVA POTTER-SHEFLD	*(See also)* **(CU/EP)** John Henry **Potter** **(Rockingham Works)**	
	Silver & Fleming Ltd. **(EP)** [(SBW) (M)] London ~ 1884 - 1898 *(See also figure: A M S)*	
SILVENE	*(See also)* **(EP)** Henry **Fielding & Son** **(Snape Street Works)**	
SILVER ASH.	*(See also)* **(CU/EP)** John **Yates & Sons**	
SILVERINE	*(See also)* **(EP)** Maurice **Baum** **(Albert Works)**	
SILVERITE	*(See also)* **(EP)** William **Page & Co.**	
SILVERMINIMUM	*(See also)* **(EP)** Arthur Egerton **Heckford**	
SILVERPRIDE **PLATE**	*(See also)* **(EP)** **Slack & Barlow Ltd.**	**S**

SILVERODE	*(See also)* John **Ingram**	**(EP)**
SILVERSTEIN	*(See also)* W. R. **Box & Co.**	**(EP)**
	Isaac **Silverston & Co.** Birmingham ~ *(See also figure: Thos. Barclay & Son)*	**(EP)** (M) (SBW)
	John Bartleet **Silvester** Birmingham (11 &12, Parade) London (30, Holborn Ely Pl) - 1872 ... *(See also figure: JBS)*	**(EP)** (K72) (S)
	William **Simkiss & Son** Birmingham (10, Kenion St) - 1862 - 1872 ...	**(EP)** (BDB) (MDG) (POB) (K72)
	Richard **Simkiss** Birmingham (10, Kenyon St) - 1878 - 1903 ...	**(EP)** (K78) (K80) (K82) (K84) (K88) (K92) (K03)
	Isaac **Simmons** Manchester (St. Ann's Sq) 1839 ... *(See also figure: IS)*	**(OSP)** (B) (SAOR)
	John **Simpson & Co.** Birmingham (7, Paradise St) - 1815 - 1818 ...	**(Coach)** (WTDB) (CD)
	Simpson & Ellis Birmingham (Livery St) - 1818 ...	**(OSP)** (WTD) (CD)
	Thomas **Simpson & Sons** (William) Birmingham (New Hall St) - 1818 - 1821 ...	(WTD) (SAOR) **(CU/CP)**
	J. **Simpson** Sheffield (Prospect Rw) - 1871 ...	**(EP)** (WDS71)
	Thomas **Simpson** Birmingham (7, Livery St) - 1823 - 1825 ... - 1835 - 1839 ... **(& Co.)**	**(CU/CP)** (WDB) (PDB) (WWDB) (WDOB)

S

Singleton & Priestman **(EP/CU)** Sheffield (Pond Hill) - 1901 - 1905 ...		(WDS01) (WDSR)
William **Sissons** **(OSP)** Sheffield (9, Eyre St) - 1841 ...		(DSRR)
William jun. & George **Sissons** **(EP)** Sheffield (9, Eyre St/75, St. Mary's Rd) London () 1858 - 1911 ... *(See also figures: WS, GS WS, WS GS)*		(B) (SAOR) (GS) (WDS79) (K80) (WDS11) (SBW) (M)

(logo: crown over S·J)	*(See also)* **(EP)** Alexander **Spear &** Sam **Jackson**	
S.J. ADDIS LONDON (compass logo)	*(See also)* **(EP)** **Ward & Payne**	
S.J.L &Cᵒ **S.J.L&Cᵒ**	*(See also)* **(EP)** S. J. **Levi & Co.** **(Squirrel Works)**	
S·K·C&Cᵒ	*(See also)* **(OSP)** **Smith, Knowles, Creswick & Co.**	
S·K&Cᵒ SK&Cᵒ	*(See also)* **(OSP)** Samuel **Kirkby & Co.**	
SK	*(See also)* **(OSP)** Samuel & W. **Kirkby**	

Skee & Co. **(EP)** Durham (39, Cuthbert St) - 1880 ...		(K80)
Alexander **Skelton** **(EP)** Birmingham (67, Spencer St) - 1903 ...		(K03)
William James **Skelton** **(EP)** Birmingham (Bell Barn Rd) - 1936 ...		(K36)

S

	Peter **Skidmore**	**(EP)**	(SAOR)
	Sheffield		
	1877 ...		
	w. **Skidmore**	**(EP)**	(B) (SAOR) (SBW)
	(Enema Works)		
	Sheffield (Cemetery Rd)		
	1861 ... *(See also figure: WS.)*		
SKINNER & Co SHEFFIELD	Albert **Skinner & Co.**	**(BM/EP)**	(E) (SAOR) (K93)
	Sheffield (9, Eyre St/217, Shoreham St)		
	1888 - 1893 ...		
	(See also figure: S&Co)		
	E. **Skinner & Co.**	**(EP)**	
	Birmingham (64, Vittoria St/Graham St)		
	- 1872 ...		
	J. **Skinner**	**(EP)**	(MDG)
	Birmingham (Icknield 7, Port Rd)		
	- 1866 ...		
	Thomas **Skinner**	**(EP)**	(GS)
	Sheffield (29, Charlotte St)		
	- 1863 ...		
	Skinner, Coulson & Branson	**(EP)**	(POS) (K54)
	Sheffield (17, Sycamore St)		
	- 1854 ...		
	John **Skip(p)**	**(CP)**	(WTDB) (CD) (WDB) (PDB) (WAB) (HTD)
	Birmingham (Hill St/52, Price St)		
	- 1815 - 1830 ...		
SKIPTON	*(See also)*	**(CU/EP)**	(E)
	T. **Fattorini**		
S.L **L**	**Not assigned!**	**(EP)**	
	London		
S·Lᴰ	*(See also)*	**(EP)**	
	William **Suckling Ltd.**		
S.LINLEY	*(See also)*	**(EP)**	
	Alldays & Onions Pneumatic		
	Engineering		
S ⚒ Lᵀᴰ	*(See also)*	**(EP)**	
	William **Suckling Ltd.**		

S

Slack & Barlow Ltd. (EP)
Sheffield (14, Sycamore St)
~ 1897 ... *(See also figures: S&B,
S&B Ltd.,* SILVERPRIDE PLATE*)*

Slack & Grinold (CU/EP) (SBW) (M)
(Bath Works)
Sheffield
~ 1900 ...
*(See also figures: BON-ACCORD,
ONWARD)*

John Edwin **Slack** (EP) (WDS01)
Sheffield (70, Sellers St)
- 1901 ...

Slack Brothers (EP) (SAOR) (SBW) (B)
(Leicester Works)
Sheffield
1862 ... *(See also figures: SB, SB LW)*

John **Slater & Son** (EP) (SAOR) (M)
Sheffield (Norfolk St) (SBW) (B) (E)
1867 - 1884 *(See also figure: J.H.S)*
(Then: Slater Brothers)

George **Slater** (EP) (K03)
Birmingham (107, Vyse St)
- 1903 ...

John Henry **Slater** (EP) (WDS71) (WDS79)
Sheffield (25, Wostenholm Rd/Ashland Rd)
- 1871 - 1879 ...

Joseph Austin **Slater** (EP) (K80)
Birmingham (74, Smith St)
- 1880 ...

Slater Brothers (EP) (SBW) (M)
(Formerly: John Slater & Son)
SLATER Sheffield (94, Scotland St/159, Fitzwilliam
BROTHERS St/105, Arundel St)
SHEFFIELD 1884 - 1911 *(See also figures: SB,
S.Bros., SLATER BROTHERS,
VENTURE, symbol "beehive")*

S

357

Slater, Son & Horton	**(EP)**	(SAOR) (B) (GS)
Sheffield (Norfolk St)		
1859 - 1863 ... *(See also figure: S&H)*		

Sleath Brothers	**(EP)**	(K88) (K92)
Birmingham (54, Hocklex St)		
- 1888 - 1892 ...		

SM&Cº

(See also) **(EP)**
Sampson Mordan & Co.
(City Road Factory)

S M & Cº Lᴰ

(See also) **(EP)**
Sampson Mordan & Co.Ltd.
(City Road Factory)

SM

(See also) **(OSP)**
s. **Mearbeck**

SMALL

Thomas **Small**	**(OSP)**	(B) (WTDB) (M)
Birmingham (Paradise St)		
1812 - 1815 ...		

Small & Hipkiss	**(CP)**	(WDB) (PDB)
Birmingham (28, Paradise St)		
- 1823 - 1825 ...		

John **Smallwood**	**(FP)**	(B) (WDB) (PDB)
Sheffield (26, Coleshill/Foredrough St/		(WAB) (DOB)
46, Navigation St)		
1823 - 1833 ... *(See also figure: JS)*		

Thomas **Smallwood**	**(CP)**	
Sheffield (29, Brittain St./39,Suffolk Rd/		
68, Woodbank Cresent)		
- 1893 ...		(K93)
- 1901 - 1905 ... **(& Co.)**		(WDS01) (WDSR)

George **Smart**	**(CP/EP)**	(BDB) (MDG)
Birmingham (15, Hampton St)		(POB)
- 1862 - 1867 ...		

Ebenezer **Smelle**	**(OSP)**	(B) (SAOR)
Derby		
1799 ... *(See also figure: ES)*		

Smith & Barlow	**(CU/CP)**	(WDB) (PDB)
Birmingham (30, Water St)		(WAB) (HTD)
- 1823 - 1830 ...		

S

SMITH&Cᵒ

Smith & Co.   **(OSP)** [B]
Birmingham
1784 ...

SMITH & Cᵒ

(See also)   **(OSP)**
Smith, Tate, Nicholson & Hoult

Smith & Co.   **(EP)** [BDB]
Birmingham (19, Northampton St)
- 1862 ...

Emma C. **Smith & Co.**   **(EP)** [CDB] [BDB] [GS]
Birmingham (50, St. Paul's Sq)
- 1861 - 1863 ...

Ernest **Smith & Co.**   **(EP)** [K36]
Birmingham (3, Warstone Parade)
- 1936 ...

G. **Smith & Co.**   **(GS/EP)** [HGDB] [HGD]
Birmingham (48, Whittall St)
- 1849 - 1850 ...

Lawrence B. **Smith & Co.**   **(EP)**
Sheffield
1887 - 1958 *(See also figure:*
L.B.S&Co)

S. W. **Smith & Co.**   **(EP)** [K82] [PC] [K03]
(Formerly: George Richmond Collis & Co)
Birmingham (57, Cambridge St)
- 1882 - 1903 ...

Smith & Eades   **(CP)** [WAB] [HTD]
Birmingham (Ludgate Hill)
- 1829 - 1830 ...

Daniel **Smith &** Robert **Sharp**   **(OSP)** [B]
London
1778 ... *(See also figure: DS RS)*

J. **Smith & Sons**   **(EP)**
Sheffield
~ 1850 ...

James **Smith & Son**   **(CU)** [B] [SAOR]
Sheffield (Arundel St/Coalpit Ln)
1829 ... *(See also figures: JSMITH,*
S SMITH S)

S

Stephen **Smith & Son** **(EP)**
Sheffield
- 1886
(Then: Amalgamated with Mappin & Webb)

Thomas **Smith & Son** **(EP)** (K80)
Glasgow (31, Queen St)
- 1880 ...

Smith & Tart **(CU/CP)** (WDB) (PDB)
Birmingham (56, Constitution Hill)
- 1823 - 1825 ...

SM ITH

William **Smith** **(CP)** (B) (WTDB) (M)
Birmingham (Lw Temple St)
1812 - 1815 ...

Benjamin **Smith** **(OSP/CU)**
Sheffield (44 & 45, South St/Duke St)   (B) (CD) (HDG)
- 1818 - 1828 ... *(See also figure: B·S)*   (NGDS) (SDG)
- 1825 - 1833 (**& Son**)   (NGDS) (GDS)
(Then: Josephus Smith)

Charles **Smith** **(EP)** (GS) (WDS79)
Sheffield (Suffolk Rd/80, Talbot St)
- 1863 - 1879 ...

Charles **Smith** **(EP)** (K78) (K80)
Birmingham (104, Vyse St)
- 1878 - 1880 ...

Daniel **Smith** **(OSP)** (B)
London
1780 ... *(See also figure: DS)*

Edward Joseph **Smith** **(EP)** (SAOR) (GS)
Birmingham (28, Regent Pl/9, Tenby St)   (POB) (K88) (K92)
1840 - 1892 ...

Frederick **Smith** **(EP)** (POB)
Birmingham (16, Summer Ln)
- 1867 ...

S

George **Smith** **(CP/EP)**
Birmingham (Bartholomew St/Scotland St)
- 1815 - 1872 ...
Then:
Mrs. George **Smith** **(EP)**
- 1884 - 1892 ...

(WTDB) (WTD)
(MDG) (POB)
(K72)

(K84) (K88) (K92)

Harry William **Smith** **(EP/CP)**
Birmingham (10, Brook St)
- 1882 - 1892 ...

(K82) (K84) (K88)
(K92)

Jabez **Smith** **(CU/CP)**
Birmingham (25, Hall St)
- 1823 - 1825 ...

(WDB) (PDB)

James **Smith** **(OSP)**
Birmingham (44, Navigation St/Constitution Hill)
- 1818 - 1839 ...

(WTD) (CD)
(WDOB)

James **Smith** **(CP)**
Birmingham (Hospital St/58, Snow Hill)
- 1815 - 1839 ...

(WTDB) (WWDB)
(WDOB)

John **Smith** **(OSP)**
Sheffield (Lambert Croft)
1775 ... *(See also figure: IS)*

(B) (SAOR)

John **Smith** **(BM/EP)**
Sheffield (19, Carver St)
- 1852 ...

(WDOS)

John Henry **Smith** **(EP)**
Birmingham (46, Frederick St)
- 1903 ...

(K03)

John Patterson **Smith** **(EP)**
Glasgow
~ 1892 ... *(See also figure: ADAMAN-TINE)*

(W)

Joseph **Smith** **(CU/OSP)**
Sheffield (Trippet Ln)
- 1829 ...

(PD)

Joseph **Smith** **(EP)**
Birmingham (11, Smith St/Gr. Hampton Rw)
- 1861 ...

(CDB)

S

Joseph **Smith** (EP) (GS) (K82) (K84) (K88) m
Birmingham (6, Mary Ann St/53, Howard St)
- 1863 - 1888 ...

Josephus **Smith** (OSP) (GDS) (SAOR) (WDS37) (HGDY) (DSRR) (SD46) (POS) (B) (GDBS) (WDOS) (K54) (SBW) (M)
(Formerly: B. Smith & Son)
Sheffield (46/47/48/141, South St Moor)
- 1833 - 1854 ..
(See also figures:
JOSEPHUS SMITH, J.S, S.S.)

Nathaniel **Smith** (CU)
Sheffield (Waingate)
1784 -
1780 - 1787 ...**(& Co.)** (GM) (ASP) (B) (M) (SAOR) (B) (GM)
(See also figures: N. Smith & Co,
NS, NS & Co.)

Peter **Smith** (CP) (DOB) (HGDB)
Birmingham (32, Navigation St/240, Aston Rd)
- 1833 - 1849 ...

Samuel **Smith** (FP) (WAB)
Birmingham (Lw. Hampton St)
- 1829 ...

Samuel **Smith** (EP) (CDB)
Birmingham (19, Northampton St)
- 1861 ...

Sarah (Mrs. George) **Smith** (EP) (K80) (K82)
Birmingham (Scotland St)
- 1880 - 1882 ...

Sidney **Smith** (EP) (K80)
Bristol (Castle Green)
- 1880 ...

Stanhope **Smith** (EP) (POB) (K72)
Birmingham (50, St. Paul's Sq)
- 1867 - 1872 ...

Thomas **Smith** (CU) (SAOR)
Birmingham
1819 ...

W. **Smith** (OSP) (B) (SAOR)
Sheffield (Coalpit Ln)
1775 ... *(See also figure: W·S)*

S

	William **Smith** (Coach/CP/GS/EP) Birmingham (58, Gt. Hampton St/21, Henrietta St/George St) 1824 - 1880 ...	(SAOR) (WAB) (MDG) (K80) (K84)
	William **Smith** (EP) Birmingham (79 & 81, Branston St./103 Augusta St.) - 1882 - 1903 ...	(K82) (K84) (K88) (K92) (K03)
	William **Smith** (EP) Birmingham (9, Richard St) - 1880 ...	(K80)
	William Arthur **Smith, Benson & Co. (EP)** London 1898 ... *(See also figure: WASB)*	(M)
SMITH KIRKBY & Cº	**Smith, Kirkby & Co.** (BM) Sheffield 1797 ...	(B)
	Smith, Knowles, Creswick & Co. Sheffield (Arundel St) **(OSP)** - 1791 - 1793 ... *(See also figure: S.K.C&Co)*	(B) (SAOR) (UBD)
	Smith, Sissons & Co. (OSP) Sheffield (9, Eyre St) - 1849 - 1854 .. *(See also figure: Symbol " bell ")*	(GDBS) (WDOS) (POS) (K54)
	Smith, Stanhope, Baynes & Co. (EP) Birmingham (50, St. Paul's Sq) - 1866 - 1878 ...	(MDG) (K78)
	Smith, Tate & Co. (OSP) Sheffield (16, Arundel St) - 1822 ...	(HDG)
	Smith, Tate, Hoult & Tate (OSP) Sheffield (16, Arundel St) - 1822 - 1829 ... *(Then: John Watson & Son)*	(PDY) (PDB) (PD) (SDG) (NGDS)
	Smith, Tate, Nicholson & Co. (OSP) Sheffield (Arundel St) - 1818 ...	(CD)

S

	Smith, Tate, Nicholson & Hoult (OSP) Sheffield (Arundel St) 1810 ... *(See also figures: SMITH & Co., ST N&H)*	(B) (SAOR) (M)
	Snell & Prideaux (EP) Birmingham (Ernest St/Holloway Head) - 1882 - 1903 ...	(K82) (K84) (K88) (K92) (K03)
SO	**Not assigned!** (OSP) ~ 1785 ...	(B)
	Son & Mitchell (CU) Birmingham 1812 ...	(SAOR)
SONORA SILVER	**Walker & Hall** (EP) Sheffield ~	(M)
	Robert **Sorby & Sons Ltd.** (EP) Sheffield (Trafalgar St) - 1901 ... *(See also figure: Symbol "kangaroo")*	(WDS01) (SBW)
	R. & W. **Sorley** (EP) Glasgow - 1907 ... *(See also figure: R&W.SORLEY)*	(E) (Rd)
S O U N D	*(See also)* (CU) Joshua **Dewsnap**	
	Benjamin **Southeran** (OSP) Sheffield (10, Norfolk Rw) - 1825 ...	(NGDS)
SOUTHERN & RICHARDSON SHEFFIELD.ENGLAND	**Southern & Richardson (CU/EP) (Don Cutlery Works)** Sheffield (Doncaster St/Ellis St) - 1901 - 1905 ...	(WDS01) (WDSR) (M)
	W. **Soutter** (EP) Birmingham (10-12, New Market St) - 1861 ...	(CDB)
S·P&C⁰	*(See also)* (OSP) **Shemeld, Parkin & Co.**	

S

SPEAR & JACKSON SHEFFIELD	Alexander **Spear &** Sam **Jackson (CU)** ^{(WDOS AD) (K72 AD) (WDS79) (WDS01)} **(Ætna Works)** Sheffield (Savile St East) - 1851 - 1901 ... *(See also figures: LLOYD DA-VIES, S&J, ÆTNA)*

J. R. **Spencer & Son (CU)** ^{(K72AD) (WDS79)}
(Albion Steel Works)
Sheffield
- 1872 - 1879 ... *(See also figure: N SPENCER SHEFFIELD)*
(Then: Matthias Spencer & Son)

Matthias **Spencer & Sons (CU)** ^{(WDS01) (SBW) (M)}
(Albion Steel Works)
(Formerly: J.R. Spencer & Son)
Sheffield (Arley St)
- 1901 ...
(See also figures: N SPEN-SER SHEFFIELD, NIMROD, MATTHIAS SPENCER)

Thomas **Spencer (EP)** ^{(MDG) (POB) (K72) (K78) (K80) (K82) (K84) (K88) (K92)}
Birmingham (52, Key Hill/405, Lodge Rd/285 then 45, Icknield St)
- 1866 - 1878 ...
- 1880 - 1892 ... **(& Co.)**

C. A. E. **Speyer & Co. (CU/EP)** ^(M)
London
~ 1880 ...
(See also figure: HERALD TRUMPETER)

Spicer & Bellamy (EP) ^{(K72) (K78) (K80)}
Birmingham (9 & 10, Gt. Russell St)
- 1872 - 1880 ...

Thomas **Spicer (CU)** ^(SAOR)
Coventry
1816 ...

F. **Spiller (CU)** ^(E)
London () Brixton ()
~ 1880 ...
(See also figure: F. SPILLER)

S

Spittle & Heape **(EP)** (K82 AD)
(Tiger Works)
Birmingham (260, Icknield St)
Sheffield
- 1882 - 1884 ...
(See figure: African Silver)

Benjamin S. **Spittle** **(GS/EP)** (K78) (K80)
(Lion Works)
(Formerly: David Cope & Son)
Birmingham (Warstone Ln)
- 1878 - 1880 ...
(Then: Frederick Whitehouse)

(See also) **(EP)**
Sheffield Nickel & Silver Plating Co.
Ltd.
(Globe Works)

Joseph **Sponner** **(OSP)** (B) (SAOR)
Sheffield (Bailey Fields)
1786 ... *(See also figure: I.S)*

William **Spooner** **(CP/EP)** (SAOR) (HGDB)
Birmingham (12, New Market St) (HGD)
1815 - 1850 ... (WTDB) (WTD)
- 1815 - 1818 ... **(& Co.)** (CD)

William **Spooner,** Thomas **Clowes & Co.** (SAOR) (WDB)
Birmingham (12, New Market St) **(CU/EP)** (PDB) (WAB)
1819 - 1833 ... (HTD) (DOB)
(Then: Edward Till)

William **Spooner,** Charles **Painter & Co.** (SAOR) (WWDB)
Birmingham (New Market St) **(CU)**
1834 - 1835 ...

Edmond **Sporle & Co.** **(OSP)** (SAOR) (B)
Sheffield (Hawley Croft)
1793 ... *(See also figure: ES&Co)*

Robert **Sporle & Co.** **(OSP)** (SAOR)
Sheffield
1792 ...

William **Spratt** **(EP)** (K36)
Birmingham (120, Hockley St)
- 1936 ...

366

Peter **Spur & Son** **(OSP)** (B) (SAOR)
Sheffield (Church Ln)
1788 ... *(See also figure: P·S)*

Spurrier & Co. **(CU/EP)** (PC)
(Holland Street Works)
Birmingham (Holland St)
- 1896 ...

Arthur Ewell **Spurrier & Co.** **(EP)** (K88)
London (35, Coleman St)
Birmingham (10, George St)
1883 - 1897 ... *(See also figures: S &*
Co., S&Co. L)

Walter **Spurrier & Co.** **(BM/EP)** (MDG) (POB)
Birmingham (52 & 53, Lionel St) (K72) (SBW) (M)
London (72, Basinghall St)
- 1866 - 1872 ...
(See also figure: GORDON SIL-
VER)

Spurrier & Co. Ltd. **(EP)** (K03)
Birmingham (Fleet St)
- 1903 ...

Spurrier & Shingler **(EP)** (K78) (K80)
(Empire Works)
Birmingham (Hall St)
- 1878 - 1880
(Then: Walter Spurrier)

SPURRIER

William **Spurrier** **(CP/BM/EP)** (HGD) (GE)
Birmingham (3 & 5, Newhall St/83, Colmo- (CDB) (BDB)
re Rw) (GS) (MDG) (K72)
- 1850 - 1903 ... (K78) (K92) (PC)
(K03)

Walter **Spurrier** **(BM/EP)** (K80) (K82)
(Empire Works)
(Formerly: Spurrier & Shingler)
Birmingham (1, Hall St)
- 1880 - 1884 ...

William **Spurrier Ltd.** **(BM/EP)** (K80) (K82) (K84)
Birmingham (81, Colmore Rw)
- 1880 - 1884 ...

S

367

	Thomas **Squire** Walsall (79, Lower Rushall St) - 1880 ...	**(EP)** [K80]
SQUIRREL BRAND	*(See also)* s. j. **Levi & Co.** **(Squirrel Works)**	**(EP)**
S·R&Cº	*(See also)* Samuel **Roberts & Co.**	**(OSP)**
S·R&Cº	*(See also)* Samuel **Roberts, Smith & Co.**	**(OSP)**
SR	*(See also)* s. **Roberts**	**(OSP)**
S R C·B	*(See also)* Samuel **Roberts &** Charles **Belk** **(Furnival Works)**	**(EP)**
S R G C&Cº	*(See also)* s. **Roberts &** G. **Cadman & Co.**	**(OSP)**
S.S&Cº	*(See also)* **Selig, Sonnenthal & Co.**	**(EP)**
S.S.	*(See also)* Josephus **Smith**	**(OSP)**
S. S. & Co	*(See also)* **Selig, Sonnenthal & Co.**	**(EP)**
S SMI TH S	*(See also)* j. **Smith & Son**	**(CU/OSP)**
S S P Lᵀᴰ	*(See also)* **Sheffield Nickel & Silver Plating Co. Ltd.** **(Globe Works)**	**(EP)**
S.TURLEY	*(See also)* s. **Turley**	**(OSP)**
St & Cº	**Not assigned!**	**(CU/EP)** [E]
	Henry **Stacey & Horton** Sheffield (Norfolk St) 1856 ... *(See also figure: S&H)*	**(EP)** [B] [SAOR]

S

Ebenezer **Stacey** **(BM/EP)** Sheffield (40/36, Garden St/Britannia Pl) 1837 - 1852 ... *(See also figure: E. STACEY)* - 1863 - 1901 ... **(& Sons)** *(See also figures: ES&S,* *E.STACEY & SONS)* *(Then: Hodges Brothers)*	(B) (GDBS) (WDOS) (GS) (WDS79) (K80) (K93) (WDS01) (M)

E. H. **Stacey** **(EP)** Sheffield (Tudor St/78, Norfolk Rd) - 1863 - 1871 ...	(GS) (WDS71)

John V. **Stacey** **(EP)** Sheffield (455, College St) - 1879 - 1901 ...	(WDS79) (WDS01)

Mrs. William **Stacey** **(GS)** Sheffield (12, Carver Ln) - 1893 ...	(K93)

Stacey Brothers **(CU)** **(Eyre Street Works)** Sheffield (Eyre St) ~ 1847 - 1851 ... - 1852 ... **(& Co.)** *(See also figures:* 𝔈𝔟𝔢𝔯𝔩𝔞𝔰𝔱𝔦𝔫𝔤, THE ARK*)*	(WDOS AD) (SBW) (M)

Stafford & Newton **(OSP)** Sheffield (Arundel St) 1787 ... *(See also figure: S&N)*	(B) (SAOR) (GM)

J. Bernard **Stagg** **(EP)** London (37 & 38, Hatton Garden) Birmingham (54, Hockley Hill) - 1936 ...	(K36)

W. D. **Stait** **(EP)** Birmingham (36, Tenby St) - 1896 ...	(PC)

STAND	*(See also)* **(CU)** Thomas **Renshaw & Co.** **(Stand Works & Sylvester Works)**

STANDARD ECLIPEPLATE	*(See also)* **(CU/EP)** George **Wheeler**

STANDARD VICTORIA SILVER	*(See also)* Frederick **Derry** **(Phoenix Works)**	**(BM/EP)**	
	Benjamin **Staniforth** Sheffield (Byron Rd) - 1871 ...	**(EP)**	(WDS71)
	James **Staniforth** Sheffield (Bridgehouse) 1804 ... *(See also figure: I·S)*	**(OSP)**	(B) (SAOR)
	John **Staniforth & Co.** Sheffield (Arundel St) 1783 ... *(See also figure: I·S)*	**(OSP)**	(B) (SAOR)
	Thomas **Staniforth & Co.** Hackenthorpe near Sheffield - 1901 ...	**(CU)**	(WDS01)
	William Thomas **Staniforth** **(Eldon Works & Ascend Works)** Sheffield (5, Eldon St/221, Ashberry Rd) - 1879 - 1901 ... *(See also figure: ASCEND)*	**(CU)**	(WDS79) (M) (SAOR) (WDS01)
STANIFORTH PARKIN&Cº	**Staniforth, Parkin & Co. (CU/OSP)** Sheffield 1784 ...		(B) (M)
STANIFORTH ' S PATENT	*(See also)* **Fenton Brothers**	**(EP)**	
	Frederick J. **Stanton** Birmingham (40 & 48, St. Paul's Sq) - 1903 - 1936 *(Then: Gray & Stanton Manufg. Co.Ltd.)*	**(EP)**	(K03) (K36)
	Josiah **Stanyard** Birmingham (Hollo Way) - 1839 ...	**(CP)**	(WDOB)
STAYBRIGHT	*(See also)* Philip **Ashberry & Sons**	**(BM/EP)**	
	William **Steel** Birmingham (Cherry St) - 1818 ...	**(CP)**	(CD)

S

370

	William **Steeley** **(EP)**	(K78) (K80) (K82) (K84) (K88)
	Birmingham (2, Mary Ann St)	
	- 1878 - 1888 ...	

	Steer & Webster **(CU)**	(K80)
	(Castle Hill Works)	
	Sheffield ()	
	London (28, Holborn Viaduct)	
	- 1851 - 1880 ...	

	Steinhart & Co. **(EP)**	(K36)
	Birmingham (70, George St)	
	- 1936 ...	

STEPHENSON & SONS	**Stephenson & Sons** **(EP)**	(E)
PALATINE PLATE	Manchester & Sheffield	
MANCHESTER & SHEFFIELD	~ 1900 ... *(See also figures: PALATINE PLATE, S&S)*	

STERLING	*(See also)* **(EP)**	
£	**Keep Brothers**	
BRAND		

STEVENS.	*(See also)* **(CU/EP)**	
	Albert J. **Beardshaw**	

	Jeremiah **Stevens** **(CP)**	(WTDB) (WTD) (CD)
	Birmingham (Aston Rd/Snowhill)	
	- 1815 - 1818 ...	

	Robert **Stevenson & Co.** **(EP)**	(WDS01)
	Sheffield (27-29, Carver St/13, Eastgrove Rd)	
	- 1901 ...	
	(See also figure: R.S & Co)	

	W. **Stevenson & Co.** **(CU/GS)**	(WDOS AD)
	Sheffield (Suffolk St, Roscoe Fields)	
	- 1852 ...	

	Stevenson & Law **(EP)**	(WDSR)
	Sheffield (103 & 105, Carver St)	
	- 1905 ... *(See also figure: S & L)*	

	Job **Stevenson** **(EP)**	(GS)
	Sheffield (Milton Ln)	
	- 1863 ...	

	John **Stevenson** **(EP)**	(MDG)
	Birmingham (Talbot Rd)	
	- 1866 ...	

S

	Stilwell & Sons Birmingham (76/44, Spencer St) - 1878 - 1888 ...	**(EP)**	(K78) (K80) (K82) (K84) (K88)
S T N&H	*(See also)* **Smith, Tate**, **Nicholson & Hoult**	**(OSP)**	
	William **Stocks** Sheffield (Hyde Park) - 1837 ...	**(CU)**	(WDS37)
STOIC	*(See also)* George **Barnsley & Sons**	**(CP/EP)**	
	Stokes & Ireland Birmingham (83, Gt. Hampton St) - 1880 ...	**(EP)**	(K80)
	Alfred Albert **Stokes** Birmingham (41, St. Paul's Sq) - 1903 ...	**(EP)**	(K03)
	Charles **Stokes** Sheffield (465, Shoreham St) - 1879 ... - 1880 - 1882 ... (**& Son**)	**(EP)**	 (WDS79) (K80) (SAOR)
	G. **Stokes** Sheffield (Moor) 1833 ... *(See also figure: GS)*	**(OSP)**	(B) (SAOR)
	Stokes, Ayres & Co. Sheffield (31, Earl St) - 1936 ...	**(EP)**	(K36)
Stot	B. **Stot** Sheffield (Duke St) 1811 ...	**(CP)**	(B) (M)
	John **Stovin** Sheffield (48, Howard St) - 1901 ...	**(EP)**	(WDS01)
	Stower & Wragg Sheffield (Eyre St) 1931 - 1967 *(See also figure: S&W)*	**(EP)**	(SI)

S

Henry **Stratford** **(EP)**
Sheffield (10, Surrey St/1, New Church St/
92, Harwood St/45, Hastings Rd)
1879 - 1900 *(See also figure: H.S)*   (SAOR)
- 1901 - 1930 (**Ltd.**)
(See also figure: H.S Ltd.)   (WDS01) (WDSR)

William & Henry **Stratford** **(EP)**   (B) (SAOR) (SBW)
Sheffield (Surrey St/1, New Church St/   (GS) (WDS79)
Harwood St)   (K80)
1855 - 1880 ... *(See also figure: WS
HS)*

(See also) **(EP)**
Baum Brothers

J. T. **Stroud & Co.** **(EP)**   (MDG)
Birmingham (140, Suffolk St)
- 1866 ...

Elizabeth **Sturges** **(BM)**   (WAB) (DOB)
Birmingham (Suffolk St/Lichfield St)
- 1829 ...
- 1833 ... (**& Son**)

John **Sturges** **(BM)**   (WDB) (PDB)
Birmingham (60, Lovedays St)
- 1823 - 1825 ...

Perey **Sturges** **(EP)**   (K03)
Birmingham (14, Hurst St)
- 1903 ...

Rd. F. **Sturges** **(MP/EP)**   (GS) (HGD)
Birmingham (46, Broad St)   (HGD)(CDB)
- 1849 - 1863 ...   (BDB) (HGDB)

S. & W. **Sturges** **(GS/CP)**   (WDOB)
Birmingham (Ashted Rw)
- 1839 ...

Sturges, Bladon & Middleton (EP)   (CDB) (BDB)
Birmingham (13 & 14, Weaman St)   (GS) (MDG)(POB)
- 1861 - 1903 ... *(See also figures:*   (K72) (K78) (K80)
SB&M, SBM)   (K82) (K84) (K88)
     (K92) (PC) (K03)

S

	William **Suckling** (EP)	
	Birmingham (40, Tenby St/35, Albion St/5, Pope St)	(K80) (K82) (K84)
	London (26-30, Holborn Viaduct)	(K88) (K92) (PC) (K03)
	- 1880 - 1903 ...	
	- 1936 ... (**Ltd.**)	(K36)
	(See also figures: KINGSWAY PLATE, REGIS PLATE, S*L^{TD})	
S U P E R	*(See also)* (CU/OSP) William **Green & Co.**	
SUPERIOR ELECTRO SILVER PLATE SHEFFIELD	*(See also)* (CU/EP) John Henry **Potter** (**Rockingham Works**)	
SUPERLATIVE	**Unwin & Rodgers** (CU) (**Globe Works**)	
SURREY EPNS	**Not assigned!** (EP) - 1911 ...	(Rd 589973)
	R. **Sutcliffe &** A. **Sporle** (OSP) (Robert **Sutcliffe & Co.**) Sheffield 1781 ... *(See also figureS: A·S, RS & Co)*	(B) (SAOR)
	Robert **Sutcliffe** (CU) Sheffield 1781 ... *(See also figure: RS)*	(B)
	Sutcliff, Sporle & Co. (CU) Sheffield (King St) 1787 ... *(See also figure: S.S&Co)*	(GM) (B)
	Suter & Woollaston (EP) Birmingham (56, Graham St) - 1872 - 1903 ...	(K72) (K78) (K80) (K82) (K84) (K88) (K92) (K03)
	Samuel **Suter** (EP) Birmingham (56, Graham St) - 1862 - 1867	(BDB) (GS) (MDG) (POB)
	Sutherland & Horne (CU/EP) Edinburgh (10, South St/Andrew St) - 1930 ... *(See also figure: S&H EDIN)* *(Then: Henry Tatton & Son)*	

S

S·W&C⁰	*(See also)* S. **Warburton & Co.**	**(OSP)**
S W &C⁰	*(See also)* Samuel **Walker & Co.**	**(OSP)**
S.WORTON	*(See also)* Samuel **Worton**	**(CP)**
SW	W. & S. **Ward** Manchester (St: Mary's Gate) 1858 ...	**(EP)** (SBW) (M) (B)
	Henry **Swadkins** Birmingham (178, Hockley St) - 1888 ...	**(EP)** (K88)
	Swain & Davis Birmingham (Whittall St) - 1818 ...	**(CP/CU)** (WTD) (CD)
	Joseph **Swain & Son** Birmingham (360, Summer Ln) - 1849 - 1850 ...	**(EP)** (HGDB) (HGD)
	George **Swain** Birmingham (263, Icknield St) - 1878 ...	**(EP)** (K78)
	Joseph **Swain** Birmingham (205, Livery St) - 1823 - 1833 ...	**(CP)** (WDB) (PDB) (WAB) (HTD) (DOB)
	William **Swain** Birmingham (15, St. Paul's Sq) - 1862 - 1863 ...	**(EP)** (BDB) (GS)
	Swain Brothers Birmingham (13, Lower Loveday St) - 1872 ...	**(EP)** (K72)
	Samuel **Swan** Birmingham (37, Swallow St) - 1823 - 1825 ...	**(CU/CP)** (WDB) (PDB)
	Swann & Adams **(Canada Works)** Birmingham ~ 1900 *(See also figure: MIXTIME)*	**(EP)** (SBW) (M)

S

John **Swann** (EP)	(K72)	
Birmingham (14-16, Exeter Rw)		
- 1872 ...		

William **Swann** (EP)	(CDB) (BDB)	
Birmingham (36, Constitution Hill/5, Regent Pd)	(GS) (MDG)(POB)	
	(K72) (K80) (K82)	
	(K84) (K88) (K92)	
- 1861 - 1903 ...	(K03)	

Joseph **Swift & Co.** (EP) (SAOR) (K80)
Sheffield (11, Arundel St)
1875 - 1880 ...

Francis **Swinden & Co.** (CP) (SAOR) (WAB) (HTD) (DOB)
Birmingham (64, Bath St)
- 1829 - 1833 ...

John **Swingler** (CP) (WAB) (DOB) (WDOB)
Birmingham (Vauxhall Rd/Heneage St)
- 1829 - 1839 ...

Samuel **Swingler** (GS) (WDOB)
Birmingham (Newhall St)
- 1839 ...

Thomas **Swingler** (CP) (WTDB) (WTD) (CD) (WDB) (PDB) (DOB) (WWDB)
Birmingham (Price St/32/52, Staniforth St)
- 1815 - 1835 ...

Thomas & William **Swingler** (CP) (WDOB)
Birmingham (Staniforth St)
- 1839 ...

William **Swingler** (EP) (HGDB) (SAOR)
Birmingham (52, Staniforth St)
- 1849 ...

Swithenbank & Stirling (EP) (K80)
Heckmondwike (High St)
- 1880 ...

Sydney Plating Co. (EP) (K03)
Birmingham (6, Warstone Parade)
- 1903 ...

SYKES &Cº

J. & D. **Sykes & Co.** (CU/OSP) (B) (SAOR) (M)
Sheffield (Pinchin Ln)
1781 ...

S

John **Sykes & Co.** **(CU/OSP)**

Sheffield (Pinston Ln/ Pinstone Ln)

1787 - 1792 ...

(GM) (B) (SAOR)

1808 ... *(See also figure: I·S&Co,*
(UBD)

JOHN SYKES&Co)
(SAOR)

SYKES " Lion " *(See also)* **(CU)**

Birks, Withers & Sykes

Dennis **Sykes** **(OSP)** (SAOR) (B) (UBD)

Sheffield

1791 ...

(See also figure: DENNIS SYKES)

S

377

T & B	*(See also)* **Thompson & Brown**	(OSP)
T & J ∗ E P	*(See also)* **Taunton & Johnson**	(BM/EP)
T.B	*(See also)* T. **Beardmore**	(EP)
T·B	*(See also)* Thomas **Blagden**	(OSP)
T·C	*(See also)* Thomas **Clayton**	(OSP)
T·C	*(See also)* Thomas **Colley**	(OSP)
T.E	*(See also)* T. W. **Eaton & Co.**	(EP)
T.E	*(See also)* Thomas **Ellis**	(EP)
T·G	*(See also)* T. **Greaves**	(OSP)
T·H	*(See also)* T. **Hoyland**	(OSP)
T.K	*(See also)* T. **Kitchen**	(OSP)
T·N **T·N** **T·N**	*(See also)* T. **Nowill**	(CU) [B]
T·S	*(See also)* Thomas **Settle**	(OSP)
T·S	*(See also)* T. **Shaw**	(OSP)
T·P	*(See also)* T. **Parkin**	(OSP)
T·P	*(See also)* T. **Prior**	(OSP)

Mark	Description	Category
T·R	*(See also)* T. **Ratcliffe**	(OSP)
T.T & C⁰ EP **T.T** **T.T**	*(See also)* Thomas **Turner** **(Suffolk Works)**	(CU/EP)
T.W.	*(See also)* **Laycock Brothers**	(EP/CU)
T.W **T.W &S**	*(See also)* Thomas **Wilkinson & Sons** **(Pelican Works)**	(EP)
T.W	*(See also)* Thomas **White** or *(See also)* Thomas **Wooley** **(Electro Plate Works)**	(EP) (CU/EP)
T.W	*(See also)* Thomas **Warris & Son**	(OSP)
T.W	*(See also)* Thomas **White** or *(See also)* Thomas **Wooley** **(Electro Plate Works)**	(EP) (CU/EP)
T	*(See also)* Robert **Bateman** **(Don Works)**	(CU/CP)
TA	*(See also)* T. **Allen**	(OSP)
	Not assigned!	(EP)
TARRATT LEICESTER	**Tarratt** Leicester ~ 1900	(EP)

T

	William **Tart** Birmingham - 1823 ...	**(CP)**	(WDB)
TAUNTON & JOHNSON	**Taunton & Johnson** **(BM/EP)** Birmingham (46, Broad St/296, Broad St) - 1872 - 1888 ... *(See also figure: T & J * EP)*		(K72) (K80) (K82) (K84) (K88) (M)
	E. W. P. **Taunton** Birmingham (46, Broad St) - 1866 - 1867 ...	**(EP)**	(MDG) (POB)
	Tay & Francis Birmingham (Leopold St) - 1872 - 1884 ...	**(EP)**	(K72) (K78) (K80) (K82) (K84)
	William **Tay & Son Ltd.** Birmingham (30 & 34, Leopold St) ~ 1900 ... *(See also figures: Medallion, WT&S)*	**(EP)**	(E)
	Thomas **Tay** Birmingham (Angelina St) - 1866 ...	**(EP)**	(MDG)
	William **Tay** Birmingham (Leopold St) - 1896 ...	**(EP)**	(PC)
	James **Taylor & Co.** London (Ely Place) ~ 1930 ...	**(EP)**	
	Taylor & Grove Birmingham (66, Scholefield St/3, St. Mary's Rw) - 1872 - 1880 ...	**(EP)**	(K72) (K78) (K80)
	Taylor & Son Birmingham (6, Augusta St) - 1903 ...	**(EP)**	(K03)
	Edward Cornelius **Taylor** Birmingham (48, Warstone Ln) - 1892 ..	**(EP)**	(K92)

	Elisha **Taylor** Sheffield (Highfield) - 1852 ...	**(EP)**	(WDOS)
	George **Taylor** Birmingham (30b, St. George's Pl) - 1936 ...	**(EP)**	(K36)
	George J. **Taylor** Birmingham (33, Tenby St) - 1888 - 1892 ...	**(EP)**	(K88) (K92)
	Gideon **Taylor** Birmingham (Park St) - 1815 ...	**(CP)**	(WTDB)
	Joseph **Taylor** Birmingham 1813 - 1825 ...	**(CP)**	(SAOR) (WTD)
	John **Taylor** Birmingham (238, Icknield St) - 1892 - 1896 ...	**(EP)**	(K92) (PC)
	Jonathan **Taylor** Sheffield (Portmahon) 1822 ...*(See also figure: IT)*	**(OSP)**	(B) (SAOR)
	John **Taylor** Sheffield (15, Philip's Rd) - 1849 ... *(See also figure: EYE WITNESS)* *(Then: Needman, Veall & Tyzack)*	**(CU)**	(GDBS)
	Thomas **Taylor** Birmingham 1814 ...	**(CU)**	(SAOR)
TAYLOR WITNESS SHEFFIELD	*(See also)* **Needham, Veall & Tyzack Ltd.** **(Eye Witness Works)**	**(EP)**	
T·B **&Cº**	*(See also)* T. **Blagden & Co.**	**(OSP)**	
T.B ★ **Lᵀᴰ**	**Not assigned!**	**(EP)**	
T·BEST	*(See also)* Thomas **Best**	**(CU/OSP)**	

TB&Cᵒ	*(See also)* T. **Badger & Co.**	**(OSP)**
TB&S	*(See also)* Thomas **Bradbury & Sons**	**(OSP/EP)**
TB &S **TB&S** **T B & S S** **T B & S S** **T B & S S EP**		
TB S B	*(See also)* Thomas **Butts**	**(CU)**
TB 2 ⅋	*(See also)* Joseph **Ash & Son**	**(CU/EP)**
TB JH	*(See also)* Thomas **Bradbury & Sons**	**(EP)**
T·C &S	*(See also)* T. **Champion & Son**	**(OSP)**
TC	*(See also)* Thomas & James **Creswick**	**(OSP)**
TC	*(See also)* Thomas **Cooper**	**(OSP)**
TCP Ltd	**Not assigned!**	**(EP)** [E]
TD	*(See also)* Thomas **Daniell**	**(OSP)**
	G. **Teasdell** London (Hatton Garden) 1859 ... *(See also figure: GT)*	**(EP)** [B] [SAOR] [SBW] [M]
	William E. **Tedd & Co.** **(Tedd & Sons)** Birmingham (97, Albion St/Kenyon St) - 1892 - 1903 ...	**(EP)** [K92] [K03]
	Terry & Oaks Birmingham (127, Suffolk St) - 1835 ...	**(CU)** [WWDB]

Mark	Details	Notes
T·F&Cº	*(See also)* T. **Fox & Co.** (Fox, Proctor, Pasmore & Co)	(OSP)
T.FATTORINI	*(See also)* T. **Fattorini**	(CU/EP) [E]
TF	*(See also)* T. **Freeman**	(OSP)
T.G & S	*(See also)* Thomas Hutchinson **Goodfellow**	(EP)
TG &M	*(See also)* **Thorpe, Glossop & Middleton**	(OSP)
TG **TG**	*(See also)* Thomas Hutchinson **Goodfellow**	(EP)
T·H &S	*(See also)* Thomas **Harwood & Son**	(EP)
T. H. ⚓	*(See also)* Thomas, James & Nathaniel **Creswick**	(OSP/EP)
T. H. DAVIES & Co	*(See also)* T. H. **Davies & Co.**	(EP)
T. H. Winder & Co Windermere	*(See also)* T. H. **Winder & Co.**	(EP)
T·H &S	*(See also)* Thomas **Harwood & Son**	(EP)
TH	*(See also)* Thomas **Hardy**	(OSP)
TH	*(See also)* Thomas **Harwood**	(CP/Coach/EP)
	Thane & Co. Sheffield (46, Carver St) - 1901 ...	(EP) (WDS01)
T H B S 🞓	Thomas Henry **Blake** Sheffield (Holly St/Carver Ln) 1887 - 1911	(EP)

T

THE ALEX. CLARK LONDON MANUFACTORING Co	*(See also)* Alexander **Clark Manufg. Co.** **(Welbeck Works)**	**(EP)**
THE ALEX^R CLARK COMPANY L_{TD} WELBECK PLATE	*(See also)* Alexander **Clark Manufg. Co. Ltd.** **(Welbeck Works)**	**(EP)** (K36)
THE ARK	*(See also)* **Stacey Brothers**	**(CU)**
THE CAVENDISH	*(See also)* Robert **Belfitt** and George **Butler & Co. Ltd.** (CU/EP) **(Trinity Works)**	**(EP)**
THE CYPRUS	*(See also)* **Judd & Co.**	**(EP)**
THE " HYGENIA "	*(See also)* **Barker Brothers** **(Unity Works)**	**(BM/EP)**
THE MASHER	*(See also)* **Bramwell & Co.** **(Bramwell Brownhil & Co. Ltd.)**	**(EP)**
The NATIONAL	*(See also)* W. S. **Savage & Co.** (W. **Savage, Smith & Co)**	**(EP)**
THEOPHILUS RICHARDS & Co	*(See also)* Theophilus **Richards & Co.**	**(EP)**
	John **Thickett** Sheffield (47 - 51, Charles St) - 1880 ...	**(EP)** (K80)
THOMAS	Francis Boon **Thomas & Co.** London (New Bond St) 1874 - 1941	**(T)** (B)

384

	Richard **Thomas & Co. Ltd.** Lydbrook, Gloucestershire ~ 1900 ... *(See also figure: ALLAWAYS)*	**(CU)**	(W)
THO MAS	S. **Thomas** Birmingham (Throp St) 1813 ...	**(CP)**	(B) (M)
	Charles **Thomas** Birmingham (24 & 26, Lionel St) - 1882 - 1903 ...	**(EP)**	(K82) (K84) (K88) (PC) (K03)
	Harold **Thomas** Birmingham (44, St. Paul's Sq) - 1903 ...	**(EP)**	(K03)
THOMAS ALDRIDGE 57 BROMPTEN ROAD LONDON	*(See also)* Thomas **Aldridge**	**(EP)**	
	E. **Thomason & Co.** (E. **Thomason & Dowler**) Birmingham (Church St) 1807 - 1815 ... *(See also figure: E. Thomason & Co.)*	**(CP)**	(B) (WTDB) (M)
	T. **Thomason & Co.** Birmingham (29 & 30, Graham St) - 1863 - 1866 ...	**(EP)**	(GS) (MDG)
THOMASON	**Sir** Edward **Thomason** Birmingham (29, Church St) 1807 - 1835 ...	**(CP)**	(CD) (WDB) (PDB) (WTDB) (WWDB) (WAB) (HTD) (DOB) (SAOR) (M)
THOMAS OTLEY SHEFFIELD	*(See also)* Thomas **Otley & Co.** **(Meadow Works)**	**(EP)**	
THOMAS OTLEY & SONS SHEFFIELD	*(See also)* Thomas **Otley & Sons** **(Meadow Works)**	**(EP)**	
THOMASS **BOND S**T	*(See also)* **Thomas & Co.**	**(T)**	
	Thompson & Barber Sheffield (Arundel St) 1809 ... *(See also figure: EB)*	**(OSP)**	(B) (SAOR)

T

Thompson & Brown   **(OSP)**   _{(SAOR) (SD46)}
_{(SBW) (B)}
Sheffield (60, Eyre Ln)
1844 - 1846 ...
(See also figures: T&B, TNB)

Edward Landers **Thompson & Co. (EP)**   (SAOR) (WDSR)
Sheffield (22, Mary St/70-76 West St)
1889 - 1905 ... *(See also figure: ELT)*

William **Thompson & Co.**   **(CU/CP)**   (WTD)
Birmingham (Gt. Brooke St)
- 1818 ...

Albert Henry **Thompson**   **(EP)**   (SAOR) (W) (K93)
(WDSR) (WDS11)
Sheffield (10-16, Regent St)
1885 - 1911 ... *(See also figure: A.H.T.)*

James **Thompson**   **(OSP/EP)**   (DSRR) (SAOR)
(Soho Plate Works)   (SBW) (M) (B)
(K80)
Sheffield (84, Lead Milll Rd/99, Napier St)
- 1841 - 1880 ... *(See also figure: J.T)*

William **Thompson**   **(CU/EP)**
Birmingham (24, Gt. Hampton St/
79, Spencer St)   (SAOR) (MDG)
1839 - 1867 ...   (POB)
- 1872 - 1880 ...   **(& Co.)**   (K72) (K78) (K80)

Thorpe, Glossop & Middleton (OSP)   (B) (SAOR)
Sheffield (Carver St)
1834 ... *(See also figure: TG&M)*

THOS BARCLAY & SON	*(See also)* **(EP)** (M) (SBW) Isaac **Silverston & Co.**
THOS BRADBURY & SONS ARUNDEL ST SHEFFIELD	*(See also)* **(EP)** Thomas **Bradbury & Sons**
THOS GOODES & Co	*(See also)* **(T)** Thomas **Goode & Co.**
THOS PARKIN 45 SYCAMORE ST SHEFFIELD	*(See also)* **(BM/EP)** Thomas **Parkin**
THOS WHITE A1 SHEFFIELD	*(See also)* **(EP)** Thomas **White**

Walter **Thowless** (EP) Walsall (George St/23, Loveday St) - 1880 - 1884 ...	(K80) (K82) (K84)
John **Thrasher & ** Robert **Mathers (CU)** Coventry 1817 ...	(SAOR)
John **Thrasher** (CU) Coventry 1813 ...	(SAOR)
Threadgill Electro Deposits Ltd. (EP) Tipton (Union St) - 1936 ...	(K36)

John **Thropp** (CP/OSP)
Birmingham (Hurst St)
1814 - 1818 ... (SAOR) (WTD)
1815 - 1818 ... (**& Co.**) (John & Ann) (SAOR) (CD)

THUR LOW **Thurlow** (EP) (E)
~
- 1896

THWN *(See also)* (OSP)
T. **Holy &** W. **Newbold**

T&I·S *(See also)* (OSP)
John & Thomas **Settle**

Joseph **Tibbitts** (OSP) (B) (SAOR)
Sheffield (Gibraltar St)
1778 ... *(See also figure: J.T)*

William **Tickle** (MP/EP) (HGDB) (HGD)
Birmingham (2, Latimer St)
- 1849 - 1850 ...

James **Tidmarsh** (EP) (SBW) (M)
London
~ 1886 ... *(See also figures: JTML MP, MEXICAN SILVER)*

James & Charles **Tidmarsh** (EP) (M)
London
~ 1886 ... *(See also figure: J&CT)*

TIFFANY & C<u>O</u> **Tiffany & Co.** (EP)

(See also) **Deakin, Reuss & Co.**	**(CU)**

Edward **Till**　　**(EP)** (CDB)
(Formerly: Spooner, Clowes & Co)
Birmingham (12 & 13, New Market St)
- 1861 ...

Thomas **Tillotson**　　**(CU)** (B) (W)
Sheffield
1774 ...*(See also figure: ALBION SILVER)*

Frederick Ellis **Timm**　　**(EP)** (SAOR) (B) (SAOR) (GS) (K54) (POS) (K80) (SBW) (M)
Sheffield (11, Hawley Croft/10, Regent St)
1857 - 1872 ...
- 1854 - 1882 ...
(See also figure: FET & Co)

Timmis & Harvey　　**(EP)** (K82) (K84)
Birmingham (23, Snow Hill/71, Slaney St)
- 1882 - 1884 ...

Timmis & Littleford　　**(EP)** (K88) (K92)
Birmingham (23, Snow Hill/71, Slany St)
- 1888 - 1892 ...

James **Timmins**　　**(OSP)** (SAOR) (CD)
Birmingham (Mount St)
1818 - 1833 ...

Thomas **Timmins**　　**(CU)** (SAOR)
Birmingham
1813 ...

Samuel **Tinker**　　**(OSP)** (B) (SAOR)
Leeds
1824 ... *(See also figure: S·T)*

James Walter **Tiptaft**　　**(EP)**
Birmingham (Holyhead Rd)
~ 1886 ... *(See also figure: J.W.T)* (M)
- 1936 ... **(Ltd.)** (K36)

T. JOWITT
SHEFFIELD
(See also) **(EP/CU)**
Alfred **Beckett & Sons**

388

TJ&NC	*(See also)* Thomas, James & Nathaniel **Creswick**	**(OSP/EP)**
T·LAW	*(See also)* Thomas **Law**	**(CU/OSP)**
	(See also) Thomas **Latham &** Ernest **Morton**	**(EP)**
TL&SS	*(See also)* Thomas **Land & Sons** **(Colonial Works)**	**(EP)**
TL	*(See also)* T. **Lamborn**	**(OSP)**
TL **DL**	*(See also)* Thomas & Daniel **Leader**	**(OSP)**
TL LAW *TL* *TL* THºLAW *TL* **TL** *TL&Co*	*(See also)* Thomas **Law**	**(CU/OSP)**
T.MᶜLELLAN Lᵀᴰ	*(See also)* T. **McLellan Ltd.**	**(EP)**
TM	*(See also)* T. **Marples**	**(EP)**
TN&Cº	*(See also)* T. **Nixon & Co.**	**(OSP)**
T N B	*(See also)* **Thompson & Brown**	**(OSP)**
	John **Tnickett** Sheffield (8, Hermitage St) - 1863 ...	**(EP)** (GS)
T.O &S **Z** **EP** **BM** **Lᵀᴰ**	*(See also)* Thomas **Otley & Son** **(Meadow Works)**	**(EP/BM)**
T. OLDHAM **MAKER** **NOTTINGHAM**	*(See also)* T. **Oldham**	**(EP)**

T. OTLEY **SHEFFIELD**	*(See also)* Thomas **Otley & Co.** **(Meadow Works)**	**(CU/EP)**
	A. F. & J. **Tofield** **(Wilsick Works)** Sheffield (129, St. Mary's Rd) - 1893 ...	**(EP)** ^(K93)

A. F. & J. **Tofield**
(Wilsick Works)
Sheffield (129, St. Mary's Rd)
- 1893 ...

(EP) (K93)

(See also) **(CU)**
John Henry **Andrew & Co.**

Tomlinson & Davies **(CP)** (WDOB)
Birmingham (Shallow St)
- 1839 ...

C. D. **Tompkins** **(CU/EP)** (PC)
Birmingham (6, Mary Ann St)
- 1896 ...

Charles **Tongue** **(CP)** (PDB)
Birmingham (1, Livery St)
- 1825 ...

John **Tongue** **(CP)** (SAOR) (WWDB)
Birmingham (12, Smith St)
1831 - 1835 ...

John & Mary **Tongue** **(CP)** (DOB)
Birmingham (36, Ludgate Hill)
- 1833 ...

Samuel **Tongue** **(CP)** (WTD)
Birmingham (Livery St)
- 1818 ...

William **Tongue** **(OSP)** (WTDB) (CD)
Birmingham (22, High St)
- 1815 - 1818 ...

William **Tongue** **(CP)** (CD) (WAB)
Birmingham (Livery St/Water St) (HTD)
- 1818 - 1830 ...

Samuel **Tonks** **(CP)** (WAB) (HTD)
Birmingham (Bromsgrove St/Bristol St) (B) (M)
1807 - 1823
1824 - 1830 ...**(& Co)**
- 1850 ... (35, Ludgate Hill) (HGD)

	Joseph **Tonks** Birmingham (Bromsgrove St/101, Bristol St) - 1815 ... - 1818 - 1825 ...(**& Co.**)	**(CP)**	(WTDB) (CD) (WTD) (WDB) (PDB)
	Robert **Toothill** Sheffield (20, Bower Spring) - 1849 - 1852 ...	**(BM)**	(GDBS) (WDOS)
TOPAZ	*(See also)* Albert Samuel **Bradley**	**(EP)**	
	Towndrow Brothers Sheffield (South St Moor) 1864 ... *(See also figure: J.T T.T)*	**(EP)**	(SAOR) (SBW) (M) (B)
	John **Townroe & Sons** Sheffield (138/188, West St) - 1880 - 1936 ... *(See also figure: JT&S)*	**(EP)**	(K80) (K93) (WDS01) (K36) (M)
	Thomas **Townsend & Co.** Birmingham (3, Upper Hockley St) - 1878 ...	**(EP)**	(K78)
	Townsend & Sleath **(Townsend & Co.)** Birmingham (91, Branston St/11, Gt. Hampton St) - 1880 - 1888 ...	**(EP)**	(K80) (K82) (K84) (K88)
	John Daniel **Townsend** Hull (12, Queen St) - 1880 ...	**(EP)**	(K80)
	John Francis **Townsend** **(Cambridge Works)** Sheffield (214, Solly St) - 1879 - 1901 ... *(See also figure: LIFE)*	**(EP/CU)**	(WDS79) (WDS01) (SBW) (M)
	Thomas **Townsend** Birmingham (23, Augusta St) - 1892 ...	**(EP)**	(K92)
	William **Toy** Birmingham (Ct. 26, Barr St) - 1878 ...	**(EP)**	(K78)

TP	*(See also)* T. **Poynton &** R. **Flower**	**(OSP)**
TPL	*(See also)* T. P. **Lowe**	**(OSP)**
TR	*(See also)* T. **Royle**	**(EP)**
TR	*(See also)* T. **Rodgers**	**(OSP)**

George **Travis & Co.**   **(BM/EP)**   ^{(K80) (K93)}
(Clarence Works)   (WDS01) (M)
Sheffield (63, Charles St/13, Bath St)
1863 - 1909 *(See also figure: GT & Co)*
(Then: Travis, Wilson & Co. Ltd.)

George **Travis &** Samuel **Russel**   **(EP)**   ^(PI)
Sheffield
1861 - 1863

Nathaniel **Travis**   **(OSP/CU)**   ^{(B) (SAOR)}
Sheffield (Whitecroft)
1774 - 1789 ...
(See also figures: IN BILBO, N·T)

George **Travis**   **(EP)**   ^{(WDS79) (WDS01)}
Sheffield (9, Broomhall Rd)
- 1879 - 1901 ...

George Roebuck **Travis**   **(EP)**   ^(WDS01)
Sheffield (31, Clarkehouse Rd)
- 1901 ...

Travis, Wilson & Co. Ltd.   **(EP)**   ^(SI)
(Clarence Works)
(Formerly: George Travis & Co.)
Sheffield (13, Bath St/85, Denby St)
1909 - 1967 ...
(See also figures: T.W&Co Ltd,
MANOR PLATE)

Walter **Trickett & Co. Ltd.**   **(EP)**   ^(K36)
Sheffield (27, Tippet Ln)
- 1936 ...

	Robert **Tricket** **(OSP/CU)**	
	Sheffield (Far Field/Hill Foot)	
	1773 ... *(See also figures: R·T, RT)*	(B) (SAOR)
	1786 ... *(See also figures: R·T,*	(B) (SAOR)
	RT&Co)	

	Tricket, Haslehurst, Whiteley & Pryor	(B)
	Sheffield (Hillfoot) **(CU)**	
	1787 ... *(See also figures: OPUS, OVA)*	

"TRUE"	*(See also)* **(EP)**	(W)
	William **Bocking**	

	Arthur **Truelove** **(GS)**	(K93)
	Sheffield (111, Carver St)	
	- 1893 ...	

TRUROX	*(See also)* **(BM/EP)**
	Atkin Brothers
	(Truro Works)

TRUSTWORTHY	*(See also)* **(BM/EP/CU)**
	John Newton **Mappin &** George **Webb**
	(Royal Plate Works)

TRY ME	*(See also)* **(EP/CU)**
	Jno. Priston **Cutts, Sutton & Sons**

T·S&Cᵒ	*(See also)* **(OSP)**
	Thomas **Settle & Co.**(Thomas Warris)

TS	*(See also)* **(OSP/CU)**
	Thomas **Sanson**

T.TURNER&Co ENGLAND	*(See also)* **(CU/EP)**
	Thomas **Turner**
	(Suffolk Works)

TU & L	**Not assigned!** **(EP)**

	William **Tucker & Co.** **(OSP)**	
	(W. **Tucker** J. **Fenton &** E. G. **Machon)**	(B) (SAOR)
	1810 ... (Norfolk St)	
	(See also figure: WT&Co)	

	W. **Tucker** J. **Fenton & Co.** **(OSP)**	(B) (SAOR)
	Sheffield	
	1796 ... (Red Hill)	
	(See also figure: WT&Co)	

T

Edward **Tuckey** (EP) [HGD]
Bordesley (152, High St)
- 1850 ...

TUDOR&Cᵒ

(See also) (OSP) [GM] [B] [M]
Tudor & Leader & Co.
Sheffield (Sycamore Hill)
1784 - 1787 ...

Henry **Tudor &** Thomas **Leader** (OSP)
(Sycamore Works)
Sheffield (Sycamore Hill)
1760 - 1773 ... [B] [SAOR] [M]
- 1791 ... **(& Co./& Nicholson**)
(See also figures: HT, ℋℐ&ℯ°, [UBD]
HT TL, TUDOR & Co)

Henry **Tudor &** S. **Nicholson** (OSP) [B] [SAOR]
Sheffield (Arundel St)
1797 ... *(See also figure: HT&Co)*

TUDOR PLATE **Not assigned!** (EP)

Samuel **Turley** (CP) [WTDB] [WTD]
Birmingham (8, Snowhill) [WDB] [PDB]
- 1815 - 1825 ... *(See also figure:* [CD] [B] [M]
S.TURLEY)

John **Turnell** (EP) [WDS79]
Sheffield (98, Fawcett St)
- 1879 ...

Turner & Bramall (EP) [GS]
Sheffield (Nursery Ln)
- 1863 ...

Turner & Co. (CU/EP) [PC]
Birmingham (Edward St)
- 1896 ...

C. R. **Turner** (EP) [GS] [CDB]
Birmingham (84, Branston St)
- 1861 - 1863 ...

James **Turner** (EP) [K80]
Sheffield (17, North Church St)
- 1880 ...

Joseph **Turner** **(CP/GS/EP)** Birmingham (4, Beak St/27, Camden St/50, Newhall Hill/Edward St) - 1825 - 1839 ... - 1850 - 1896 ...		(WDB) (PDB) (HTD) (WDOB) (HGD) (MDG) (POB) (K72) (K78) (K80) (PC)

Joseph **Turner** (jun) **(EP)** Sheffield (185, Ann's Rd) - 1901 ...		(WDS01)

Thomas **Turner** **(CU/EP)** **(Suffolk Works)** Sheffield (Suffolk Rd) 1853 - 1864 *(See also figure: T.T)* 1865 - 1921 **(& Co)** *(See also figures: T.T&Co, T.TURNER, ENCORE)*		(B) (SAOR) (SBW) (M) (B) (SAOR) (WDS79) (WDS01) (SBW) (M)

Richard William **Turner** **(EP)** Birmingham (28, St. Mary's St/Caroline St) - 1872 - 1880 ...		(K72) (K78) (K80)

Richard **Turner** **(EP)** Birmingham (40, St. Paul's Sq) - 1882 ...		(K82)

William **Turner** **(BM)** Birmingham 1827 - 1833 ...		(SAOR) (GDS)

William **Turner** **(EP)** Birmingham (100, Buckingham St) - 1872 ...		(K72)

Hammond **Turner Ltd.** **(EP)** Birmingham - 1936 ... *(Then: Lion Works Ltd.)*		(K36)

Joseph **Turney** **(CP)** Birmingham (Beak St) - 1829 ...		(WAB)

John **Turton** **(CP)** Birmingham (40, Church St) - 1818 - 1833 ...		(SAOR) (WTD) (WDB) (PDB) (WAB) (HTD) (DOB) (B) (M)

John **Turton** **(EP)**
(Australian Works)
Sheffield (Bow St)
- 1880 ...   (K80) (M)
~ 1898 - 1910 (**& Co.**)   (WDS01)
(See also figures: JT&Co S, JTS EP)
~ 1910 -1923 (**& Co. Ltd.**)
(See also figure: JT&CoLd S)

TV   *(See also)* **(OSP)** (B)
T. **Vaughan**

T·W & Co   *(See also)* **(EP)**
Thomas **White & Co.**
(Squirrel Works)

T.W & Co.L^TD   *(See also)* **(EP)**
Thomas **Wilkinson & Co. Ltd.**
T.W & Co Ld.S   or
Travis, Wilson & Co. Ltd. **(EP)**

T. W. EATON & Co   **(EP)**T. W. **Ea-**
SHEFFIELD   **ton & Co.**

T.W &S   **Not assigned!** **(EP)**
Possibly:
Thomas **Wilkinson & Sons** **(EP)**
(Pelican Works)

T. Worthington   *(See also)*
Burton on Trent   T. **Worthington** **(T)**

TW&Co   *(See also)* **(CP/EP)**
Thomas **Wilkinson & Co.**
(Wilkinson & Co)

TW &Co   *(See also)* **(OSP)**
Thomas **Watson**, James **Fenton &**
Thomas **Bradbury**

T W   **Not assigned!** **(CU)** (E)

TW   *(See also)* **(CU/EP)**
Thomas **Wooley**
(Electro Plate Works)

Twells & Podmore **(CP)** ^(WAB)
Birmingham (New St)
- 1829 ...

W. J. **Twining & Son Ltd.** **(EP)** ^(K03)
Birmingham (1, Graham St)
- 1903 ...

Thomas & John **Twiss** **(CP)** (WTDB) (CD)
(WTD) (WDB)
Birmingham (29/33, Gt. Charles St) (PDB) (WAB)
- 1815 - 1830 ... (HTD)

Thomas **Twiss** **(CP)** (DOB) (WWDB)
(WDOB)
Birmingham (33, Gt. Charles St)
- 1833 - 1839 ...

Thomas & H. **Twiss** **(CP)** (HGDB) (HGD)
Birmingham (32, Gt. Charles St)
- 1849 - 1850 ...

Elisabeth **Twist** **(OSP)** (WTD) (CD)
Birmingham (Newhall St)
- 1818 ...

James **Twist** **(OSP)** (WTDB)
Birmingham (Newhall St)
- 1815 ...

Thomas **Twist** **(EP)** (CDB)
Birmingham (Caroline St)
- 1861 ...

Edwin **Tye** **(EP)** (K72) (K78) (K80)
Birmingham (18, Union Passage)
- 1872 - 1880 ...

John **Tyler** **(BM/OSP)** (WDG) (GDBS)
(WDOS) (M)
Sheffield (17, Joiner Ln)
- 1819 - 1852 ...
(See also figure: I.TYLER)

John Benjmain **Tyler** **(EP)** (WDS01)
Sheffield (32, Gray St)
- 1901 ...

William **Tyler** **(BM/EP)**
Sheffield (11/13 & 15, Brunswick Rd)
- 1880 - 1893 ... (K80) (K93)
- 1901 - 1905 ... (**& Sons**) (WDS01) (WDSR)

Joseph **Tyndall**
Birmingham (Moseley St)
1813 - 1815 ...

(CP) (B) (WTDB) (M)

Edward **Tyzack**
Sheffield (Edge Mount View)
- 1871 ...

(EP) (WDS71)

U·W &Cº	*(See also)* **(OSP)** Underdown, Wilkinson & Co.	
U ✳ S	*(See also)* **(EP)** Isaac **Barnes**	
	Thomas **Underdown** **(OSP)** Sheffield (97, Eyre St/South St/Burgess St) - 1833 - 1841 ...	(GDS) (WDS37) (DSRR)
	Underdown, Wilkinson & Co. **(OSP)** Sheffield (9, Sycamore St) 1826 - 1833 ... *(See also figure: U.W&Co)*	(SAOR) (PD) (SDG) (GDS) (B)
	George **Underhill** **(EP)** Birmingham (80, Buckingham St/139, Hampton St) - 1866 - 1903 ...	(MDG) (POB) (K82) (K84) (K88) (K92) (PC) (K03)
UNETT PLATE MADE IN ENGLAND	**Not assigned!** **(EP)** 1920 ...	(E)
	George **Unite** **(CP/CU/EP)** Birmingham (65, Caroline St) London (Holborn Circus) 1834 - 1861 ... 1863 - 1928 (**& Sons**) 1928 .... (**Sons & Lyde Ltd.**) *(See also figure: GU)*	(SAOR) (B) (K80) (SBW) (M)
	Unity Electro Plating Co. **(EP)** Birmingham (16, Frankfort St) - 1903 ...	(K03)
UNITY QUALITY PLATE	*(See also)* **(BM/EP)** **Barker Brothers** (**Unity Works**)	
	Unwin & Rodgers **(CU)** (**Rockingham Works & Globe Works**) Sheffield (Penistone Rd) - 1851 - 1901 ... - 1879 ... (**Ltd.**) *(See also figure: SUPERLATIVE)*	(WDOS AD) (WDS01) (WDS79)
	William **Urton** **(OSP)** Sheffield (Hall St) 1788 ... *(See also figure: WU)*	(B) (SAOR)

U

USE

(See also)
Richard **Groves & Sons**
(Beehive Works)

(CU/EP)

	Vale & Charles Birmingham (181, Hockley St) - 1936 ...	**(EP)**	(K36)
	Vale & Hardy Birmingham (Charlotte St) - 1818 - 1823 ...	**(OSP)**	(CD) (WDB)
	Henry **Vale** Sheffield (131, Charles St) - 1879 ...	**(EP)**	(WDS79)
	Jabez **Vale** Coventry 1813 ...	**(CU)**	(SAOR)
	Joseph **Vale** Birmingham (Edmund St) - 1815 - 1818 ...	**(CP)**	(WTDB) (WTD)
	Samuel **Vale** Coventry 1816 ...	**(CU)**	(SAOR)
	Vale Brothers & Sermon Birmingham (27, Spencer St) - 1888 - 1896 ... *(See also figure: VB&S)*	**(EP)**	(K88) (K92) (PC) (M)
VALIANT PLATE	*(See also)* **Priestley & Moore Ltd.**	**(EP)**	
VALOR	*(See also)* Theophilus **Richards & Co.**	**(EP)**	
	Thomas **Vaughan** Sheffield (Lady's Walk) 1818 ... *(See also figure: TV)*	**(OSP)**	(B) (SAOR)
	(See also) **Vale Brothers & Sermon**	**(EP)**	
VENETIA GOLD PLATE	*(See also)* N. C. **Reading & Co.**	**(EP)**	
VENETIAN SILVER	*(See also)* **Deykin & Harrison**	**(EP)**	
VENTURE	*(See also)* **Slater Brothers**	**(EP)**	

	James **Vernon & Brothers** (EP) ^(SBW)	

Wigtown

~

W. H. **Armitage & Co.** **(EP)**
(Vesuvius Works)

Not assigned! **(CU/EP)** ^(E)

VICEROY PLATE **Not assigned!** **(EP)** ^(E)

James **Vickers** **(BM)** ^(B)
Sheffield
1787 - 1817
(See also figure: I.VICKERS)

John **Vickers** **(CU/BM)** ^{(B) (PDB) (PD)}
(Britannia Place) ^{(SDG) (GDS)}
^(WDS01)
Sheffield (42, Garden St/38, Barretta St)
1817 - 1901 ...
(See also figure: I VICKERS)
(Then: E.Stacey)

Victoria Plating & Manufacturing Co.
(EP)
Birmingham (Sherbourne Rd/6, Albion St) ^{(K88) (K92)}
- 1888 - 1892 ... ^(K36)
- 1936 ... (**Ltd**.)

VICTORY *(See also)* **(EP)**
Henry **Rossell & Co.**
(Wallace Works)

S. **Viener** **(EP)** ^(K36)
(Wentworth Works)
Sheffield (Andrew St)
- 1936 ...

Viner's Ltd. **(EP)** ^(K36)
(Successors to Th. Turner. From 1924 used the
VINERS *Harrison Bros & Howson Alpha trademark)*
of Sheffield Sheffield (Bath St)
- 1900 - 1985 ...
(See also figures: VLtd, V.LD)

VINER & HALL **SHEFFIELD**	**Viner & Hall** Sheffield ~	**(EP)**
VIRGINIAN SILVER	*(See also)* John **Yates & Sons**	**(CU/EP)**
	H. H. **Vivian & Co. Ltd.** **(Parade Works)** Sheffield (107 & 109, Arundel St) Birmingham (43 & 46, George St) - 1884 - 1905 ...	**(GS)** (K84) (K88) (K93) (WDSR)
V. LD V LTD	*(See also)* **Viner's Ltd.**	**(EP)**
	P. H. **Vogel & Co.** Birmingham (Warstone Parade) ~ 1920 *(See also figure: P.H.V&Co)*	**(EP)** (S)
VULCAN.	*(See also)* Thomas **Ellin & Co.** **(Sylvester Works)**	**(CU)**
VOLUNTEER	*(See also)* Edwin **Blyde & Co.**	**(EP)**
V. W. S & Co.	*(See also)* Van **Wart, Son & Co.**	**(EP)**

V

W&C° (and variants)	*(See also)* George **Waterhouse & Co.**	**(OSP)** ^{(SBW) (M) (B)}
W&F	*(See also)* J. **Wright &** G. **Fairbairn**	**(OSP)** (B)
W & **G**	*(See also)* **Watson & Gilliott**	**(EP)**
W&H	*(See also)* **Walker & Hall** **(Electro Works)**	**(EP)**
W & **J**	**Not assigned!** Sheffield	**(EP)**
W&K	*(See also)* **Wardell & Kempson**	**(OSP)**
W & R	*(See also)* Henry **Wilkinson &** John **Roberts**	**(OSP)**
W&S	*(See also)* George **Waterhouse & Co.**	**(OSP/EP)**
W.B	*(See also)* William **Briggs**	**(CU/OSP/EP)**
W.B	*(See also)* William **Brearley**	**(EP)**
W·C	*(See also)* William **Coldwell**	**(OSP)**
W.C	*(See also)* Walter Charles **Cox**	**(EP)**
W·D	*(See also)* W. **Damant**	**(OSP)**
W·D	*(See also)* W. **Darby**	**(OSP)**
W.D	*(See also)* W. **Dewsnap**	**(OSP)**

Mark	Description	Category
W·D S (shield)	*(See also)* Frederick **Wilson &** William **Davis** **(Hattan Works)**	(EP)
W·F	*(See also)* W. **Fox**	(OSP)
W.G	*(See also)* William **Gallimore & Co.** **(Electro Plate Works)**	(OSP)
W·H	*(See also)* W. **Hoyland & Co.**	(OSP)
W·J	*(See also)* W. **Jervis**	(OSP)
W·L	*(See also)* William **Linley**	(OSP)
W·M	*(See also)* W. **Marsden**	(OSP)
W·M	*(See also)* William **Morton**	(EP)
W.P	*(See also)* William **Parkin**	(BM/CU)
W·P	*(See also)* William **Patten**	(OSP)
W·S	*(See also)* W. **Smith**	(OSP)
W.W	*(See also)* W. **Wrangham**	(OSP)
W.A&Cº	*(See also)* W. **Allanson & Co.**	(OSP)
W A & S G (gothic letters)	*(See also)* William **Alexander & Sons**	(EP)
W A (shields) **W·A**	*(See also)* William **Adams Inc.**	(EP)
WADE & BUTCHER SHEFFIELD	*(See also)* William & Samuel **Butcher**	(CU)

George **Walker & Co.**   **(EP)**   (SD46) (GDBS)
(Electro Works)   (WDOS AD)
Sheffield (11, Howard St)
- 1846 - 1852 ...

C. P. **Walker & Co. Ltd.**   **(CU)**   (E)
~ 1900... *(See also figure: C. P. WAL-KER & Co. LTD)*

Walker & Hall   **(BM/CU/EP)**   (B) (POS) (GS)
(Electro Works)   (K54) (WDS79)
Sheffield (9 & 15, Howard St/10-18, Eyre   (K93) (WDS01)
St)   (M) (SAOR)
London (45, Holborn Viaduct/165, Fren-   (SBW)
church St)
- 1854 - 1936 ...
- 1936 ... **(Ltd.)**
(See also figures: HH&JEB, W&H, W&H S, symbol " flag ")

Walker   **(EP)**
Sheffield
1861 - 1890 *(See also figure: W&H.S)*

Albert **Walker**   **(EP)**   (K92)
Birmingham (3, Hall St)
- 1892 ...

Edward **Walker**   **(BM)**   (SAOR) (WDB)
Birmingham/Coventry
1822 - 1829 ...

Frank **Walker**   **(EP)**   (K03)
Birmingham (Gem St)
- 1903 ...

Jno. **Walker**   **(BM)**   (HGD)
Birmingham (45, Woodcock St)
- 1850 ...

James **Walker**   **(CU/EP)**   (Rd)
London
- 1907 - 1928 ...
1929 - 1984 **(Ltd.)** (Rd.748743)
(See also figure: CENTURYPLATE)

Richard & James **Walker** **(OSP)** ^(WTDB)
Birmingham (Newhall St)
- 1815 ...

S. **Walker** **(GS)** ^(MDG)
Birmingham (Lower Fazeley St/3, Church St)
- 1866 ...

Samuel **Walker** **(FP/OSP)**
Birmingham (29, Park St/25, Burgess St) ^{(DOB) (HGDB)}
- 1833 - 1849 ...
1836 - 1837 ... ^{(B) (SAOR)}
(See also figure: SW&Co) ^{(HGDY) (WDS37)}

Thomas **Walker** **(EP)** ^(WDS01)
Sheffield (66, Sutton St)
- 1901 ...

William **Walker** **(BM)** ^{(WDB) (WAB)}
Birmingham (40, Water S) ^{(DOB) (WDOB)}
- 1823 - 1839 ...

Walker Brothers **(EP)** ^{(K82) (K84) (K88)}
Birmingham (69, Victoria St) ^{(K92) (PC) (K03)}
- 1882 - 1903 ...

Walker, Knowles & Co. **(OSP/EP)** ^{(SAOR) (B)}
Sheffield (55, Burgess St) ^{(SD46) (GDBS)}
London (Strand) ^{(WDOS) (POS)}
1840 - 1863 ... *(See also figures:* ^{(K54) (GS)}
WK&Co, Globe) ^{(M) (SBW)}

H. S. **Wall & Co.** **(EP)** ^(K36)
Sheffield (136, West St)
- 1936 ...

Wallbank & Bassett **(CP)** ^{(WAB) (DOB)}
Birmingham (Gt. Charles St/James St) ^(WWDB)
- 1829 - 1835 ...

Charles **Wallbank** **(CP)** ^(WDOB)
Birmingham (James St)
- 1839 ...

Markham **Wallis** **(EP)** ^(GS)
(Cleveland Works)
Sheffield (191, Rockingham St)
- 1863 ...

Walsam & Co. (EP) ^(K03)

Birmingham (9, George St)
- 1903 ...

G. E. **Walton & Co. Ltd.** (EP) ^(SBW)

Birmingham
~ *(See also figure: IXION)*

John **Walton** (EP) ^(K88)

Birmingham (30, Princip St)
- 1888 ...

William **Walton** (FP) ^{(WAB) (DOB)}

Birmingham (9, Doe St)
- 1829 - 1833 ...

Samuel **Warburton & Co.** (OSP) ^{(B) (SAOR)}

Sheffield (Bridgehouse)
1775 ... *(See also figures: S·W, S·W&Co)*

Samuel **Warburton** (BM) ^(GDS)

Sheffield (6, Broad Ln)
- 1833 ...

Frederick **Ward & Co.** (CU) ^{(WDS79) (K93)}

Sheffield (37, George St/Tudor Pl)
- 1879 - 1893 ...
(See also figures: A "pistol", B4 ANY)

Ward & Payne (CU) ^(WDOS AD)
(Ward's Works & Limbrick Works) ^{(SBW) (W)}
(Formerly: David Ward & Co.)
Sheffield (West St)
- 1852 - 1901 ...
(See also figures: S.J.ADDIS, W P)

Arthur John **Ward** (EP) ^(POB)

Birmingham (Lower Fazeley St/114, Bradford St)
- 1867 ...

George **Ward** (OSP) ^{(B) (SAOR) (SBW)}
 ^(M)
Sheffield (Exchange St)
Manchester
1846 ... *(See also figure: GW)*

John **Ward** (GS) ^(WDOB)

Birmingham (Windsor St)
- 1839 ...

Salomon **Ward** **(FP/CP)** (WTDB) (WDB)
Birmingham (6, Nova Scotia St/Duke St) (PDB) (WAB)
- 1815 - 1829 ...

S. H. **Ward** **(EP)** (SAOR)
Manchester
1858 ...

Thomas **Ward** **(CP/BM/EP)** (K80)
(Argan Plate Works)
Sheffield (Rockingham St)
- 1880 ... *(See also figure: WARD ⑤)*

W. & S. **Ward** **(EP)** (SAOR) (SBW)
Sheffield (St. Mary's Gate) (M) (B)
1858 ... *(See also figure: SW)*

William **Wardell &** Peter **Kempson (OSP)** (B) (SAOR)
Birmingham
1811 - 1813 ... *(See also figure: W&K)*

Wards, Brown & Co. **(OSP)** (PD)
Sheffield (Howard St)
- 1829 ...

Waring & Gillow **(EP)**
London
- 1938 ... (Reg.826878)
~ **(Ltd.)**

William & Alfred **Warrall** **(EP)** (MDG)
Birmingham (10, Upper Hockley S)
- 1866 ...

Henry **Warren & Co.** **(EP)** (K36)
Birmingham (44, St. Paul's Square)
- 1936 ...

James **Warren** **(EP)** (BDB) (POB)
Birmingham (Ct. 11, Thorp St) (K72) (K78) (K80)
- 1862 - 1892 ... (K82) (K84) (K88)
(K92)

George **Warren** **(EP)** (K03)
Birmingham (Ct. 11, Thorp St)
- 1903 ...

Thomas **Warris & Son** **(OSP)** (B) (SAOR)
Sheffield (Church Ln)
1796 ... *(See also figure: T.W)*

	George **Warriss** **(CU/EP)** **(School of Art Works)** Sheffield (32, Howard St/19, Eyre Ln/40, Cresent Rd) - 1876 - 1905 ... - 1911 ...	(K76) (WDS79) (K80) (SAOR) (WDS01) (WDSR) (WDSR11)
	Van **Wart, Son & Co.** **(EP)** Birmingham ~ *(See also figure: V.W.S&Co)*	(SBW) (M)
	Thomas **Warwick** **(GS/EP)** Birmingham (21, Bread St/1, St. Mark's St) - 1849 - 1861 ...	(HGDB) (HGD) (CDB) (MDG)
WARWICK PLATE	**Not assigned!** **(EP)** London ~	(E)
WASB	*(See also)* **(EP)** William Arthur **Smith, Benson & Co.**	
	Robert **Wass** **(OSP)** Sheffield (High St) 1810 ... *(See also figure: RW)*	(B)
WATCH HUMBLE	*(See also)* **(CU)** M. **Hunter &** J. **Twig(g)**	
WATERHOUSE&Cº	George **Waterhouse** **(CP/OSP)** Birmingham (1, Horse Fair) 1807 - 1839 ...	(SAOR) (WWDB) (M) (WDOB)
	Benjamin **Waterhouse & Co.** **(EP)** Birmingham (51, Charlotte St) - 1850 ...	(HGD)
	George **Waterhouse & Co. (OSP/CU)** Sheffield (75, Carver St) 1842 - 1846 ... *(See also figures: W&Co, W&S, Homeland)*	(SAOR) (SBW) (M) (B) (SD46)
	I. & I. **Waterhouse & Co.** **(OSP)** (J. & J. **Waterhouse, Hodgson & Co.)** Sheffield (Portobello Pl/near St. George Church) 1820 - 1833 ... *(See also figures: I&I WATER-HOUSE & Co., I&IW&Co)*	(ASP) (PDB) (M) (B) (SAOR) (PD) (SDG) (GDS) (NGDS)

T. **Waterhouse & Co.** **(CP)** (WWDB) (WDOB)
(Waterhouse & Thomas **Parker)** (SAOR)
Birmingham (45, St Paul's Sq)
- 1835 - 1839 ...

Waterhouse & Ryland **(CP)** (WTD) (WTDB)
Birmingham (26/26, Hill St) (WDB) (PDB)
- 1818 - 1830 ... (WAB) (HTD)
(CD)

Thomas **Waterhouse & Son** (George) **(CP)** (SAOR) (DOB)
Birmingham (Hill St) (WWDB) (WDOB)
1830 - 1839 ...

John **Waterhouse,** E. **Hatfield & Co.** (B) (SAOR)
(Waterhouse & Co.) **(OSP)** (HGDY) (WDS37)
Sheffield (203, Portobello St) (DSRR) (SD46)
1836 - 1846 ... *(See also figures: J.W*
E.H, symbol "phoenix")

Thomas **Waterhouse** **(OSP/CU)** (B)
Birmingham
1830 ...

Hannah **Watkinson &** William **Watson** (B) (SAOR)
(Hannah **Watkinson & Co.)** **(OSP)**
Sheffield (Silver St)
1793 ... *(See also figure: H.W&Co)*

Hannah **Watkinson** **(OSP)** (B) (SAOR)
Sheffield (Silver St)
1792 ... *(See also figure: H.W)*

J. **Watkinson** **(OSP)** (B)
Sheffield (Silver St)
1776 ... *(See also figure: I.W)*

W. **Watson &** T. **Bradbury** **(OSP)** (B) (SAOR) (CD)
Sheffield (Mulberry St) (HDG)(PDY) (PD)
- 1818 - 1829 ... (PDB) (SDG)
(See also figure: WW&TB) (NGDS)

Watson & Co.   **(OSP)**   (UBD) (B) (SAOR)
(Th. **Watson**, J. **Fenton** & Th. **Bradbury**)   (M)
(Formerly: Fenton, Creswick Oates & Co.)
Sheffield (Methodist Meeting Yard/ Mulberry St)
1791 - 1801 ...
(See also figure: TW&Co)
(Then: Thomas Bradbury & Son)

WATSON&Cᵒ

William **Watson & Co.**   **(OSP)**   (B) (SAOR) (GDS)
Sheffield (15, Arundel St)
1832 - 1852 ...
(See also figure: W.W&Co)

Watson & Gilliott   **(EP)**   (WDSR) (Rd 379519)
Sheffield (26, Eyre Ln)
- 1901 - 1935 *(See also figure: W & G)*

John **Watson & Son**   **(OSP)**   (SAOR) (HGDY) (B) (PD) (NGDS) (SDG) (GDS)
Sheffield (Baker's Pool/Burgess St/16, Arundel St/ 43, Fargate)
1822 - 1837 ... *(See also figure: I.W)*

John **Watson**   **(OSP)**   (B) (SAOR)
Sheffield (Furnace Hill)
1795 ... *(See also figure: I.W)*
(Then: Watson, Pass & Co)

John **Watson**   **(OSP)**
Sheffield (53, Broad Ln/16 & 51, Arundel St)   (DSRR)
- 1841 ...   (NGDS) (WDS37)
- 1825 - 1846 ... **(& Son)**   (DSRR) (SD46)
(See also figure: Symbol "hand")

Joseph Henry **Watson**   **(EP)**   (K82) (K84)
Birmingham (50, St. Paul's Square)
- 1882 - 1884 ...

Thomas **Watson**   **(CU)**   (NGDS)
Sheffield (5, George St)
- 1825 ...

Thomas Henry **Watson**   **(EP)**   (MDG) (POB) (K72) (K78) (K80) (K88) (K92)
Birmingham (17, Great Barr St/Upper Priory/18, Bath St/371, Summer Ln)
- 1866 - 1892 ...

	William **Watson**	**(CP)**	(WAB) (HTD) (HGDB)
	Birmingham (Staniforth St/29, Key Hill) - 1829 - 1849 ...		
	William **Watson**	**(EP)**	(K80)
	Sheffield (43, Darnall Green) - 1880 ...		
	William **Watson**	**(OSP)**	(B)
	Sheffield (15, Arundel St) 1833 ... *(See also figure: W.Watson)*		
WATSON PASS&Cᵒ	John **Watson, Pass & Co.** *(Formerly: John Watson)* Sheffield (Watson's Walk/Hartshead/Burgess St) 1811 - 1825 ...	**(OSP)**	(CD) (HDG) (PDY) (PDB) (B) (M)
	Watts & Deacon Birmingham (9, George St) - 1903 ...	**(EP)**	(K03)
WATTS & HARTON LONDON	**Watts & Harton** London ~ 1854 ...	**(EP)**	(M)
W·B &Cᵒ	*(See also)* W. **Birks & Co.**	**(CU/OSP)**	
W.B&S Lᵀᴰ	**Not assigned!**	**(EP)**	
W. B. STRAND	**Not assigned!** ~ 1815 - 1825	**(CU/OSP)**	(B)
W.BAILY & SONS	*(See also)* William **Baily & Sons**	**(EP)**	
W.BELK	*(See also)* Walter **Belk & Son** **(Kingsley Works)**	**(EP)**	
W.BINGLEY **W. BINGLEY**	*(See also)* William **Bingley**	**(CU/OSP)**	
W.BUTCHER SHEFFIELD	*(See als)* William & Samuel **Butcher**	**(CU)**	
W.B L	**Not assigned!** London ~	**(EP)**	(E)

WB&Cᴼ	*(See also)* William **Blackwell & Co.**	(OSP)
WB & **Cᴼ** **WB&CoS** 𝔚 𝔅 & 𝕮ᴼ	*(See also)* William **Briggs & Co.**	(BM/EP)
WB&S	*(See also)* w. **Birks & Son**	(CU/OSP)
WB & **S** **EP**	*(See also)* William **Batt & Sons**	(EP)
𝔚 𝔅 👑 𝔐 𝔰	*(See als* William **Briggs**	(CU/OSP/EP)
𝐖 𝐁 ✶ 𝐁 **EP NS**	Not assigned!	(EP)
WB	*(See also)* w. **Bagshaw**	(OSP)
W.COLDWELL.	*(See also)* William **Coldwell**	(OSP)
𝔚 𝕮 👑 𝔊	*(See also)* William **Clarke**	(EP)
WC	*(See also)* w. **Carter**	(OSP) [B]
𝐖 & 𝐃 𝐋 & 𝐒 𝐖 & 𝐃 𝐒 **BP**	*(See also)* Frederick **Wilson &** William **Davis** **(Hattan Works)**	(EP)
WD&Cᴼ	*(See also)* **Webster, Danby & Co.**	(OSP) [B] [PDB]
𝐖 𝐃 & 𝐂ᴼ	Not assigned!	(EP) [E]
WD	*(See also)* w. & m. **Dodge**	(EP)
W.E.W.	*(See also)* **Perry & Co. Ltd.**	(EP)

John **Webb** **(GS/EP)** (MDG) (PC)
Birmingham (91, Barr St/40, St. Paul's Sq)
- 1866 - 1896 ...

William **Webb** **(EP)** (K78) (K80) (K82)
Birmingham (40, Howard St/73, Tower St) (K84) (K88) (K92)
- 1878 - 1903 ... (K03)

William **Webster** **(EP)**
(Sycamore Works)
Sheffield
~ 1880 ...
(See also figure: WILLIAM (M)
WEBSTER)
1871 ... (**& Son**) (SAOR)

Webster, Danby & Co. **(OSP)** (B) (SAOR) (PDB)
Sheffield (Lea Croft/Howard St)
1822 - 1825 ... *(See also figure:*
WD&Co)

𝔚𝔈𝔇&𝔠 **Not assigned!** **(EP)** (E)

WELBECK.A1
WELBECK Alexander **Clark** Manufacturing **Co. Ltd.**
PLATE **(Welbeck Works)** **(EP)**

Daniel **Welby & Co.** **(EP)**
London
- 1897 ... *(See also figure: D.W.&Co.)*

G. **Welch & Co.** **(CU/CP)** (HGDB) (HGD)
Birmingham (11, Dean St)
- 1849 - 1850 ...

George **Welch** **(EP)** (CDB) (BDB) (GS)
Birmingham (13, Edgbaston St)
- 1861 - 1863 ...

Henry **Welch** **(EP)** (MDG) (K72)
Birmingham (Sampson Rd/56 & 56, Summer Ln)
- 1866 - 1872 ...

Thomas **Welch** **(CP)** ^{(DOB) (WWDB)}
Birmingham (Prospect Rw)
- 1833 ... (John & Thomas)
- 1835 ...

D. & J. **Wellby Ltd.** **(EP)** ^(E)
London
~ 1920 ...
(See also figure: D & J. WELLBY)

W

WELL DONE

(See also) **(EP)** ^{(K80) (K93) (M)}
Francis **Howard** ^(SBW)
(West End/Aberdeen Works)

William **Weller** **(EP)** ^(K80)
Brighton (38, Bond St)
- 1880 ...

Charles **Wells** **(BM)** ^(WAB)
Birmingham (Oxford St)
- 1829 ...

E. S. **Wells** **(EP)** ^(M)
Birmingham
~ 1899 ... *(See also figure: E·S·W)*

Edward **Wells** **(EP)** ^(K03)
Birmingham (100, Nursery Rd)
- 1903 ...

Joseph **Wells** **(CU)** ^(DSRR)
Sheffield (91, Wentworth Terrace)
- 1841 ...

Joseph **Wells** **(CP)** ^(WTD)
Birmingham
- 1818 ...

Joseph & Thomas **Wells** **(EP)** ^{(CDB) (BDB)}
Birmingham (1, Carver St/15, Gt. Hampton St) ^{(POB) (K72)}
- 1861- 1872 ...

M. R. **Wells** **(BM)** ^{(DOB) (WDOB)}
Birmingham (61, Oxford St)
- 1833 - 1839 ...

Richard **Wells** **(CP)** ^{(WAB) (HTD)}
Birmingham (65, Edmund St) ^{(DOB) (WDOB)}
- 1829 - 1839 ...

Thomas **Wells** **(EP)**
Birmingham (15, Gt. Hampton St)
- 1878 - 1892 ...
- 1880 ... **(& Co.)**

(K78) (K82) (K84)
(K88) (K92)
(K80)

Thomas **Welsh** **(CP)** (WDOB)
Birmingham (Gt. Brook St)
- 1839 ...

Wenlock Electro Platers Ltd. (EP) (K36)
(Wenlock Street Works)
Hull (Wenlock St)
- 1936 ...

Wentworth Plate Co. Ltd. **(EP)** (K36)
(Wentworth Works)
Sheffield (Andrew St)
- 1936 ...

Not assigned! **(EP)** (E)

Thomas **West** **(EP)** (GS)
Birmingham (66, Caroline St)
- 1863 ...

West of England Electro Plate Co. (K80)
Glasgow (Bothwell St) **(EP)**
- 1880 ...

West of Scotland Electro Plate Co. (K80)
Glasgow (97 & 99, Bothwell St) **(EP)**
- 1880 ...

Joseph **Westbrooke** **(CP)** (WDB)
Birmingham
- 1823 ...

Charles **Westwood & Son** **(GS)** (K88) (K92)
Birmingham (14, Hall St)
- 1888 - 1892 ...

Joshua Frederick **Westwood**   **(EP)**
Birmingham (62, Gt. King St/11, Gt. Hampton St/
76, Tower St)   (K88)
- 1888 ...   (K80)
- 1880 ... (**& Co.**)   (K36)
- 1936 ... (**& Son**)

W

W.F.C	*(See also)* W. F. **Casewell**	**(EP)**
W.F.JOHNSON **LEICESTER**	*(See also)* W. F. **Johnson**	**(EP)** (E)
W.F.W	*(See also)* W. F. **Wostenholme**	**(EP)**
W. GREEN & Co."pistol"	*(See also)* William **Green & Co.**	**(CU/OSP)**
WG &Co	*(See also)* William **Gallimore & Co.** (**Electro Plate Works**)	**(EP)**
W G & Cº	*(See also)* William **Green & Co.**	**(CU/OSP)**
WG	*(See also)* William **Gallimore** (jun.)	**(EP)**
WG	*(See also)* William **Gough**	**(EP)**
W&H·H	*(See also)* W. & H. **Hutchinson**	**(OSP)**
W·H&Cº	*(See also)* William **Harwood & Co.**	**(OSP)**
W.H.H **S**	Not assigned! Sheffield ~	**(EP)**
W.H.H.S SHEFFIELD ORIENT PLATE	Not assigned! Sheffield ~	**(EP)**
W·HIP· **WOOD**	*(See also)* William **Hipwood**	**(CP)**

W·H I·R (logo)	*(See also)* W. **Hancock** & J. **Rowbotham**	**(OSP)**
W.H L (shield logo)	*(See also)* William Henry **Lyde**	**(CU/EP)**
WH & Cº (logo)	*(See also)* W. **Hoyland & Co.**	**(OSP)**
W H & Cº S (logos)	*(See also)* William **Howe & Co.**	**(EP)**
W H & S **WH & S B P** **WH & S B P** (logos)	*(See also)* William **Hutton & Sons**	**(CU/EP)**
WH (oval logo)	*(See also)* William C. **Hutton & Sons**	**(EP)**
WH (logo)	*(See also)* William **Hutton**	**(OSP)**

Henry G. **Whall** Birmingham (Prospect Rw) - 1823 - 1825 ...	**(CP)**	(WDB) (PDB)
Thomas & Edward **Wharton** Birmingham (5, Gt. Charles St) - 1849 - 1872 ...	**(EP)**	(CDB) (HGDB) (HGD) (BDB) (POB) (K72)

WHB (logos)	*(See also)* William Henry **Beaumont & Co.**	**(BM/EP)**

Wheatley Brothers (CU/BM/EP) **(Eclipse Works)** Sheffield (New Goerge St) - 1880 ...		(WDS79) (K80)
George **Wheeler** (CU/EP) Birmingham (20, Northwood St/53, Vyse St/ 131, Barr St/33, Harford St/10/11, James St) - 1862 - 1896 ... *(See also figure: Standard Elipse- plate)*		(BDB) (GS) (MDG) (POB) (K72) (K80) (K92) (PC) (M)
George & Sarah **Wheeler** (EP) Birmingham 1846 ...		(SAOR)

W

419

J. **Wheeler** **(EP)** (HGDB)
Birmingham (16, Fordrough St)
- 1849 ...

John **While** **(GS)** (MDG)
Birmingham (Johnston St)
- 1866 ...

W

J. **Whip &** J. **Rose** **(OSP)** (B) (SAOR)
Sheffield (Cross Burgess St)
1822 ... *(See also figure: IW IR)*

WH IR&C⁰

(See also) **(OSP)**
W. **Hancock &** J. **Rowbotham**

George Henry **Whitaker** **(EP)**
Sheffield (1, Cavendish St)
1881 ...
- 1893 - 1901 ... **(& Co.)**
(See also figure: GHW EPNS) (K93) (WDS01)

WHITBY PLATE
LONDON
ENGLAND

Whitby Plate Works **(EP)** (K36)
London (Hackney Road 232)
- 1936 ...
(See also figure: Symbol " snail ")

Thomas **Whitcombe** **(EP)**
Birmingham (Berners St/59, Constitution
Hill/69 & 70, Northwood St)
- 1867 - 1872 ... (POB) (K72)
- 1878 - 1888 ... **(& Son)** (K78) (K80) (K82)
(K84) (K88)

White & Allgood **(CP)** (B) (WTD)
Birmingham (9, Gt. Charles St) (WTDB) (CD) (M)
1811 - 1818 ...

White & Barnett **(EP)** (BDB)
Birmingham (20, Key Hill)
- 1862 ...

White & Hawkins **(EP)** (CDB) (GS)
Birmingham (95, Albion St/15 & 16, Legge (MDG) (POB)
Ln) (K72) (K78) (K80)
- 1861 - 1884 ... (K82) (K84)

White & Johnstone **(EP)** (B) (SAOR)
Sheffield (North St)
1859 ... *(See also figure: W.W T.J)*

John **White** **(CU)** (SAOR) (HGDB)
Birmingham (77, Palmer St)   (HGD)
1826 - 1850 ...

Thomas **White** **(EP)** (K80) (M)
Sheffield (21, Westfield Terrasse)
- 1880 ... *(See also figure: THOS*
WHITE)

Thomas **White** **(EP)**
(Squirrel Works)
Birmingham (59, Barr St/51, Brearley St)   (CDB) (K80) (K82)
- 1861 - 1888 ... *(See also figure: T.W)*   (K84) (K88)
- 1892 - 1896 ... (**& Co.**)
(See also figure: T.W&Co)   (K92) (PC) (M)
(Then: S. J. Lewi & Co)

William **White** **(EP)** (K80) (K82) (K84)
Birmingham (Ludgate Hill)
- 1880 - 1884 ...

White, Henderson & Co. **(EP)** (B) (SAOR) (SBW)
(Elcho Works)
Sheffield (Burgess St)
1866 ... 1878 *(See also figure:*
W·W&J·H)

White, Sons & Co. **(EP)** (SAOR) (K80)
(Echo Works)
Sheffield (Burgess St)
1878 - 1880 ...

Henry Cox **Whitehead** **(EP)** (WDS01)
Sheffield (80, Milton St)
- 1901 ...

William **Whitehead** **(CU)** (DSRR)
Sheffield (New George St)
- 1841 ...

Benjamin **Whitehouse** **(BM)**
Birmingham (Bordesley Mills/ 51, Charlotte
St/24, Exeter Rw)
- 1833 - 1839 ...   (DOB) (WDOB)
- 1850 - 1872 ... (**& Co.**)   (HGD) (K72)

Frederick **Whitehouse** **(CU/EP)**
(Lion Works)
(Formerly: Benjamin Spittle)
Birmingham (Warstone Ln)
- 1882 - 1903 ...
(See also figures: Electro Imperial, Imperial FW)

(K82) (K84) (K88) (K92) (PC) (K03) (SBW) (M)

George **Whitehouse** **(EP)**
Birmingham (19, Holloway Head/13, Victoria St/24, Exeter Rw)
- 1882 - 1884 ...
- 1861 - 1880 ... **(& Co.)**

(K82) (K84) (CDB) (GS) (MDG) (K78) (K80)

Isaac **Whitehouse** **(BM)**
Birmingham (41, Park St)
- 1823 - 1825 ...

(WDB) (PDB)

William **Whitehouse** **(EP)**
Birmingham (Ct. 1, Sherlock St)
- 1872 - 1878 ...

(K72) (K78)

William **Whiteley** **(EP)**
London
~ 1885 ... *(See also figure: W.Whiteley)*

(M)

Henry **Whitelock & Co.** **(OSP)**
Sheffield (Broad Ln)
1792 ... *(See also figure: H.W&Co)*

(B) (SAOR)

John **Whitmore** **(CP)**
Birmingham
- 1823 ...

(WDB)

James **Whitworth** **(OSP/BM)**
Birmingham (Aston Rd/Bagot St)
- 1815 - 1825 ...

(WTDB) (CD) (WTD) (WDB) (PDB)

James Higham **Whitworth** **(EP)**
Sheffield (286, Townsend St)
- 1901 ...

(WDS01)

Not assigned! **(EP)**
Sheffield
~

John **Wigfall & Co.**   **(CU)** (WDS01)
Sheffield (37, Eldon St)
- 1901 ... *(See also figure:* BONA-
FIDE*)*

Thomas **Wigfall**   **(CU)** (WDOS AD)
(Atlantic Works)
Sheffield
- 1852 ...

Henry **Wiggin & Co.**   **(GS)**
Sheffield (57, Charles St)
Birmingham (55, George St)
- 1884 - 1892 ...   (K84) (K88) (K92)
1893 ... **(Ltd.)**   (K93)

Christopher **Wight**   **(CP)** (WTDB) (CD)
Birmingham (Bromsgrove St)
- 1815 - 1818 ...

Thomas **Wigley**   **(EP)** (K88)
Birmingham (49, Ellis St)
- 1888 ...

Joseph **Wignall**   **(FP)** (WAB)
Birmingham (Islington Rw)
- 1829 ...

WIGNALL HEELEY & CO   **Wignall Heeley & Co.**   **(EP)** (M)
Sheffield
~ 1895 ...

William **Wild & Co.**   **(OSP)** (B) (SAOR)
Sheffield (Trinity St)
1784 ... *(See also figure:* W.W&Co*)*

Wilder & Co. Ltd.   **(EP)** (K36)
Birmingham (59, Key Hill)
- 1936 ...

Edward William **Wild**   **(EP)** (WDS01)
Sheffield (107, Kent Rd)
- 1901 ...

William **Wilding**   **(EP)** (K78) (K80) (K82)
Birmingham (72, Vyse St)   (K84)
- 1878 - 1884 ...

George C. **Wildman** **(EP)** (PC)
Wolverhampton (Peel St)
- 1896 ...

Wilkes & Doley **(EP)** (CDB)
Birmingham (38, Camden St)
- 1861 ...

Charles **Wilkes** **(EP)**
Birmingham
1893 - 1934 *(See also figure: C W)*

John **Wilkes** **(CP)** (WAB) (HTD)
Birmingham (91, Hill St) (DOB) (WWDB)
- 1829 - 1839 ... (WDOB)

John Aston **Wilkes** **(CU/CP)**
Birmingham (16, St. Paul's Sq) (WTD)
- 1818 ... (CD)
- 1818 ... **(& Co.)**

Walter **Wilkes** **(EP)** (GS) (POB) (K72)
Birmingham (11, George St)
- 1863 - 1872 ...

George **Wilkin** **(EP)** (M) (SBW)
(Palmerston Works)
Sheffield
~ 1900 ...
(See also figure: DEFIANCE)

Thomas **Wilkinson & Co.** **(CP/EP)**
(Pelican Works) (DOB) (WWDB)
Birmingham (13 & 15/45 & 46 /49, Gt. (HGD) (CDB)
Hampton St) (BDB) (GS)
- 1833 - 1903 ... (MDG) (POB)
(See also figure: TW&Co) (K72) (K03) (M)
- 1872 - 1936 ... **(& Sons)**
(See also figures: T.W &S, symbol (K72) (K78) (K82)
"pelican") (K84) (K88) (K92)
~ 1915 - 1932 **(& Co. Ltd.)** (PC) (K03) (K36)
(See also figures: Symbol "peli-
can", T.W & Co L^{TD})
(Then: A. L. Davenport)

Henry **Wilkinson &** John **Roberts (OSP)** (B) (SAOR) (GDS)
Sheffield (Low St Park)
1831 - 1833 ... *(See also figure: W & R)*

Thomas **Wilkinson &** James **Shaw**   (SAOR)
Birmingham   **(CU/BM)**
1835 - 1839 ...

Wilkinson & Taylor   **(EP)**   (WDS01)
Sheffield (157, Division Ln)
- 1901 ...

Benjamin **Wilkinson**   **(EP)**   (WDS01)
Sheffield (61, Witney St)
- 1901 ...

Frederick William **Wilkinson**   **(EP)**   (K93)
Sheffield (57, Trafalgar St)
- 1893 ...

Henry **Wilkinson (CU/OSP/BM/EP)**   (SDG) (PD) (GDS)
Sheffield (South St/Park/Pond Hill   (GDBS) (WDOS)
Terrace/46, Castle Mills/13, Wicker/ 36,   (POS) (K54) (GS)
Arundel St/Howard St/13, Eyre Ln/65, Divi-   (WDS79) (K80)
sion St/69/20/38, Norfolk St)   (K93)
- 1828 - 1893 ...   (SAOR) (GDS)
1831 - 1893 ... **(& Co.)**   (WDS37) (WDOS)
(See also figures: H.W.&Co,   (GDBS) (POS)
NEILL, symbol "keys")   (K54) (K93) (B)
1872 - 1892 **(& Co. Ltd.)**   (M) (GS) (SBW)
(See also figure: H.W Ltd.)   (HGDY)
(Then: Walker & Hall)   (M) (WDS79)
   (K80)

Henry **Wilkinson**   **(GS)**   (WDOB)
Birmingham (Woodcock St)
- 1839 ...

Henry Dawson **Wilkinson (OSP/CU/EP)**
(Electro Plate Works & Shrewbury   (GDBS) (WDOS
Works)   AD) (POS)
Sheffield (5, Union Ln/Broad St)   (HGDY) (SD46)
- 1832 - 1854 ...   (K54)
- 1837 - 1841 ... **(& Co.)**   (WDS37) (DSRR)

J. **Wilkinson**   **(OSP)**   (B)
Sheffield (Lambert Croft)
1790 ... *(See also figure: I.W)*

John **Wilkinson** **(GS/EP)** ^(K72)
(Branston Street Metal Works)
Birmingham (Branston St/10, Gt. Hampton Rd)
- 1872 ...
- 1884 - 1888 ... (**& Sons**) (K84) (K88 AD)

Robert **Wilkinson** **(EP)** (GS)
Sheffield (Norfolk Ln)
- 1863 ...

R. F. **Wilkinson** **(CU)** (SAOR)
Sheffield
1805 ...

Thomas **Wilkinson** **(GS/CU/BM/EP)**
Sheffield (17, New Church St/13, Kenyon
Alley, Allen St/95, New Edward St) (K80)
- 1880 ...
- 1851 - 1852 ... (**& Son**) (WDOS AD)

William **Wilkinson** **(EP)** (K80)
Birmingham (11, Gt. Hampton St)
- 1880 ...

Wilkinson Brothers **(EP)** (K93) (WDS01)
Sheffield (9, Eyre St)
- 1893 - 1901 ...

W. **Wilkinson Ltd.** **(EP)** (S)
London (Skinner St/Clerkenwell Rd)
1925 - 1936 *(See also figure: WW L^{TD})*

Wilkinson, Sword Co. Ltd. **(EP)** (WDSR)
Sheffield (14 & 16, Arundel Ln)
- 1905 ...

Charles **Wilks** **(EP)** (K80) (K82) (K84)
Birmingham (15 & 16, Mott St) (K88) (K92) (K03)
- 1880 - 1936 ... (K36)

Jacob **Wilks** **(EP)** (BDB)
Birmingham (38 & 39, Camden St)
- 1862 ...

Walter **Wilks** **(EP)** (MDG)
Birmingham (11, George St)
- 1866 ...

WILLIAM.S.BURTON OXFORD STREET LONDON	*(See also)* William S. **Burton**	**(EP/OSP)**
WILLIAM BECKETT & Co CUTLERS SHEFFIELD	*(See also)* William **Beckett & Co.**	**(CU/EP)**

Williams & Fowler **(EP)**
(Formerly: William Williams)
Birmingham (13, Mary St/St. Paul's Sq)
- 1882 - 1884 ...
(Then: Williams & Son)
(K82) (K84)

Williams & Son **(EP)** (K88)
(Formerly: William & Fowler)
Birmingham (13, Mary St/St. Paul's Sq)
- 1888 ...
(Then again: William Williams)

Alfred **Williams** **(EP)** (K80)
Walsall (New St)
- 1880 ...

Arnold Edward **Williams** **(EP)** (K36)
Birmingham (84 & 84a, Vyse St)
- 1936 ...

James & Joshia **Williams** **(EP)** (K80)
Bristol (14, Small St/18, St. Augustine's
Parade)
- 1853 - 1880 ...
- 1881 ... (**Williams & Co.**)
(See also figure: J & J W)

William **Williams** **(EP)**
Birmingham (2, Howard St/77, Caroline St/
13, Mary St)
1842 - 1880 ...
(Then: Williams & Fowler)
- 1888 - 1892 ...
(SAOR) (MDG)
(K72) (K78) (K80)
(K88) (K92)

Henry **Williamson** **(EP)** (SBW) (W) (M)
London
~ 1892 ... *(See also figure: ACME.)*

WILLIAM SYKES & Co. *A.B.* SHEFFIELD	*(See also)* W. H. **Armitage & Co.** **(Vesuvius Works)**	**(EP)**

WILLIAM WEBSTER SYCAMORE WORKS	*(See also)* William **Webster** **(Sycamore Works)**	**(EP)**	
	Charles **Willetts** Birmingham (86, Spencer St) - 1862 ...	**(EP)**	(BDB)
	Mrs. Harriett **Willington** (Mrs. Harriett Luisa **Wellington**) Birmingham (67, Spencer St) - 1866 - 1880 ... - 1878 - 1884 ... **(& Son**)	**(EP)**	(MDG) (POB) (K72) (K80) (K78) (K80) (K82) (K84)
	Thomas **Willington** Birmingham (67, Spencer St) - 1861 - 1863 ...	**(EP)**	(CDB) (BDB) (GS)
	Arthur **Willis** Sheffield ~ 1897 ... *(See also figure: A.W)*	**(EP)**	(M)
	Mark **Willis** **(Exchange Works)** Sheffield (56, Fargate/Tudor Pl/207, Ro-ckingham St) 1875 - 1880 ... *(See also figure: MW)* - 1905... **(& Son**) *(See also figure: MW&S)* - 1911 ... **(& Son Ltd.**) (William)	**(EP)**	(SAOR) (WDS79) (K80) (M) (WDSR) (WDS11)
WILLMORE & WILKES PATENT	**Willmore & Wilkes** Sheffield 1807 ...	**(CU)**	(B) (M)
WILLMORE	Joseph **Willmore** Birmingham 1807 - 1832 ... *(See also figure: JW)*	**(OSP)**	(M) (B) (SAOR)
	Thomas **Willmore** Birmingham (New St) - 1818 - 1829 ...	**(CP)**	(WTD) (WAB)
	Willms Brothers Birmingham (17, Horse Fair) - 1878 ...	**(EP)**	(K78)

W

Edward **Wilmot &** Charles **Roberts (CU)** ^(SAOR)
Birmingham
1848 ...

John **Wilmot &** William **Roberts (CU)** ^(SAOR)
Birmingham
1835 ...

John **Wilmot** **(CP)** ^(WTDB)
Birmingham (St. Paul's Sq)
- 1815 ...

John E. **Wilmot** **(EP)** ^(PC)
Birmingham (32, Hylton St)
- 1896 ...

Joseph **Wilshaw** **(EP)** ^{(CDB) (BDB) (GS)}
Birmingham (65, Hospital St) ^{(MDG) (POB)}
- 1861 - 1872 ... ^(K72)

Frederick **Wilson & Co.** **(EP)** ^{(SAOR) (K93)}
Sheffield (32, Eyre St/9-13, Cavendish St) ^{(WDS01) (WDSR)}
1883 - 1905 ... *(See also figure: FWS)*

Frederick **Wilson &** William **Davis (EP)**
(Hattan Works)
London ^{(SAOR) (SBW)}
Sheffield (19-21, Sycamore St/43, Norfolk St/ ^{(M) (WDS79)}
32, Eyre St) ^(K80)
1871 - 1880 ... *(See also figures: FW*
WD, W&D L&S, W·DS)

WILSON & GILL
Wilson & Gill **(T)**
London (139, Regent St)
~ 1900

C. **Wilson & Sons** **(EP)** ^(K93)
(Carlton Works)
Leeds (Exeter Pl)
- 1893 ...

S. **Wilson & Son** **(BM/OSP)** ^(SDG)
Sheffield (Charles St)
- 1828 ...

WILSON
Richard **Wilson** **(CP)** ^{(B) (WDB)}
Sheffield
- 1823 ...

W

	Joseph **Wilson** (OSP)	(B) (SAOR)
	Sheffield (Highfields/Fargate)	
	1773 ... *(See also figure: IW)*	
	1793 ... **(& Co.)***(See also figure: I.W*	(B)
	& Co)	

	John **Wilson** (CU)	(WDS79) (WDS01)
	Sheffield (32, Sycamore St)	
	- 1879 - 1901 ...	

	Matthew **Wilson** (EP)	(E)
	Liverpool (White Chapel)	
	~ 1885 *(See also figure: Matthew*	
	Wilson)	

	Thomas **Wilson** (EP/CU)	(WDSR)
	Sheffield (49, Arundel St/46, Montgomery	
	Rd)	
	- 1905 ...	

WILSON HAWKSWORTH ELLISON & COMPANY	**Wilson, Hawksworth, Ellison & Co. (Carlisle Works)** (EP)	(WDS79) (WDS01)
	Sheffield (Carlisle St/Sutherland St)	
	- 1879 - 1901 ...	
	(Then: Kayser, Ellison & Co. Ltd)	

	T. H. **Winder & Co.** (EP)	(E)
	Windermere	
	- 1880 ...	

WINGFIELD	**Wingfield & Rowbotham & Co. (CU) (Harp & Crown Cutlery)**	(K88AD) (K93 AD)
	Sheffield (82, Tenter St)	
	London (321, High Holborn)	
	- 1888 - 1893 ...	

	John **Winter** (OSP)	
	Sheffield	
	1778 ... *(See also figure: I.W)*	(SAOR) (M) (B)
	1765 - 1773 ... **(& Co.)**	
	(See also figures: IW symbol	(SAOR) (M) (B)
	"crown", IW&Co)	

	Winter, Parsons & Hall (OSP)	(B)
	Sheffield	
	- 1783	
	(Formerly: J. Parsons & Co.)	

	Joseph **Wiseman** Birmingham (87, Branston St) - 1880 ...	**(EP)**	(K80)
	George **Wish** **(Denmark Works)** Sheffield (Norfolk Ln/Burgess St/75, Cherry Tree Rd) 1879 - 1911 ...*(See also figure: GWS)*	**(EP)**	(SAOR) (WDS79) (K80) (K93) (WDS01) (WDSR) (WDSR11) (M)

	William Arthur **Witheford** Sheffield (Brittain St) - 1936 ...	**(EP)**	(K36)
	Benjamin **Withers** Sheffield (Cheney Sq) 1781 ...	**(OSP)**	(B) (SAOR)
"EYE" WITNESS	*(See also)* John **Taylor**	**(CU)**	
WITNESS	*(See also)* **Needman, Veall & Tyzack** **(Eye Witness Works)**	**(EP)**	
	P. H. **Witton** Birmingham - 1823 ...	**(CP)**	(WDB)
W. J. BELCHER & Co **SHEFFIELD**	*(See also)* William **Beckett & Co.**	**(CU/EP)**	
W. J. SUPERIOR QUALITY	**Not assigned!**	**(EP)**	
W·JER VIS	*(See also)* W. **Jervis**	**(OSP)**	
WJ	*(See also)* W. **Jessop**	**(OSP)**	
WJM &Co	*(See also)* William James **Myatt & Co.**	**(EP)**	
WK &C⁰	*(See also)* **Walker, Knowles & Co.**	**(OSP/EP)**	
W·LIN WOOD	*(See also)* W. **Linwood**	**(CP)**	

W& MD	*(See also)* W. & M. **Dodge**	**(EP)**
W·MARKLAND	*(See also)* W. **Markland**	**(CU/CP)** (B) (CD)
WM &Co	*(See also)* W. **Marsden & Co.**	**(OSP)**
WM 👑 **S** **WM & S**	*(See also)* William **Marples & Sons**	**(CU/EP)**
WM	*(See also)* William **Mammatt** **(Albion Works/Portland Works)**	**(EP)**
Wм BRIGGS&Cᴼ SHEFFIELD	*(See also)* William **Briggs & Co.**	**(BM/EP)**
Wᴹ H & S	*(See also)* William **Hutton & Sons**	**(EP)**
Wᴹ NEWBOULD & SONS	*(See also)* William **Newbould & Sons**	**(OSP)**
Wᴹ PAGE & Cᴼ	*(See also)* William **Page & Co.**	**(EP)**
WmTAY & Son (SHEFFIELD) Lᵀᴰ	*(See also)* William **Tay & Son Ltd.**	**(EP)**
W. NEWBOULD & SONS	*(See also)* William **Newbould & Sons**	**(OSP)**
W N & Cᴼ	*(See als* William **Naylor & Co.** **(Caledonian Works)**	**(BM/CP/GS/EP)**
	John **Wollin** Sheffield (71, Westbar Green) - 1825 - 1828 ...	**(OSP)** (NGDS) (SDG)
	Wolstenholme & Biggin Sheffield (41, Matilda St) - 1879 ...	**(EP)** (WDS79)
	W. **Wolstenholme & Son** **(Ecclesall Works)** Sheffield (Rockingham Ln) - 1893 ...	**(EP)** (K93)

W

Charles James **Wolstenholme (BM/EP)** (K78) (K80) (K82)
Birmingham (K84)
- 1878 - 1882 ...

James **Wolstenholme** (EP) (SAOR)
Sheffield (70, Navigation St)
1850 ... *(See also figure: J.Wolstenholme)*

Joseph **Wolstenholme** **(EP/BM)** (B) (PDB) (SDG)
Sheffield (36, Spring St/8/10/31, Broad St) (GDS) (GDBS)
1821 - 1854 ... *(See also figure: J.W)* (WDOS AD) (POS)
(K54) (M)

W. F. **Wolstenholme** (EP) (SAOR) (SBW) (B)
Sheffield (Broad St)
1858 ... *(See also figure: W.F.W)*

Wolverhampton Electro Plate Co. (K72)
(Peel Works) **(BM/EP)**
Wolverhampton
- 1872 ...

Benjamin **Wood** (CP) (WDB)
Birmingham
- 1823 ...

Frank **Wood** (CU) (WDS01)
Sheffield (41, Arundel St)
- 1901 ... *(See also figure:* I GUIDE*)*

Thomas Henry **Wood** (EP) (MDG) (POB)
Birmingham (45, Hall St/77, Spencer St/ (K72) (K78) (K80)
174, Warstone Ln) (K92)
- 1866 - 1892 ...

Eglon **Woodall & Co.** (EP) (K78) (K82) (K84)
Birmingham (Warstone Ln/258, Brearley St)
- 1878 - 1884 ...

Mary Ann **Woodall** (EP) (K80)
Bristol (14 & 15, Lower Castle St)
- 1880 ...

Woodcock & Hardy (EP) (K93)
(Eldon Works)
Sheffield (145, Eldon St)
- 1893 ...

Thomas **Woodcock & Sons** **(EP)** (K36)

Sheffield (90, Eyre St)
- 1936 ...

George **Woodcock** **(CP)** (WAB) (HTD)
(DOB) (WDOB)

Birmingham (Church St/Gt. Charles St/69,
Constitution Hill)
- 1829 - 1839 ...

James **Woodhouse** **(CU)** (WDOS AD)
(Old Rockingham Works)

Sheffield (175, Rockingham St)
- 1852 ...

Horace **Woodward & Co.** **(EP)**
(Atlas Works)

Birmingham (Paradise St/Edmund St)
London (Holborn Viaduct)
- 1878 - 1882 ...   (K78) (K80) (K82)
(See also figure: H.W&Co)   (M)
- 1884 - 1903 ... **(& Co. Ltd.)** (K84) (K88) (K92)
(See also figure: HW&Co Ltd)   (PC) (K03) (M)

WOOD WARD

William **Woodward** **(CP/CU)** (B) (WDOB)
(HGDB) (M)

Birmingham (Bishopsgate St/108, Broad St)
1814 - 1849 ...

E. **Woolf & Son** **(EP)** (K80)

Birmingham (94, Smallbrook St)
- 1880 ...

Woolf Brothers **(EP)** (MDG)

Birmingham (11, Mount St)
- 1866 ...

Thomas **Woo(l)ley** **(CU/EP)** (CDB) (GS)
(Electro Plate Works)   (MDG) (K72)
                                   (K78) (K80) (K84)
Birmingham (226, Camden St/33, St. Paul's (K88)(PC) (K03)
Sq/18, Caroline St/Mary St)
- 1861 - 1903 ... *(See also figure: T.W)*

James **Woolley** **(EP)** (K92)

Birmingham (18, Caroline St)
- 1892 ...

James **Woolley, Sons & Co.** **(EP)** (M) (SBW)

Manchester
~ *(See also figure: BOVAL)*

J. S. **Woolrich** **(MP)** [HGD]
Birmingham (12, James St)
- 1850 ...

John **Wootton** **(EP)** [K78]
Birmingham (51, Loveday St)
- 1878 ..

Robert **Wootton** **(EP)** [HGDB]
Birmingham (7, Cross St)
- 1849 ...

Charles **Worrall** **(EP)** [K72] [K78] [K80] [K82] [K84]
Birmingham (77, Caroline St/54, St. Paul's Sq)
- 1872 - 1884 ...

T. **Worthington** **(T)** [E]
Burton on Trent
- 1900 ...

Wort & Son **(EP)** [MDG]
Birmingham (100, Ryland Rd)
- 1866 ...

B. **Worth & Sons** **(EP)** [S]
Sheffield
1899 - 1916 *(See also figure: BW&S)*

Samuel **Worton** **(CP)** [B] [WDB] [WAB] [HTD] [M]
Birmingham (Near Fife Ways/Snow Hill)
1821 - 1830 ...
(See also figure: S.WORTON)

George **Wostenholm & Sons Ltd. (CU)** [M] [SBW]
(Washington Works)
Sheffield
~ *(See also figure: +I.XL)*

Gregory **Wostenholme** **(OSP)**
Sheffield (Rockingham St)
1809 ... *(See also figure: G.W)* [B] [SAOR]
1809 ... **(& Co.)** [B] [SAOR]
(See also figure: GW&C)

(See also) **(CU)**
Ward & Payne

WP	*(See also)* **(EP)** **Parkin & Marshall** **(Telegraph Works)**
WP	*(See also)* **(OSP)** W. **Proctor**
WP / **W P & Cº**	*(See also)* **(EP)** William **Page & Co.**
W P & S (symbols)	William **Padley & Son** **(EP)**
W.R.H &CºS " Lamp " W.R. HUMPHREYS &Co RADIANT PLATE SHEFFIELD ENGLAND	*(See also)* **(EP)** William R. **Humphreys & Co.** **(Haddon Works & Eyre Street Works)**
W.R. SILVERO & Co	*(See also)* **(EP)** William **Rae & Co.**
WR.N & Cº	*(See also)* **(EP)** William R. **Nutt & Co.** **(Wentworth Works)**
	William **Wrangham** **(OSP)** [(B) (SAOR)] Lincolnshire (Louth) 1817 ... *(See also figure: W.W)*
	George **Wreaks** **(CU/OSP)** [(CD) (GDS)] Sheffield (7, Norfolk Rw) - 1818 - 1833 ...
WRIGHT& FAIRBAIRN	J. **Wright &** G. **Fairbairn** **(OSP)** [(B) (SAOR) (M)] Sheffield (Park) 1809 ... *(See also figure: W&F)*
	Christopher **Wright** **(CP)** [(DOB)] Birmingham (Ct. 2, Livery St) - 1833 ...
	Henry **Wright** **(CP/EP)** [(WDOB) (CDB)] Birmingham (Upper Hospital St/Hockley St) - 1839 - 1861 ...

John **Wright** Sheffield (Smithfield) 1789 ... *(See also figure: IW)*	**(OSP)**	(B) (SAOR)
John **Wright** Birmingham (43, Ashted Rw) - 1829 - 1833 ...	**(CP)**	(WAB) (HTD) (DOB)
Thomas **Wright** Sheffield (Highfield) - 1829 ...	**(OSP)**	(PD)

W. & S. BUTCHER

(See also) **(CU)**
William & Samuel **Butcher**

W.S&S

(See also) **(EP)**
William **Shirtcliffe & Sons**

W.S&S **A1**
W S & S

(See also) **(EP)**
William **Shirtcliffe & Sons**

WS.

(See also) **(EP)**
W. **Skidmore**
(Enema Works)

WS

(See also) **(EP)**
William & George **Sissons**

WS

(See also) **(OSP)**
W. **Sansom**

W S
G S

(See also) **(EP)**
William jun. & George **Sissons**

W S
H S

(See also) **(EP)**
William & Henry **Stratford**

WT&C⁰

(See also) **(OSP)**
W. **Tucker** J. **Fenton & Co.**
(W. **Tucker** J. **Fenton &** E. G. **Machon**)

X I E S A	*(See also)* <small>Samuel</small> **Ashforth**	(OSP)
XL ALL	*(See also)* <small>William</small> **Parkin & Marshall** **(Telegraph Works)**	(CU/EP)
XX	*(See also)* <small>John</small> **Copley & Sons** **(Richmond Works)**	(EP)
X y	*(See also)* **Boswell, Hatfield & Co.** **(Hope Works)**	(EP)

X

Y&D	*(See also)* (OSP) **Younge & Deakin**	
Y & S	*(See also)* (CU/EP) _{John} **Yates & Son(s)**	
YG & H **YG&H**	*(See also)* (OSP) **Younge, Greaves & Hoyland**	

	_{Joseph} **Yarnall** (GS/BM) Birmingham (Ct. 6, 17, Buck St) - 1839 - 1866 ...	(WDOB) (HGD) (MDG)
	Yates & Davis (BM) Birmingham (Ct. 16, Park St) - 1829 ...	(WAB)
YATES & SONS **YATES** **EP.CROWN** YATE'S NEW METAL **YATES'S** VIRGINIAN SILVER	_{John} **Yates & Son(s)** (CU/EP) Birmingham (37 & 38, Coleshill St/56, Pritchett St/Highgate St) - 1850 - 1936 ... *(See also figures: J Y & S,* SIL- VER ASH., VIRGINIAN SILVER, Y&S, J.YATES & SONS, *)*	(B) (HGD) (CDB) (GS) (MDG) (K78) (K80) (K82) (K84) (PC) (K03) (K36) (SBW) (M)
	_{John} **Yates** (BM/GS) Birmingham (38, Coleshill St) - 1829 - 1839 ...	(WAB) (WDOB)
	_{Thomas} **Yates** (BM/EP) Birmingham (37 & 38, Coleshill St) - 1850 - 1880 ...	(HGD) (MDG) (K80)
	Yates, Birch & Spooner (BM) Birmingham (38, Coleshill St) - 1833 ...	(DOB)
	Yates Brothers (EP) Birmingham (43 & 44, Coleshill St/Pritchett St) - 1861 - 1892 ...	(CDB) (BDB) (MDG) (POB) (K72) (K78) (K80) (K82) (K84) (K88) (K92)
YEOMAN PLATE	**Yeoman of England Co.** (EP) Herfordshire 1897 ...	

439

David Curtis **Yewdall** **(EP)** [K80]
Bradford (Ct. Albion St)
- 1880 ...

Robert **Youle** **(CU)** [W]
Sheffield
1787 ... *(See also figure: ALO*)*

Charles Henry **Young** **(EP)** [K88] [K92] [K03]
Birmingham (20 & 24, Summer Hill Terrace)
- 1888 - 1903 ...

John **Younge & Co.** **(OSP)** [B] [SAOR] [UBD]
(John T. **Younge & Sons & Co.)**
Sheffield (Union St)
1779 - 1791 ...
(See also figures: IY, IY Co)

John T. **Younge & Co.** **(OSP)** [B] [SAOR]
(Younge, Walker & Crowder)
Sheffield (Union St)
1797 ...
(See also figures: ITY&Co, YWC)

S. & C. **Younge & Co.** **(OSP)**
Sheffield (Union St)
1811 ... *(See also figure: SCY&Co)*
1813 ... [B] [SAOR]
(See also figure: .C.YOUNGE&Co) [B] [M]

Younge & Deakin **(OSP)** [B] [SAOR]
Sheffield (Union St)
1813 ... *(See also figure: Y & D)*

John **Younge & Sons** **(OSP)** [B] [SAOR]
Sheffield (Union St)
1788 ... *(See also figure: ITY&Co)*

Charles Frederick. **Younge** **(OSP/CU)** [NGDS] [GDS]
Sheffield (45, High St) [SDG] [WDS37]
- 1825 - 1846 ... *(See also figure: C.F.Y)* [B] [SAOR]
[DSRR] [SD46]

G. S. **Younge** **(OSP)** [HDG]
Sheffield (45, High St)
- 1822 ...

Younge, Greaves & Hoyland (OSP) ^(B)
(Formerly: J. Hoyland & Co)
Sheffield (Union St)
1779 ... *(See also figure: YG & H)*

S. **Younge,** C. **Walker & Co. (OSP)** (SAOR) (CD)
(S. **Younge,** C. **Walker & Kitchen & Co)** (HDG) (PDY)
Sheffield (Union St) (NGDS) (PDB)
1818 - 1829 ... (PD) (SDG)

(See also) **(OSP)** ^(B)
J. T. **Younge & Co.**

Y

441

Z.BARRACLOUGH&SONS **LEEDS**	*(See also)* z. **Barraclough & Sons**	**(EP)**
Z.BARRACLOUGH&SONS **LTD** **LEEDS**	*(See also)* z. **Barraclough & Sons Ltd.**	**(EP)**
ZEITZ & Co SHEFFIELD	**Zeitz & Co.** (EP/CP) **(Carlisle Works)** Sheffield (St. Peter's Close, Harthead/ Carlisle St) - 1893 - 1901 ...	(K93) (WDS01)
ZENITH **SILVER PLATE**	**Not assigned!** (CU/EP)	(E)
	Arthur & John **Zimmerman** (EP) Birmingham (37, Regent Pl) 1879 ... 1928 *(See also: Marke: A.J.Z.)*	(S) (K88)
$\bar{7}$ **W A**	*(See also)* John **Ashforth** (OSP)	(B)

Z

442

Pictorial Marks

It is not uncommon to find the occasional piece of silver plate bearing only a pictorial mark of either an animate or inanimate object.
These can vary from a bear to a building!
Even Old Sheffield Plate and close plated wares were subjected to this form of marking.
While there may be considerably more electro plate in existence than the earlier fused and close plate, it is fair to say that there will probably be more fused and close plate bearing only character or pictorial marks, than can be found on electro plated wares.
The pictorial marks herein have been shown in as much a logical alphabetical order
as possible e.g.
A bat would appear before a bell, which would precede a building etc.

3423	*(See also)*	**(CU/CP/EP)**
	Joseph **Rodgers & Sons** (George)	
	(See also)	**(EP)**
	Army & Navy Cooperative Society	
	(See also)	**(EP)**
	John Batt & Co.	
	(See also)	**(EP)**
	Slater Brothers	
	Brookes & Crookes	**(CU)**
	(Atlantic Works)	
	(See also)	**(OSP)**
	S. **Roberts,** G. **Cadman & Co.**	
	(See also)	**(OSP)**
	Roberts, Samuel **Smith & Co.**	
	(See also)	**(OSP)**
	Smith, Sissons & Co.	
	(See also)	**(EP)**
	William jun. & George **Sissons**	
	(See also)	**(EP)**
	(The) **Potosi Silver Co.**	
	(See also)	**(OSP)**
	John **Waterhouse,** E. **Hatfield & Co.**	

	(See also) **(EP)** Jonathan W. **Hukin &** John Th. **Heath**
	(See also) **(CU)** Alfred **Field & Co.** **(Continental Works)**
	(See also) **(EP)** (K72) (K78) (PC) Thomas **Wilkinson & Sons** (K03)(K36) **(Pelican Works)**
	Not assigned! **(EP)** (In combination with R. Martin, E. Hall & Co.)
	(See also) **(CU)** S. S. **Brittain & Co.** **(St. George's Work)**
	(See also) **(EP)** Frederick Charles **Asman**
	(See also) **(CU)** E. **Blaydes & Co.**
	(See also) **(EP)** J. & J. **Beal** **(Redhill Works)**
	(See also) **(EP)** George **Bowen & Son** **(Victoria Works)**
	(See also) **(BM/EP)** Philip **Ashberry & Sons**
	(See also) **(EP)** John **Moreton & Co.**
	(See also) **(CU)** Charles **Cammell & Co. Ltd.** **(Cyclops Steel & Iron Works)**
	(See also) **(EP)** **Parkin & Co. Ltd.** **(Cornwall Works)**

PM

Logo	Company	Type
	(See also) **Barker & Ellis** - 1912 ...	(EP)
DEFIANCE	*(See also)* Charles S. **Green & Co. Ltd.** and George **Wilkin**	(EP) (EP)
	(See also) Israel Sigmund **Greenberg**	(EP)
	(See also) William **Jackson & Co.** **(Sheaf Island Works)**	(EP)
	(See also) **Cooper Brothers & Sons Ltd.**	(EP)
	(See also) Joseph **Rodgers & Sons**	(CU/CP/EP)
	(See also) **Creswick & Co.** and William C. **Hutton & Sons**	(EP) (CP)
	(See also) **Creswick & Co.** and William C. **Hutton & Sons**	(EP) (CP)
	(See also) **Viner's Ltd.** *(This trademarke is in use since 1924)*	(EP)
	Generic mark used only till 1897	(EP)
	(See also) John **Grinsell & Sons** **(Victoria Works)**	(EP)
CYCLOPS	*(See also)* Charles **Cammell & Co. Ltd.** **(Cyclops Steel & Iron Works)**	(CU)

	Not assigned!	**(EP)**
	(See also Walker & Hall (Electro Works)	**(BM/CU/EP)**
	Generic mark for EPNS	
	(See also) **Barker & Ellis** - 1932 ...	**(EP)**
	(See also) Philip **Ashberry & Sons**	**(BM/EP)**
	(See also) Thomas H. **Daniel &** Thomas R. **Arter** (Globe Nevada Silver Works)	**(EP)**
	(See also) William R. **Deykin &** Walter A. **Harrison**	**(EP)**
	(See also) John **Watson & Son**	**(OSP)**
	(See also) **Padley, Parkin & Co.** and **Padley, Parkin & Staniforth** and William **Padley & Son**	**(OSP)** **(EP)** **(EP)**
	(See also) Samuel **Osborn & Co.** (Clyde Steel Works & Iron Works)	**(CU/EP)**
	(See also) **Hale Brothers** (Moorfields Works)	**(CU)**
	(See also) **Atkinson Brothers** (Milton Works)	**(EP)**

PM

(See also) (CU)
Robert **Sorby & Sons Ltd.**

(See also) (OSP)
J. **Green & Co.**
and
H. **Wilkinson & Co.** (OSP/EP)

(See also) (OSP/EP)
J. **Parson & Co.**
and
H. **Wilkinson & Co.** (OSP/EP)

(See also) (EP)
Samuel **Roberts &** Charles **Belk**
(Furnival Works)

(See also) (EP)
William R. **Humphreys & Co.**
(Haddon Works & Eyre Street
Works)

(See also) (BM/EP)
James **Deakin & Sons**
(Sidney Works)

(See also) (CU)
John **Bedford & Sons**

(See also) (EP)
Barker & Ellis
- 1912

(See also) (OSP/EP)
Walker, Knowles & Co.

(See also) (OSP)
Blagden, Hodgson & Co.

(See also) (CU)
Wilson, Hawksworth, Ellison & Co.
(Carlisle Works)
and
Kayser, Ellison & Co. (EP)

	(See also) **Cooper Brothers & Sons Ltd.**	(EP)
	(See also) **Barker & Ellis** - 1906 ...	(EP)
	(See also) **Atkin Brothers** **(Truro Works)**	(BM/EP)
	(See also) **Lewis, Rose & Co. Ltd.**	(EP)
	(See also) John **Wilson**	(CU)
	(See also) **Whitby Plate Works**	(EP)
	(See also) **Barker & Ellis** - 1912 ...	(EP)
	(See also) Thomas **Hands & Sons**	(EP)
	(See also) S. J. **Levi & Co.** **(Squirrel Works)**	(EP)
	(See also) Matthew **Boulton & Plate Co.**	(OSP)
	(See also) Joseph **Mappin & Brothers** and John **Mappin &** George **Webb** (BM/EP/CU)	(EP)
	(See also) John **Jenkins &** Herbert **Timm** **(Pensilvia Works)**	(EP)
	(See also) Francis **Howard** **(West End & Aberdeen Works)**	(EP)

	(See also) (EP)
	Joseph **Ridge & Co.**
	(Ridge, Allcard & Co)
	(Lion Works)
	then
	(See also) (EP)
	John **Round & Son Ltd.**
	(Tudor Works & Arundel Works)
	(See also) (CU/BM/EP)
	James **Dixon & Sons**
	(See also) (CU/EP)
	Richard **Groves & Sons**
USE	**(Beehive Works)**
	(See also) (EP)
	George **Ibberson & Co.**
	(See also) (CU)
	William. J. **Bingham**
	(Clough Works)
	then
	(See also) (CU)
	Linley, Linacre & Bingham
	(Conbar Works & Clough Works)

PM

(GM)   1787 Gales & Martin Business Directory of Sheffield
(UBD)   1791 Universal British Directory
(POAD)   1808 Post Office Annual Directory, B. Critchett
(AB)   1812 Abstract of the Evidence, London, J. Mcqcreery
(WTDB)   1815 Wrightson's New Triennial Directory of Birmingham, R. Wrightson
(WTD)   1818 Wrightson's New Triennial Directory of Birmingham, R. Wrightson
(CD)   1818 The Commercial Directory for 1818-19-20, James Pigot
(WDG)   1819 White's Directory & Gazetteer of Birmingham
(HDG)   1822 History, Directory & Gazetteer of the Country of York, Edward Baines
(PDY)   1822 Pigot's Directory of Yorkshire, Pigot & Co.
(WDB)   1823 Wrightson's Triennial Directory of Birmingham, R. Wrightson
(NGDS)   1825 New General & Commercial Directory of Sheffield, R. Gell
(PDB)   1825 Pigot's Directory of Merchants & Manufactures of Sheffield & Birmingham
(SDG)   1828 Sheffield Directory & Guide, John Blackwell
(PD)   1829 Pigot's Directory of Professions and Trades, Sheffield
(WAB)   1829 Wrightson's Annual Directory of Birmingham, R. Wrightson
(HTD)   1830 History, Topography and Directory of Warwickshire, William West
(GDS)   1833 The General Directory of the Borough of Sheffield, William White
(DOB)   1833 The Directory of Birmingham, Wrightson & Webb
(WWDB)   1835 The Directory of Birmingham, Wrightson & Webb
(HGDY)   1837 History Gazetteer & Directory of the West-Riding of Yorkshire, Wm. White
(WDS37)   1837 Directory of Sheffield and Rotherham, William White
(WDOB)   1839 The Directory of Birmingham, Wrightson & Webb
(DSRR)   1841 The Directory of Sheffield and Rotherham, Henry & Thomas Rodgers
(SD46)   1846 Slater's Directory of Sheffield
(JPC)   1847 Journal für praktische Chemie, Erdmann & Marchand, Leipzig
(HGDB)   1849 History & General Directory of the Borough of Birmingham, F. White & Co.
(GDBS)   1849 General Directory of the Town and Borough of Sheffield, William White
(HGD)   1850 History Gazetteer & Directory of Warwickshire, Francis White & Co.
(GE)   1851 Official descriptive and illustrated catalogue, Great Exhibition, London
(WDOS)   1852 Gazetteer & General Directory of Sheffield, William White
(POS)   1854 Post Office Directory of Sheffield, Kelly & Co.
(K54)   1854 Post Office Directory of Sheffield, Kelly & Co.
(CDB)   1861 Corporation, General & Trades Directory of Birmingham, Wm. Cornish
(BDB)   1862 Business Directory of Birmingham, J. S. C. Morris
(MHM)   1862 International Exhibition Medals & Honorable Mentions, London
(GS)   1863 The Goldsmith's & Cutler's Directory, W. Hogg & Co.
(MDG)   1866 Morris & Co. Commercial Directory & Gazeteer of Warwickshire
(POB)   1867 Post Office Directory of Birmingham, Kelly & Co.
(WDS71)   1871 Directory of Sheffield and Rotherham, William White
(K72)   1872 Directory of Birmingham, Staffordshire & Warwickshire, Kelly & Co.
(CHAF)   1874 Hallmarks on Gold and Silver Plate, Dryden Press, England
(K76)   1876 Post Office Directory of Worcestershire, Kelly & Co.
(K78)   1878 Post Office Directory of Birmingham, Kelly & Co.
(WDS79)   1879 General and Commercial Directory of Sheffield & Rotherham, William White

(K80)   1880 Directory of the Watch & Clock Trades of England, Kelly & Co.
(K82)   1882 Directory of Birmingham, Staffordshire, Warwickshire, Kelly & Co.
(K84)   1884 Directory of Birmingham, Staffordshire, Warwickshire, Kelly & Co.
(K88)   1888 Directory of Birmingham, Staffordshire, Warwickshire, Kelly & Co.
(K92)   1892 Directory of Birmingham, Staffordshire, Warwickshire, Kelly & Co.
(K93)   1893 Directory of Leeds, Sheffield & Rotherham, Kelly & Co.
(CRI)   1894 Old English Plate, London, W. J. Cripps
(PC)   1896 Circular Trades Directory of Birmingham, W. E. Peck
(WDS01) 1901 General & Commercial Directory of Sheffield & Rotherham, William White
(K03)   1903 Directory of Birmingham, Kelly & Co.
(HBSP)   1903 Illustrated Handbook of Old Pewter & Sheffield Plate, W. Redman
(WDSR) 1905 Directory of Sheffield and Rotherham, William White
(VOSP)   1906 The Values of Old English Silver and Sheffield Plate, J. W. Caldicott
(SAOR)   1911 The Sheffield Assay Office Register
(WDS11) 1911 Directory of Sheffield and Rotherham, William White
(B)   1912 History of Old Sheffield Plate, London, Frederick Bradbury
(RO)   1922 Der Goldschmiede Merkzeichen, Frankfurt, M. Rosenberg,
(K36)   1936 Directory of Merchants, Manufactures & Shippers of the World, Kelly & Co.
(OS)   1937 The Book of old Silver, Crown Pub. USA, S. B. Wyler
(OSP5)   1946 Old Silver & Old Sheffield Plate, Doubleday & Co. USA, H. P. Okie
(SBW)   1949 The book of Sheffield Plate, New York, Seymour B. Wyler
(OSP2)   1955 Old Sheffield Plate, Bell & Sons, London, E. Wenham
(SAS)   1957 Small Antique Silverware, New York, G. B. Hughes
(BUR)   1957 Silver, Pewter and Sheffield Plate, New York, F. W. Burgess
(VSP)   1963 Victorian Silver and Silverplate, Jenkins, London, P. Wardle
(KSS)   1964 Schönes Silber, Keysersche, München, M. Meinz
(JEP)   1969 Illustrated History of English Plate, Vol.: I New York, C. J. Jackson
(JEP2)   1969 Illustrated History of English Plate, Vol.: II New York, C. J. Jackson
(ASP)   1970 Antique Sheffield Plate, London, B. Hughes
(RCS)   1971 Silber, Parkland, Stuttgart, R. Came
(GSM)   1971, The Great Silver Manufactory M. Boulton, November Book Ltd. London
(FR)   1971 The Price Guide to Old Sheffield Plate, Baron Publishing, T.W. Frost
(FAL72) 1972 Marks of the London Goldsmiths & Silversmiths, J.P. Fallon
(SV)   1973 Silver, Peerage Books, London, M. Holland
(TZB)   1974 Tafelzier des Barock, Edition Schneider, München, St. Bursche
(KAM)   1977 Kerzenleuchter aus Metall, Callway, München, V. Baur
(ABC)   1978 Alte Bestecke, Callway, München, G. Benker
(SAAW)   1978 Silberstempel aus aller Welt, Dausien, Hanau, Jan Divis
(RSS)   1980 Ein rheinischer Silberschatz, Köln, Heuer, Klesse & Schürmann
(MERI)   1982 The Meriden Britannia Silver-Plate Treasury, USA, E. P. Hogan
(BAT)   1979 Silber, Battenberg, München, H. Domdey-Knödler
(EAS)   1986 Encyclopedia of American Silver Manufacturers, Shiffer Pub., D.T. Rainwater
(ASO)   1987 Sterling Silver, Silverplate and Souvenir Spoons, LW Books, USA
(BAS)   1988 Buying Antique Silver & Sheffield Plate, Macdonald Orbis, England, R. Feild
(OSP3)   1988 Old Sheffield Plate, England, A. Bambery

(E)	1989 Own Collection
(SF)	1990 Silverplated Flatware, Tere Hagan, USA
(SPFW)	1990 Silverplated Flatware, Collector Books, USA, T. Hagan
(W)	1991 Trademarks on Basemetal Tableware, Ontario, Eileen Woodhead
(EB)	1991 Historisches Essbesteck, Hamburg, J. Amme
(MIL)	1993 Silver & Sheffield Plate Marks, Octopus Pub. London, J. Bly,
(BNMS)	1994 Silber & Gold, Augsburger Silberschmiedekunst für Höfe Europas, München
(CM)	1995 Coffee Makers, Quiller Press, London, E. & J. Bramah,
(UASP)	1996 Understanding Antique Silver Plate, England, St. J. Helliwell,
(MTM)	1997 Mesters to Masters - History of the Company of Cutlers in Hallamshire, Oxford Uni Press, England, B. & D. Hey,
(TSM)	1998 The Soho Mint, Spink, London, R. Doty,
(M)	1999 Electroplated Nickel Silver, OSP, Makers' Marks, George Mappin, London
(Made)	Indication of articles by fabrication after 1920
(Dia)	Diamond registration marks
(MB)	2009 Math. Boulton, Silver & Sheffield Plate, Birmingham, Kenneth Quickenden,
(NA)	National Archives UK
(Rd)	Registration marks
(S)	Silver Assay Offices, Sheffield
(SDB)	Directory of Birmingham, Showell's
(SH)	Sheffield History

THE ANTIQUE TRADE CALENDAR

BRITAIN'S GUIDE TO ANTIQUE FAIRS MARKETS AND CENTRES

Published quarterly, order by subscription from:
G.P. London, 32 Fredericks Place
North Finchley, London N12 8QE
Telephone 020 8446 3604

Notes

Notes

Notes